INFORMATION USERS AND INFORMATION SYSTEM DESIGN

Information Users and Information System Design

VOLUME III OF THE SELECTED WORKS OF

Marcia J. Bates

PROFESSOR EMERITA, DEPARTMENT OF INFORMATION STUDIES
GRADUATE SCHOOL OF EDUCATION AND INFORMATION STUDIES
UNIVERSITY OF CALIFORNIA, LOS ANGELES

Ketchikan Press
BERKELEY

Edited by Marcia J. Bates

Published by Ketchikan Press, Berkeley, CA

SERIES DESIGN & PRODUCTION
Chris Hall

ISBN 978-0-9817584-3-5

PUBLISHER CATALOGING-IN-PUBLICATION DATA
Names: Bates, Marcia J.
Title: Information users and information system design: volume III of the selected works of Marcia J. Bates / edited by Marcia J. Bates.
Description: Berkeley, CA : Ketchikan Press, 2016. | Series: Selected works of Marcia J. Bates | Includes index.
Identifiers: ISBN 978-0-9817584-3-5
Subjects: LCSH: Information science. | Information storage and retrieval systems. | Information behavior. | User-centered system design. | Search engines. | Digital libraries.
Classification: LCC Z665.B316 2016 v. 3 | DDC 020—dc23

Text set in Calluna 9.5/12.5; heads and captions set in Calluna Sans

To my mentors

Carl Baumann
POMONA COLLEGE

William J. Paisley
STANFORD UNIVERSITY

Contents

ALL ENTRIES BY MARCIA J. BATES UNLESS OTHERWISE NOTED

TWO   User-centered design of information systems

Acknowledgments

My heartfelt thanks go to the talented people who worked with me in preparing these volumes: Chris Hall for his book design, illustrations, and typesetting, Nicholas Carroll and Chris Hall for production management, Leonard Rosenbaum for indexing, and Doris Lechner for proofreading.

I also want to thank my parents, especially my mother, for their hard work in putting me through college. My mother made it possible for me to have the education she could only dream of.

—*Marcia J. Bates*

Introduction to the series

The iconic image associated with Silicon Valley's new world of information technology is that of two guys in a garage tinkering with and launching new inventions that revolutionize the world. The founders of Hewlett-Packard, the founders of Apple, and, more recently, the founders of Google all fit the mold. Investors pour millions, nay, billions of dollars into these projects, with subsequent phenomenally great reward, as the products are taken up and used throughout the world. Many of these products involve information storage, transfer, and use. The average person's sense of how information can be found and utilized, sent to friends, or support study has changed drastically.

But there was a prehistory to this story. People have needed and used information since prehistoric times. They even needed it—a lot—just before the Internet exploded in people's consciousness in the 1990's. What did they do then?

It turns out that the several forms of limited information technologies available then—when investment in information retrieval research was a pittance—forced those of us who thought about these questions to become very knowledgeable about the inner workings of information seeking, the expressing of information needs, the methods of describing and indexing information, as well as the acts of searching, retrieving and utilizing information. In the field of information science, we had to understand the process at a granular level, in order to take advantage of the then-available technologies, which were usually vastly more limited than today's capabilities. We were forced to understand the process deeply, in the way that pilots used to develop a bone-deep feel for flying, before the advent of the automatic pilot and the disengagement by pilots from the core processes of keeping a plane in the air.

Many of the directions we took are now difficult to pursue, because the giant search corporations like Google and Yahoo have labeled all this intellectual territory as proprietary. In a *New Yorker* article ("When G.M. Was Google," *New Yorker*, Dec. 1, 2014), Nicholas Lemann describes a technical problem that Google's engineers "solved." But that problem was well known for decades in the information sciences, and had been addressed in a number of ways in both manual and automated systems. Google might have solved it simply by *doing a search* on the research literature of the subject.

The purpose of these volumes is to republish selected significant publications of mine, representing my work on the topics of information, the information professions, information seeking and searching, information organization, and user-centered design of information systems. The papers demonstrate the work we in my field did to understand information behavior and information system development and use, back when we had to burrow deeply into the human relationship with information in a way that is seldom done these days. There is a great deal to learn from that earlier work, and a great deal of knowledge that is being overlooked in these days of rapture with the new technologies. When the intoxication fades a bit, and people return to wanting to improve the actual ways people find and use information, then perhaps some of the approaches explored in these papers will regain prominence.

One of the "problems" of information science is that it continues to have associations with the discipline that has dealt with information storage and retrieval the longest: library science. It makes sense: There were decades of transition from all-paper information storage to various sorts of electronic storage and retrieval. The transition involved many stages of development, using various combinations of paper and electronic information processing. The computers we worked with started out with minuscule amounts of storage and processing power, and gradually managed to handle vastly more of our storage-intensive resources.

This association of information science with library science is not a problem because of the latter field's expertise and long experience with information. Rather, it is a problem only because of the astounding degree of negative stereotyping conventionally associated with the field. Could there be a greater contrast than that between the two guys in a garage, and the hermetic librarian hunched over his desk, protecting his collection from defilement by users, or the virginal spinster with the pencil stuck in the bun at the back of her head, presiding over the reference desk?

I have been astonished countless times in my life at the stubborn persistence of these stereotypes, despite all facts to the contrary. Every Christmas we are treated to a showing on television of the film *It's a Wonderful Life*, wherein, during the dream sequence, the wife of Jimmy Stewart's George Bailey, who would now have never married without him, becomes a librarian, and is shown locking the library door at night, as she comes home from her lonely work. An analysis of the social role of this librarian stereotype has yet to be written. It is a charged and deeply meaningful archetype in the popular consciousness, and deserves full analysis. In the meantime, however, this stereotype has largely doomed any chance that the new information technology world learns from what librarians know about information and people. I recall recently being in a symposium and observing a graduate student from another field, who had become interested in what we do, hastily denying—indeed, almost panicking at the thought—that her new interest had anything to do with library science.

Information science, when it launched in the 1960's, was the exciting new field that would take the old librarianship into the new world of automation. And it did do that, with great success. But information science had another "flaw" that doomed it in the thinking of many computer scientists. Not only were there more women in the field than in computer science, there was also a great deal of attention to the so-called soft side of technology, its use and integration with people's lives and work, the psychology and sociology of information.

I sat in the audience at a conference while Gerard Salton, the father of modern information retrieval, explained that it was not possible to study the human factors in information system use, because these social aspects were too squishy and unmanageable (not his exact words). It is hard to maintain a balance in a discipline between people with a social and psychological perspective and those with an engineering, technical perspective when applying their expertise to a problem. As a rule, they have fundamentally different cognitive styles, which do not necessarily mix well. Yet both these perspectives are needed where information systems are concerned. Information science has retained that balance, but consequently sometimes puts off computer scientists, many (not all) of whom literally do not see the social side of information, are not interested in it, and are happy to purge that perspective from their university departments.

For all these reasons, the extensive knowledge that has built up within information science is frequently ignored in today's research and scholarship, and in the popular consciousness. The publication of these articles of mine is my bid to draw attention to some of what has been learned in information science about information-related behavior and good information system design. In what follows, the technologies may indeed have been superseded, but pay attention to the thinking around the technologies—what we learned about people and information, what we learned about dissecting an information query and searching on it, what we learned about how people process information when approaching an information system, and what we learned about how to design an information system to support information seeking well. Much of what we learned has *still* not been implemented in information systems, despite the billions of dollars poured into the information technology world.

Finally, these papers are also of interest as a historical record of that time of transition in information research between the 1960's and the early twenty-first century. Coincidentally, the arc of my professional career happened to parallel the arc of development of modern information retrieval, and some of that history is represented in these volumes. I hope you find material of interest and value herein.

The papers reproduced here represent, in my rough estimate, about half my published work, the half I felt would be of most use today. I have always had wide interests within information science, and many of the papers could arguably fall in more than one category. I have grouped them as best I can in the categories below, arranged by volume. One popular article, on "berrypicking," appears in both Volumes II and III. Otherwise, all articles are unique.

Articles and chapters are carefully reproduced exactly as they originally appeared in print, with two exceptions: errors are corrected, and citations in reference lists that were originally listed as "in press" have been supplied with their subsequent publication information. Consequently, a few citations will be more recent than the original publication date of the article in which they appear.

Volume III: *Information Users and Information System Design*
Information Seeking and Interaction (8 articles)
User-centered Design of Information Systems (8 articles)
Appendix: Content Lists and Index for all volumes

It can be difficult to see things from the user's perspective . . .

"It was a good rotting carcass, but it wasn't a great rotting carcass."

Preface to Volume III

This volume completes the attention to users, information seeking, and information system design begun in volume II of this series. All these elements, as well as the searching and indexing vocabulary addressed in the prior volume, need to be considered simultaneously in the design of quality information systems.

SECTION ONE: INFORMATION SEEKING AND INTERACTION

In "Toward an integrated model of information seeking and searching," which was a Keynote Address to the Information Seeking in Context conference in Lisbon in 2002, I argue for recognizing that people operate at many levels simultaneously, and that a complete sense of their information seeking cannot be gained without recognizing these several layers. I have seen work, for example, that seems to assume that information searching operates only at the level of conscious thought, and is completely unconnected with the *behaviors* of moving through information resources or online databases—as if there were no physical substrate whatsoever to our thought processes. This paper makes the argument for an integrated vision of information seeking.

I wrote the "Information behavior" entry for the *Encyclopedia of Library and Information Sciences, 3rd Ed.*, wherein I covered the history of information seeking research, and described the status of the work at the time of the 2010 publication date of the encyclopedia.

The next four articles address information seeking behavior in various contexts. The Bates, Wilde, and Siegfried article, "Research practices of humanities scholars in an online environment: The Getty Online Searching Project report no. 3," describes the results of extensive interviews with visiting scholars in the humanities in their sabbatical year at the Getty Research Institute in Santa Monica, CA. In the project, scholars had complete funded access to a large set of databases. Their research practices and uses of online searching were studied closely. Altogether, six articles were written out of the large data set from the Getty project. "The Getty end-user Online Searching Project in the humanities: Report no. 6: Overview and conclusions," summarizes the results from all six papers for academic librarians.

One of the least well-understood categories of users is that of people doing interdisciplinary research. Yet prior research has demonstrated that they have dramatically much more difficulty locating relevant material for their research than do other scholars. In the 1996 article, "Learning about the information seeking of interdisciplinary scholars and students," these issues are discussed, and suggestions are provided for further research, as well as techniques for assisting interdisciplinary researchers.

At the dawn of widespread use of the World Wide Web, I participated in a study organized by Yasmin Kafai on Web searching by elementary school students ("Internet Web-searching instruction in the elementary classroom: Building a foundation for information literacy"). Our results, published in 1997, were some of the earliest that linked World Wide Web use with educational practices.

In an article that was similarly early in the World Wide Web age, my then doctoral student, Shaojun Lu, and I wrote a paper on the presentation of self by people on their personal home page in "An exploratory profile of personal home pages: Content, design, metaphors." We were surprised to see that there was virtually no prior research on website genres before the 1997 publication date.

Working with me on her doctoral dissertation research, Diane Mizrachi carried out a revealing study of "Undergraduates' personal academic information management and the consideration of time and task-urgency." In our current era of continual transition from paper to digital forms of information, Mizrachi analyzed the personal information ecology of each of her student respondents, from dormitory room to classroom. We learned much about how students cope with the myriad information forms used by their professors, and the resulting mix of forms and technologies they preferred in their own studying.

SECTION TWO: USER-CENTERED DESIGN OF INFORMATION SYSTEMS

This topic is where all the various elements of good information system design come together in a finished product. In this section, I address the design of a complete, coherent information system from several perspectives.

As a kind of general introduction to this section, the OpEd piece written for the *Los Angeles Times* in 1999, "Another information system fails—Why?," provides a brief discussion of the problems that arise with the design of information systems in public agencies. "The design of browsing and berrypicking techniques for the online search interface," the sole repeat across the three volumes of this series, is a popular article describing ways of matching system design with searching options for the user.

"Where should the person stop and the information search interface start?" addresses specifically the question of the amount of support to be given by the system in relation to the user's own actions to promote searching success. Four levels of system support are described, and research recommendations made for this area of system design.

It happened that, around 1990, I was able to implement the approach I had recommended in a 1986 article on improving subject access in online systems ("Subject access in online catalogs: A design model," *Journal of the American Society for Information Science, 37*(6), 357–376; reproduced in vol. II of this series). The implementation occurred in association with consulting work I did on a $30,000,000 project to develop a multi-million-item records management database and information system at the Los Angeles Department of Water and Power. The design is described in "Design for a subject search interface and online thesaurus for a very large records management database." The approach described in this 1990 article is an implementation of the techniques recommended in the 1986 article. The approach involves creating a thesaurus for the searcher, which has important design differences from thesauri for indexers, and needs to be implemented in the interface in a very different way from indexer thesauri. The system was actually completed and made available to the 10,000-person staff at the DWP.

Unfortunately, the fall of the Soviet Union in 1989–91, which led to a recession in most of the United States, led to a depression in California, which was heavily dependent on the defense industry. Regrettably, before I had an opportunity to do testing of actual success rates with real users of the DWP system, the organization went through a drastic downsizing with massive staff layoffs, while we at UCLA were likewise distracted by having to cope with severe cuts at the University of California. Within a few months, the DWP had so changed that any hope of continuity with the earlier management regime was lost, and the organization seemed unlikely to be receptive to testing.

I felt considerable vindication, however, for the approach promoted in my articles when, in 2015, Tuukka Ruotsalo and colleagues published the results of their research on a novel means of making appropriate searcher vocabulary available to users in an online search system they created

("Interactive intent modeling: Information discovery beyond search," *Communications of the ACM 58*(1): 86–92). They achieved the system design I had argued for through a completely different means than I had used. Their results led to *100 percent* improvement in searcher success (p. 86), a result stunningly much higher than typical studies of new retrieval system designs. As of this writing, approaches that achieve what was intended in the Bates and in the Ruotsalo work have yet to be implemented for widespread use.

"The design of databases and other information resources for humanities scholars: The Getty Online Searching Project report no. 4," is, I believe, an undervalued paper of mine. The needs of science and technology are so dominant in the thinking of designers of information resources that the distinctive characteristics of humanities research and humanities resources are seldom recognized and designed for properly. In this paper, I discuss these differences and show how resources of different kinds could be designed for these scholars.

In "Document familiarity in relation to relevance, information retrieval theory, and Bradford's Law: The Getty Online Searching Project report no. 5" (1996) I show how what we learned in the Getty humanities searching project produces a fundamental challenge to basic assumptions in the world of information retrieval theory. Prior familiarity with documents found in a search is assumed to be rare, and is not much discussed in the information retrieval literature, yet we found that humanities scholars expected to know, and already did know, a substantial portion, sometimes almost all, of the items found in an online search. Some of the implications of this challenge to information retrieval theory are discussed in the article.

As Internet use surged in the late 1990's, and the popular assumption arose that "information retrieval has been solved," I decided to write about a range of issues that we had learned about in information science in relation to information retrieval, issues that appeared to be mostly ignored in the new excitement about online searching by the general and scholarly public. That work appears in the 1998 article, "Indexing and access for digital libraries and the Internet: Human, database, and domain factors."

Finally, in the 2002 article, "The cascade of interactions in the digital library interface," I brought together many insights about the several layers of system structure that need to be designed in conjunction with each other, in order to produce a truly effective information system. All too often, one or two of these layers, usually the most technical parts, dominate the design for the other layers, especially the portions addressing human needs, with the consequence that sub-optimal systems consistently, and persistently, result.

ONE

Information seeking
and interaction

Toward an integrated model of information seeking and searching

ABSTRACT

The emphasis in much information seeking research at the current time is on the social and cultural context of human interaction with information. This effort is highly desirable, but is incomplete. The model to be developed here has integration as its objective in two senses: 1) to provide a single model that incorporates both information seeking and searching within it, and 2) to integrate the social and cultural with the underlying biological and physical anthropological layers of human experience with respect to information seeking and searching.

Introduction

In information studies currently, there is a burst of exciting work being done on information seeking in a social and cultural context. Indeed, that emphasis on context has been sufficiently important that an entire conference, namely, this one, has been dedicated over several years to studying information seeking in context. As a result of this interest, we have learned much about the rich social texture surrounding people and imbuing their information seeking. This research has added immensely to our understanding of information-related behavior by people, and I expect it to continue to do so, as more and more work along this line comes out.

First published as Bates, M. J. (2002). Toward an integrated model of information seeking and searching. *New Review of Information Behaviour Research, 3,* 1–15.

| Spiritual (religion, philosophy, quest for meaning) |
| Aesthetic (arts and literature) |
| Cognitive/Conative/Affective (psychology) |
| Social and Historical (social sciences) |
| Anthropological (physical and cultural) |
| Biological (genetics and ethology) |
| Chemical, Physical, Geological, Astronomical |

FIG. 1. *Levels of understanding*

However, I have been troubled by an apparent almost complete absence of awareness of and attention to a scientific perspective, as distinct from a social sciences or humanities perspective, on these information seeking questions in our field of late. See also the discussion in Sandstrom and Sandstrom (1995). Scientific approaches are frequently seen as inherently reductive, that is, they are assumed to be explanations that seek to reduce understanding of the social and spiritual in life to the merely physical. While there have long been, and probably always will be, people who attempt such a reduction, there are also many who do not, including myself. Studying something from a natural science point of view does not automatically mean that one is claiming that only the natural science matters or can teach us something. In my view, our understanding of information seeking is not complete as long as we exclude the biological and anthropological from our study. To focus only on the social and humanistic is simply to be reductionist in the other direction!

Surely, it is desirable to build our understanding of information seeking behavior on all the levels in Figure 1, not just some, whether upper levels or lower ones.

So the phrase, "integrated model," in the title has a dual meaning in this paper. I am attempting to 1) integrate our understanding of information seeking across the several levels, or layers, of human life, and 2) develop an integrated model of information seeking in relation to information searching.

The biological and anthropological levels

Because I believe that the biological and anthropological levels have been neglected in the study of information seeking, I will emphasize them here

FIG. 2. *Interpenetration of the levels*

today. But the intention is not to reduce information seeking in context to only these levels. Rather, I hope to re-introduce these levels to our thinking, and integrate them with the social levels.

This approach is best illustrated by Figure 2, "Interpenetration of the Levels." This diagram illustrates how the several levels are, in reality, often interpenetrating each other, and doing so in a variety of ways. For example, for a person with severe schizophrenia, the biological reaches all the way through all layers of life, and may impede the ability to operate effectively in life, to relate socially, and so on. In other cases, say, a high level of intelligence, or a propensity to migraine headaches, the biological may benefit or at least not harm too much the living at the other levels.

Other aspects of human life show complex interrelations between these several levels. For example, it is generally agreed in the field of psycholinguistics that human beings have some sort of in-born language capacity that puts some constraints on the nature of the languages that can be developed. Within those constraints, however, language can and does have the huge variety that real-world languages show. See Jackendoff (2002), Pinker (1995). Thus, the particulars of the language a person speaks, the grammar and vocabulary, must all be learned during an individual's lifetime, and vary tremendously from culture to culture. So language capacity is neither totally biological nor totally social, but a complex mixture of both. Many other aspects of human behavior could be described with similar complex mixes across the levels.

For this reason alone, the study of information seeking will never be complete until we integrate the social levels with the underlying ones. To ignore the latter is to be incomplete at best, and seriously distorting at worst. The best way I can demonstrate what I have in mind is to attempt to develop a model of information seeking and searching.

Information seeking and searching

So where does information seeking come into this general context of integrated levels? First of all, let us consider information seeking with respect to all the information that comes to a human being during a lifetime, not just in those moments when a person actively seeks information.

We, along with other mammals, are capable of learning a great deal during our lifetimes. We have very large, general-purpose brains, and so can adapt to a great range of environmental conditions and social arrangements. We have some general mental structures, as with the language example above, which enable us to learn various types of things, but the specifics of what we learn come with our experiences. We, also like most mammals, learn particularly much from family or clan. These are emotionally intense relationships—because our very survival depends on their succor—and so family learning makes a great impression. We are a very social species and draw much learning and experience from such social interactions. For most people, most of the time, information-related behavior consists of absorbing and using the learning and information that comes our way during the course of our daily lives.

Looking at us as a species that exists physically, biologically, socially, emotionally, and spiritually, it is not unreasonable to guess that we absorb perhaps 80 percent of all our knowledge through simply being aware, being conscious and sentient in our social context and physical environment.

With that as a foundation, let us consider Figure 3, "Modes of Information Seeking" (adapted from an earlier paper by the author [1986]). "Directed" and "Undirected" refer, respectively, to whether an individual seeks particular information that can be specified to some degree, or is more or less randomly exposing themselves to information. "Active" and "Passive" refer, respectively, to whether the individual does anything actively to acquire information, or is passively available to absorb information, but does not seek it out.

Awareness An enormous part of all we know and learn surely comes to us through passive undirected behavior, or simply *being aware* (cell "D" of Figure 3).

The work of Virginia Walter (1994), a colleague at UCLA, is illustrative of the value of the above perspective. The few studies of children's information seeking had mostly concentrated on instances where children seek information or books to read in libraries. But Walter saw that children had much larger needs—that even a two-year-old really has enormous information needs. She talked with people who work a lot with children, as children often cannot articulate their needs themselves, to discover what things children need to know at what ages.

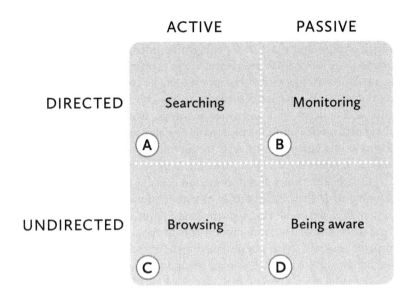

ACTIVE   PASSIVE

DIRECTED   Searching   Monitoring

(A)   (B)

UNDIRECTED   Browsing   Being aware

(C)   (D)

FIG. 3. *Modes of information seeking*

It is one thing to think of children's information needs as the questions they ask about dinosaurs when they go to the library. It is quite another to see the full array of learning that must occur for a child to emerge successfully into adulthood. In a dysfunctional family, with parents on drugs, for example, there may be no one to tell the child to look both ways when crossing the street—something as simple as that. The children of thieves think thievery is natural; it is what people do. That comes from simply soaking up what is in their environment, especially from the emotionally meaningful people around them.

In this context, then, when we determine what services to offer in the public library, we may have a substantially different view of the way in which that library can serve children. Specifically, the library can constitute not only a good education and entertainment resource for children, but also may constitute a critical additional venue for children to get essential life information that they are not getting anywhere else. We see here how a view of children in terms of the learning they must take in as offspring, in order to develop into successful adult members of the species, changes our perspective on what they need, and has immense implications for policy at the social level.

Monitoring Monitoring and browsing are complementary to each other, opposites, in a way. Monitoring is directed and passive, while browsing is undirected and active. In monitoring (cell "B" of Figure 3), we maintain a back-of-the-mind alertness for things that interest us, and for answers to questions we have. We do not feel such a pressing need that we engage in an active effort to gather the information we are interested in; we are content to catch as it goes by, so to speak. We also may have a question in mind and not act to find an answer, but notice when information comes along that is relevant to the question. (The activity that has been called "maintaining current awareness" in the information seeking literature may use monitoring, directed searching or browsing.)

One of the things the information seeking in context research is teaching us is that, intentionally or unintentionally, we often arrange our physical and social environment so as to provide the information we need when we need it. From grocery lists to the arrangement of dials in airplane cockpits, to the physical placement of and organization of tools and offices, we make it possible to be reminded, when we need reminding, of next steps or appropriate behaviors. See Hutchins (1995), Sellen and Harper (2002), and Star and Ruhleder (1996) for examples of research into these sorts of contextual supports. The availability of these supports cuts down on the need for active information seeking. Here it is hard to draw a line between simple awareness and monitoring. Presumably, the more experienced one is with a particular action or process, the more likely one is to be monitoring the environments for the infrastructural triggers for the next behavior.

The elaborate social infrastructure of academic disciplines (Garvey, 1979; Wiberley & Jones, 1989; Bates, 1994), of hobbyist groups (Hartel, 2002), and of work groups (Hutchins, 1995; Star & Ruhleder, 1996) is very supportive of monitoring. A person is likely to come across a great deal of useful information just in the process of interacting socially and physically within the relevant milieu. In academic departments, scientific laboratories, as well as at conferences and over listservs, the typical participant in a discipline or work group continually runs into people who have a lot of common areas of knowledge, people who can suggest information or resources of use to the participant. See Menzel (1959) for excellent examples. These serendipitous encounters are not truly by chance, in the usual sense of the term. Rather, they are the product of proximity, either electronically or physically, that has come about through people organizing for common goals and needs.

Browsing Browsing is the complementary opposite of monitoring. Here we have no special information need or interest, but actively expose ourselves to possibly novel information (Figure 3, cell "C"). It can be said that **monitoring** and **directed searching** are ways we find information that we know we need to know, and **browsing** and **being aware** are ways we find information that we do not know we need to know.

Curiosity may lead to browsing behavior. Curiosity poses an interesting dilemma for animals over the course of biological evolution. Curiosity *has* killed a few cats. See also discussion in Loewenstein (1994). Curiosity may lead to discovering new food sources or mates, but it can also lead an animal to unexpected dangers. It seems likely, then, that there is a trade-off, a balance between too much and too little curiosity in a species. We may presume that the amount of curiosity in a given species is approximately right for at least some of the conditions that that species evolved under.

It pays to examine closely the actual physical behavior engaged in by a browsing person. Barbara Kwasnik (1992), in work that has been too little recognized, identified the actual physical activities associated with browsing. She noted that people do not just scan the horizon in one single movement, but rather take a glimpse, look further at things that interest them, then take another glimpse, and so on. She identified actions within browsing, such as orientation, place-marking, comparison, resolution of anomalies, and so on. This is a complex behavior, charged with meaning. And it shows up in many human behaviors, not only in interaction with recorded information. See also discussion in Rice et al. (2001).

My doctoral advisee, Jenna Hartel, has been developing an approach to browsing in which she has identified a variety of behaviors that can all be seen as similar to browsing, that is, the same underlying impulse is translated into a generic behavior we call "sampling and selecting." Behaviors she has identified to date include browsing, berrypicking, mingling, dating, shopping, nibbling, sightseeing, wayfinding, channel surfing, and Web surfing.

In each of these cases, a person samples from a number of possibilities and then selects from among the options. In another paper, we are arguing that this sampling and selecting behavior may have evolved out of mating and foraging behavior. Indeed, some of the things on this list *are* mating and foraging!

Sandstrom (1994, 1999) and Pirolli and Card (1999) have written extensively on what they call "information foraging." It is a common pattern, recognized in evolutionary biology, that a feature adapted for one purpose in a species is used for another purpose when the environment puts different demands on the species. Gould and Vrba (1982) call this "exaptation."

We have no way to prove this, but it may be that foraging behavior has exapted to browsing or other information seeking behavior. We suspect that, in the act of browsing, human beings have applied a general propensity to sample and select, evolved through millions of years, to sampling and selecting from information objects or sources.

Directed searching Finally, we come to directed search—active attempts to answer questions or develop understanding around a particular question or topic area (Figure 3, cell "A"). If being aware gives us 80 percent of all we know, then directed searching probably gives us one percent, with browsing and monitoring taking up the rest. Countless studies have shown that people use the principle of least effort in their information seeking, even to the point that they will accept information they know to be of lower quality (less reliable), if it is more readily available or easier to use. A large number of these studies are reviewed in Poole (1985).

We have long puzzled in this field over this human perverseness. Why do physicians not use the medical literature, rather than relying on the drug company salesperson for information about a new drug? Why will our students not get up and walk a hundred meters to access a key journal article in the library? Well, put in the context presented here, we can see that throughout human history, most of the information a person needed came to him or her without requiring active efforts to acquire it. Picture the hunter-gatherer: raised in a family group or clan, most learning came through interaction with one's mates and with the environment, that is, through being aware and monitoring. As one's clan moved around, looking for food, one would forage in new environments, that is, one would essentially browse for food, for materials for shelter, for possible mates, etc., wherever one happened to wander.

Once in a while, one would have a specific problem to be solved that required some information to answer. One would ask others, or try to discover an answer on one's own, through experiment or exploration. So, throughout human history, active searching for information has actually been a relatively rare act in most lives. Or, to put it differently, we get so much information through the natural conduct of our lives, from the flow of people and events around us, that it is easy to fall back on those rather passive habits, to expect that the needed information will just come along, rather than having to expend energy to acquire it.

Directed searching is further complicated by another factor in our modern lives. It has only been in the last 200 years or so that the amount of recorded information available has grown to such an extent that complex and sophisticated access mechanisms have had to be developed to enable access. So, people accustomed to mostly passive ways of learning new information not only have to search actively for the information, but also have to master a fair amount of ancillary skills and knowledge just to be able to search for the information, with no guarantee that that effort will actually lead to an answer.

Put in this way, I think we can see why the overwhelming propensity of most people is to invest as absolutely little effort into information seeking as they possibly can. It is only in moments of great urgency or great interest that they spontaneously begin investing seriously in acquiring the information skills needed to satisfy their needs.

Information farming

Sandstrom's research showed that, not surprisingly, people sought to reduce their information seeking effort (Sandstrom, 1999). However, her foraging model makes it possible to explain effort reduction more fully than we have otherwise been able to do to date. She found that "such searching behaviors as regular reading, browsing or the deliberate information foray (relatively solitary information-seeking activities) yielded resources belonging mostly to the peripheral zones of scholars' information environments" (p. 19). She found that core resources, by contrast, were often resident in the scholar's own personal collection, or came through colleagues, article reviewing, and other socially mediated channels.

Put in the terms used earlier in this article, much information comes through the social milieu one works in—just as it came in hunter-gatherer times through the family or clan, and much of the rest comes from personal collections. It is only rarely that the scholar forages alone into truly new territory.

However, hunter-gatherers have no "personal collections." In their case, life is lived in a nomadic manner, and collections of objects cannot realistically be carried along. Collecting things did not really begin until nomadic peoples became sedentary, that is, began farming (Harris & Hillman, 1989).

The items one collects personally can be seen in analogy to farming, because the scholar "tends" the farm by organizing the materials for later use. Whether the resources are simply sorted in meaningful piles on a desk, or filed in various systems of organization, the scholar typically creates and exploits a system of organization for personally owned materials. This process is called "enrichment" by Pirolli and Card (1999). Also compare Case (1991a, 1991b), Soper (1976), and Sellen and Harper (2002). Sandstrom was studying researchers, but there are many examples of people in other walks of life and in pursuit of hobbies who collect a great deal of information and organize it for their continuing uses.

The integrated model

The four-part model of awareness, monitoring, browsing, and searching in Figure 3 may be seen to incorporate both information seeking in general, as well as explicit acts of information searching; in other words, it may be seen as an integrated view of information seeking and searching.

The two passive modes of information seeking—awareness and monitoring—almost certainly provide the vast majority of information for most people during their lives. The child soaks up what is in its environment, and even adults, who have full freedom of movement, often rely almost entirely on whatever information comes their way socially and culturally in order to solve life or work problems. As Sandstrom noted, much information comes to the scholar through the social structures within which the scholar is embedded—service on editorial boards, graduate training, discussion with colleagues (Sandstrom, 1999, p. 19).

In the model, active information seeking occurs with the other two methods of browsing and directed searching. In both of these cases, it appears that a fundamental behavior, which Hartel and I call "sampling and selecting," has likely been exapted from mating and foraging behaviors to the more socially and cognitively sophisticated human behavior of information seeking. I suggested in 1989 (Bates, 1989) that what I called "berrypicking"—which I would now see as one more manifestation of sampling and selecting—was the more common and natural way people actually engaged in active directed searching. I argued against formalistic models in which the searcher submitted a query to an information system and the system found what the searcher wanted. Rather, I suggested, the searcher typically finds information a bit at a time, uses a variety of sources—diet breadth, in the parlance of foraging theory (Pirolli & Card, 1999)—and a variety of search methods to find everything wanted, i.e., engages in berrypicking.

In the more comprehensive context of both this four-part model and of the concept of "sampling and selecting," it can be seen that both browsing and berrypicking are types of sampling and selecting. Browsing is undirected, while berrypicking is more directed. In fact, one could argue that berrypicking is the natural mode for doing all directed searching, though, for one reason or other, not everyone is able to engage in berrypicking to solve directed search needs. So, left to their own devices, most people resort to sampling and selecting techniques for both directed (berrypicking) and undirected (browsing) active information searching.

Thus, in terms of information seeking as behavior, people operate in two general modes—sampling and selecting (Figure 3, "A," "C") or passive absorption ("B," "D"). When they know what information they want, people generally either actively search for it (A), or monitor environmental information for it (B). When they do not know what they want, people browse (C) or remain passively aware (D). Thus the natural propensities of human beings are to collect information passively through absorption from the environment or actively through sampling and selecting.

The role of the social structure of information access

Let us suppose, then, that the natural predilection of most people is to fall back on passive absorption or sampling and selecting as a way to find needed information. What happens when this propensity encounters the complex structures of libraries, classifications, metadata, and so on? It was not until approximately the late eighteenth or early nineteenth century that the quantity of publications available became so large that libraries began to have to find more powerful means of access to the contents of book and other collections. Before then, the knowledgeable librarian or scholar often knew of all the relevant materials for a given research interest.

However, in the modern industrial world, when more powerful methods of printing and distribution were developed, it became possible for libraries to collect far larger numbers of items than had been dreamed of before. More effective access became a pressing need, and all the systems developed in the nineteenth and twentieth centuries—classified and alphabetico-specific catalogs, subject headings and thesaurus terms, online database searching and the World Wide Web—constituted efforts to make a small slice of information accessible within ever-larger enveloping collections.

An enormous amount of energy has gone into the design and application of these various systems—yet the information seeking literature continues to show that people avoid or ignore these monumental access systems to a great extent—even people with doctorates, who we would expect to be very skilled in information searching. With the biological/anthropological approach taken in this paper, perhaps we can now see this human propensity in the following way: The natural human tendency in information seeking is to fall back on passive and sampling and selecting behaviors derived from millions of years of evolutionary development. Information seeking has thus generally been done in a rather unconscious or automatic way. To put it differently, passive absorption and sampling and selecting have been around so long that they are carried out in a completely natural, unselfconscious way.

On the other hand, complex intellectual systems of access are only a century or two old, at most. To use them effectively, they require that the searcher master quite a bit of both substantive knowledge about the systems of access, as well as technical searching skills, known as "declarative" and "procedural" knowledge, respectively (Bhavnani & Bates, 2002). As people are generally quite unaware of their usual information seeking behaviors, they do not even have as a part of their conscious thought the idea that one needs searching skills and search planning—let alone know of specific strategies they can follow to find what they want. In that case, it is not surprising, then, that the methods of access designed by librarians are generally little used.

Perhaps, finally, this biological/anthropological perspective on information seeking can go some way in explaining the persistent results we find in studies of information seeking and searching. People use least effort because they have always used it, and because, until very recently, it has worked adequately, if not optimally.

Integrated model redux

I have endeavored to provide an example in which some of the levels in Figure 1 are at least partially integrated in our thinking about the information seeking and searching of human beings. I would like now to return to the philosophical question of how these levels should properly be integrated. How we do so can be interpreted in many ways. Briefly, I would like to compare this approach to those of two other papers presented recently, which also discuss types of integrated models—those of Tuominen, Talja, and Savolainen (2002), on the one hand, and of Hjørland (2002) on the other hand.

In their 2002 conference article entitled "Discourse, cognition, and reality. . .," Tuominen, Talja, and Savolainen discuss three metatheories, which they term the "information transfer" model, the constructivist model, and the constructionist model. To put it in simplistic, but not seriously distorting terms, they equate the first model with a classically scientific approach, the second with a cognitivist approach in which the individual experiencing person is the focus of attention, and the third with the socially and linguistically negotiated production of knowledge and discourse communities. They see the three theories as following upon each other in time, each constituting a "correction" of the prior ones (Tuominen, Talja, & Savolainen, p. 279). They argue for the third, and most recent, in this series, constructionism, as being superior, and as a good metatheory upon which to base present library and information science research. We could thus say that they are writing within a historical perspective, in which each new metatheoretical development improves upon and enriches the prior metatheory. Thus, the scientific approach of the "information transfer" model is passé, retro—good in its time, to be sure, but now superseded twice over by successive superior metatheories, cognitivism and then constructionism.

Hjørland, on the other hand, takes a different strategy. In his 2002 paper, "Epistemology and the socio-cognitive perspective in information science" (Hjørland, 2002), he contrasts the cognitive metatheory with the socio-cognitive, or, "domain-analytic" metatheory. As he says, "In domain analysis, we are less inclined to speak about mental models and more inclined to talk about knowledge, (pre)understanding, theories, paradigms, and epistemologies" (Hjørland, 2002, p. 261). He argues for the latter approach, just as do Tuominen et al. (2002).

Hjørland astutely points out that:

The cognitive view tends to psychologize the epistemological issues (to study knowledge by studying the individual), but what is needed is the socio-cognitive view, which tends to epistemologize psychological issues (to see individual knowledge in a historical, cultural, and social perspective). (p. 268)

Let us examine the logical and rhetorical strategies used in these two articles. Tuominen et al. argue that constructionism has grown up as a correction, and by implication, a clear improvement on, prior scientific and cognitivist metatheories. Hjørland, on the other hand, argues that the cognitive view has psychologized epistemological questions, that this is wrong, and that what is needed now is a socio-cognitive metatheory that epistemologizes psychological issues. In other words, in our field, epistemology should lead and dominate psychology.

I want to take a third logical and rhetorical position. The scientific, the cognitive, and the socially constructed metatheories need not struggle for dominance. The epistemological issues should not be psychologized and the psychological issues should not be epistemologized. Nor should these metatheories be viewed in a solely historical context, in which whatever came earlier is automatically inferior. The very fact that we have at some point in human history, explored and learned much that is meaningful from these various metatheoretical perspectives should suggest that there may be a *valuable continuing role for all of them.*

Each of these three perspectives, as well as the several others referred to in Figure 1, constitute distinctive types of learning, research, and understanding that human beings have developed over the course of our history. The paradigms of the various disciplines, as well as the range of distinctive sub-paradigms that develop within these disciplines over time, represent human explorations in mind, in the social world, and in nature. Each of these distinctive intellectual perspectives constitutes a wonderfully enriching means of understanding human experience.

Not infrequently, different philosophical perspectives and metatheories lie behind the understanding at each level. I would venture to say that the typical physicist has a different kind of mind, a different cognitive style, from the psychologist, and the psychologist a different one from the literary scholar. These differences are developed and sharpened through decades of study and intellectual development in individuals and in whole intellectual communities and disciplines.

We should not be surprised, therefore, if we find conflicts between these perspectives. I would argue, however, that we should address the conflicts directly through a dialogue leading to mutual understanding, rather than through an approach that seeks to enforce the triumph of one metatheory over another.

Conclusions

In this article, it has been argued that a more complete understanding of information seeking behavior requires attention to the several levels of human existence, not only to the social or individual perspectives. Biological and anthropological levels have been discussed in relation to previously known social behaviors of human beings with regard to information seeking.

Information seeking has been conceptualized in terms of all the ways in which information comes to people, including much that is absorbed passively. It has been argued that more active efforts to acquire information, such as browsing and berrypicking, are probably applications of a generic human behavior known as sampling and selecting. Sampling and selecting, in turn, may be an exaptation (though I cannot prove it) from original animal food foraging and mating behavior.

Searching thus becomes one behavior within a general model of human information-related behaviors (see Figure 3). Human tendencies to use the principle of least effort, and more generally, to be quite passive in information seeking, may come about because so much needed information has come automatically from the social milieux of most people throughout the history of humanity.

Finally, it has been argued that the several metatheories driving research in information seeking each have much of value to offer, and should not be placed in a life or death struggle for dominance in our thinking and research.

REFERENCES

Bates, M.J. (1986). An exploratory paradigm for online information retrieval. In B.C. Brookes (Ed.), *Intelligent information systems for the information society. Proceedings of the Sixth International Research Forum in Information Science (IRFIS 6), Frascati, Italy* (pp. 91–99). Netherlands: North-Holland.

Bates, M.J. (1989). The design of browsing and berrypicking techniques for the online search interface. *Online Review, 13*(5), 407–424.

Bates, M.J. (1994). The design of databases and other information resources for humanities scholars: The Getty Online Searching Project report no. 4. *Online & CDROM Review 18*(6), 331–340.

Bhavnani, S., & Bates, M.J. (2002). Separating the knowledge layers: Cognitive analysis of search knowledge through hierarchical goal decompositions. *Proceedings of the 64th ASIST Annual Meeting, 39,* 204–213.

Case, D.O. (1991a). Collection and use of information by some American historians: A study of motives and methods. *The Library Quarterly 61*(1), 61–82.

Case, D.O. (1991b). Conceptual organization and retrieval of text by historians: The role of memory and metaphor. *Journal of the American Society for Information Science 42*(9), 657–668.

Garvey, W.D. (1979). *Communication: The essence of science: Facilitating information exchange among librarians, scientists, engineers, and students.* New York: Pergamon Press.

Gould, S.J., & Vrba, E.S. (1982). Exaptation—A missing term in the science of form. *Paleobiology 8*(1), 4–15.

Harris, D.R., & Hillman, G.C. (Eds.). (1989). *Foraging and farming: The evolution of plant exploitation.* London: Unwin Hyman.

Hartel, J. (2002). *Appetite for information in the hobby of cooking.* Poster at Information Seeking in Context: The Fourth International Conference on Information Needs, Seeking and Use in Different Contexts, Lisbon, Portugal.

Hjørland, B. (2002). Epistemology and the socio-cognitive perspective in information science. *Journal of the American Society for Information Science and Technology 53*(4), 257–270.

Hutchins, E. (1995). *Cognition in the wild.* Cambridge, MA: MIT Press.

Jackendoff, R. (2002). *Foundations of language: Brain, meaning, grammar, evolution.* New York: Oxford University Press.

Kwasnik, B.H. (1992). *Descriptive Study of the Functional Components of Browsing.* Paper presented at the Proceedings of the IFIP TC2\WG2.7 Working Conference on Engineering for Human-Computer Interaction, Elivuoi, Finland, August 10–14, 1992.

Loewenstein, G. (1994). The psychology of curiosity: A review and reinterpretation. *Psychological Bulletin 116*(1), 75–98.

Menzel, H. (1959). Planned and unplanned scientific communication. In *Proceedings of the International Conference on Scientific Information* (Vol. 1, pp. 199–243). Washington, D.C.: National Academy of Sciences, National Research Council.

Pinker, S. (1995). *The language instinct.* New York: Harper Perennial.

Pirolli, P., & Card, S. (1999). Information foraging. *Psychological Review 106*(4), 643–675.

Poole, H.L. (1985). *Theories of the middle range*. Norwood, NJ: Ablex.

Rice, R.E., McCreadie, M., & Chang, S.-J.L. (2001). *Accessing and browsing information and communication*. Cambridge, MA: MIT Press.

Sandstrom, A.R., & Sandstrom, P.E. (1995). The use and misuse of anthropological methods in library and information science research. *The Library Quarterly, 65*(2), 161–199.

Sandstrom, P.E. (1994). An optimal foraging approach to information seeking and use. *The Library Quarterly, 64*(4), 414–449.

Sandstrom, P.E. (1999). Scholars as subsistence foragers. *Bulletin of the American Society for Information Science 25*(3), 17–20.

Sellen, A.J., & Harper, R.H.R. (2002). *The myth of the paperless office*. Cambridge, MA: MIT Press.

Soper, M.E. (1976). Characteristics and use of personal collections. *The Library Quarterly 46*(4), 397–415.

Star, S.L., & Ruhleder, K. (1996). Steps toward an ecology of infrastructure—design and access for large information spaces. *Information Systems Research 7*(1), 111–134.

Tuominen, K., Talja, S., & Savolainen, R. (2002). Discourse, cognition, and reality: Toward a social constructionist metatheory for library and information science. In H. Bruce, R. Fidel, P. Ingwersen, & P. Vakkari (Eds.), *Emerging frameworks and methods: Proceedings of the Fourth International Conference on Conceptions of Library and Information Science (CoLIS 4)* (pp. 271–283). Greenwood Village, CO: Libraries Unlimited.

Walter, V.A. (1994). The information needs of children. *Advances in Librarianship 18*, 111–129.

Wiberley, S.E., Jr., & Jones, W.G. (1989). Patterns of information seeking in the humanities. *College & Research Libraries, 50*(6), 638–645.

2

Information behavior

ABSTRACT

"Information behavior" is the currently preferred term used to describe
the many ways in which human beings interact with information, in particular, the ways in which people seek and utilize information. The broad
history of research on information-seeking behavior over the last 50–60
years is reviewed, major landmarks are identified, and current directions
in research are discussed.

Introduction

"Information behavior" is the currently preferred term used to describe the
many ways in which human beings interact with information, in particular, the ways in which people seek and utilize information. Information
behavior is also the term of art used in library and information science (LIS)
to refer to a subdiscipline that engages in a wide range of types of research
conducted in order to understand the human relationship to information.

Interest in this area developed out of several streams. Librarians
wanted to understand library users better, government agencies wanted
to understand how scientists and engineers used technical information

First published as Bates, M. J. (2010). Information Behavior. In M. J. Bates & M. N. Maack
(Eds.), *Encyclopedia of library and information sciences* (3rd ed., Vol. 3, pp. 2381–2391). Boca
Raton, FL: CRC Press.

in order to promote more rapid uptake of new research results, and social scientists generally were interested in the social uses of information in a variety of senses. In more recent years, social studies of information technology (IT) and social informatics have contributed to this area as well. Within LIS, these various streams of research are drawn on for what they can contribute to a richer understanding of information behavior.

Information

What, then, is information? Here, rather than review the many senses in which this term has been interpreted in the field, we will rely on a sense of the term that is an extended understanding of the concept as used in general conversation. We all recognize that people search for information on, say, the history of a small town, the population of Turkey, or how to do foreign exchange trading online. All these examples make a reasonable match with the generally understood sense of information as being factual, statistical, and/or procedural (See the entry on "Information," p. 2347).

"Information," however, is used in a broader sense as well in the world of information behavior research. The term is generally assumed to cover all instances where people interact with their environment in any such way that leaves some impression on them—that is, adds or changes their knowledge store. These impressions can include the emotional changes that result from reading a novel, or learning that one's friend is ill. These changes can also reflect complex interactions where information combines with preexisting knowledge to make new understandings, or enables the individual to deduce or induce new thoughts and ideas. As the Hans Christian Andersen tale suggested, the ugly ducking did not realize that he was a swan until he came in contact with swans, saw his reflection in water, and figured out that he was himself a swan, too (Andersen, 1907).

These information interactions can also leave a negative impact—one may ignore, deny, or reject information (Case, Andrews, Johnson & Allard, 2005). (See also an excellent early analysis of relations to information by Atkin [1973].) One may also simply discover that nothing has changed—the university admissions letter still hasn't come in the mail. This negative news is, of course, informative in its own way, just as a person who has ignored information has often, in some way or other, nonetheless absorbed it. In fact, probably the largest amount of all information taken in by human beings is that received passively—simply through being aware—that is absorbed in the context of daily living (Bates, 2002).

Is this not a very broad understanding of information behavior? Indeed, does it not cover all interactions people have with their environment? Bates has argued:

In comparison to other social and behavioral science fields, we are always looking for the red thread of information in the social texture of people's lives. When we study people we do so with the purpose of understanding information creation, seeking, and use. We do not just study people in general.... In communications research, a cousin to our field, the emphasis is on the communication process and its effects on people; in information science we study that process *in service of information transfer.* (Bates, 1999)

Bates goes on to provide a specific example:

... [T]here are social scientists today who are observing people doing collaborative work through new types of networked systems in the field of computer-supported cooperative work (CSCW). The sociologist or social psychologist identifies and describes the network of relationships and the social hierarchy that develops under these circumstances....

The information scientist, on the other hand, follows the information.... That's the red thread in the social tapestry. When we look at that social hierarchy, we are not interested in the hierarchy per se, but, rather, we ask how it impedes or promotes the transfer of information. We ask what kinds of information people prefer to communicate through this or that new channel of information technology. We always follow the information. (Bates, 1999)

Thus, the study of information behavior can cast a very wide net, looking into both individual interactions as well as large-scale complex group and societal interactions with information. Indeed, as we shall see, the variety of contexts in which information behavior has been studied demonstrates this breadth. But information behavior research is not communication, psychology, education, sociology, or social impacts of technology research, though all those disciplines may find the work interesting to discover. Rather, information behavior research actually studies—and largely limits itself to—information-related behavior.

History of information behavior research

From the earliest days, librarianship in the United States had a commitment to care about and serve the users of libraries. In the founding year of American professional librarianship, 1876, Samuel Green wrote to encourage librarians to "mingle freely" with the library's users "and help them in every way" (Green, 1876). In the mid-twentieth century, the great Indian librarian, S.R. Ranganathan, promulgated his Five Laws of Librarianship, which were very much oriented to the library user:

1. Books are for use
2. Every reader, his book
3. Every book its reader
4. Save the time of the reader
5. The library is a growing organism (Ranganathan, 1957)

However, for many decades that commitment remained largely on the plane of values and had little other than anecdotal data upon which to develop library services. In the 1930s, the Graduate Library School at the University of Chicago (Richardson, 1982) introduced the first doctoral degree in library science in the United States. Sophisticated social science researchers, such as Douglas Waples and Bernard Berelson, brought their skills to the field. Waples (1938) did research on reader preferences, and Berelson, among other things, produced a compendium of results from dozens of studies on public library use (Berelson, 1945, 1949).

The experiences associated with the operation of "Big science" during World War II—major projects such as the development of the atom bomb—led government leaders to see the advantages in improving the distribution and transfer of information on new discoveries to other scientists and engineers. Major conferences on scientific information, in 1948 and 1959, led to a substantial amount of money being invested during the 1950s and 1960s in research on how scientists gathered and used information in their research work. Major example publications were the proceedings of the two science information conferences (Royal Society of London Scientific Information Conference, 1948; Proceedings of the International Conference on Scientific Information, 1959), the 21-report series "Project on Scientific Information Exchange in Psychology" from the American Psychological Association (1968), and the work of Garvey et al. on several disciplines (Garvey & Griffith, 1967; Garvey, 1970). Other influential early works include publications by Derek de Solla Price (1963, 1965), Diana

Crane (1972), and A.J. Meadows (1974). (Note: In order to keep this entry's long bibliography from being even longer, referenced items are often only a sample of a person's work, and when a series of articles comes out from a project, generally only the last article in the series is referenced.)

Early on, studies on information behavior were called "use studies" (Davis & Bailey, 1964), studies of "information seeking and gathering," or studies of "information needs and uses" (Menzel, 1966). Gradually, the term "information-seeking research" was used to include all kinds of research on people's interaction with information.

More recently, however, some researchers came to feel that "information seeking" suggested only explicit efforts to locate information, and did not include the many other ways people and information interacted. In the 1990s, the term "information behavior" came into wide use to replace "information seeking." The Old Guard objected that the phrase is a non-sequitur—information does not "behave"—but, they lost out, and "information behavior" remains the most commonly used term today.

During the 1960s, in particular, generous funding was available in the United States for social science research, and a great deal of knowledge, based on large, well-designed studies, was developed regarding the social aspects of scientific communication and information use (Paisley, 1968; Garvey, 1979; Poole, 1985). Important studies were also produced on information use and library use by the general public (Bundy, 1967; Warner et al., 1973; Dervin, 1976). Focus in the larger society during the 1960s and 1970s on identity politics of race, gender, sexual orientation, and the economically underprivileged also led to research attention being directed to information seeking of the corresponding population groups.

In the late 1960s and early 1970s, this research began to be taught in library and information educational programs in North America (Bates, 2004). As scientists had been studied according to their disciplines—physics, biology, etc.—and many members of the general public had been studied by their social identities—the poor, the elderly, etc.—there was a tendency to study information-related behavior by looking at groups of these sorts. For example, an invited conference on "information service needs of the nation" was funded by the U.S. National Commission on Libraries and Information Science in 1973. Presentations were structured in a parallel format to address the needs of a number of groups, including people working in science, agriculture, business, labor, biomedicine, the arts, social services, as well as children, the geographically remote, the economically and socially deprived, the institutionalized, and the mentally and physically handicapped, among others (Cuadra & Bates, 1974).

After the earlier attention to the natural sciences, during the 1970s research attention turned to information transfer in the social sciences. Grant funding in the United States receded, and pride of place went to Great Britain, where several researchers engaged in creative and revealing research on information seeking and use in the social sciences (Blake, Morkham & Skinner, 1979; Brittain, 1979; Streatfield & Wilson, 1982).

Finally, in the 1980s and 1990s the underfunded humanities at last got their due (Wiberley, 1989; Case, 1991; Cobbledick, 1996; Chu, 1999), particularly with the support of large institutions such as the J. Paul Getty Trust (Bates, 1996). In the 1990s interdisciplinary and area studies researchers were addressed (Westbrook, 2003). See, especially Carole Palmer, as Issue Editor, of an issue of *Library Trends* on interdisciplinary information seeking (Palmer, 1996), as well as her subsequent book (Palmer, 2001).

In the 2000s, Kari and Hartel made a persuasive case for studying the information behavior of people engaged in activities aimed at fulfillment and self-realization, and their own research provided examples of what could be learned along this line (Kari & Hartel, 2007).

Over the decades, varying amounts of information behavior research has been done in various professional contexts as well, including the health sciences (Davies, 2007), law (Sutton, 1994), and business (Auster & Choo, 1993). Among the professions, it is almost certainly the health sciences where the largest body of information behavior research has been done— probably due to abundant funding—while the education profession, despite the importance of information seeking for teachers, seems, mysteriously, to have drawn very little attention (Summers, Matheson & Conry, 1983; Williams & Coles, 2007).

Throughout the years, a number of models have been proposed to characterize various aspects of information behavior. Paisley beautifully characterized the subjective world of the scientist, as constituting a series of contexts—local work environment, research specialty, discipline, larger cultural and political world, etc. (Paisley, 1968). In 1981, Tom Wilson described information seeking in general in a model (Wilson, 1981) that was subsequently very widely used, and also reviewed a wide range of information behavior models in 1999 (Wilson, 1999). Belkin et al. propounded the concept of "anomalous state of knowledge," or ASK (Belkin, Oddy & Brooks, 1982), as characterizing many information needs. That is to say, they argued that the information need is often complex and requires an extensive description to cover all the factors really at play in people's requests. Kuhlthau's Information Search Process model, based on extensive research, demonstrated how intricately the conceptualization of a paper or project was bound up with confusions and problems in searching for information (Kuhlthau,

1991). Bates' "berrypicking," i.e., picking up a bit of knowledge here and a bit of knowledge there, was seen to be an appropriate description of much of human searching to meet information needs (Bates, 1989), in contrast to the previous generally assumed simple query that could be answered by a single retrieval from just one database.

Though extensive research on information seeking inside and outside of LIS had been going on since the 1950s, it was an article by Dervin and Nilan in 1986 (Dervin & Nilan, 1986), however, that seemed to provide the impetus for a great increase in interest in the subject in LIS. The authors articulated the value of placing the user/searcher at the center of research, and paying close attention to the internal motivations and needs of the information seeker. From a minority interest of a relatively few people, information behavior research exploded in LIS after that article appeared, and doctoral students flocked to the subject area. For example, the number of articles dubbed "Use studies," the standard term used in Wilson Web's article database *Library Literature and Information Full Text*, doubled per year in the 5 years between 1985 and 1990—from 76 to 155—while in the subsequent 18 years, the annual number has gone up by less than 60% to 245 in 2008 (author's database search). (Of course, these results could be artifacts of the publisher's indexing practices, and a fuller exploration would be needed to verify this conclusion.)

In particular, Dervin's conception of "sensemaking," the effort of people to make sense of many aspects of their lives through information seeking and use, has been a dominating force in recent research on information behavior (http://communication.sbs.ohio-state.edu/sense-making/AAauthors/authorlistdervin.html [accessed June 2008]).

Dervin dismissed prior studies on grounds that "the studies assumed that the information brick was being thrown into the empty bucket"—i.e., into the user of information (Dervin, 1983). In one blow, this clever metaphor both characterized and caricatured much of the more classically empirical scientific approaches to research on information behavior, and gave qualitative research techniques and philosophies a boost. Dervin's "brick" image was unfair to the many researchers who did not take a simplistic view of information transfer, including many of the people mentioned in this entry to this point (Talja & Hartel, 2007). However, her emphasis on the importance of sense-making in motivating information seeking legitimated the subsequent emphasis on qualitative techniques in the field, and enlarged the perspective of the whole subdiscipline of information behavior.

Indeed, over the years, increasing dissatisfaction was expressed by some researchers toward the prior orientation either to the individual seeking information, or to studying the tendencies and preferences of large social groups, such as physicists or older people. These researchers sought to expand information behavior research, drawing on several theoretical paradigms of interest in the social sciences, such as social constructivism, social constructionism, and ethnographic techniques (Talja, Tuominen & Savolainen, 2005).

The surest sign of this broader interest came in the form of the "Information Seeking in Context" (ISIC) conference that came to be presented every other year, mostly in Europe, beginning in 1996 (http://www.kf.vu. lt/~isic2008/?page_id=4 [accessed June 2008]). Conference attendees have sought to study information behavior in a way that goes beyond traditional research designs. They argue that context must be understood in a much fuller sense; they argue for rich, detailed, qualitative study of specific situations and contexts, in order to understand the very nuanced ways in which people might receive and shape information.

They draw upon many different information-related theories and models (Fisher, Erdelez & McKechnie, 2005), as well as on the many varieties of metatheoretical and philosophical perspectives that have become popular in the social sciences and humanities (Bates, 2005). See, as examples of these newer approaches, Ellis' grounded theory approach (Ellis, 1993), Talja's discourse analysis of the culture of music in relation to libraries (Talja, 2001), Xu's application of activity theory to interactive information retrieval (Xu & Liu, 2007), Reddy and Jansen's ethnographic study of collaborative information behavior in health care (Reddy & Jansen, 2008), Limberg's (1999) and Ford's (1986, 2004) use of educational theory, and Srinivasan and Pyati's critical reexamination of information environments for diasporic groups (Srinivasan & Pyati, 2007).

At the same time, research drawing on other, more classically scientific and engineering methodologies did not disappear. See Fidel and Pejtersen's use of the Cognitive Work Analysis Framework (Fidel & Pejtersen, 2004), Sandstrom and Sandstrom's analysis of the methods of scientific anthropology as applied in LIS (Sandstrom & Sandstrom, 1995), Nicholas et al.'s study of online information seeking through transaction log analysis (Nicholas, Huntington, Jamali & Watkinson, 2006), and even Bates' use of biological and evolutionary concepts in her recent work on information (Bates, 2005) and browsing (Bates, 2007).

Perhaps the greatest sign of maturity of the field of information behavior research came with the publication—at last!—of the first book comprehensively addressing information seeking, by Donald Case, in 2002, with a second edition in 2007 (Case, 2007).

The popularity of the ISIC conferences demonstrates the recent efflo-rescence of qualitative information behavior research beyond the borders of the (sometimes self-absorbed) research culture of the United States. Scholars from the United Kingdom (Tom Wilson, David Ellis, Nigel Ford, and Elizabeth Davenport), Ireland (Crystal Fulton), Scandinavia (Louise Limberg, Olof Sundin, and Annelise Mark Pejtersen), and Finland (Pertti Vakkari, Reijo Savolainen, Sanna Talja, and Jannica Heinström) have presented and published at ISIC and elsewhere. Australian (Kirsty Williamson and Theresa Anderson) and Canadian researchers (Heidi Julien, Karen Fisher, Gloria Leckie, Lynne McKechnie, Pam McKenzie, Roma Harris, and Chun Wei Choo) have also been very active in recent years. Recently, Savolainen may have marked the beginning of a new phase in information research when he urged that the qualitative research on information behavior be called instead the study of "information practice" (Savolainen, 2007, p. 109). He argued that the concept of "information behavior" is primarily associated with the cognitive viewpoint, while "information practice is mainly inspired by the ideas of social constructivism" (Savolainen, 2007).

> The concepts of information behavior and information prac-
> tice both seem to refer to the ways in which people "deal with
> information." The major difference is that within the discourse
> on information behavior, the "dealing with information" is
> primarily seen to be triggered by needs and motives, while
> the discourse on information practice accentuates the con-
> tinuity and habitualization of activities affected and shaped
> by social and cultural factors. . . . (Savolainen, 2007, p. 126)

In the last several years, there has also been a very active Special Interest Group on Information Behavior (SIG-USE), founded by Barbara Wildemuth and Karen Fisher, among others, in the American Society for Information Science and Technology, which has held a number of preconferences and conference sessions, and offered awards for research in the area.

Information searching vs. information seeking

The above discussion addressed research on how people interact with information, how and when they seek information, and what uses they make of it. But it should be understood that throughout this period of time a parallel body of research and practical application was continuing that addressed the specifics of *the act of searching itself.* That is, in working with paper and online resources, many problems were encountered and skills needed to succeed in the specific acts associated with locating information in a paper or online resource. Bates' articles on information searching tactics and search techniques (Bates, 1979, 1981) promoted greater attention to the complexities of identifying sources and working one's way through resources to locate the desired information. A long line of research followed that addressed both search success and desirable design features in information systems to promote ease of use (Cochrane & Markey, 1983; Fidel, 1984; Hsieh-Yee, 1993; Marchionini, 1995; Spink, Wolfram, Jansen & Saracevic, 2001). Even browsing, normally seen as the most unstructured method of information searching, came in for considerable attention (O'Connor, 1993; Rice, McCreadie & Chang, 2001; Bates, 2007) (See the entry on "Information Searching and Search Models," p. 2592).

Role of technology in information behavior research

In order to simplify the narrative line, the above discussion made little mention of the role of technology in information seeking and research on information seeking. But, in fact, the extraordinary changes in IT over the last 50–60 years have meant that a great deal of information behavior research has also been concerned with impacts of and reactions to the kinds of interactions people experience when using new technologies for finding and communicating information.

Focus on impacts of, and roles of, IT in information behavior has been intertwined to a greater and lesser extent with the information behavior research over these decades. Early studies took a fairly stable, largely paper-based environment for granted. Indeed, Garvey's research (Garvey, 1979) made salient, perhaps for the first time for many readers of his work, the huge, complex scientific publication cycle, from early tentative verbal presentation at talks all the way through conference presentations, summary reports, journal publication, annual reviews, and finally, incorporation of the scientific results into the established canon in textbooks.

But consciousness of the complexity of the production and publication of science was soon joined by efforts to improve, especially to speed up, the collection, storage, organization, and dissemination of that information.

Indeed, the entire discipline of information science has, in one sense, been the story of the successive absorption of a long series of IT innovations, followed, in each case, by research on the impacts of those innovations, and efforts to improve access to information through optimal design of those innovations. With the excitement generated by each new technology, the relatively stable underlying human behaviors and reactions were sometimes forgotten, and the new technology instead was seen as the source of a totally new information-seeking landscape. One thing we now know, however, after a lot of research on those successive waves of new technology, is that underlying human propensities with regard to information emerge again and again, as each new technology becomes familiar and its use second nature. Often, in the end, the new technologies offer speed and ease of use, while otherwise replicating previous social structures and interactions.

We know, for example, that people are willing to commit very little energy and effort to seeking information, in contrast, say, to seeking a fortune, a family, or a reputation. In fact, the truly explosive popularity of the World Wide Web as an information source may be due to the fact that the level of effort the searcher must engage in to find an answer to a question on the Web is at last so very little as to slip in under that minimal level of (least) effort that feels "natural" in information seeking. Most of the information that people eagerly seek online was once available in their local public or academic library, but the effort required to locate that information was seen as excessive in the vast majority of cases.

In the rest of this section, we will follow several IT innovations and consider their impact on information behavior research.

The first major technology in modern times to affect information seeking was the computer. Initially, its use for library information systems was limited—computers were used to capture machine-readable versions of library catalog records ("MARC" records), which, in turn, enabled the publication of computer-produced print-on-paper book catalogs. This was followed, in short succession, by so-called "COM cats," that is, computer output microfiche catalogs, which could update book catalogs between publications of paper editions (Hodges & Bloch, 1982).

It will be forgotten today, that in the age of card catalogs, while in one library, one could not access the catalog of any other branch of the academic or public library, or of any other library, for that matter. In academic libraries, a comprehensive copy of all the materials on campus was generally available only in the main library. Disseminating multiple copies of the full set of library records through book catalogs and COM cats in branch libraries was a significant, time-saving innovation.

These catalog innovations during the late 1960s and 1970s were followed by a true revolution in catalog accessibility—the online catalog, which was developed in the early 1980s. These constituted the first widely available end-user information search systems, and much was learned about how untrained people did and did not succeed in this form of online searching (Matthews, Lawrence & Ferguson, 1983; Lynch, 1992).

For a variety of reasons, the card catalog structure could not be simply translated into online form. Questions of redesign of catalog access in the new context, and the development of new and faster system designs to improve access occupied many in LIS research over the next 10–15 years (Bates, 1986; Hildreth, 1989; Borgman, 1996) (See the entry on "Online Catalog Subject Searching," p. 3953).

In the meantime, (at least) four other overlapping information-related revolutions were occupying the field as well. The first revolution occurred in the area of information retrieval, where various forms of automatic indexing and retrieval were experimented with over decades from the 1950s forward, gradually improving the speed and effectiveness of both retrieval and ranking algorithms (Salton & McGill, 1983; Voorhees & Harman, 2005). In the 1990s, search engines, such as Alta Vista and Google, drew upon these retrieval techniques to design their Web systems.

Second, in the early 1970s, online database searching was made practicable through searching against large databases on "dumb" terminals receiving and sending data over telephone wires. "Online searching" as then understood, and as then implemented by database vendors, was a complex skill that required considerable training to do well. Teaching these skills became an important part of LIS education, and drew a lot of research interest as well. That type of searching required a mix of gifts that not everyone has, and numerous studies of online searching behavior resulted (Fidel, 1984, 1991; Saracevic & Kantor, 1988).

The third revolution was the development of the Internet and World Wide Web, which enabled access to information all over the world from anywhere in the world. We are still working through the many impacts and implications of this capability for all prior information technologies and sources of information (Cronin & Hert, 1995; Xie, 2003; Rich, 2004).

The fourth revolution occurred with the widespread interest in creating digital libraries of all manner of textual and image material—and sometimes online portals to access those resources. The Digital Libraries Initiative in the 1990s marked the moment when, at last, truly substantial amounts of research money entered the information science field. Ann Bishop and colleagues addressed at book length the sociotechnical factors of digital library use (Bishop, Van House, & Buttenfield, 2003). The new capability of storing and easily accessing previously unimaginably large bodies of information in digital libraries led to innovative experiments in the storage and use of primary resources materials. Example studies are those of children using primary archival materials (Gilliland-Swetland, Kafai & Landis, 1999), uses of texts in the field of classics in a digital library (Marchionini & Crane, 1994), and use of a medical portal (Roderer, Zambrowicz, Zhang & Zhou, 2004).

During the 1970s to the present, many studies of information behavior involved, to a greater or lesser extent, research on people's use of and success with, these innovations in information access. On the whole, more behavioral research was done in the areas of online catalogs and online database searching than in information retrieval. For a long time, IR researchers were not particularly receptive to, or interested in, the human side of the equation, though in the 1990s, they came to realize that people needed attention, too, in the overall effort to improve retrieval. See, for example, the contrasting emphases in the two entries in this encyclopedia by Salton ("SMART System: 1961–1976") and Järvelin and Ingwersen ("User-Oriented and Cognitive Models of Information Retrieval").

With the development of frequent interaction with microcomputers in the early 1980s, the already-thriving field of human–computer interaction research, or HCl, exploded and became a still larger field. HCl paid little attention to LIS research, however, and LIS paid little attention to HCl research, probably to the detriment of both fields. However, there may have been good reasons for this mutual indifference. The specific circumstances of needing and seeking information are not well understood, for the most part, outside of LIS, and required the focused attention of LIS researchers. At the same time, HCl researchers were working to discover general principles applicable to all online and computer access, and therefore tended to ignore the distinctive features of various "application" fields, including information seeking (See the entry on "Human–Computer Interaction in Information Retrieval," p. 2183).

In this encyclopedia, Diane Nahl's two entries on early and recent "User-centered design," as well as entries by Elaine Toms ("User-Centered Design of Information Systems") and Judith Weedman ("Design Science in the Information Sciences") address, in much greater detail, the efforts and results in this area at the intersection of IT and the study of information behavior.

Range of topics of information behavior research

What have we learned over the years from the study of information seeking behavior? This is a hard question to answer briefly, to put it mildly, but a description of the sequence of research topics of interest over the years may give a hint of the growing understanding over time of the human relationship with information. What follows is a mere sampling.

In the 1940s and 1950s information seeking and gathering tended to be viewed implicitly as the study of the use of various forms of literature—books, journals, handbooks, etc.—and of various types of institutions and their services. How many books were circulated, how many reference questions were asked, how many people of what economic strata used the public library, and so on (Berelson, 1949).

In the 1960s and beyond, studies of information seeking and use by the general public opened out the research to incorporate many sources of information, of which the library was only one (Warner et al., 1973; Chen & Hernon, 1982). The first surprise was to discover how much information—in both personal and professional contexts—people got from friends and colleagues. In a study looking at how scientists learned of things serendipitously, Menzel found that fellow scientists were immensely important in that process (Menzel, 1959). In fact, in a large number of studies, the human preference to get information from other people was soundly demonstrated.

From early on, the dominance of the "principle of least effort" in human information seeking was demonstrated over and over (Poole, 1985). It may not seem surprising that people try to minimize effort in finding information, but the research demonstrated that ease of access and ease of use mattered more to people than the quality of the information they found. People have a (sometimes unjustified) belief in their ability to filter the good and valid information from the faulty, hence their tendency to undersearch to find the highest quality information available.

Further, information seeking is often quite unselfconscious. People are trying to solve problems in their lives, not "seek information." Activities that involve information seeking are seldom differentiated from the other actions taken to solve problems. Good research design for the study of information seeking *must* recognize this reality; asking people what they have done lately in the way of information seeking is therefore not the way to get data with high internal validity, as a rule. Dervin has made this point repeatedly and insightfully. For a prime example of her research technique, see Dervin, Harpring, and Foreman-Wernet (1999).

Thus, as a rule, people—even including Ph.D. scholars—develop what search skills they have incidentally to their primary efforts at research or problem-solving, and often fail to develop a conscious repertoire of search skills and techniques to help them over difficult stages. Particularly among college students, discomfort regarding library research has been found to be severe enough to merit the term "library anxiety," and a number of studies have been done on this topic. Along with the evidence of student difficulties with libraries, a large literature has developed on the goals and techniques of teaching "information literacy," i.e., the capability of finding and effectively evaluating desired information. In sum, people often vastly underutilize available resources and are often quite inefficient in finding what they do find (See the entries on "Library Anxiety," p. 3298, "Information Literacy," p. 2421 and "Information Literacy Instruction," p. 2429).

In the study of various academic disciplines, the close attention in the 1960s to the rich complexity of the culture of science enabled a subtler analysis of the information seeking in all the academic disciplines studied from the 1970s to the present time. See, for example, Patrick Wilson on the concept of "cognitive authority" (Wilson, 1983), Julie Hurd on implications of information use patterns for library design (Hurd, 1992), Paisley on "information and work" (Paisley, 1980), Robert Taylor on "information use environments" (Taylor, 1991), Cronin on invisible colleges (i.e., informal groups of researchers with shared interests [Cronin, 1982]), the model by Leckie et al. of information seeking in the professions (Leckie, Pettigrew & Sylvain, 1996), and Budd (1989) and Bates (1994) comparing the cultures of science and humanities. In the understudied area of archival resources, Barbara Orbach (1991) and Wendy Duff and Catherine Johnson (2003) have provided insightful descriptions of the use of historical archival materials.

During the 1980s and 1990s, several researchers deepened the understanding of various aspects of information behavior by exploring questions and areas previously not as well understood. Elfreda Chatman looked at the information environments of janitors, women in a retirement home, and prisoners (Chatman, 1987, 1992, 1999). Cheryl Metoyer-Duran applied the concept of gatekeeping to five minority groups in Southern California, and developed sophisticated (and sometimes counterintuitive) understandings about information flow within minority communities, and between them and the larger society (Metoyer-Duran, 1993). The challenge of studying unconventional groups and domains even extended to abused women (Harris & Dewdney, 1994) and abused children (Hersberger, Murray & Sokoloff, 2006).

Carol Kuhlthau is another researcher who has had very wide influence in the information behavior world. She developed a model of student information seeking, which she refined over several studies that are themselves models of the art of research. Her model runs counter to many assumptions in both education and LIS about how people tackle researching a paper or project, and how that experience can be substantially improved over past approaches (Kuhlthau, 2004). Specifically, she discovered that the combined process of researching and writing a paper is complex and difficult for most people—indeed, the library research is inextricably bound with the understanding and gradual formulation of the thesis of the paper. Consequently, the simple idea of "picking a topic," like picking an apple off a tree, then going to research it in the library, is not how the process reasonably can or should be expected to proceed. Yet generations of teachers and professors have left students floundering and frustrated as they moved, essentially without guidance, through this core process in paper-writing.

David Ellis' empirically based model of common actions associated with scholarly information seeking (Ellis, 1989) has also been influential, spurring several follow-on studies to test for similar activities in the work of people in other circumstances. And, of course, Brenda Dervin's concept of "sensemaking" as a motivation for information seeking constituted the underlying model for much information behavior research (http://communication.sbs.ohio-state.edu/sense-making/AAauthors/authorlistdervin.html [accessed June 2008)]).

In the 1990s and 2000s, along with the growth of the ISIC community, researchers expanded their look at information behavior by incorporating the whole environment—physical, social, and technological—in the study of people's interactions with information. Social context and social situation were recognized as essential to the understanding of information seeking (Cool, 2001; Courtright, 2007). Karen Fisher (née Pettigrew) developed the concept of "information grounds"—the joint creation of social environments by people in which to share conversation and information (Fisher, Durrance & Hinton, 2004). Disciplinary examples of these rich analyses include science (Palmer, 2001) and business (Choo, Detlor & Turnbull, 2000).

Several recent studies have demonstrated particularly creative approaches to the study of children's information seeking, traditionally an underpopulated area of research. Virginia Walter demonstrated that children's information needs were immense, and were in no way limited to requests made of school librarians (Walter, 1994)! Joanne Silverstein studied unconventional forms of information use (Silverstein, 2005), and Ciaran Trace studied informal information creation and use by children (Trace, 2007).

During recent decades, a more sophisticated understanding has also developed of information genres and the ways they are shaped by practice. In a particularly elegant study, Kling and McKim showed how preexisting social information practices shaped the design of post-Web online information support in three scientific disciplines (Kling & McKim, 2000). Peiling Wang studied at the microlevel how scientists actually make use of and subsequently cite other literature in the course of their research (Wang &

White, 1999), Ann Bishop (1999) and Lisa Covi (1999) studied closely the interactions between people and the structure and genres of information.

Conclusions

Information behavior research has grown immensely from its scattered beginnings earlier in the twentieth century. We now have a much deeper and less simplistic understanding of how people interact with information. We understand information behavior better within social contexts and as integrated with cultural practices and values. The further complexity of information seeking through the use of various technologies and genres is coming to be better understood, though there is much more to be studied. In fact, even as I write, some six billion people are interacting with information worldwide, drawing on cognitive and evolutionarily shaped behaviors, on social shaping and environmental expectations, and interacting with every IT from the book to the wireless handheld "smartphone." There is unimaginably much more to learn about information behavior.

The state of our current understandings on these topics is reviewed in over 30 entries in this encyclopedia. See, especially, the section titled "People Using Cultural Resources" in the topical contents list of the encyclopedia.

REFERENCES

American Psychological Association. (1968). *Project on Scientific Information Exchange in Psychology, 1963-1968* (21 reports). Washington, DC: American Psychological Association.

Andersen, H.C. (1907). The ugly duckling. In *Fairy Tales from Hans Christian Andersen*, (E. Lucas, Trans., 3rd ed., pp. 379-387). London: J.M. Dent.

Atkin, C. (1973). Instrumental utilities and information seeking. In P. Clarke (Ed.), *New Models for Mass Communication Research* (Vol. 2, pp. 205-239). Beverly Hills, CA: SAGE.

Auster, E., & Choo, C.W. (1993). Environmental scanning by CEOs in two Canadian industries. *Journal of the American Society for Information Science, 44*(4), 194-203.

Bates, M.J. (1979). Information search tactics. *Journal of the American Society for Information Science, 30*(4), 205-214.

Bates, M.J. (1981). Search techniques. *Annual Review of Information Science and Technology, 16*, 139-169.

Bates, M.J. (1986). Subject access in online catalogs: A design model. *Journal of the American Society for Information Science, 37*(6), 357-376.

Bates, M.J. (1989). The design of browsing and berrypicking techniques for the online search interface. *Online Review, 13*(5), 407-424.

Bates, M.J. (1994). The design of databases and other information resources for humanities scholars: The Getty Online Searching Project report no. 4. *Online & CDROM Review 18*(6), 331-340.

Bates, M.J. (1996). The Getty end-user online searching project in the humanities: Report no. 6: Overview and conclusions. *College & Research Libraries, 57*(6), 514–523.

Bates, M.J. (1999). The invisible substrate of information science. *Journal of the American Society for Information Science, 50*(12), 1043–1050.

Bates, M.J. (2002). Toward an integrated model of information seeking and searching. *New Review of Information Behaviour Research, 3*, 1–15.

Bates, M.J. (2004). Information science at the University of California at Berkeley in the 1960s: A memoir of student days. *Library Trends, 52*(4), 683–701.

Bates, M.J. (2005). Information and knowledge: An evolutionary framework for information science. *Information Research, 10*(4), paper 239. Retrieved from http://InformationR.net/ir/10-4/paper239.html.

Bates, M. J. (2005). An introduction to metatheories, theories, and models. In K. E. Fisher, S. Erdelez, & L. McKechnie (Eds.), *Theories of information behavior* (pp. 1–24). Medford, NJ: American Society for Information Science and Technology.

Bates, M.J. (2007). What is browsing—really? A model drawing from behavioural science research. *Information Research, 12*(4), paper 330. Retrieved from http://InformationR.net/ir/12-4/paper330.html.

Belkin, N.J., Oddy, R.N., & Brooks, H.M. (1982). ASK for information retrieval: Part I. background and theory. *Journal of Documentation, 38*(2), 61–71.

Berelson, B. (1945). The public library, book reading, and political behavior. *The Library Quarterly, 15*(4), 281–299.

Berelson, B. (1949). *The library's public.* New York: Columbia University Press.

Bishop, A.P. (1999). Document structure and digital libraries: How researchers mobilize information in journal articles. *Information Processing & Management, 35*(3), 255–279.

Bishop, A.P., Van House, N.A., & Buttenfield, B.P. (2003). *Digital library use: Social practice in design and evaluation.* Cambridge, MA: MIT Press.

Blake, B., Morkham, T., & Skinner, A. (1979). Inside information: Social welfare practitioners and their information needs. *Aslib Proceedings, 31*(6), 275–283.

Borgman, C.L. (1996). Why are online catalogs still hard to use? *Journal of the American Society for Information Science, 47*(7), 493–503.

Brittain, J.M. (1979). Information services and the structure of knowledge in the social sciences. *International Social Science Journal, 31*(4), 711–728.

Budd, J.M. (1989). Research in the two cultures: The nature of scholarship in science and the humanities. *Collection Management, 11*, 1–21.

Bundy, M.L. (1967a). Metropolitan public library use. *Wilson Library Bulletin, 41*, 950–961.

Bundy, M.L. (1967b). Factors influencing public library use. *Wilson Library Bulletin, 42*, 371–382.

Case, D.O. (1991). Conceptual organization and retrieval of text by historians: The role of memory and metaphor. *Journal of the American Society for Information Science, 42*(9), 657–668.

Case, D.O. (2007). *Looking for information: A survey of research on information seeking, needs, and behavior* (2nd ed.). Amsterdam: Elsevier Academic Press.

Case, D.O., Andrews, J.E., Johnson, J.D., & Allard, S.L. (2005). Avoiding versus seeking: The relationship of information seeking to avoidance, blunting, coping, dissonance, and related concepts. *Journal of the Medical Library Association, 93*(3), 353–362.

Chatman, E. (1987). The information world of low-skilled workers. *Library & Information Science Research, 9*, 265–283.

Chatman, E.A. (1992). *The information world of retired women.* Westport, CT: Greenwood Press.

Chatman, E.A. (1999). A theory of life in the round. *Journal of the American Society for Information Science, 50*(3), 207–217.

Chen, C., & Hernon, P. (1982). *Information seeking: Assessing and anticipating user needs.* New York: Neal Schuman Publishers.

Choo, C.W., Detlor, B., & Turnbull, D. (2000). *Web work: Information seeking and knowledge work on the World Wide Web.* Boston, MA: Kluwer Academic.

Chu, C.M. (1999). Literary critics at work and their information needs: A research-phases model. *Library & Information Science Research, 21*(2), 247–273.

Cobbledick, S. (1996). Information-seeking behavior of artists: Exploratory interviews. *The Library Quarterly, 66*(4), 343–372.

Cochrane, P.A., & Markey, K. (1983). Catalog use studies—Before and after the introduction of online interactive catalogs: Impact on design for subject access. *Library & Information Science Research, 5*(4), 337–363.

Cool, C. (2001). The concept of situation in information science. *Annual Review of Information Science and Technology, 35,* 5–42.

Courtright, C. (2007). Context in information behavior research. *Annual Review of Information Science and Technology, 41,* 273–306.

Covi, L.M. (1999). Material mastery: Situating digital library use in university research practices. *Information Processing & Management, 35*(3), 293–316.

Crane, D. (1972). *Invisible colleges: Diffusion of knowledge in scientific communities.* Chicago, IL: University of Chicago Press.

Cronin, B. (1982). Invisible colleges and information transfer: A review and commentary with particular reference to the social sciences. *Journal of Documentation, 38*(3), 212–236.

Cronin, B., & Hert, C.A. (1995). Scholarly foraging and network discovery tools. *Journal of Documentation, 51*(4), 388–403.

Cuadra, C.A., & Bates, M.J. (Eds.). (1974). *Library and information service needs of the nation: Proceedings of a conference on the needs of occupational, ethnic, and other groups in the United States.* Sponsored by the National Commission on Libraries and Information Science, University of Denver, CO. Washington, DC: U.S. Government Printing Office.

Davies, K. (2007). The information-seeking behaviour of doctors: A review of the evidence. *Health Information and Libraries Journal, 24*(2), 78–94.

Davis, R.A., & Bailey, C.A. (1964). *Bibliography of use studies.* Philadelphia, PA: Drexel Institute of Technology, Graduate School of Library Science.

Dervin, B. (1976). *Development of strategies for dealing with the information needs of urban residents: Phase I—Citizen study. Final report.* (ERIC ED 125 640). Seattle, WA: Department of Communication, University of Washington.

Dervin, B. (1983). Information as a user construct: The relevance of perceived information needs to synthesis and interpretation. In S.A. Ward & L.J. Reed (Eds.), *Knowledge structure and use: Implications for synthesis and interpretation* (pp. 155–183). Philadelphia: Temple University Press.

Dervin, B., & Nilan, M. (1986). Information needs and uses. *Annual Review of Information Science and Technology, 21,* 3–33.

Dervin, B., Harpring, J.E., & Foreman-Wernet, L. (1999). In moments of concern: A sense-making study of pregnant, drug-addicted women and their information needs. *Electronic Journal of Communication, 9*(2–4). Retrieved from http://www.cios.org/www/ejc/v9n23499.htm.

Duff, W.M., & Johnson, C.A. (2003). Where is the list with all the names? Information-seeking behavior of genealogists. *American Archivist, 66*(1), 79–95.

Ellis, D. (1989). Behavioural approach to information retrieval system design. *Journal of Documentation, 45*(3), 171–212.

Ellis, D. (1993). Modeling the information-seeking patterns of academic researchers: A grounded theory approach. *The Library Quarterly, 63*(4), 469–486.

Fidel, R. (1984). Online searching styles: A case-study-based model of searching behavior. *Journal of the American Society for Information Science, 35*(4), 211–221.

Fidel, R. (1991). Searchers' selection of search keys: III. Searching styles. *Journal of the American Society for Information Science, 42*(7), 515–527.

Fidel, R., & Pejtersen, A.M. (2004). From information behaviour research to the design of information systems: The Cognitive Work Analysis framework. *Information Research, 10*(1), paper 210. Retrieved from http://InformationR.net/ir/10-1/paper210.html.

Fisher, K.E., Durrance, J.C., & Hinton, M.B. (2004). Information grounds and the use of need-based services by immigrants in Queens, New York: A context-based, outcome evaluation approach. *Journal of the American Society for Information Science and Technology, 55*(8), 754–766.

Fisher, K.E., Erdelez, S., & McKechnie, L. (Eds.). (2005). *Theories of Information Behavior.* Medford, NJ: American Society for Information Science and Technology.

Ford, N. (1986). Psychological determinants of information needs: A small-scale study of higher education students. *Journal of Librarianship, 18*(1), 47–62.

Ford, N. (2004). Towards a model of learning for educational informatics. *Journal of Documentation, 60*(2), 183–225.

Garvey, W.D. (1970). Communication in the physical and social sciences. *Science, 11,* 1166–1173.

Garvey, W.D. (1979). *Communication: The essence of science: Facilitating information exchange among librarians, scientists, engineers, and students.* New York: Pergamon Press.

Garvey, W.D., & Griffith, B.C. (1967). Scientific communication as a social system. *Science, 157,* 1011–1016.

Gilliland-Swetland, A.J., Kafai, Y., & Landis, W.E. (1999). Integrating primary sources into the elementary school classroom: A case study of teachers' perspectives. *Archivaria, 48,* 89–116.

Green, S.S. (1876). Personal relations between librarians and readers. *American Library Journal, 1,* 78.

Harris, R.M., & Dewdney, P. (1994). *Barriers to information: How formal help systems fail battered women.* Westport, CT: Greenwood Press.

Hersberger, J.A., Murray, A.L., & Sokoloff, S.M. (2006). The information use environment of abused and neglected children. *Information Research, 12*(1), paper 277. Retrieved from http://InformationR.net/ir/12-1/paper277.html.

Hildreth, C.R. (1989). *Intelligent interfaces and retrieval methods for subject searching in bibliographic retrieval systems.* Washington, DC: Library of Congress Cataloging Distribution Service.

Hodges, T., & Bloch, U. (1982). Fiche or film for COM catalogs—two use tests. *The Library Quarterly, 52*(2), 131–144.

Hsieh-Yee, I. (1993). Effects of search experience and subject knowledge on the search tactics of novice and experienced searchers. *Journal of the American Society for Information Science, 44*(3), 161–174.

http://communication.sbs.ohio-state.edu/sense-making/AAauthors/authorlistdervin.html (accessed June 2008).

http://www.kf.vu.lt~isic2008/?page_id=4 (accessed June 2008).

Hurd, J.M. (1992). Interdisciplinary research in the sciences: Implications for library organization. *College & Research Libraries, 53*(4), 283–297.

Kari, J., & Hartel, J. (2007). Information and higher things in life: Addressing the pleasurable and the profound in information science. *Journal of the American Society for Information Science and Technology, 58*(8), 1131–1147.

Kling, R., & McKim, G. (2000). Not just a matter of time: Field differences and the shaping of electronic media in supporting scientific communication. *Journal of the American Society for Information Science, 51*(14), 1306–1320.

Kuhlthau, C.C. (1991). Inside the search process: Information seeking from the user's perspective. *Journal of the American Society for Information Science, 42*(5), 361–371.

Kuhlthau, C.C. (2004). *Seeking meaning: A process approach to library and information services* (2nd ed.). Westport, CT: Libraries Unlimited.

Leckie, G.J., Pettigrew, K.E., & Sylvain, C. (1996). Modeling the information seeking of professionals: A general model derived from research on engineers, health care professionals, and lawyers. *The Library Quarterly, 66*(2), 161–193.

Limberg, L. (1999). Experiencing information seeking and learning: A study of the interaction between two phenomena. *Information Research, 5*(1). Retrieved from http://informationr.net/ir/5-1/paper68.html.

Lynch, C.A. (1992). The next generation of public access information retrieval systems for research libraries: Lessons from ten years of the MELVYL system. *Information Technology and Libraries, 11*, 405–415.

Marchionini, G. (1995). Information seeking in electronic environments. Cambridge, UK: Cambridge University Press.

Marchionini, G., & Crane, G. (1994). Evaluating hypermedia and learning: Methods and results from the Perseus project. *ACM Transactions on Information Systems, 12*(1), 5–34.

Matthews, J.R., Lawrence, G.S., & Ferguson, D.K. (Eds.). (1983). *Using online catalogs: A nationwide survey: A report of a study sponsored by the Council on Library Resources.* New York: Neal-Schuman.

Meadows, A.J. (1974). *Communication in science.* London: Butterworths.

Menzel, H. (1959). Planned and unplanned scientific communication. In *Proceedings of the International Conference on Scientific Information* (Vol. 1, pp. 199–243). Washington, DC: National Academy of Sciences, National Research Council.

Menzel, H. (1966). Information needs and uses in science and technology. *Annual Review of Information Science and Technology, 1*, 41–69.

Metoyer-Duran, C. (1993). *Gatekeepers in ethnolinguistic communities.* Norwood, NJ: Ablex.

Nicholas, D., Huntington, P., Jamali, H.R., & Watkinson, A. (2006). The information seeking behaviour of the users of digital scholarly journals. *Information Processing & Management, 42*(5), 1345–1365.

O'Connor, B. (1993). Browsing: A framework for seeking functional information. *Knowledge: Creativity, Diffusion, Utilization, 15*(2), 211–232.

Orbach, B.C. (1991). The view from the researcher's desk: Historians' perceptions of research and repositories. *American Archivist, 54*(1), 28–43.

Paisley, W.J. (1968). Information needs and uses. *Annual Review of Information Science and Technology, 3*, 1–30.

Paisley, W.J. (1980). Information and work. *Progress in Communication Sciences, 2*, 113–165.

Palmer, C.L. (1996). Navigating among the disciplines: The library and interdisciplinary inquiry. *Library Trends, 45*(2), 129–366.

Palmer, C.L. (2001). *Work at the boundaries of science: Information and the interdisciplinary research process.* Dordrecht, Boston, MA: Kluwer Academic.

Poole, H. (1985). *Theories of the middle range.* Norwood, NJ: Ablex.

Price, D.J. de Solla. (1963). *Little science, big science.* New York: Columbia University Press.

Price, D.J. de Solla. (1965). Networks of scientific papers. *Science, 149*, 510–515.

Proceedings of the International Conference on Scientific Information. (1959). Washington, DC (2 Vols.). Washington, DC: National Academy of Sciences, National Research Council.

Ranganathan, S.R. (1957). *The Five Laws of Library Science*, (2nd ed.). London: Blunt & Sons. See also http://dlist.sir.arizona.edu/1220/ (Retrieved December 2008).

Reddy, M.C., & Jansen, B.J. (2008). A model for understanding collaborative information behavior in context: A study of two healthcare teams. *Information Processing & Management, 44*(1), 256–273.

Rice, R.E., McCreadie, M., & Chang, S.L. (2001). *Accessing and browsing information and communication.* Cambridge, MA: MIT Press.

Richardson, J.V., Jr. (1982). *The spirit of inquiry; the Graduate Library School at Chicago, 1921–1951,* (ACRL Publications in Librarianship No. 42). Chicago, IL: American Library Association.

Rieh, S.Y. (2004). On the web at home: Information seeking and web searching in the home environment. *Journal of the American Society for Information Science and Technology, 55*(8), 743–753.

Roderer, N.K., Zambrowicz, C., Zhang, D., & Zhou, H. (2004). User information seeking behavior in a medical web portal environment: A preliminary study. *Journal of the American Society for Information Science and Technology, 55*(8), 670–684.

Royal Society of London Scientific Information Conference. (1948). *Report.* London: Royal Society.

Salton, G., & McGill, M.J. (1983). *Introduction to modern information retrieval.* New York: McGraw-Hill.

Sandstrom, A.R., & Sandstrom, P.E. (1995). The use and misuse of anthropological methods in library and information science research. *The Library Quarterly, 65*(2), 161–199.

Saracevic, T., & Kantor, P. (1988). A study of information seeking and retrieving. III. Searchers, searches, and overlap. *Journal of the American Society for Information Science, 39*(3), 197–216.

Savolainen, R. (2007). Information behavior and information practice: Reviewing the umbrella concepts of information-seeking studies. *The Library Quarterly, 77*(2), 109–132.

Silverstein, J. (2005). Just curious: Children's use of digital reference for unimposed queries and its importance in informal education. *Library Trends, 54*(2), 228–244.

Spink, A., Wolfram, D., Jansen, B.J., & Saracevic, T. (2001). Searching the web: The public and their queries. *Journal of the American Society for Information Science and Technology, 52*(3), 226–234.

Srinivasan, R., & Pyati, A. (2007). Diasporic information environments: Reframing immigrant-focused information research. *Journal of the American Society for Information Science and Technology, 58*(12), 1734–1744.

Streatfield, D.R., & Wilson, T.D. (1982). Information innovations in social services departments: A third report on Project INISS. *Journal of Documentation, 38*(4), 273–281.

Summers, E.G., Matheson, J., & Conry, R. (1983). The effect of personal, professional, and psychological attributes, and information seeking behavior on the use of information sources by educators. *Journal of the American Society for Information Science, 34*(1), 75–85.

Sutton, S.A. (1994). Role of attorney mental models of law in case relevance determinations: An exploratory analysis. *Journal of the American Society for Information Science, 45*(3), 186–200.

Talja, S. (2001). *Music, culture, and the library: An analysis of discourses.* Lanham, MD: Scarecrow Press.

Talja, S., & Hartel, J. (2007). Revisiting the user-centered turn in information science research: An intellectual history perspective. *Information Research, 12*(4). Retrieved from http://InformationR.net/ir/12-4/colis/colis04.html.

Talja, S., Tuominen, K., & Savolainen, R. (2005). "Isms" in information science: Constructivism, collectivism and constructionism. *Journal of Documentation, 61*(1), 79–101.

Taylor, R.S. (1991). Information use environments. In B. Dervin, & M. Voigt (Eds.), *Progress in Communication Sciences*, (Vol. 10, pp. 217–255). Norwood, NJ: Ablex.

Trace, C.B. (2007). Information creation and the notion of membership. *Journal of Documentation, 63*(1), 142–164.

Voorhees, E.M., & Harman, D.K. (Eds.). (2005). *TREC—Experiment and evaluation in information retrieval*. Cambridge, MA: MIT Press.

Walter, V.A. (1994). The information needs of children. *Advances in Librarianship, 18,* 111–129.

Wang, P.L., & White, M.D. (1999). A cognitive model of document use during a research project. Study II. Decisions at the reading and citing stages. *Journal of the American Society for Information Science, 50*(2), 98–114.

Waples, D. (1938). *People and print; Social aspects of reading in the Depression*. Chicago, IL: University of Chicago Press.

Warner, E.S. (1973). *Information needs of urban residents*, (ERIC ED 088 464). Baltimore and Rockville, MD: Regional Planning Council and Westat Research, Inc.

Westbrook, L. (2003). Information needs and experiences of scholars in women's studies: Problems and solutions. *College & Research Libraries, 64*(3), 192–209.

Wiberley, S.E., Jr., Jones, W.G. (1989). Patterns of information seeking in the humanities. *College & Research Libraries, 50*(6), 638–645.

Williams, D., & Coles, L. (2007). Evidence-based practice in teaching: An information perspective. *Journal of Documentation, 63*(6), 812–835.

Wilson, P. (1983). *Second-hand knowledge: An inquiry into cognitive authority*. Westport, CT: Greenwood Press.

Wilson, T.D. (1981). On user studies and information needs. *Journal of Documentation, 37*(1), 3–15.

Wilson, T.D. (1999). Models in information behaviour research. *Journal of Documentation, 55*(3), 249–270.

Xie, H.I. (2003). Supporting ease-of-use and user control: Desired features and structure of web-based online IR systems. *Information Processing & Management, 39*(6), 899–922.

Xu, Y., & Liu, C. (2007). The dynamics of interactive information retrieval, Part II: An empirical study from the activity theory perspective. *Journal of the American Society for Information Science and Technology, 58*(7), 987–998.

3

Research practices of humanities scholars in an online environment: The Getty Online Searching Project report no. 3

ABSTRACT

Use of online databases by humanities scholars searching as end users was monitored in a 2-year project conducted by the Getty Art History Information Program. Visiting Scholars at the Getty Center for the History of Art and the Humanities in Santa Monica, California, were offered the opportunity to do unlimited subsidized searching of DIALOG® databases. This third report from the project presents results of interviews conducted with the scholars regarding their experiences with searching, the role the searching took in their broader research activities, and their attitudes about the future of online searching in the humanities. Scholars found the experience stimulating and novel, with comments ranging from its "addictive" properties to a "Sorcerer's Apprentice" quality to complaints about the "industrialization of scholarship." Generally, the scholars saw DIALOG searching as supplementing their usual research methods, and not changing them in a fundamental way. Online searching was seen as particularly useful for interdisciplinary research, and as possibly setting a new standard for the extent of literature that should be reviewed. Identified problems were about equally divided between difficulties with the search

First published as Bates, M. J., Wilde, D. N., & Siegfried, S. (1995). Research practices of humanities scholars in an online environment: The Getty Online Searching Project report no. 3. *Library and Information Science Research, 17*(1), 5–40.

interface and lack of desired types of resources. All foresaw online searching being used in the future by arts and humanities scholars.

Introduction

The Getty Art History Information Program (AHIP) launched a 2-year program in 1989 to study how humanities scholars, engaging in their characteristic modes of research, would use online databases when given the chance to do unlimited searching, unconstrained by cost. The study, conducted with the cooperation of visiting scholars at the Getty Center for the History of Art and the Humanities,[1] Santa Monica, California, was intended to probe a number of aspects of the scholars' experiences with online searching, including their reactions to the use of the online databases, the role the searching had in their research work, their search techniques and learning curve, their queries, and the search terms they used. The results of the study are being reported in a series of articles, of which this is the third.[2]

The first report (Bates, Wilde, & Siegfried, 1993) analyzed the vocabulary used by the scholars in their searches, and the second report (Siegfried, Bates, & Wilde, 1993) analyzed and profiled the online searching record itself. The purpose of this report is to present analyses of the interviews with the scholars about the role of the online searching in their research, and their reactions to DIALOG® and online searching generally. The succeeding sections present the background of this research, the methodology used, the results, and, finally, discussion and conclusions.

Background

As the basic outlines of information-seeking behavior in the natural and social sciences became clear through research done in the 1960s and 1970s, the gap in research on humanities scholars became apparent. Since the beginning of the 1980s, when Sue Stone (1982) reviewed the work done to

---

1   The J. Paul Getty Trust is a private operating foundation. Two of its programs are the Getty Art History Information Program and the Getty Center for the History of Art and Humanities. These two entities collaborated on this subject.

2   Marilyn Schmitt conceived the Getty Online Searching Project; she designed the study together with Susan Siegfried and Deborah N. Wilde. Siegfried and Wilde carried out the collaborative project plan and oversaw the gathering of data throughout the project. Marcia J. Bates designed the interview schedule for the second year's data, analyzed the data for both years, formulated conclusions, and contributed insights from the discipline of information science. Katherine Smith transcribed the interviews for subsequent analysis.

that date, growing interest in the humanities has been evidenced by a great many reviews, research studies, and commentaries on the information needs and information seeking of humanists (Broadbent, 1986; Case, 1986, 1991; Corkill & Mann, 1978; Crawford, 1986; Fabian, 1986; Guest, 1987; Katzen, 1986; Loughridge, 1989; Lowry & Stuveras, 1987; Rahtz, 1987; Stam, 1984; Stam & Giral, 1988; Stone, 1982; Tibbo, 1991, 1993; Wiberley, 1991; Wiberley & Jones, 1989).

Particularly perceptive commentary on humanistic scholarship from the perspective of the scholar has been provided in Weintraub's discussion (Weintraub, 1980) and in the papers in the symposium volume *Humanists at Work* (1989). Systematic and extensive interviews of faculty, librarians, and others associated with humanities research form the basis of an analysis of the information needs in eight humanistic disciplines (Gould, 1988), while in-depth interviews provide the basis of an extensive and detailed description and analysis of the art historian at work (Schmitt, 1988).

Much of the research on humanists has dealt with the research behavior of scholars in general, including the general context of automation of information, but with little attention to their use of online database systems. However, in the last few years, serious attention has also been given to online searching in the humanities—its particular requirements, problems with databases and vendors, and search techniques (Everett & Pilachowski, 1986; Horner & Thirlwall, 1988; Hurych, 1986; Krausse & Etchingham, 1986; Mackesy, 1982; Ruiz & Meyer, 1990; Stern, 1988; Stielow & Tibbo, 1988; Tibbo, 1993; Walker, 1988, 1990; Walker & Atkinson, 1991).

In a few cases, empirical studies have been done on actual uses of online searching by or for scholars in the humanities. Woo (1988) studied how three graduate students at Columbia University made online use of the *Avery Index to Architectural Periodicals*. Krausse and Etchingham (1986) elicited the reactions of scholars to database searching when those scholars received the searches under a grant. Horner and Thirlwall (1988) tested several hypotheses regarding uses of online searching by social science and humanities scholars, and Hurych (1986) compared information-seeking patterns across the spectrum of disciplines (sciences, social sciences, and humanities) through an analysis of formally submitted online search requests.

Schmitt (1990a, 1990b) argued for a closer working relationship among humanities scholars, information managers, and systems experts. Optimal design of information retrieval systems for the humanities cannot take place until a thorough understanding of the humanistic research process drives the design of online systems. It was the purpose of the research presented here to discover what happens when scholars confront an established online information system. Where is the good and bad fit with their research pattern? What does the system do for them and fail to do for them? What more do the scholars want from it? Increasingly, scholars will expect the system to conform to their needs, rather than the other way around. The research presented in this article highlights some of those directions for change.

Methodology

Population

In the first year of the study, henceforth known as the 1989 group, 11 of the 15 scholars visiting the Center agreed to participate in the online searching project; in addition, two of the spouses of these 11—scholars in their own right—also participated, for a total of 13. In the second year, henceforth known as the 1990 group, 12 of the 18 scholars agreed to participate; three spouses did also, for a total of 15. Some who trained did no searching subsequently.

One of the scholars from the first year stayed over the second year. Thus, the actual total number of different individuals involved was not 28 (13 in 1989 plus 15 in 1990), but rather 27, as this scholar participated both years. She did minimal searching in the first year and was interviewed only in the second year. There is no evidence from the interviews that the presence of this slightly more experienced searcher had any impact on the 1990 group.

There were 8 men and 5 women in the 1989 group and 9 men and 6 women in the 1990 group. The participants came from France, Germany, Great Britain, Hungary, Italy, the Netherlands, and the United States. In 1989, 5 of the 13 were native English speakers, as were 6 of the 15 in 1990. All had a good command of English, although some nonnative speakers had greater mastery than others. (Note: Because more of the scholars produced data relevant to the factors analyzed in this report than was the case for Report No. 1, the population analyzed is slightly different in the two reports. Hence, the descriptions of the populations differ slightly between the reports as well.)

The scholars' research interests included the history of art and architecture, film history, social history, philosophy, comparative literature, classics, history of music, social and cultural anthropology, and psychology. In terms of occupation, the groups comprised university professors, independent scholars, curators, an architect, postdoctoral scholars, and doctoral candidates.

The training, setting, and arrangements

The first year's group of scholars was given a full day of DIALOG training in late January and early February of 1989, and did all their searching between then and June 1989. One scholar in the first year arrived late and was trained by Jeanette Clough of the Getty, rather than by the DIALOG trainer, Amy Greenwood. He was counted in the group of participants. Twelve of the second year's group were given DIALOG training at the end of November 1989, and the remaining three during January and February of 1990. They did their searching between the time of training and July 1990.

After taking the training, the scholars had access 24 hours a day to the workstation for DIALOG searching in the Getty Center Library near their offices up until the time they left in the summer. Next to the workstation were placed thesauri for several arts and humanities databases, as well as documentation for the DIALOG search service. The former included *RILA (International Repertory of the Literature of Art) Subject Headings, Architectural Keywords,* and *Historical Abstracts Index.*

The Getty Trust arranged for a limited DIALOG account, which gave the scholars access to a large subset of about 60 of the DIALOG databases. Databases in the package, drawn from the social sciences, arts, and humanities, included all those thought to be of interest to arts and humanities scholars, such as *Art Literature International (RILA), The Architecture Database (RIBA),* and *Historical Abstracts.* Bibliographic databases covered journal articles, books, and dissertations. Some directories (e.g., *Marquis Who's Who*) and some full-text databases (e.g., *Academic American Encyclopedia,* no longer available on DIALOG) were also included. DIALINDEX, the database of DIALOG databases, was included, as were citation databases (e.g., *Arts & Humanities Search*).

The participants were encouraged to have an "assisted search" by appointment sometime during the months after the training: that is, a search in which an experienced online searcher would sit next to the scholar and answer questions and help in any way desired while the scholar searched. During the first year, six scholars requested an assisted search during the spring of 1989, and one of these had a second one as well. In 1990, one scholar had three assisted searches, three had two, five had one, and six had none.

During the first year, scholars were also offered the opportunity to have an experienced searcher do a "comparative search," that is, redo one of the searches already done by a scholar. The scholar first submitted a written search request to the expert, who then conducted the search (without discussing with the scholar what he or she had done). The results of the comparative searches were then discussed in an interview with the scholar. In 1989, seven scholars requested comparative searches (performed by Kathleen Salomon of the Getty Center Library). These comparative searches took place after the scholars had done most of their searching for the year; none occurred earlier than May 4, 1989. They were discontinued in the second year.

Two group review sessions were offered during the second year. Three people attended the first one in January 1990, and five people (including one who also attended the first session) attended the second one in March. (In both years, help with assisted searches was provided by Jeanette Clough of the Getty Center Library, who also conducted the two group review sessions.) Overall, the project was designed to encourage scholars to do their own searching, and, generally, other than these opportunities, assistance was available only through the DIALOG help line, not locally.

Objectives of interviews

Objectives for the interviews were developed prior to the 1989 interviews, and then, based on experience with the first year's interviews, refined for the second year. They are:

1. Determine the researchers' subjective reactions to DIALOG online searching, specifically:
   - How they felt about DIALOG online searching in general.
   - How they saw DIALOG searching fitting with their usual research process, both currently and prospectively.

2. Determine researchers' reactions to certain specific features of DIALOG online searching:
   - Search commands and other features of DIALOG.
   - Databases available on DIALOG.

3. Determine researchers' reactions to certain specific features of the Getty online search program:
   - Assistance provided by Getty staff (individual and group).
   - Documentation supporting searching.

4. Record background information on participants:
   - Their research projects and needs.
   - The stage of their research.
   - Their previous experience with computers and online searching.

Interview design

In the first year, interviewers Deborah Wilde and Susan Siegfried developed broad objectives for the interviews, then interviewed the scholars in a wide-ranging, qualitative mode. They made certain they touched on all areas of interest with each scholar, but did not use a formally developed interview schedule. In the second year, Bates was asked to draw on the first year's experience and develop a more formal interview schedule, based on social/behavioral science methodological practices, which she did.

The experience of using the two different approaches to interviewing, the one more humanistic and the other more social scientific, was interesting from several standpoints. For one, we researchers had to learn to communicate across the methodological divide between our respective backgrounds. For another, by using significantly different interviewing methods in the 2 years, we were able to achieve some of the value of what is variously known as "triangulation," or "multiple operationism" in the behavioral sciences. That is, if the results produced by two different methods on a population are similar, we may have greater confidence in the results. To put it another way, we may be more confident that we are actually testing what we think we are testing, rather than discovering results that are merely artifacts of the research method or research conditions themselves. In the event, results from the two years were broadly similar (the different techniques used did not allow for exact comparison), and no significant differences in overall response patterns were found.

In the second year, although the emphasis was on a behavioral science approach through the development of carefully worded and designed interview schedules in which questions were asked in a prescribed order, we also determined to use the strengths of Deborah Wilde, our interviewer, in qualitative techniques, by a careful introduction of some qualitative techniques into the interviews. The behavioral sciences, in general, have become more open to qualitative techniques in recent years, and there are ongoing debates about how and when to use such techniques effectively. We decided to experiment methodologically in the design of the interview.

The general approach we took was to have Wilde follow the interview schedule carefully, asking the questions in order, and checking to see that they had been answered, at the same time allowing the respondents considerable freedom in answering the questions. A conversational atmosphere was created, where respondents felt free to make discursive replies in the general topic area of the interview. The openness of the atmosphere meant that occasionally scholars did not answer a question, but more often it enabled them to revisit a particular question at several points during the interview. It was as if the interview stimulated the respondents' thinking generally about the DIALOG use, and, as their reactions and awareness crystallized around some aspect of the experience, they felt free to comment at whatever point they became aware of their reactions.

We feel that this approach was quite successful. The interview schedule itself probed the questions of interest from several different angles, and the open atmosphere of the interviews allowed the scholars to flesh out their experiences and reactions from still more perspectives.

Two carefully worded and sequenced interview schedules were developed. "Participation" in the online searching project was defined operationally as having taken the training. If scholars chose not to use the searching thereafter, then that reaction was one we wanted also to probe. Therefore, the first schedule was for those scholars who had done any unassisted online searching at all, apart from the training; the other was for those who had done the training but no unassisted searching. Both interview schedules are reproduced in the Appendix.

As many questions as possible were kept the same on the two schedules. A "funnel" approach was used, in which very general, or "grand tour" (McCracken, 1988) questions were asked at first, allowing respondents to give whatever reactions were most salient in their minds, followed by increasingly specific questions. In this way the interview would not initially channel the scholars' reactions along predetermined routes and divert their responses from aspects of their experience that were important to them and previously unrecognized by us.

Subsequent more specific questions enabled us to focus in detail on questions we wanted to be sure were answered as well. Key topics, such as the relationship between their general research practices and DIALOG searching, were probed from several angles through a succession of questions on the topic. Respondents were put at ease initially by asking them questions about something very familiar, viz., their research projects; responses to these questions were needed in any case. Finally, simpler, more factual information needed was gathered by giving the scholars a brief eight-question questionnaire.

Conduct of the interviews

All participants were given code numbers, which are used consistently throughout all reports of this online searching project. Participants in 1989 were assigned numbers 1-13; 1990 participants were assigned numbers 14-28. Code numbers were assigned in order of amount of searching done by each scholar, counted in number of search statements entered. Thus, lower numbers each year always represent the most active searchers.

The scholar, mentioned earlier, who returned a second year, had number 10 in the first year and number 17 in the second. Thus, again, 27, not 28, different people were involved.

Of the 13 participants in 1989, 11 were interviewed, 6 of them twice. The two who were not interviewed included one individual who did no searching of any kind (scholar #13) and scholar #10 mentioned earlier who returned in 1990 and was interviewed in 1990. Thus, among the 1989 group, interviewed individuals are numbered 1–9, 11–12. First and second interviews for the 1989 group were conducted in April through June of that year. In 1990, all 15 participants were interviewed; 11 received the "searcher" interview and 4 received the "nonsearcher" (i.e., no unassisted searching) interview. The 1990 interviews were all conducted between mid-May and mid-June of 1990.

As noted, code numbers were assigned based on the total number of search statements produced by the scholars during their tenure at the Getty. During the second year, one of the individuals who had done no searching at the time of the interview, and thus received the "nonsearcher" interview, subsequently did some searching. Therefore, she, as a "nonsearcher," has a lower code number (because she input a few more search statements in her subsequent search) than two other searchers who input fewer statements but did all their searching before their interviews. Those receiving the searcher interview are numbered 14–22, 24–25, and the nonsearcher interviewees are numbered 23, 26–28.

One final complication: #25 was timid about her English and wanted to be interviewed with her husband, #20. She responded to only some of the questions. Her responses are included where available.

All interviews in 1990 were tape recorded. The responses were transcribed by Katherine Smith. Transcription was not verbatim; rather the essential contents, with some direct quotations, were extracted. The few questions that arose during data analyses were checked against the original tapes.

Results

As noted earlier, the amount of searching varied across the individuals studied, and some scholars did no unassisted searching at all. To provide a baseline for all subsequent discussion, Table 1 presents data on the search histories of all participants in the project both years.

Results are grouped in the following into the broad areas of desired information that were described in the methodology section for the 1990

TABLE 1. *Search histories of the scholars*

SEARCHER	TOTAL SEARCH STATEMENTS	UNASSISTED SESSIONS	TIME ONLINE (IN HOURS)	NO. OF ASSISTED SEARCHES
1	703	33	7.7	1
2	436	19	7.1	0
3	164	5	1.8	1
4	127	10	1.0	1
5	91	3	1.9	0
6	87	10	1.5	0
7	66	5	1.4	0
8	57	3	0.8	0
9	53	1	1.5	1
10	51	1	1.2	0
11	7	1	0.3	2
12	0	0	0.0	1
13	0	0	0.0	0
1989 TOTALS	1,842	91	26.2	7
14	1,035*	134	71.1	2
15	882	22	13.4	1
16	331	9	7.5	1
17	327	24	5.2	1
18	210	11	5.7	3
19	179	7	1.9	0
20	140	5	2.8	0
21	109	4	1.7	2
22	103	3	1.2	2
23	36	1	0.7	0
24	25	3	0.4	1
25	10	1	0.2	0
26	0	0	0.0	1
27	0	0	0.0	0
28	0	0	0.0	0
1990 TOTALS	3,387	224	111.8	14
GRAND TOTALS	5,229	315	138.0	21

NOTE: *Only the first 1,035 statements of this scholar (equal to 28.7 hours) were analyzed; total statements for all sessions for this individual were not calculated.*

interviews. Interview questions referred to in section titles are questions for searchers. Relevant nonsearcher responses are identified and discussed, where appropriate, with searchers' responses. Refer to the Appendix for full searcher and nonsearcher interview schedules.

Because the approach taken in the 1989 interviews was very different from that in the 1990 interviews, it was not possible to coordinate responses on a given topic consistently between the 2 years. The decision was made, therefore, to present the results in accordance with the design of the more systematic 1990 interview schedule. Comments and reactions from scholars during 1989 are added where they clearly relate to the content of the 1990 questions.

Scholars' previous experience with computers and database searching: Questionnaire questions 3–7

All 15 scholars interviewed in 1990 responded to these questions. Just two had ever had an online search done for them (Question 3), and not one had ever done online searching for himself or herself before (Question 4). Comments on this question were noted from about half the 1989 group and followed a similar pattern. The participants' personal familiarity with online searching before participating in this program was minimal.

On the other hand, familiarity with online catalogs and personal computers was quite high. Eight of the 15 scholars in 1990 had used online catalogs before. Because most of the scholars are from Europe, where online catalogs are less widespread, such a result might not have been anticipated. Seven of the eight had used online catalogs at two or three different libraries, so most of these would have had the experience of adapting to different information retrieval systems before tackling DIALOG. Both searchers and nonsearchers were among those who had used online catalogs, so online catalog familiarity was not, in any striking way, associated with the tendency to use DIALOG. Six of the 11 people interviewed in 1989 also mentioned having used online catalogs. Three of these mentioned use of more than one catalog.

No fewer than 14 of the 15 1990 respondents had used computers for writing. Their average (mean) starting date for using a computer for writing fell between 1985 and 1986; these people can be presumed to be very experienced in using computers. Five of the 15 had used computers for something other than word processing. Most of these uses were for developing small databases. Overall, these patterns regarding computer use and online searching are quite similar to those found by Wiberley and Jones (1989).

Research projects and status: Interview questions 1–3

These questions were asked principally for reference or background purposes. It was thought that comments made elsewhere in the interview might be elucidated through referral to information about the topics of research being pursued by the scholars. However, the data proved to have additional value as well. Answers to the questions were analyzed to see if any relationship could be discerned between the stage or phase of research being done on a project by a scholar and the amount of online searching he or she did in this study. It might be surmised, for example, that scholars would do more searching in the early phases of research when they are attempting to identify the literature relevant to their topic of interest.

Drawing from the 1990 data, the number of distinct research projects being worked on by each scholar during their Getty year was first recorded. Then each project was assessed according to whether the work on it could be said to be in early, middle, or late stages while the scholar was at the Getty. These judgments were of necessity broad and approximate, as the wording of the responses varied. Projects in which the scholar was involved in initial literature searching and interpretation of materials were considered to be "early," those with some research done and some remaining to be done, usually with some writing begun, were considered "middle," and projects primarily involving writing or editing, with research completed except for finishing up odds and ends were considered "late."

The first result of this analysis was the discovery that most scholars were working on more than one project. Twelve of the 15 scholars were engaged in two or more projects and 6 of the 12 in four or more. Excluding some cases where scholars said they were working on some "other" unspecified projects, there were 39 projects mentioned altogether among the 15 scholars. This pattern of working on multiple overlapping projects at different stages has also been found in research on the social and natural sciences (Garvey, 1979).

Each project was then coded with respect to the stages covered while at the Getty. Some projects were done entirely at the Getty, and so were marked in all three categories; others had begun or ended at the Getty. In the case of three of the projects, there was some ambiguity regarding the status of one or two of the stages. These ambiguous cases were treated as half a mark for the relevant stages.

Twelve of the 15 scholars had one or more projects at the early stage while they were at the Getty, 11 of 15 had project(s) in the middle stage, and 13 had project(s) in the late stage. Analysis of the relationship between stage of research and amount of online searching done is clouded by the fact that almost everyone had work at two or three stages during their year at the Getty, even though work on a particular project may have been at only one stage.

Scholars were also grouped into three categories by amount of searching done: high (over 5 hours of searching and over 200 online search statements produced), medium (1 to 3 hours—no one did between 3 and 5 hours—and between 100 and 200 search statements), and low (under 1 hour and fewer than 100 search statements). Scholars falling in each group were nos. 14–18, 19–22, and 23–28, respectively.

The total marks for each stage of the research were then added up for each group of scholars. It should be kept in mind that any one project could be marked in one, two, or three of the stages, depending on whether the scholar did all or part of the work on the project while at the Getty. The following sums represent the total project marks for each research stage for all projects being working on by members of the applicable group:

- High Searching Group: 17 projects
  - 13   Early Stage
  - 4½   Middle Stage
  - 6   Late Stage

- Medium Searching Group: 7 projects
  - 1   Early Stage
  - 3½   Middle Stage
  - 4   Late Stage

- Low Searching Group: 15 projects
  - 9   Early Stage
  - 6½   Middle Stage
  - 7   Late Stage

There would appear to be no clear-cut pattern. There are a lot of projects in the early stages for the first group, the heavy users of online searching, but there are also for the third group, the lightest users. Thus, according to this admittedly crude measure, it would appear that there is no strong, unambiguous association between research stage and amount of online searching done by the scholars under study.

Scholars' reactions to DIALOG
searching in general: Interview questions 4–8

Among the 1990 cohort, when asked why they decided to participate in the online searching project, five searchers and two nonsearchers responded that they were curious and/or wanted to take advantage of the opportunity

(#15, 16, 18, 21, 22, 26, 27). Three searchers and one nonsearcher (#14, 19, 20, 23) saw it as a way to expand their research materials in one fashion or another. For #14 it was a way of researching topics in an interdisciplinary way; #20 wanted to explore neighboring areas, while #19 had wanted to use it to develop course materials.

One searcher and one nonsearcher expected it to have some impact on their research mode. Scholar #17 wanted to find a new work method—"not to be lazy in the way researchers sometimes are"—and hoped it would help her overcome a "very strong resistance to computers." Scholar #23 thought it could help her with her "chaotic way of working." Two minimal searchers and one nonsearcher said they had not expected to use it much, which proved out in their low use (#24, 25, 28). In sum, curiosity, expectations of increased research materials, and hope to supplement research techniques motivated the participants.

Results from questions 5, 6, and 7 are considered together here. These all dealt with expectations and results from the online searching. Specific search queries discussed in Question 7 are not analyzed, but comments made in the course of responding to Question 7 regarding scholars' reactions to the searching experience are included in the analysis.

Questions 5 and 6 are actually significantly different: The first deals with expectations met or unmet and the second with degree of actual help provided in meeting research needs. The fact that responses meshed closely between the questions suggests that the scholars' expectations largely centered around getting good results from searches and not, say, around developing their online searching skills. Thus good research retrievals equaled expectations met in most minds.

With respect to Question 5, five 1990 respondents got what they expected or more than what they expected (#15, 17–19, 22), three got partially what they expected (including answers that took the general form of "Yes, but"—#14, 16, 20), three got little or nothing of what they expected (#21, 24, 25), and four said they did not have much need this year for online searching (#23, 26–28).

All three who gave the "partial" answer added that they were disappointed that the databases did not cover earlier materials, but were otherwise positive about it. Two people in the 1989 group, #2 and #6, gave highly positive mention to the benefits from DIALOG searching. (Otherwise much of the discussion the first year was directed to identifying problems respondents had.)

Overall, these responses track fairly closely to the amount of use made of DIALOG. That is, high users report that DIALOG met or exceeded their expectations, while low users found it disappointing. There is a chicken and egg problem here; it is difficult to tell whether initial positive (or negative) experiences led to greater (or lesser) use, or scholars were more or less predisposed to like and use DIALOG before they began and acted accordingly. The four nonsearchers all said they had not had much need for DIALOG this year.

Not everyone specifically mentioned surprises and disappointments, but negative comments were more common in both years. In the 1990 group, negative comments were divided about half and half between complaints about the unavailability of desired resources in the databases and difficulties with the search interface. More specifics on these reactions will be provided later in the discussion of the questions dealing with specific issues.

Comments on pleasant surprises included these:

- Scholar #15 noted the power of combining different concepts. He provided an example from his research where he created two concept sets and then ANDed them to get six references, all in a few minutes. "It would take you literally a full day to do this manually."

- Scholar #15 also noted that "the most creative" type of search is to search the same topic across several databases to get an interdisciplinary search.

- Scholar #17 liked that books and articles are combined in DIALOG. "Having that through DIALOG is really wonderful, absolutely great. This has been a great surprise."

On the whole, it would appear that the searchers did not gain the full benefit that they might have because they did not become skilled enough in searching to get the maximum benefit out of the databases. Only one individual, #15, who was also the most enthusiastic generally, mentioned one of the most powerful features of Boolean systems, namely, combining different concepts.

Because the scholars had committed a full day to learning DIALOG, these reactions would seem to confirm a pattern found elsewhere with end-user searching: It is difficult to master and retain DIALOG searching well enough in a fairly short time to be really successful with it. The searchers clearly got benefit from using DIALOG, as we will see in more detail in the next question, but their enthusiasm is restrained by the difficulty in using it and by the incompleteness of arts and humanities resources in the databases.

Three scholars, #1 and #7 in 1989 and #20 in 1990, mentioned problems with entering dates successfully. Scholar #20 suggested that it would be helpful to have sheets that mentioned the main keywords for different topics including dates. As noted in *Report No. 1* (Bates et al., 1993), dates are an important and common part of the descriptions of online search topics given by the scholars; 16% of the natural language descriptions of subject searches contained some mention of dates. Yet development of consistent procedures for describing dates—especially procedures that facilitate good online searching—has typically been paid relatively little attention by thesaurus developers and database producers.

Regarding Question 6, the degree to which online searching has been helpful to the respondent in meeting his or her research needs this year, responses from all 11 searchers (#14–22, 24–25) largely adumbrated those of Question 5. Most found it helpful, some quite so, but most of those who found it helpful also noted some body of desired literature missing in the databases (#14–18, 20–21). Three scholars said they did not need to do much information searching of any kind this year (#19, 22, 25). One scholar said she did need to search, but the kinds of materials needed were not in any of the available databases (#24).

The four nonsearchers were asked the question, "Why did you not search this year?" All four (#23, 26–28) said they had little or no need for DIALOG this year. Three made reference to not having time or not wanting to spend the time experimenting with it (#23, 26, 28). Not finding an hour or two to experiment with DIALOG in the better part of a year at the Getty hints at something more than lack of time—perhaps discomfort, unwillingness to switch gears, or lack of fundamental interest.

Scholar #23 made some additional comments that suggested a more complicated response. She felt that if the procedure had been simpler, she would have used DIALOG more: "There's something about not wanting to go over, switch it on, see if there's enough paper, do all of that. . . . It's somehow less user-friendly to me than something sitting right here that I'm not bothered about." She said she could see herself using DIALOG with colleagues, or with a research assistant. So much material of no interest to her came out that she would like a research assistant to do the culling for her.

There is a sense here of the discomfort that most people feel when beginning to use something very new to them. This discomfort might be fairly easily overcome with just a little more experience, perhaps with individualized assistance. After this interview, perhaps stimulated by the discussion, scholar #23 did do her first unassisted search of the year.

There are striking parallels between the responses to this cluster of questions and the results of interviews with "a small group of scholars" who responded to questions on their use of the RLIN national cataloging database at the University of Pennsylvania (Lehmann & Renfro, 1991). Humanities faculty expressed a strong desire for expansion of coverage to earlier materials; they wanted easy, right-at-hand access (implicit in #23's comments), and would like greater user-friendliness.

Question 8 asked for general reactions to using DIALOG. The interviewer was instructed to probe for emotional responses on this question, and the emphasis in the analysis of this question is on those emotional responses. Feeling reactions are likely to have an important role in whether people use these resources again, and may also shed some light on what needs to be done to help end users be more comfortable with online searching.

Many of the comments touched on the theme of enjoyment or discomfort of one sort or another. First, let us get a sense of the positive reactions:

- "I feel like an explorer. . . . I enjoy it" (#14).

- After saying that he enjoyed using DIALOG very much, #15 described it as "Las Vegas for the intellectual," and "a very exciting process."

- #17, who is the scholar who stayed for a second year, felt "very strange in the beginning," "suspicious." By her second year she felt comfortable using DIALOG and enjoyed it.

- DIALOG was fun and very easy to use (#20).

- Scholar #22, who encountered some system problems, said "When it worked I found it fun."

- The assisted search was "fun," but she was uncomfortable with searching on her own (#26, to be discussed more shortly).

- Scholar #7, of the first year, said she enjoyed using DIALOG, although she had not done much on it.

The positive expressions took their most extreme form in comments on how "addictive" online searching is:

- "I might be an addict" (#14). Later, in response to another question, #14 said that it became harder as the year went on to resist the temptation to search more and more—that there was a danger of being diverted from one's chosen research path.

- #17, who had begun being "suspicious," noted that "If you use a lot of it, then you get absolutely enthusiastic, and you can't [be] without [it]. It's a kind of addiction. . . ."

Expressions of discomfort took various forms:

- Scholar #14, who was later "addicted," noted that "At first you are a bit concerned whether you are doing the right thing."

- DIALOG searching was "too complicated" (#16). She had fun reading the printouts but did not enjoy working through the steps that generate the printout.

- Scholar #18 indicated that he was not entirely at home with DIA-LOG, and felt this was due to the fact that he had not had enough practice with it. "It seems slightly alien to me. . . ."

- Scholar #19 summed up many of the issues about access to online searching by end users, saying: "I found it cumbersome. It never became transparent for me in the way ORION [UCLA's online catalog] has. I think that's partially due to the fact that I didn't use it enough. . . . I think there are some built in barriers toward its easy access." When asked to clarify what he meant by "transparent," he explained that he has a relatively precise conception of exactly what ORION can and cannot do. He doesn't have to think up strategies for getting information out of it. With DIA-LOG he never got to the point where he "plumbed the depths."

- The overall tone of #21's response was one of wariness. When asked how he felt about using DIALOG, he replied jokingly, "Observed." (Incidentally, this was the only explicit expression in the study of discomfort with the awareness of being studied.) He was hesitant to express any feelings about using DIALOG, and finally said he had not searched enough to give a meaningful answer.

- Scholar #26 who had not done unassisted searches, expressed discomfort with the location of the DIALOG workstation:

  I always felt inhibited about going over there and going on the machine myself, being an unmechanical type of person who fought against using a computer. . . . I had the feeling that sitting out there with DIALOG, in front of everybody else walking around, if I did something stupid, or I couldn't figure something out, everybody would see. So there was a certain public presence that for me, anyway, was sort of an inhibitor.

On the other hand, she thought her assisted search was "really fun." Working with Jeanette in the training class she found a wealth of relevant material: "That one training class kept me going for months."

- Elsewhere, #26 mentioned that she found searching DIALOG to be "daunting," and #28 referred to it as "threatening" at two different points in his interview.

- Even though access to DIALOG was free for the scholars, two mentioned an awareness of time pressure. Scholar #17 said she was always worried about using too much time, not spending time well. After mentioning that he felt the pressure of time, #15 explained why: "Because time translates into money. . . . Next year I'm on my own."

Discomfort with online searching took one particular form in the responses of several scholars. Several made reference to the large quantities of information produced by the searches, and some referred, in one way or another, to its "Sorcerer's Apprentice" quality (#12, 17, 19, 20, 23, 26). Examples:

- "Once it starts spewing out, and you look at [the records]. . . . It just seems so incredibly bulky to yield so little of the kind of thing I want" (#23).

- "A person can be so overwhelmed with the two thousand references that come pouring out like the "Sorcerer's Apprentice" . . ." (#26).

It should be noted that the study was designed so that all information from the searches was printed out locally from the workstation. In this way, complete transaction logs of the searches could be captured and retained for later analysis. The consequence was that large searches could produce great quantities of printout paper right in front of the scholar, rather than remotely at DIALOG headquarters.

There were several other interesting expressions having to do with the scholar's relation to the machine:

- Two commented on their awareness of being connected to a global network, one negatively and the other positively: After noting that he was used to working in university libraries, where the information is in-house and directly accessible, #18 commented: "To get into this 'global network' strikes me as slightly odd." On the other hand, #26 noted: "It [DIALOG] puts you in touch with a network. You sort of feel connected. . . . Scholars can tend to get isolated in their little niches doing their work, and all of a sudden the database and this searching connects you with a whole network of people working in your area all over the world. . . ."

- Scholar #17 liked the idea of having her own password, "which is a kind of intimate relation to the machine."

- Of the first year's group, #12, who did one assisted search and no unassisted searches, reacted very strongly and extensively against the whole idea of online searching: "I resist what strikes me as a kind of industrialization of scholarship." He felt the premise of DIALOG is of quantity and totality. "It's a perverse form of consumerism." He imagined DIALOG being used by promotion and tenure committees to make decisions about tenure. "How many citations does someone have? If this is what scholarship is about, I don't want to be a part of it." This was, he said, professionalization, in the most dangerous sense of the word, being applied to academics.

On the basis of these comments it appears that providing ways for people to feel more mastery over the system could go a long way toward increasing their comfort level. An improved, more user-friendly interface would help and, specifically, provision of easy, effective means to increase and reduce output set size would moderate feelings of threat considerably.

The relative isolation of humanities scholars has long been noted in the literature of scholarly communication, and contrasted with the collaborative nature of much of the natural sciences, in particular. Database vendors might consider enhancing and promoting the networking aspects of online searching as a way of attracting more humanities users.

Impact of online searching on the scholars' usual research behavior: Interview questions 9–17

Question 9 asked how online searching fit in with the scholar's usual process of doing research. Responses reveal a fairly sharp demarcation between those who had integrated the use of online searching into their thinking and those for whom, for one reason or another, the online search was still external, "other." Scholars #14, 15, 16, 17, 20, and, possibly, 22 fall into the former category, and the rest (#18, 19, 21, 23–24, 26–28) into the latter. In addition, #12, from 1989 foresaw DIALOG as having a very marked negative impact on his scholarship. In a sense, he had integrated DIALOG meaningfully and significantly into his thinking, but in a negative, or rejecting manner.

Following are some sample particulars from scholars in the first group:

- "It [online searching] doesn't fit in. It revolutionized it" (#15). He went on to explain that his successful experience with online searching has changed his approach to research. "I will always, in the future, start out with a DIALOG search, particularly in inter-disciplinary topics." His usual method of building a bibliography has been "by accumulation"—going through indexes and bibli-ographies in hard copy, and looking at bibliographies in books he is reading. He pointed out that when he is researching different fields at the same time, this manual method can be extremely time-consuming. In the future, he will use DIALOG "for what it does best, namely, to combine databases from different fields, to see at one glance, within a few seconds, what has been done in connecting field A and field B."

- For #20, accumulating information in libraries was always a first step in his research, which meant searching in card catalogs or going directly to the shelves to find what had been written on the topic. He would like to begin his future projects with a general DIALOG search, using multiple databases.

Scholar #12's negative reaction nonetheless demonstrated an intense engagement with the idea of online searching. Even if he ends up rejecting it forever, he has certainly involved himself with the idea more than a number of the other scholars did. Because the first year's interviews were not tape recorded, the following comments of #12's are paraphrases:

- There is a kind of thinking in DIALOG; it takes thinking from scholars. This is why when you go on DIALOG, you have to be more careful [intellectually].

- The perversity has to do with the ease of it—it eliminates my judgment and insight.

- A lot of my thinking about [my topic] goes on piecemeal in works that seem irrelevant. Thinking goes on in trying to accumulate material. My methods are haphazard. That's where thinking occurs. DIALOG eliminates my thinking.

- DIALOG makes you align up scholarship with what it does.

On the whole, those who had not integrated DIALOG in their research thinking had done the least online searching; and felt they had little use for DIALOG during their year. Examples:

- "Most of the [research] work I did this year was either through clearly defined bodies of theoretical writing which were all making references to each other and I was getting citations from there, or it was primary source material, and DIALOG is useless for that" (#19).

- "My first inclination is to go get a book and look through it. This [DIALOG] would have been somewhat more abstract." Later in the interview: "It would involve redoing some habits, because my sense is that it's far more valuable to me to look through journals than to look at a screen" (#24).

Question 10 asked if the respondent had ever browsed or experimented with a topic to see what might be found. Of the 10 1990 scholars who responded to this question (#14–22, 24), one, who had done the least searching, said she had not worked enough with DIALOG to do it. Eight of the remaining nine said they had done so. Here are some comments:

- In response to a different question, #14 said he preferred not to be too specific in his searches because he values serendipity, and it plays an important role in his research. "You throw out a net to the sea, and you are waiting for a special kind of fish . . . but you are catching all these other things too, and that can be very useful."

- Scholar #15 said he often browsed and experimented while using DIALOG. Sometimes he would think of another topic of interest in the middle of a search and take a few minutes to find what he could on that subject.

One scholar (#21), the one individual who did not say he browsed on DIALOG, had a very different reaction to the whole idea of browsing in DIALOG. Here, and in response to another question, he saw DIALOG as *restricting* his ability to browse. He saw manual research methods as being much more "open" than online searching. DIALOG would provide him with information about a particular article in a particular journal, but it would not let him know about other articles in that journal. He also appeared to think of browsing only as browsing within the full text of the book or article. Because the databases being searched were mostly not full text, he could not browse. He said:

- When I'm working with books it's . . . an immense quantity of information which I bring with me, and then I look on something which is related to the topic. When I work in DIALOG I have to define it as short as possible. I have to try to go with less information into the topic. . . .

Question 11 asked whether the scholar had changed his or her typical research pattern in order to make use of DIALOG. The overwhelming reaction among the 10 scholars responding (#14–22, 24) was no, they did not change their patterns in order to make use of DIALOG. There is an apparent contradiction here with the responses to Question 9, about how DIALOG fitted in with the scholar's usual research procedure. This is most vividly seen in #15's reaction to the two questions. For Question 9, he said "It doesn't fit in. It revolutionized it." Yet, in Question #11, he said no, DIALOG "fits exactly my interdisciplinary research patterns."

The difference in these responses may have to do with the precise wording of the two questions. The first asks how DIALOG searching fits in with the scholar's usual process of doing research. In the analysis of that question's responses, a half-dozen people were found to have integrated DIALOG into their research behavior, or at least their thinking about research. Question 11, on the other hand, asks if they had changed their typical research patterns *in order* to make use of DIALOG. One could presumably integrate online searching into one's research patterns without having to change one's patterns first in order to use DIALOG. This is a subtle difference, but one that might well have made a difference in the responses.

The only two comments that suggested a change in order to use DIA-LOG were to the effect that the scholar had to think through the search terms carefully, and come up with synonyms (#16, 17).

In Question 12, scholars were asked if they had followed a line of inquiry through DIALOG that they would not have attempted had they only had noncomputerized sources. Responses were strongly associated with amount of use. Of the eight 1990 scholars who responded to this question (#14–19, 21, 24), the top five searchers (in number of search statements—#14–18) said they had done so. Most were not specific about why they chose to make the online search, although one (#15) did mention the benefit of searching simultaneously across several disciplines at the same time. After initially saying yes, #17 reconsidered and said, "No, it's only the quickness which gives me the impression that I would have done it in a different way, but probably not."

Question 13 asked if the scholar had had to do any extra offline research by hand because of the information found in DIALOG. The only extra work mentioned by any of the 10 1990 scholars who responded to this question (#14–22, 24) was looking up the articles and other materials found in the DIALOG search—mentioned by five people.

Question 14 asked if the experience of doing research with the help of DIALOG had changed how the scholar thinks about the research process. Out of the eight who responded in 1990 (#14–18, 20–21, 24), three said the experience had not changed how they thought about the research process. A fourth individual said his experience had not changed his thinking about research, but "it made it much easier and made the spectrum much much broader, and with much more information, which is, of course, a qualitative change" (#20).

One reason the searching experience may not have changed how some of these scholars think about research is that other research has shown that the print indexes and abstracting services on which most online databases are based are not very important to scholars. If the scholar does not use a resource in its print form, then it is not surprising that changes in availability of the online form have relatively little impact on search behavior. Scholars most frequently find references for additional reading in other books and articles they read, in book reviews, and in conversation or correspondence with colleagues. In Guest's study (1987), in fact, these three sources ranked first, second, and third, respectively, whereas abstracts and indexes ranked seventh (p. 163). Tibbo (1993) found in her study of 25 historians that 84% used footnotes and bibliographies of recent monographs, while only 24% used abstracts and indexes (p. 117). Scholars may use online databases more than the print forms, as access becomes easier.

Other comments:

- Scholar #14's experience had changed his attitude because his expectations have grown. Now he is looking for "the utmost" in bibliographic information. In the past he was content with less.

- According to #15, "It has made it possible to integrate even more literature that would definitely have been outside of my orbit, that's for sure." DIALOG has made his research richer, more interdisciplinary. He felt that his use of DIALOG would result in an increase in the number of footnotes in his articles and books, and this could be helpful to readers.

- Scholar #18 would feel a researcher's obligation to use it. " . . . [I]f you're a serious scholar, you should preclude any omissions by actually [using] it."

The scholars were asked, in Question 15, what they did with the search results after finishing an online search session. There were no surprises here from the 10 1990 scholars who responded to this question (#14–22, 24). Most saved the results; some reviewed them immediately and marked references of interest; others planned to take the material back to their home base for future use.

Question 16 asked if there had been any instances where the scholar found that the DIALOG search produced a "gold mine" of useful information. Of the nine 1990 respondents to this question (#14–18, 20–22, 24), five said yes and four no. There was no relationship to the amount of searching done by the scholars; both frequent and infrequent users gave each response. It would appear to be a matter of the luck of the draw whether individual searchers happened to hit a gold mine—rather like prospecting in real life!

Question 17 asked if there had been any instances where the scholar concluded that it would have been easier to do the work by hand than through DIALOG. Eight of the 10 1990 respondents (#14–22, 24) either said they had not so concluded, or else that their work was of a nature that the necessary materials were not in the databases. In two cases, however, problems with online searching were identified. One scholar (#17) said that for a major topic of research of hers she found nothing of value to her on DIALOG. Scholar #19 did not respond to this question, but elsewhere in his interview he stated that given his present state of proficiency in DIALOG, if he were to have a complete research library at his disposal and he had a choice between using DIALOG and going to offline sources, he would choose the latter.

DIALOG databases and search techniques:
Interview questions 18–27, questionnaire questions 1–2

Asked, in Question 18, which databases had been particularly useful, scholars gave varying responses. Some mentioned specific databases, others mentioned categories of databases. Of the 10 1990 respondents

(#14–22, 24), five mentioned as most useful the databases that were central to their research interests. Another four mentioned databases both in the center of their interests and at the periphery. One respondent, who had used the system for less than half an hour total, did not remember the databases examined.

Asked, in Question 19, which databases they thought would be useful but proved not to be, 9 of the 10 1990 respondents (#14–22, 24) said either that there had been no examples of databases they thought would be useful and were not, or else they could not remember whether there had been any. The tenth (#24) said she had wanted to find a database of early journals, ones that were no longer being published, then learned that DIALOG did not contain any such databases. Realizing that she could not find historical materials in general had been a big disappointment for her.

Asked, in Question 20, if they had found useful databases that were new to them, the responses were not particularly striking. Ten 1990 scholars responded to this question (#14–22, 24). Four said that all the databases were new to them. It is unclear whether they meant that the entire databases were new to them or just the online forms of them. Most scholars did not mention specific databases, and among those that were mentioned, no notable pattern emerged. Only three databases were mentioned more than once: *Social SciSearch, Magill's Survey of Cinema,* and the *Avery Index to Architecture Periodicals* database were each mentioned twice.

Question 21 was intended as a follow-on to Question 20. The latter had asked whether the scholar had found useful databases that were new to him or her. If so, Question 21 asked: Will you continue to use them, either online or in printed form? Answers appear to have been given with respect to the use of DIALOG generally, not just to any new databases found. Nine of the 1990 searchers were asked this question. Eight said they would continue to use the databases (#14–16, 18–22); the ninth said they were not available in her home city in Europe (#17).

Question 22 asked if there were other types of information, or particular databases, the scholar would like to see added to DIALOG. Five people in 1989 commented on this matter (#1, 3, 4, 5, 9) and 10 in 1990 (#14–22, 24—nonsearchers were not asked). Only one of these 1990 respondents had no additional desired material to suggest. An individual could make indefinitely many suggestions but, in fact, comments were fairly evenly distributed across the respondents:

- *International Literature* Fifteen comments were made regarding a desire for more international literature, including German (the most popular suggestion), European, French, Spanish, and Latin American. The suggestion was also made to include more international literature in the dissertation database.

- *Earlier Literature* Six comments were made with respect to earlier literature of one kind or another: Two comments regarded earlier literature in general, and one each mentioned art, architecture (journals back to 1850), music, and French.

- *Art and Architecture Databases* Six comments referred to desired changes in art and architecture databases: More information on early art and architecture, very current art topics, both art and architecture in the same database (*RILA* in fact does this), and *Art Index* online (*Art Index* is available online but not on DIALOG).

- *Other* Other comments suggested a film literature index, Library of Congress databases (these were, in fact, available to the scholars), and bibliographies of classical archeology and philology.

Question 23 asked the scholar to think back on his or her experience overall with online searching during the year and say how easy or hard it was to use as a way of getting information. The answers of the 10 1990 respondents (#14–22, 24) to the question broke out as follows:

- Fully positive reaction, without qualification, for example, "Extremely easy" (#15): 15, 17, 20.

- Positive reaction with some (usually very small) qualification, for example, "The more you deal with it, the easier it is" (#14): 14, 18, 21, 22.

- Equivocal whether hard or easy, for example, needed 3 more hours online to become relatively fluent in DIALOG use (#19): 19, 24.

- Hard to use: 16.

Comments elsewhere in the responses to interview questions indicate that use of DIALOG was somewhat more difficult than these reactions would suggest. For that reason, it may be important to pay attention to the presence of slight or substantial qualifications in all but the first group of reactions.

Question 24 asked: Did it get easier or harder to use as the year went on? To put it differently, did you learn more and more DIALOG commands and search techniques as you went along, or did you tend to forget things as time passed after the fall training session? Nine people in the 1990 group (#14–22) had used DIALOG enough to feel they could answer this question. Their overall reaction was that the searching got easier as the year went on. They tended to forget commands if there was a gap in their use of DIALOG, but they generally found it easy to recoup what they had forgotten. One noted: "DIALOG impresses me as being complex enough that for occasional use it's hard to maintain the set of skills and strategies necessary for efficient use" (#19).

Four people also mentioned using just a small core of commands to achieve, as one put it, a fairly stable but "low level" of proficiency (#19). One of the nine had a more activist approach: Scholar #20 attended review sessions and went through the manual on his own to learn new techniques.

Question 25 asked if the scholar found any of the search commands, or any aspects of DIALOG, confusing or difficult to use. The 1989 group had more criticisms than the 1990 group in response to this question. Comments dealt with databases, the command language, and the system as a whole:

- *Databases*
  - Foreign language problems: variant spellings, knowing whether a term will be translated into English or not (#2).
  - Different structure and standards in databases (#4).
  - Different databases have different "syntaxes" (#7).
  - Lack of uniformity between databases makes it difficult to use OneSearch (the multidatabase search command) (#19).

- *Command Language*
  - Boolean logic is too rigid (#1).
  - Resorted to a lot of personal name searches because of the difficulty of formulating subject searches (#6).
  - Need a way to express sophisticated ideas, like "history of anthropology" (#6), or history of philosophy, not philosophy of history (#1). (The latter criticism could be handled by DIALOG's "w" operator.)
  - Hard to formulate a query (#7).
  - Commands confusing, not natural (#14, 16).

- *System as a Whole*
  - Hard to winnow down retrieved sets (#2).
  - Thrown off DIALOG because spent too much time reading the printout (#3).

- Need an interface between the system and the casual user. Why not develop an interface with artificial intelligence so the searcher can use a natural language query? (#4).
- You cannot know when you have made a mistake (#5).
- Error messages "insulting" and "impolite" (#6).

Many of these criticisms have been heard many times before from other searchers. The comments that are most likely to reflect the particular concerns of arts and humanities researchers are those dealing with foreign languages and personal name searching.

Question 26 asked if the scholar had found any of the search commands, or any other aspects of DIALOG, particularly easy or powerful to use. Nine 1990 scholars responded to this question (#14–22). Favorable comments were made about the following features, in descending order of popularity—none received more than three comments: OneSearch, "Expand" command, truncation, parentheses, Boolean operators, OR chains ("hedges"), "f" ("same field") operator, DIALINDEX, date limitation, and journal title limitation.

Asked, in Question 27, if they would like to see other commands or search capabilities added to DIALOG, most of the nine respondents in 1990 (#14–21, 24) had no suggestions, often feeling insufficiently experienced or knowledgeable about such systems to contribute anything. Three did make suggestions, however. Here they are:

- Weighting terms in the abstracts by their importance (#14).

- Articles ordered by length. Offered as a way to provide better discrimination among items in retrieved set (#18).

- Scholar #19 would like to be able to flag desired references on the screen, paste them to a file of his own, and print them out. (There are ways, in fact, to do this.) He would also like for there to be uniformity across databases in how they are accessed, and no barrier between them—essentially, one giant database.

Question 1 of the questionnaire asked scholars whether they used the DIALOG training manual, the DIALOG "blue sheets" (short summaries of the features of databases), or the DIALOG database chapters (longer descriptions of the database characteristics and search techniques to be used with them). They replied on all of these in a range of Always/Usually/

Sometimes/Seldom/Never. All 11 searchers responded (#14–22, 24–25). (Responses of the nonsearchers were not applicable.)

With just 11 responses spread over five possible answers, we decided that our best approach was to look simply for main tendencies. Use of the training manual tied at three each for always and usually, with smaller numbers in the other categories. Use of the blue sheets tied at four each for usually and sometimes, while use of database chapters got the largest number of marks, four, in never. In sum, the scholars used the training manual very frequently, the blue sheets often, and rarely used the database chapters.

Question 2 concerned use of thesauri. Respondents were asked for yes or no answers on whether they had ever used *RILA Subject Headings* (Repertory of the Literature of Art), *Architectural Keywords,* and *Historical Abstracts Index* in connection with DIALOG searching. All three thesauri were available at the workstation. Ten (#14–20, 22, 24–25) responded to this question. Six, six, and seven of the respondents, respectively, had never used each of the three thesauri in connection with their online searching. Among those responding yes, individuals had used one or another thesaurus at some time. Altogether, these results are fairly good. Many end users (and professionals as well) do not understand how important it is to consult these sources. The training apparently taught the scholars good searching practices, although greater use of the database chapters would have been helpful to them. Some of their difficulties in finding information might have been relieved had they had a deeper understanding of the unique strengths and limitations of particular databases.

Training and assistance while at the Getty: Interview questions 28–30

Questions 28–30 asked whether the scholar had received personal assistance in searching or had attended a group review session, and asked how helpful these had been. Ten (#14–22, 24) 1990 searchers responded to these questions. Two neither requested individual help nor attended a group review session. Of the remaining eight, seven got personal help and five went to a group review session. Among the four 1990 nonsearchers, one had personal help and two went to a group review session.

The general reaction was that these forms of assistance were helpful. Both searchers and nonsearchers expressed the strongest enthusiasm for the personal assistance. Scholar #16 suggested that DIALOG training should be geared more to the specific needs of the scholars, and that they should be taught the various "tricks," such as the use of parentheses and question marks, in the first training session. She felt that some of the information dispensed in the initial training session was useless.

Scholar #15 put forth an even more specific training proposal. He felt that the assisted search was the most valuable way to learn DIALOG. He much preferred it to the full-day training session, which he felt was "too academic" and "too concentrated." He favored a completely individualized training program, with 1 hour of learning search techniques, starting with the most basic of these and progressing to more difficult and creative searches. This experience could be followed by perhaps another hour for the researcher to work on his or her own searches with a training assistant nearby.

Scholars' projections regarding future use and impact of online searching: Interview questions 31–34

Question 31 asked whether the scholar planned to do online database searching in the future. Eight out of 10 searchers (#14–22, 24) and three out of four nonsearchers (#23, 26–28) who responded said that they did plan to use online searching in the future, although several qualified these statements by saying they would use it if available or if affordable.

This very positive result should be accepted cautiously. People commonly say that they will use projected information resources or capabilities in the future, then fail to use them when they become available. Use of socially valued resources, like libraries and information retrieval systems, is seen as a "good thing," and so people tend to say yes if they anticipate any chance at all of using them.

What actually most often conditions a person's use of information sources is the Principle of Least Effort: To a surprising degree, people—including researchers, physicians, and others who need information professionally—use those sources they see as easiest to use and most accessible (Poole, 1985). Evidence in this study, in both interviews and search protocols, shows that DIALOG was fairly difficult for the scholars to use. Therefore, they may actually not use it much in the immediate future—until and unless it becomes much easier to use. Nonsearchers, who could have experimented for free, could not find an hour or two all year to do so.

Comments that they would use online databases "if available" or if they could afford them may indicate a fairly passive attitude toward online searching. Many scholars in the program came from Europe, where systems equivalent to DIALOG are widely available and relatively inexpensive, although cost and difficulty of access vary from country to country. (Of course, expense will always be an issue with poorly funded humanities

TABLE 2. *Search mode preferences of 1990 scholars*

PREFERENCE	SEARCHERS	NON-SEARCHERS	TOTAL
Self-searching alone	2 (#15, 20)	1 (#27)	3
Self with someone nearby to answer questions	4 (#14, 16, 17, 21)	0	4
Self with someone sitting next to one	2 (#22, 24)	1 (#26)	3
Intermediary searching with scholar sitting there giving feedback	1 (#18)	1 (#28)	2
Intermediary searches without scholar present	1 (#19)	1 (#23)	2
No response	1 (#25)	0	1
TOTAL	11	4	15

research.) An information hotline to DIALOG was available to the scholars all year where they could have learned about the availability of DIALOG or other systems in their home cities. Yet only two searchers had looked into the possibility of doing DIALOG searching in their home institutions at the time of the interview. As scholar #18 noted, computers are not "an instinctive part of my armory."

In Question 32 scholars were asked if they preferred to do online database searching themselves or have librarians or research assistants do it for them. Responses to this question were intriguing in that they were so varied. Among the 1990 group, five different preferences were mentioned, which were broadly distributed among the respondents (see Table 2). Searcher numbers are provided in parentheses after the count.

Scholar #19, the only one willing to turn over the search to someone else, noted that before experiencing DIALOG firsthand, he probably would have objected to the idea of someone else conducting searches for him. Now, however, after seeing how DIALOG works, he would prefer to just submit a request and have someone well trained in DIALOG do the search for him. He would want to be able to communicate with the intermediary if needed, however.

The six scholars in 1989 (#1, 2, 4, 6, 7, 11) who commented on this question showed an equally wide range of responses; among them they added two other options. One said he would assign simple searches to someone else and do the complex queries himself (#2). The other said he would like to do both—conduct the search himself and have a professional searcher do it too (#4). Data for 1989 scholars are not included in Table 2 because the interview conditions for that group were significantly different with respect to this question. The 1989 scholars had comparative searches done and the 1990 group did not.

Question 33 asked: In the future, as systems like DIALOG become more widely available, what impact from them do you foresee on research in the arts and humanities in general? All 15 1990 respondents commented. All saw online searching as having at least some impact on research, with some envisioning a very substantial effect. Most foresaw neutral or positive effects, but some predicted negative effects. The scholars' perceptive comments are discussed here in terms of the themes raised, with quotation and paraphrase where appropriate.

Overwhelmed by information, effect on research and publication Several scholars (#12, 21, 22, 26) commented on the effects of the large quantities of information that DIALOG searching can provide. All said such quantities were difficult to control or manage. Scholar #26 made some particularly thoughtful comments:

- On the down side, creativity has to do, to a very large extent, with selectivity, and flooding people with masses of data is just as bad as not having any, in a way, so that it becomes a complicated issue. In the humanities you want to leave room for the unexpected and the surprise—that's probably just as true in the sciences.

Elsewhere in the interview she comments in greater detail:

- I think that it's very interesting psychologically. . . . The whole DIALOG experience can be very daunting. . . . On the one hand, it can be tremendously exciting to know that there is this vast literature. I was amazed at how much had been done in my area. . . . But I think that it can also be stiflingly daunting. A person can be so overwhelmed with the two thousand references that come pouring out like the "Sorcerer's Apprentice". . . . When you're actually in the throes of creative experience you might want to put blinders on at that point and say "Forget it. What I've got is inside of me, at this point."

Others talked about the quantity of materials in relation to the *product* of the research:

- Scholar #20 felt that the vast amount of information that DIALOG can provide is one of its advantages, but there is also the danger that a "terrible amount of information is accumulated" and simply put into printed form without any thought or analysis. He said he had read several dissertations that were written with the aid of online search systems, and he found them extremely bulky. "Now because it's much more easy, I think, authors are always using full quotations, not abbreviated—a half page, or one page—and it's a terrible amount of written material, and you are lost in the details, somehow." His wife, #25, agreed: "Only quantity, without any quality."

- Scholar #23 saw the potential impact of online search systems as "enormous." She added, however: "I'm afraid there are going to be more very boring articles of the sort that just quote thousands of other articles." She went on: "Of all the twelve thousand things on [my topic], there are about ten that are interestingly written and worth referring to."

Relationship to scholarly creativity Some respondents (#6, 21, 23, 28) made a point of distinguishing how one gets information from what one does with it. The general point was that even if acquiring information is eased, scholarly creativity lies in what one does with it.

- "DIALOG is tangential to the creative process . . ." (#6).

- Scholar #23 felt that the massive amounts of information made available through online sources could make it very difficult for scholars to make wise judgments as to what to include and what to discard. "It's not going to tell you which [articles or books] are good or interesting, or anything. . . . I don't think it's going to help originality any. I'm not optimistic about that."

- "Whatever a database will provide, it won't eliminate that second phase of putting the information together in an interesting way and doing new things with it" (#28).

- One scholar noted that he would not recommend that students use DIALOG because he feels they should develop their research methodology manually, using their intuition, their imagination, and their ability to make associations. "I think it's very important for a student to go into the library, to be stimulated by books, and to work with books" (#21).

Finally, one respondent (#17) felt that the impact on research could be very positive, in that systems such as DIALOG may encourage scholars to think in a different way. She noted how computers have changed our way of writing in comparison to typewriters, qualitatively as well as quantitatively. In the same way, she felt DIALOG could change the way scholars do research and the way they think about research.

Speed of research Three scholars (#19, 27, 28) noted that research would be speeded up. Scholar #19 believed that the drudge work of going through periodical indexes volume by volume would be saved.

Increase in competitiveness, standards of scholarship Four people commented on the theme of competitiveness and standards. Database searching could intensify research (#14); the expectations of degree of awareness of the literature would increase: "The level of scholarship will have to keep pace" (#26).

An information gap could develop between those who use DIALOG and those who do not (#22). Scholar #21 felt that the prohibitive cost of DIALOG would make it an elite system, available to a very limited number of researchers, so that a small number of people would have access to masses of information. He could envision a competitive atmosphere developing around this quest for more and more information.

Impact on content of research materials Three people (#15, 18, 24) noted the increase in interdisciplinary research that could result from online searching. Here are some reflections by #15:

- "DIALOG, or something like DIALOG, will become more and more useful, and needed even—at the moment it's helpful, but I think it's going to be *needed* within ten years—because the humanities are moving in a direction that almost makes bibliographic research of the old kind impossible, because the old kind [of research] has always been one discipline, one bibliography. Now that we are combining things [such as] architecture and film, or the image of medicine in the fine arts, or the perception of urban space in the early movies. . . .These are [topics] that are truly interdisciplinary [and] they have to be researched along those lines."

Three others (#16, 18, 27) commented on research materials as well. Online searching would make it easier to survey a discipline (#27), it would be useful as an entree to a new area of study (#18), and it would enable scholars to become more aware of what is being written on their topics in other countries (#16).

Summary The scholars believed that online searching could overwhelm researchers with materials and require that they exercise more judgment than ever in identifying the worthy sources and useful material to include in their writings. Although research could be speeded up and competitiveness increased as a greater number of background sources come to be expected in humanities writing, the scholar must still make creative use of the materials. Interdisciplinary research and entree into new fields could be particularly benefited by online searching.

Question 34 asked if the scholar thought that other arts and humanities scholars would use these systems. All respondents, both searchers (#14–22, 24) and nonsearchers (#23, 26–28), thought other scholars would use online databases. Some mentioned hindrances such as cost and availability problems that might impede things for a while, but they saw the basic pattern as one of future use. Three (#14, 17, 28) foresaw some hesitancy or resistance on the part of scholars at first, but they did not see this as lasting indefinitely. Closely related to this point, one scholar remarked that the first step for scholars is to use the computer: "Once they are used to the computer, they will start to use the databases" (#22). Another noted that for younger people growing up "in this world of high-tech," using systems like DIALOG will not require any major adjustments (#26).

Summary and conclusions

This study's results are summarized according to the broad topics of interest covered in the various questions of the 1990 searcher interview schedule. For the sake of brevity, code numbers for scholars are given in the previous results section, but not in the conclusions section. Questionnaire results are interspersed where appropriate. After the areas are reviewed, final conclusions are presented.

Background experience of the scholars (from questionnaire)

Experience of the 1990 respondents with online database searching, whether done by themselves or others, was virtually nil. On the other hand, virtually all had used computers for word processing, and half had used online catalogs.

Research projects and status

Most of the 15 1990 scholars were engaged in two or more projects while they were at the Getty. By a rough measure, in which stage of research was categorized into early, middle, and late, no relationship could confidently be identified between stage of research and amount of online searching being done by the scholars.

Reaction to DIALOG searching in general

Curiosity, expectations of increased research materials, and hope to supplement research techniques motivated the scholars to agree to participate. Four of the 15 1990 participants said they had little use for DIALOG searching this year and did none. Of the remainder, responses were about equally divided between those who got as much or more than they expected from the program and those who got less.

Comments on disappointments with the experience are divided about half and half between complaints about the unavailability of desired resources in the databases and difficulties with the search interface. Positive comments mentioned the power of combining distinct concepts with Boolean logic and the value and ease of interdisciplinary research online.

Feeling reactions are likely to have an important role in whether people use these resources again, so one question probed for the emotional side of the experience. The scholars made a number of positive expressions, including even comments by a few respondents that they might be becoming "addicts."

The respondents' expressions of discomfort can be recognized as the familiar ones of people who have (a) not yet really mastered something new to them, and (b) are contending with the not fully user-friendly features of DIALOG. DIALOG and other major database vendor systems designed for use by trained intermediaries are difficult to master and use effectively without quite a bit of training and experience. The one day's training the scholars got was very helpful but did not produce accomplished searchers.

One respondent summed up the problems well:

l found it cumbersome. It never became transparent for me
in the way ORION [UCLA's online catalog] has. l think that's
partially due to the fact that l didn't use it enough. . . . l think
there are some built-in barriers toward its easy access.

Another recurring theme in the scholars' reactions was the description of database searching as a sorcerer's apprentice. Several scholars used terms like "overwhelmed" with reference to the information "spewing" or "pouring" out of the machine. One scholar resented what he called the "industrialization of scholarship" represented by automated searching, and called it a "perverse form of consumerism." On the other hand, these very features could also be enjoyable in their serendipitous production of resources not previously known to the scholar. One called it "Las Vegas for the intellectual."

Impact on and relation to usual research behavior

Overall, the 1990 scholars viewed online searching as supplementing their usual research methods and making some small changes around the edges in their current and projected searching behavior. Online searching did not lead to fundamental shifts in how they think or go about their research. They saw online searching as enriching or extending their research; some felt that they would have the scholar's obligation to check these additional resources in surveying the literature of their topics in the future. Most said they had used DIALOG to browse, but gave few specifics. Browsing did not seem to be an important part of their thinking about DIALOG use.

Reaction to resources in DIALOG

Scholars liked the databases they used and did not single out any particular databases as disappointing their expectations. However, they had many suggestions for additional resources that should be covered in DIALOG to meet their research needs. Recommendations centered strongly on a need for additional European materials, especially German. There was also a strong desire for more historical (primary) materials, and coverage of journals well before 1975.

DIALOG search techniques, ease of use, database manuals, and thesauri

On the whole, 1990 respondents felt DIALOG was fairly easy to use. However, a number of complaints surfaced, more from 1989 than 1990 respondents. Some problems they identified included the rigidity of Boolean logic, difficulty with formulating search queries, different structures and standards between databases, and difficulty in winnowing down retrieved sets. They liked the OneSearch (simultaneous multiple database searching) and the "Expand" command (viewing alphabetically or conceptually related terms) features in DIALOG.

Responses to questionnaire questions on use of DIALOG manuals and database thesauri showed that scholars' use of these sources was fairly extensive in connection with their online searching. Most had used the DIALOG materials, and half of those who searched had used one or more thesauri.

Training and assistance

Most scholars took advantage of group review sessions and personal assistance offered them; they were most enthusiastic about having personalized assistance.

Projected use of online searching

Eleven of the 15 1990 respondents said they planned to do online searching in the future. This is a very positive result, but should be accepted with caution. Statements on planned use of information sources in research on information-seeking behavior are regularly higher than actual use. Human information seeking is governed largely by the Principle of Least Effort; people, including researchers, use sources that are easy to use and accessible before they use harder-to-use sources. Although a large number said they planned to use database searching in the future, only two respondents, a husband and wife, actually investigated how they might do so when they returned home.

When asked whether they preferred to do online searching themselves or have it done for them, respondents favored a wide variety of solutions to this question, rather than a single approach. Between the 1989 and 1990 respondents, no fewer than seven different responses to this question were given: self searching alone, self with someone nearby to answer questions, self with someone sitting next to one, intermediary searching with scholar sitting there giving feedback, intermediary searching without scholar present, scholar searching difficult queries and intermediary searching easy ones, and both scholar and intermediary independently searching the query.

Projected impact on arts and humanities research

In response to these questions, the scholars discussed the impact of the large quantities of information produced by online searching, and the relationship of online searching to scholarly creativity and publication, the speed of research, and competitiveness. They saw online searching as speeding the identification and retrieval of research information.

They identified the danger of getting great quantities of information and not being selective enough in using the material. As one noted: " . . . creativity has to do, to a very large extent, with selectivity, and flooding people with masses of data is just as bad as not having any, in a way. . . ." Another said: "I'm afraid there are going to be more very boring articles of the sort that just quote thousands of other articles." Others pointed out that scholarly creativity—" putting the information together in an interesting way and doing new things with it"—is different from the mere gathering of the information.

Several respondents felt that the availability of online searching would increase the standards of scholarship, and make it necessary for scholars to be aware of a wider range of literature. Two expressed concern about a gap developing between information haves and have nots. Three people felt online searching would have a particularly strong positive impact on interdisciplinary research, by making it easy to search across many fields. All 1990 respondents, both searchers and nonsearchers, thought that other scholars would use online databases.

Conclusions

Altogether, the scholars' response to online searching was positive, if fraught with some anxiety about getting used to a new system and some discouragement at not finding some of the resources they would like. Like many before them, they found DIALOG searching "cumbersome" for beginners. Those who searched enough to become comfortable, however, were very enthusiastic about it.

Generally, the scholars saw DIALOG searching as supplementing their usual research methods, not changing them in any fundamental way. Online searching was seen as particularly useful for interdisciplinary research.

They were impressed, even taken aback, by the quantities of information DIALOG could produce. They felt the availability of online searching would raise expectations on the amount of material that should be reviewed in humanities scholarship, but noted that scholarly creativity requires selectivity and imaginative use of what is found. All foresaw online searching being used in the future by arts and humanities scholars.

Despite these promising prognostications by the participants in the project, these results also demonstrate that online searching of DIALOG— even when completely free to the scholar—did not take on an intimate, familiar, frequent role in these scholars' work life. The resources available do not yet match fully with the information needs of the scholars, particularly for historical and primary research materials, and the search interface is still difficult to negotiate for these end users. No doubt they will continue to use this resource for the materials it has, but adaptations are needed before the use of such online systems by humanists grows explosively.

APPENDIX: INTERVIEW SCHEDULES

Interview for individuals who had done some or a lot of searching.
(Note: Notes and suggestions to the interviewer are deleted.)

1. Now that you have been at the Getty for several months, how would you describe the topic(s) or problem(s) you are researching?

2. At what stage of the research were you when you came, and at what stage are you now?

3. Has your topic or research shifted in any way during the course of your work here at the Getty?

4. Why did you decide to participate in this online searching project?

5. Have you gotten what you expected from your participation in the online searching project? Were there any surprises or disappointments?

6. To what degree has the online searching been helpful to you in meeting your research needs this year?

7. As you think back on your work here these last months, tell me some of the points you can remember in your research where you decided to use DIALOG. What kinds of research needs did you have—what were you trying to find out—at those moments that you went online?

8. What, in general, are your reactions to using DIALOG?

9. As you reflect on the uses you have made of DIALOG during these months, how would you say online searching fitted in with your usual process of doing research?

10. Did you ever browse or experiment with a topic just to see what you might find?

11. Did you change your typical research patterns in any way in order to make use of DIALOG?

12. Were there any instances where you looked for information or followed a line of inquiry through DIALOG that you would not have attempted had you only had noncomputerized sources?

13. Did you have to do any extra *offline* work, that is, additional research by hand, of any kind because of the information you found on DIALOG?

14. Has the experience of doing research with the help of DIALOG changed how you think about the research process in any way?

15. What do you do with the search results after you finish an online search session?

16. Were there any instances where you would say that your DIALOG search produced a "gold mine," that is, where you found a very useful or very extensive body of information?

17. On the other hand, were there any instances where, after using DIALOG, you concluded that it would have been easier to do the work by hand?

18. What databases did you find particularly useful? Why?

19. What databases did you think would be useful but proved not to be? Why?

20. Did you find useful databases that were new to you?
[If so]: 21. Will you continue to use them, either online or in printed form?

22. Are there other types of information, or particular databases, you would like to see added to DIALOG?

23. Thinking back on your experience overall with online searching this year, how easy or how hard would you say it was to use as a way of getting information?

24. Did it get easier or harder to use as the year went on? To put it differently, did you learn more and more DIALOG commands and search techniques as you went along, or did you tend to forget things as time passed after the fall training session?

25. Did you find any of the search commands, or any other aspects of DIALOG, confusing or difficult to use?

26. Did you find any of the search commands, or any other aspects of DIALOG, particularly easy or powerful to use?

27. Are there other commands or search capabilities you would like to see added to DIALOG?

28. Did you receive personal assistance in searching? [yes/no]

29. Did you attend a group review session? [yes/no]

30. How helpful were these forms of assistance?
[If so]: How were they helpful?

31. Do you plan to do online database searching in the future?

32. Do you prefer to do online database searching yourself or would you rather have librarians or research assistants do it for you?

33. Now I have a couple of more general questions. In the future, as systems like DIALOG become more widely available, what impact from them do you foresee on research in the arts and humanities in general?

34. Do you think other arts and humanities scholars will use these systems?

Interview for individuals who had done no searching beyond training session. (*Note: Notes and suggestions to the interviewer are deleted.*)

1. Now that you have been at the Getty for several months, how would you describe the topic(s) or problem(s) you are researching?

2. At what stage of the research were you when you came, and at what stage are you now?

3. Has your topic or research shifted in any way during the course of your work here at the Getty?

4. Why did you decide to participate in this online searching project?

5. Have you gotten what you expected from your participation in the online searching project? Were there any surprises or disappointments?

6. Why did you not search this year?

7. Did you have no need this year for the kind of information provided in the databases?

8. Did you find DIALOG hard to use?

9. Did you find it easier to use your accustomed methods for finding citations?

10. Did you prefer to have someone else do the online searching?

11. Did you have insufficient time?

12. Did you forget how to search?

13. Any other reasons?

14. Did you receive personal assistance in searching?

15. Did you attend a group review session?

16. How helpful were these forms of assistance?
    [If so]: How were they helpful?

17. Do you plan to do online database searching in the future?

18. Do you prefer to do online database searching yourself or would you rather have librarians or research assistants do it for you?
19. Now I have a couple of more general questions. In the future, as systems like DIALOG become more widely available, what impact from them do you foresee on research in the arts and humanities in general?
20. Do you think other arts and humanities scholars will use these systems?

REFERENCES

Bates, M.J., Wilde, D.N., & Siegfried, S. (1993). An analysis of search terminology used by humanities scholars: The Getty Online Searching Project report no. 1. *The Library Quarterly, 63*(1), 1–39.

Broadbent, E. (1986). A study of humanities faculty library information seeking behavior. *Cataloging & Classification Quarterly, 6*(3), 23–36.

Case, D.O. (1986). Collection and organization of written information by social scientists and humanists: A review and exploratory study. *Journal of Information Science, 12*(3), 97–104.

Case, D. O. (1991). Collection and use of information by some American historians: A study of motives and methods. *The Library Quarterly 61*(1), 61–82.

Corkill, C., & Mann, M. (1978). *Information needs in the humanities: Two postal surveys. CRUS Occasional Paper No. 2.* (BLR & DD Report No. 5455). Sheffield, England: Centre for Research on User Studies.

Crawford, D. (1986). Meeting scholarly information needs in an automated environment: A humanist's perspective. *College & Research Libraries, 47*(6), 569–574.

Everett, D., & Pilachowski, D.M. (1986). What's in a name? Looking for people online—humanities. *Database, 9*(5), 26–34.

Fabian, B. (1986). Libraries and humanistic scholarship. *Journal of Librarianship, 18*(2), 79–92.

Garvey, W.D. (1979). *Communication: The essence of science: Facilitating information exchange among librarians, scientists, engineers, and students.* New York: Pergamon Press.

Gould, C.C. (1988). *Information needs in the humanities: An assessment.* Stanford, CA: Research Libraries Group.

Guest, S.S. (1987). The use of bibliographical tools by humanities faculty at the State University of New York at Albany. *Reference Librarian, 7*(18), 157–172.

Horner, J., & Thirlwall, D. (1988). Online searching and the university researcher. *Journal of Academic Librarianship, 14*(4), 225–230.

Humanists at work: Disciplinary perspectives and personal reflections: Symposium, April 27–28, 1989. Chicago, IL: University of Illinois.

Hurych, J. (1986). After Bath: Scientists, social scientists, and humanists in the context of online searching. *Journal of Academic Librarianship, 12*(3), 158–165.

Katzen, M. (1986). The application of computers in the humanities: A view from Britain. *Information Processing & Management, 22*(3), 259–267.

Krausse, S.C., & Etchingham, J.B., Jr. (1986). The humanist and computer-assisted library research. *Computers and the Humanities, 20*(2), 87–96.

Lehmann, S., & Renfro, P. (1991). Humanists and electronic information services: Acceptance and resistance. *College & Research Libraries, 52*(5), 409–413.

Loughridge, B. (1989). Information technology, the humanities and the library. *Journal of Information Science, 15*(45), 277–286.

Lowry, A., & Stuveras, J. (1987). *Scholarship in the electronic age: A selected bibliography on research and communication in the humanities and social sciences.* Washington, DC: Council on Library Resources.

Mackesy, E.M. (1982). A perspective on secondary access services in the humanities. *Journal of the American Society for Information Science, 33*(3), 146–151.

McCracken, G.D. (1988). *The long interview.* Newbury Park, CA: SAGE.

Poole, H. (1985). *Theories of the middle range.* Norwood, NJ: Ablex.

Rahtz, S. (Ed.). (1987). *Information technology in the humanities: Tools, techniques and applications.* Chichester, England: Ellis Horwood-Wiley.

Ruiz, D., & Meyer, D.E. (1990). End-user selection of databases—part III: Social science/arts & humanities. *Database, 13*(5), 59–64.

Schmitt, M. (Ed.). (1988). *Object, image, and inquiry: The art historian at work.* Santa Monica, CA: The Getty Art History Information Program.

Schmitt, M. (1990a). Alas, the failure to communicate: Thoughts on the symbiosis of scholars, information managers and systems experts. *Art Documentation, 9*(3), 137–138.

Schmitt, M. (1990b). Scholars must take the lead in computerization in the humanities. *Chronicle of Higher Education, 37*(12), A44.

Siegfried, S., Bates, M.J., & Wilde, D.N. (1993). A profile of end-user searching behavior by humanities scholars: The Getty Online Searching Project report no. 2. *Journal of the American Society for Information Science, 44*(5), 273–291.

Stam, D.C. (1984). How art historians look for information. *Art Documentation, 3*(4), 117–119.

Stam, D.C., & Giral, A. (Eds.). (1988). Linking art objects and art information. *Library Trends, 37*(2), 117–264.

Stern, P. (1988). Online in the humanities: Problems and possibilities. *Journal of Academic Librarianship, 14*(3), 161–164.

Stielow, F., & Tibbo, H. (1988). The negative search, online reference and the humanities: A critical essay in library literature. *RQ, 27*(3), 358–365.

Stone, S. (1982). Humanities scholars: Information needs and uses. *Journal of Documentation, 38*(4), 292–312.

Tibbo, H.R. (1991). Information systems, services, and technology for the humanities. *Annual Review of Information Science and Technology, 26*, 287–346.

Tibbo, H.R. (1993). *Abstracting, information retrieval, and the humanities.* Chicago, IL: American Library Association.

Walker, G. (1988). Online searching in the humanities: Implications for end users and intermediaries. *Proceedings of the 12th International Online Information Meeting* (pp. 401–412). Oxford, England: Learned Information.

Walker, G. (1990). Searching the humanities: Subject overlap and search vocabulary. *Database, 13*(5), 35–46.

Walker, G., & Atkinson, S.D. (1991). Information access in the humanities: Perils and pitfalls. *Library Hi Tech, 9*(1), 23–34.

Weintraub, K.J. (1980). The humanistic scholar and the library. *The Library Quarterly, 50*(1), 22–39.

Wiberley, S.E., Jr. (1991). Habits of humanists: Scholarly behavior and new information technologies. *Library Hi Tech, 9*(1), 17–21.

Wiberley, S.E., Jr., & Jones, W.G. (1989). Patterns of information seeking in the humanities. *College & Research Libraries, 50*(6), 638–645.

Woo, J. (1988). The Online Avery Index End-User Pilot Project: Final report. *Information Technology and Libraries, 7*, 223–229.

4

The Getty end-user Online Searching Project in the humanities: Report no. 6: Overview and conclusions

ABSTRACT

Over a two-year period, the Getty Information Institute (formerly the Getty Art History Information Program) sponsored and carried out a major study of end-user online searching by humanities scholars. Complete logs of the searches and output were captured, and the twenty-seven scholars involved were interviewed in depth. An overview of the study and its results is presented, with particular emphasis on matters of interest to academic librarians. Implications are drawn for academic library reference service and collection development, as well as for cataloging in the online and digital environment.

Introduction

Over a two-year period, the Getty Information Institute (formerly the Getty Art History Information Program, or Getty AHIP) sponsored and carried out a major study of end-user online searching by humanities scholars. Complete logs of their searches and output were captured, and the twenty-seven scholars involved were interviewed in depth.

The results of the study have appeared in a series of five articles to date (Bates, Wilde & Siegfried, 1993, 1995; Siegfried, Bates & Wilde, 1993; Bates, 1994, 1996). It is the purpose of this article to (1) provide an overview of the

First published as Bates, M. J. (1996). The Getty end-user Online Searching Project in the humanities: Report no. 6: Overview and conclusions. *College & Research Libraries,* 57(6), 514–523.

entire project, (2) review major findings of the study, and (3) draw implications of the study research for the practice of academic librarianship in reference and online searching services, collection development, and cataloging.

Marilyn Schmitt, Deborah Wilde, and Susan Siegfried, of the Getty Information Institute, who originated and carried out much of the study, brought me into the project to design the second year's interview schedule and to analyze this immense body of data. (Wilde and Siegfried are no longer with the Institute. Vanessa Birdsey, Nancy Bryan, Brian Sullivan, Jeanette Clough, and Katherine Smith also assisted in various parts of the study.)

In the space of this necessarily brief article, it is feasible neither to recapitulate all the results nor, especially, to present all the supporting data that appeared in five lengthy articles elsewhere. The purpose here is to extract the information of use to the busy academic librarian; the reader interested in more detail will be directed to the appropriate article(s). As can be seen in the notes, the articles are numbered Reports #1 through 5 to make it easier to distinguish and locate them; they will also be referred to by number here.

Succeeding sections describe the study methodology, state the content areas of each of the five prior reports, extract the principal results from the five prior articles, and draw implications from these results for academic library service to humanities researchers.

Background

Literature reviews are provided in the various earlier reports, especially #1 through 3. The reader interested in learning more in general about humanities information-seeking is directed to the recent review article by Rebecca Watson-Boone (1994), the earlier extensive review by Sue Stone (1982), and research by Stephen Wiberley and William Jones (1989, 1994).

Methodology

Visiting scholars at the Getty Research Institute for the History of Art and the Humanities[1] are invited for a one-year stay, and come from all over

---

1 The J. Paul Getty Trust is a private operating foundation. Two of its programs are the Getty Information Institute (formerly the Getty Art History Information Program) and the Getty Research Institute for the History of Art and the Humanities (formerly the Getty Center for the History of Art and the Humanities). These two entities collaborated on this research.

the world. To do research at the institute is a prestigious opportunity, and the institute draws a range of qualified researchers, from people finishing their doctorates to internationally renowned senior scholars. In return for the opportunity to do unlimited, free (i.e., subsidized by the Getty) online searching as end users on about 60 humanities and social sciences databases, participating scholars agreed to be interviewed and to have their search logs captured for study. During 1988–89 and 1989–90, all visiting scholars at the research institute were invited to participate.

Over the two years, about two-thirds of them agreed to participate, as well as five spouses (scholars in their own right), for a total of twenty-seven participants, seventeen male and ten female. (One of the first-year scholars stayed a second year; see Report #2 for information on where her second-year data are or are not included in various tallies.) Scholars came from all over Europe and the United States. Eleven were native English speakers; English language proficiency of the non-native speakers ranged from adequate to excellent. Research interests of the scholars ranged across the arts and humanities, with some working in the social sciences.

All took a one-day training session in DIALOG® searching with a DIALOG trainer. The scholars also had available some other opportunities for search assistance, which they utilized, but, overall, the study design encouraged scholars to do their own searching and further self-education once the training was over. (See Report #2 for more details on general study design.)

Scholars recorded their own natural language descriptions of their queries at the beginning of their searches. A specially written computer program captured these statements, as well as the entire search, including printout results. In other words, full searches and search results were printed out locally, rather than at DIALOG; the program kept a record of (1) the user's natural language query statement (meaningless to DIALOG), (2) all DIALOG search statements by the end user, and (3) all printout retrieval results.

The terminology used in natural language statements and search formulations was analyzed in detail. (Methodological issues associated with terminology analysis are discussed in Report #1.) An elaborate set of about one hundred codes was developed to analyze the various aspects of DIALOG searching that was done by the scholars, including use of commands and use of Boolean logic. (The codes are presented in Report #2.) Scholars were also interviewed in depth. (See Report #3 for interview schedules used and methodological issues involved in the interviewing.)

Overview of reports to date

The terminology used in the natural language statements and in search formulations was analyzed in detail; these data form the bulk of what is reported on in Report #1. The character of the vocabulary, and the implications for cataloging and online searching, were surprising in some ways. Cataloging is now in flux as libraries enter the era of digital resources. Catalogers may be called upon to make substantial changes in descriptive and subject cataloging for this new age. The results in Report #1 may be of particular interest to catalogers designing for new approaches to subject cataloging.

An analysis of length and character of the online searches, including use of search commands and Boolean logic, forms the heart of Report #2. Search records also were sampled over time to determine whether the scholars demonstrated a learning curve with experience. Those librarians engaged in online searching and bibliographic instruction may find the results in Report #2 revealing.

The results of the interviews with scholars are presented in Report #3. Scholars were interviewed on their experiences with online searching, the role the searching took in their broader research activities, their reactions to DIALOG, and their attitudes about the future of end-user online searching. Reference librarians may find Report #3 of particular interest.

As one who has taught science and engineering literature and has some sense of the culture and values of the sciences, this author was struck by the distinctive characteristics of the humanities' culture, values, and expectations, in contrast to those of the sciences, as they appeared in our study.

These differences are commented on in Reports #1, 4, and 5, in particular. Much of the database world has been developed on the science model. Report #4 draws implications from the study for the design of databases and other information resources for humanities scholars. Librarians may find the points in this report of value for their future collection development in reference departments or main collections.

Report #5 addresses the possible impact of features of online searching in the humanities on the (characteristically science-based) theory of information science, especially information retrieval theory and Bradford's Law.

Principal results

In this section, the study results of interest to academic librarians will be extracted from the various reports and discussed. The points made are not necessarily associated with any one prior report.

The distribution of amount of end-user online searching by the scholars falls out into a familiar pattern of a few using it a lot, and most using it little.

It has commonly been found that where end users have the opportunity to learn online searching and search on their own, some few will take it up with enthusiasm, whereas, in a sharply descending curve of use, many will use it little or not at all after training (Pfaffenberger, 1990). This pattern emerged with the Getty scholars. All who participated were required to attend a one-day training session for DIALOG. Yet, of the twenty-seven scholars, only five spent a *total* of seven or more hours (each) actually doing online searching over their year's stay after their training session (i.e., only five searched about as long as, or longer than, their training session lasted). Five others did no further searching on their own at all after their training session, and most of the rest searched less than two hours.

With regard to their background use of computers, the scholars had had vanishingly little prior experience with online searching, but many had used online catalogs before, and most had begun using personal computers for writing.

Positive reactions to online searching dealt mostly with the power of DIALOG to cover many topics or bodies of literature; negative comments dealt mostly with difficulty with the command language and the lack of desired resources available online.

Scholars liked Dialindex, DIALOG's database of terms covering all databases at once, and OneSearch, which allowed them to search several databases at once. One said, "I feel like an explorer. . . . I enjoy it." Another called online searching "Las Vegas for the intellectual," referring to the surprises he found in the output. This same scholar became experienced and comfortable enough with searching that he recognized and commented on the power of Boolean logic to search on combinations of two or more topics.

Negative comments expressed the beginner's hesitancy in using the system, as well as some of the problems that have been touched on repeatedly by critics of the conventional online Boolean-type systems. The scholars had difficulty converting their queries into Boolean logic; they found the DIALOG commands confusing, not natural. Searchers found it "too complicated," "daunting," and "cumbersome," and one compared it unfavorably to UCLA's online catalog, ORION, which he found easier to understand. Another scholar said, "I resist what strikes me as a kind of industrialization of scholarship."

A separate interview schedule was used for those scholars who had not searched at all during the months after their training session. They said they had little need to do it, and/or did not want to spend the time experimenting with it. Not finding an hour or two for cost-free experimentation with DIALOG over the course of the better part of a year suggests something more than just lack of time or immediate need—perhaps discomfort or a lack of fundamental interest.

Overall, judging by both the scholars' comments and the character of their searching, most did not become skilled enough in online searching to get maximum benefit from it. All search statements were coded for "probable errors" and "certain errors." In the case of the latter, something about the search statement would have guaranteed failure; with regard to the former, there might conceivably have been some reason to do what the searcher did, but it did not appear to be a wise way to search. Over the two years, 17 percent of all search statements contained one or more probable or certain errors, roughly evenly divided between the two classes of error. This is not too bad a rate, considering that most scholars did not search enough to build up expertise. Further, errors did not seem to be a major inhibiting factor for the searchers; in fact, one of the most active searchers had the highest personal error rate. Overall, 32.8 percent of that person's search statements contained one or more errors.

At the same time, the searching done was not very sophisticated. Search terms used were mostly (62.5 percent) single-word terms, and only 3.1 percent of the "Select" statements contained parentheses, which are a mark of more sophisticated searching. However, use of the "building block" technique was emphasized in the scholars' training. This technique of entering the elements, or building blocks, of the query one at a time is an excellent one for beginners to use, and may account for the apparent simplicity of the scholars' search statements.

Three of the twenty-two scholars who searched subsequent to their training never used a single Boolean operator; another five used only ANDs when they did do Boolean searching. So these eight, a third of the active searchers, were unable to take advantage of the common searcher technique of inputting "hedges" (strings of terms ORed together) of multiple term variants for a single concept in order to get full coverage of a topic.

The other main body of scholars' criticisms of online searching concerned the contents of the databases. Available databases often proved not to be what the scholars wanted. They wanted access to more European literature, earlier literature, and primary research materials. Most databases cover only literature going back to the early 1970s, which is often just a small part of the range that a humanities scholar is interested in. Earlier literature is generally not in machine-readable form, so is much more expensive for the vendor to mount. (See Report #4 for some suggested ways to meet both scholar needs and vendor interest in the bottom line.)

> For these scholars, use of DIALOG searching was valuable largely at the margins.

There were a number of spontaneous comments to the effect that the scholar searchers were pleased to find something of value at all in the searching—not because they doubted the effectiveness of the retrieval system but, rather, because they considered themselves experts on their subjects of interest and therefore did not expect to come across anything they did not already know.

The standard assumption behind much of information retrieval theory is that the person making a query will be familiar with little or none of the literature found in a bibliographic search. In fact, this assumption is so fundamental that it is hardly ever articulated. It is just assumed that people would not be searching if they already had found what they wanted. That may be reasonably accurate for many nonhumanities researchers, but for a variety of reasons having to do with fundamental differences in the very nature of humanities scholarship and scientific research (discussed in depth in Reports #4 and #5), it may be more common for the scholar to know, and know very thoroughly, the literature respecting his or her subject of inquiry than is the case for the scientist.

Other research on humanities scholars has found that they use the indexes that are the basis for bibliographic databases little in print form either, and gather much of their key references through a variety of other channels, such as references in articles, specialized bibliographies, colleagues, etc. (Wiberley & Jones, 1989; Guest, 1987). One might nonetheless make the straightforward assumption that once scholars had discovered the power and scope of online database searching, they would happily move to it and abandon older, more scattershot methods. This may yet happen, but did not occur during the year the scholars had their free opportunity, with the possible exception of one or two of the most enthusiastic searchers.

Another reason for low usage could have been that the scholars already had done their research before arriving, and came only to write during their year at the Getty. However, this proved not to be the case. The fifteen scholar-participants during the second year were asked about the status of their research projects. It turned out that the fifteen were engaged in thirty-nine different projects among them, at all stages of development. No discernible association was found between stage of project and amount of online searching.

Upon being asked, several of the scholars said they expected that online databases would raise the expectations of thoroughness in scholarly preparation in the field. Nonetheless, at the time of their interview, only two scholars had actually looked into how they might be able to continue searching once they returned home.

Five scholars mentioned the value of online searching to explore interdisciplinary topics or topics in neighboring disciplines. So it would appear that in a very clear-cut way, the use of DIALOG served indeed to benefit the scholars at the margins of their interests. They often found little at the core of their interest area(s), because they had developed extensive bibliographies of materials in those areas over the years, and over many projects and papers. But the power of online searching enabled them to discover their topic being discussed in another field, and some of the best finds were materials found outside their own discipline.

Scholars' search mode preferences varied over five distinct options.

One of the most striking results of the study was the wide range of preferences the scholars expressed for modes of online searching. The following question was asked of the second year's fifteen visiting scholars: "Do you prefer to do online database searching yourself, or would you rather have librarians or research assistants do it for you?"

The interview style was conversational, and scholars responded in a variety of ways to this question. Their preferences can be summarized as follows, with *searcher* referring to those who searched by themselves at some point after their training session and *nonsearcher* referring to those who did not search by themselves after their training session:

- *self-searching alone:* two searchers, one nonsearcher;
- *self with someone nearby to answer questions:* four searchers, zero nonsearchers;
- *self with someone sitting next to one:* two searchers, one nonsearcher;
- *intermediary searching with scholar sitting there giving feedback:* two searchers, one nonsearcher;
- *intermediary searching without scholar present:* one searcher, one nonsearcher;
- *no response:* one searcher.

This remarkable range of preferences suggests that librarians doing online searching may need to expect to work out a variety of arrangements with their users, rather than assuming that one arrangement will work best.

> The logical, engineering-oriented design of online systems is generally not well matched with the talents of the humanities scholar.

The humanities scholar is a genius at detecting the trend or nuance that is not explicitly expressed in the text being studied, at reading through and between the lines. The design of current online retrieval systems, by contrast, is intended to be explicit, rigorously consistent, and logico-mathematical in design. In analyzing the data, the researchers were struck, again and again, by the "simple" logical and other errors made by these brilliant scholars as they attempted to master DIALOG searching.

One small example is telling: In the DIALOG manual available at the time (this has since been changed), the "N" operator was shown as "nN." The "N" operator is one with which the searcher can ask the system to search for two words in either direct or reverse order. The "nN" model was meant to show that the searcher could put a number before the N operator to indicate how many words could be between the two search words and still retrieve the record. For example, "Child (1N) psychology" would mean that the phrases "Child psychology" and "Psychology of children," among others, would both be retrieved by such a formulation. One of the scholars input this operator directly as "nN" in a search, however, without converting the "n" to a number, and consequently retrieved nothing.

Now this usage is essentially algebraic. The small letter can be substituted for by many numbers. In the author's experience teaching online searching, she has been struck by the ease with which students with a strong mathematics or engineering background pick up Boolean searching, and the difficulty that many, though not all, people with a humanities background have in learning this skill. The humanities scholar might well point out that the engineer is never again required to repeat the poem he or she memorized in ninth-grade English. Why, then, should the humanities scholar be required to remember ninth-grade algebra?

The humanities scholar *will* experience online searching differently. Referring to online searching as "the industrialization of scholarship," as mentioned earlier, is the sort of conceptualization of the searching experience not likely to be foremost in the mind of the engineer. Another scholar liked the idea of having her own password, which, she said, "is a kind of intimate relation to the machine." Others were conscious of a sense of being connected in to a network—one scholar commenting positively on that sensation, and one negatively. This sophisticated awareness of social and aesthetic dimensions of this particular human activity of online searching is bound to have some impact on the reactions of scholars to its use.

> The character of humanities search terms varies considerably from that of the sciences. Humanities thesauri probably should be designed on different principles from conventional thesauri, and humanities search interfaces should be designed differently as well.

Stephen Wiberley argued, beginning in 1983, that humanities subject terms are mostly not the characteristically vague, hard-to-define terms that they are generally assumed to be (Wiberley, 1983, 1988). He provided convincing evidence that terms of importance to humanities scholars in reference books and indexes are often highly precise proper names.

In this study, both the vocabulary in the natural language descriptions of queries given by the scholars, as well as the actual terms used in searching, were analyzed in detail (Report #1). The data confirmed Wiberley's findings and demonstrated a number of other differences from conventional thesaural vocabulary and search vocabulary as well.

In the natural language statements, the scholars' descriptions of their queries were expressed in the most natural, native way, not yet converted into search statements. Ninety-one percent, or 150, of the 165 natural language statements indicated a subject search of some kind. These subject queries were the focus of the author's analysis.

After reviewing the data, these categories of subject terms were developed: (1) works or publications as subject, (2) individuals as subject, (3) geographical term, (4) chronological (date) term, (5) discipline term, (6) other proper term, and (7) other common term. "Discipline term" refers to terms comparable to academic disciplines, such as "history," "philosophy." "Other proper" refers to proper nouns (normally capitalized words) that do not fall into any of the preceding categories, and "other common" referred to any common (uncapitalized) terms that do not fall into the preceding categories.

Data analyzed from these 150 subject statements were then compared to the text of thirty-eight real natural and social science queries that had been gathered for a National Science Foundation-funded study of online searching carried out by Tefko Saracevic and others (Saracevic & Kantor, 1988). For the researchers' study, the Saracevic queries were analyzed in the same way as the Getty natural language statements. The data are summarized in table 1. The figures in each row represent the percentage of queries that contained one or more terms of the designated type. (More detail on the methodology of counting these terms is found in Report #1.) An indefinite number of terms and term types can be in a single query.

The dramatic difference in terminological profile between the two bodies of data is immediately evident in the table. All the Saracevic queries contained one or more common terms; only 57 percent of the Getty

TABLE 1. *Frequencies of subject categories in NSF and Getty studies*

	NSF		GETTY	
	N	%	N	%
Total subject queries	38	100%	150	100%
Works or pubs. as subject	1	3	8	5
Individuals as subject	0	0	74	49
Geographical name	3	8	37	25
Chronological term	1	3	26	17
Discipline term	0	0	35	23
Other proper term	4	11	11	7
Other common term	38	100	85	57

NOTE: *Percentages are the percentage of total query statements in each sample in which one or more terms of a given category appeared.*

queries did. Consider a typical Saracevic study query: "the relationship and communication processes between middle-aged children and their parents" (Saracevic & Kantor, 1988, p. 195). All terms in this query are common; there are none of any other type. This is typical of the science queries. Note what small percentages of the queries in the Saracevic sample contain any other type of term.

Now consider one of the Getty queries: "image of the tree in literature, art, science, of medieval and renaissance Europe." This query contains geographical, chronological, and discipline terms, in addition to the common terms. As noted above, only 57 percent of the Getty statements contained any common terms at all. On the other hand, high rates of all the noncommon term types appear in the Getty column, in sharp contrast to the data in the Saracevic column. This general pattern carried over into the actual search terms used by the scholars as well.

Much of the theory of thesaurus design focuses on the development of what are here called "common" terms. Given the profile of the science data, and the historic importance of science databases in online searching, this is understandable and reasonable. But it is also clear that if the needs of humanities scholarship are to be well served, much more attention needs to be given to the design of terminology of the other types as well. (The study results inadvertently confirmed the value of two Getty databases that were already in development at the time of the study, *The Union List of Artist Names* and *The Thesaurus of Geographic Names*.)

Good design of such terminology *in the online searching context* is not obvious. Consider dates, for example, which would seem to be the most straightforward possible type of search term. However, the producers of the database *Historical Abstracts* experimented for several years before finding optimal ways of coding and searching on dates to provide good retrieval under many circumstances. (See Bates for a more extensive discussion [1992]).)

The broad categories of subject term found in this study lend themselves well to a faceted approach to index terminology. (The choices that had been made earlier to design the Getty's *Art & Architecture Thesaurus* on a faceted basis are strongly confirmed by this study's data.)

Likewise, the scholars frequently attempted to create search terms that were, in effect, strings of facet elements. Unfortunately, because they did not fully understand the use of Boolean logic and proximity operators, and because current indexing is often not well suited to such strongly faceted subject matter, they frequently produced strings that would not work online, for instance:

humanities(w)(method? OR methodology)(w)(comparison usa europe)

Suppose that the searcher could instead have entered elements of this query into a prompt screen with labeled slots for geographical term, date, topic, named individuals, etc. In that case, the system could carry out the Boolean work; the user need only know what he or she knows best—the elements of the query.

The indexing in many current databases does not recognize and build on these facet elements well, thus making it difficult to form a good search statement, even when one is an expert searcher. Many of the humanities queries work like the example above—that is, they consist of several elements, each one of which is conceptually quite broad ("humanities," "Europe"), but when the elements are all brought together (in effect, ANDed), they form a highly specific query. Yet, precisely because of the breadth of many of these terms, indexers are discouraged from using them. Database producers need to recognize that with queries of the distinctive sort found in the humanities, indexing terms and policies may need some adaptation to produce indexing that is optimally effective for online users.

Implications for library service

Keeping in mind the relatively small sample upon which these conclusions are drawn, consider the following points regarding academic library services for humanities scholars:

- Because online searching has been powerful in discovering work of interest for scholars in other disciplines, give particular attention to providing interdisciplinary information in online searching for humanities scholars. Use multidisciplinary databases such as DIALOG's Dialindex and ISI's citation databases.

- Recognize that humanities searches are often composed of several facet elements. Because the indexing for many databases is not optimally designed for queries of this sort, good online database searching in the humanities may actually be harder than for the sciences, even for the skilled online intermediary, and will almost certainly be difficult for the typical humanities end user.

- Expect a wide array of preferences among humanities users for database searching arrangements—from the scholar searching alone, through various mixes of scholar and intermediary working together, to the intermediary doing the search alone for the scholar.

- Look to acquire reference materials in CD-ROM or other automated forms that show a sensitivity to the unique characteristics of humanities scholars and scholarship, specifically, that provide indexing sensitive to the typical kinds of facets of interest to scholars, that have *very* user-friendly interfaces, and that contain resources with historical and geographical depth.

REFERENCES

Bates, M.J. (1992). Implications of the subject subdivisions conference: The shift in online catalog design. In M.O. Conway (Ed.), *The future of subdivisions in the Library of Congress Subject Headings system* (pp. 92–98). Report from the 1991 Subject Subdivisions Conference sponsored by the Library of Congress. Washington, DC: Library of Congress Cataloging Distribution Service.

Bates, M.J. (1994). The design of databases and other information resources for humanities scholars: The Getty Online Searching Project report no. 4. *Online & CD-ROM Review 18*(6), 331–340.

Bates, M.J. (1996). Document familiarity in relation to relevance, information retrieval theory, and Bradford's Law: The Getty Online Searching Project report no. 5. *Information Processing & Management, 32*(6), 697–707.

Bates, M.J., Wilde, D.N., & Siegfried, S. (1993). An analysis of search terminology used by humanities scholars: The Getty Online Searching Project report no. 1. *The Library Quarterly, 63*(1), 1–39.

Bates, M.J., Wilde, D.N., & Siegfried, S. (1995). Research practices of humanities scholars in an online environment: The Getty Online Searching Project report no. 3. *Library & Information Science Research, 17*(1), 5–40.

Guest, S.S. (1987). The use of bibliographical tools by humanities faculty at the State University of New York at Albany. *Reference Librarian, 7*(18), 157–172.

Pfaffenberger, B. (1990). *Democratizing information: Online databases and the rise of end-user searching* (pp. 111–112). Boston, MA: G.K. Hall.

Saracevic, T., & Kantor, P. (1988). A study of information seeking and retrieving. II. users, questions, and effectiveness. *Journal of the American Society for Information Science, 39*(3), 177–196.

Siegfried, S., Bates, M.J., & Wilde, D.N. (1993). A profile of end-user searching behavior by humanities scholars: The Getty Online Searching Project report no. 2. *Journal of the American Society for Information Science, 44*(5), 273–291.

Stone, S. (1982). Humanities scholars: Information needs and uses. *Journal of Documentation, 38*(4), 292–312.

Watson-Boone, R. (1994). The information needs and habits of humanities scholars. *RQ, 34*(2), 203–216.

Wiberley, S.E., Jr. (1983). Subject access in the humanities and the precision of the humanist's vocabulary. *The Library Quarterly, 53*(4), 420–433.

Wiberley, S.E., Jr. (1988). Names in space and time: The indexing vocabulary of the humanities. *The Library Quarterly, 58*(1), 1–28.

Wiberley, S.E., Jr., & Jones, W.G. (1989). Patterns of information seeking in the humanities. *College & Research Libraries, 50*(6), 638–645.

Wiberley, S.E., Jr., & Jones, W.G. (1994). Humanists revisited: A longitudinal look at the adoption of information technology. *College & Research Libraries, 55*(6), 499–509.

5

Learning about the information seeking of interdisciplinary scholars and students

ABSTRACT

The information needs and information-seeking behavior of scholars and students in interdisciplinary fields has been studied very little. The few scattered studies available suggest that such fields may require striking and distinctive information-seeking adaptations by researchers that mark this area as different and very much deserving of research. Kinds of research needed at both basic and applied levels and with respect to both scholars and students are discussed.

Introduction

Successive decades of research on information needs and information-seeking behavior have emphasized the study of different broad constituencies of specialists. In the 1950s and 1960s—in part because of the availability of U.S. Federal grant money—the emphasis was on the needs of scientists and engineers (see Meadows, 1974). Needs in the social sciences were attended to in the 1970s, especially with some major research studies that were performed in Great Britain (see review in Hogeweg-de-Haart, 1984). Finally, in part through the support of, and activity of, the Getty Trust in

First published as Bates, M. J. (1996). Learning about the information seeking of interdisciplinary scholars and students. *Library Trends, 45*(2), 155–164.

the arts, attention turned to the arts and humanities in the 1980s and 1990s (see Watson-Boone, 1994; Bates, 1994; Bates et al., 1993, 1995).

At least two more broad constituencies remain woefully lacking in research on information seeking:

1. The performers—as distinct from the scholars in the arts—the artists, designers, musicians, actors, dancers.

2. Interdisciplinary researchers—people engaged in the study of fields that span two or more of the established academic disciplines.

It is the second of these two groups that is the focus of this article.

Prior suggestive research

Research on information use and information-seeking behavior of people in interdisciplinary fields is sparse to non-existent. To those whose studies have been missed, my apologies, but a literature review in the conventional places and under conventional terms resulted in the same low hit rate encountered in the past. With increasing interest in interdisciplinary work in scholarship, in fields such as popular culture, film studies, ethnic studies, gay and lesbian studies, and women's studies, it is high time research on information seeking was done in this area.

But research on the information-seeking behavior of scholars and students in interdisciplinary fields would do even more than fill in an obvious gap in our knowledge of this segment of academia. There is reason to suspect that the problems and information-seeking patterns of this group may be dramatically different from those of the scholars in the classical academic disciplines such as history, literature, etc. even where an interdisciplinary field may draw its inspiration and researchers from people trained in these very same established disciplines.

In 1962, L. J. B. Mote published a study which contained some provocative results. Mote divided the scientific users of the Shell Thornton Research Centre Library (United Kingdom) into three groups according to whether their fields of research were low, medium, or high scatter. Low scatter fields were defined as those in "which the underlying principles are well developed, the literature is well organized, and the width of the subject area is fairly well defined" (p. 170). In high scatter fields, the number of different subjects is great and the organization of the literature is almost non-existent. The medium group fell between the other two in degree of scatter.

Mote (1962), drawing from a sample of 178 people, found that the average number of inquiries requiring thirty or more minutes to answer per person during a three-year period was, for the low to high scatter group, 1.4, 3.6, and 20 (yes, twenty!), respectively. No one in the low scatter group made more than six inquiries and no one in the high scatter group made fewer than ten inquiries (p. 172). In a smaller sampling, the same pattern was found with requests that required under thirty minutes to resolve.

The low and high scatter groups diverged from each other by a factor of over ten to one. This is a most striking and suggestive result. Even though the study was done in the sciences and engineering, we may well wonder if such divergences might also be found in "high scatter" fields such as area and ethnic studies where the researcher must cross several disciplines to locate all relevant background material for a research project. Could it thus be the case that a researcher in an interdisciplinary field could have ten times as many problems with the process of gathering information for research as people in conventional disciplinary fields?

More recently, Packer and Soergel (1979) also studied scientists (chemists, in this case) in fields with low and high scatter. They focused on techniques used for keeping up to date, or "current awareness" techniques. They found that taking advantage of selective dissemination of information (SDI) services helped the scientists' efficiency in high scatter fields and actually *reduced* efficiency for those in low scatter fields. To put it differently, diametrically opposing strategies were optimal for researchers in high versus low scatter fields. (SDI is a technique whereby bibliographic citations or copies of new materials received in the library are selectively sent to individual researchers. The selection is based on profiles prepared of each researcher's interests.) So again we see the high/low scatter difference in the character of fields producing a marked effect—in this case, scientists needing to engage in different strategies depending on how focused or scattered the field.

Support comes from another quarter as well for the premise that interdisciplinary information seeking is particularly plagued by problems. The Group on Interdisciplinary Searching of the International Council for Scientific and Technical Information studied the problems specific to interdisciplinary information seeking. Their *Journal of Documentation* article (Weisgerber, 1993) consists of a dense twenty pages of problems and possible remedies in six areas: "1) coverage and technical content of the database, 2) bibliographic information, 3) textual content, 4) numeric data, 5) file organization, and 6) interdisciplinary searching on multiple hosts" (p. 231). An example of an information-seeking problem is that conference proceedings are cited in a number of different ways within and across databases (p. 238).

Still another study produced results that have enormous implications for the provision of information services to researchers. Again, working in the sciences, Julie M. Hurd (1992) studied the journal citation patterns in the research papers produced by chemistry faculty at her university (University of Illinois at Chicago). She found that a great many of the citations were to work outside the researcher's discipline. Over 49 percent of the journals cited in her sample's publications were in fields outside chemistry. Individual chemistry professors differed in what percentages were from the outside—the range was 0 to 100 percent. On the other hand, there were practically no citations outside the sciences (1992, p. 293) (earlier, Paul Metz [1983] had found similar outside-of-field circulation of books to faculty. Also, Howard Pikoff [1991] found that professors, when offered the opportunity to see new acquisitions lists for subject areas all over the Library of Congress classification, frequently selected topics outside their discipline as well as intradiscipline areas).

Hurd (1992) found, further, that chemistry researchers with high citation rates outside the field of chemistry were those researchers who were working in fields that were, by definition, interdisciplinary—e.g., biochemistry and physical chemistry. These chemists cited, respectively, 85 percent and 64 percent of their references to nonchemistry journals, mostly in biology and physics. On the other hand, chemists at the core of the discipline, in inorganic and organic chemistry, cited nonchemistry journals only 29 percent and 24 percent of the time, respectively (p. 294). These results suggest that there is indeed higher scatter in interdisciplinary fields but also that even core fields have connections outside the core.

Hurd (1992) describes some of the implications of her results for provision of information services to scientists as follows:

> The high level of interdisciplinary information use measured
> for those chemists appears to argue against the narrow
> departmental library type of organization. A chemistry library,
> narrowly defined and stocked, would only partially meet their
> needs; a broader, divisional library seems better suited to
> support their highly interdisciplinary research. (1992, p. 295)

Over the years there has been a strong pattern at major universities of developing discipline-sized libraries in parallel to discipline-oriented departments. Hurd's results suggest that the assumption behind that practice—that libraries, in their size and organization, would do best to mirror the intellectual "turf" organization of disciplines—is misguided.

Prospective possibilities in basic research

All the studies discussed in the previous section are notable for their striking results. In each case, the implications are major, not minor, ones involving small adjustments. These results suggest that there may be dramatic differences in the kinds of strategies needed and the amount of effort needed to seek information, depending on the degree of coherence of the bibliographic resources of a field. In sum, studying researcher information seeking in interdisciplinary fields may tell us not only about the needs and problems of people in those fields—something we very much need to learn about—but also about what factors, in general, contribute to ease and difficulty in information seeking in scholarship.

In fact, the results of the Mote study touch on one of the most fundamental—and therefore rarely examined—assumptions in our field. It is taken as a given in library and information science that the organization, description, and indexing of information in indexes, catalogs, and reference books contributes to the successful and speedy retrieval of information by users. Do we know that it does this in fact? Both the Mote (1962) and Packer and Soergel (1979) studies indirectly suggest that such information organization does make a tremendous difference.

On the other hand, Stoan (1984) has argued persuasively that the model librarians have developed of information searching in academic libraries bears little resemblance to actual research techniques used by scholars and their graduate students. Our conception of the kinds of information access and library organization that will be useful to scholarly users might, in fact, match poorly with their real needs. Thus the question remains open as to whether libraries' access apparatus is, in fact, optimally supportive of scholars' library research.

We might learn much more about just what kinds of organization produce what sort of an effect were we to compare fields that are well controlled—such as conventional academic disciplines—against fields that are not well controlled—such as interdisciplinary concentrations.

The Mote (1962), Packer and Soergel (1979), and Hurd (1992) studies were all done in the sciences and engineering, and we know that there are major differences between the sciences and the humanities and humanistically-oriented social sciences that are the emphasis in this article (see Bates, 1994; Bates et al., 1993). Nonetheless, these studies are highly suggestive.

It certainly seems to be a reasonable preliminary hypothesis that scholars in interdisciplinary fields may have to engage in both substantially more information seeking—and of a different kind—than scholars in a conventional discipline.

In reflecting on the activities of scholars in these fields, one can identify several possible sources of these differences. A scholar can be seen as the cynosure of an extensive social and documentary infrastructure. Academic fields develop a common vocabulary and research style, establish journals, found academic departments, create professional associations, hold conferences, and communicate informally in a number of ways. Libraries, special collections in libraries, and archives are set up with a focus or emphasis that may influence the kind of research done. (For instance, what might be the impact on historical or political science research of having separate presidential libraries around the country, making it easy to concentrate on a single administration, and hard to cut across several administrations?) Bibliographic and other research reference sources are published and collected in scholars' own libraries and in academic libraries. When failures, changes, and gaps anywhere in this extensive scholarly communication apparatus can be identified in interdisciplinary—in contrast to conventional—academic fields, these differences could reasonably be expected to have a substantial impact on the conduct of research.

This scholarly apparatus is in fact so extensive that one could generate dozens of hypotheses about possible differences among the fields. Instead, whole classes of hypotheses will be condensed by talking about broad areas where we might expect differences to be found.

First, we need basic descriptive information: *Are* there differences between interdisciplinary fields and conventional disciplines in the information needs and information-seeking behavior of their member scholars? Is research and "keeping up" harder for people in interdisciplinary fields? Must the scholar know two or three times as many information resources of each type to cover the territory of interest across two or more fields, or, likewise, must the scholar know and stay in touch with two or three times as many fellow researchers?

Or do compensatory mechanisms develop, mechanisms unique to interdisciplinary research, that make the scholar's task no more difficult than that of scholars in conventional fields? We do not know the answer to these questions at this point.

Second, we might ask whether there is a natural life cycle to the study of a research specialty topic. Diana Crane (1972) found this to be so in her investigation of communication among scientists in subfields of sociology and mathematics. She charted periods of initial slow growth, followed by explosive growth as new researchers are drawn into the field, and finally, a tapering off of research and publication as a subject matures as a topic of interest (p. 172).

Is an interdisciplinary field simply a new field that has not yet earned full separate-field status? In other words, do disciplines generally feel "interdisciplinary" when they are new? This might evolve because scholars are often drawn to a new field from existing fields, and ideas and research problems in existing fields may be the stimulus for the development of the new field. On the other hand, might some fields remain genuinely interdisciplinary through time, continuing to draw on people from several fields and continuing to need nourishment from several different intellectual traditions? These are hard questions to answer and should probably be left to researchers in scholarly communication and the sociology of science.

For our purposes in information science, these questions might be constructed in the following manner: What is the life history of development of various channels of communication and various forms, or genres, of information resources in a field? Do interdisciplinary fields go through characteristic stages of development, each stage associated with certain typical patterns of ease and difficulty in gathering primary and secondary information for research purposes? Have different interdisciplinary fields responded differently to the challenges of such research with some fields, perhaps, more successful in their response than others?

In the process of studying these various questions, much work needs to be done to define "interdisciplinarity" operationally. Is it, in fact, detectable through high scatter of information resources? Or is there some more essential measure that is closer to the heart of the meaning of the concept?

Do we start from formal theoretical categories and define what the real-life consequences should be based on the theory, and then test the theory? Or do we take a bottom-up approach and identify one or more characteristics, such as Hurd's out-of-field citation rate, study that statistic in a variety of environments, and develop hypotheses to test further? There are so many possible measures to be taken and questions to be tested in this area that a final decision on methodology must await more specific hypotheses in each.

However, this author confesses to a bias toward the latter approach at this stage of our knowledge. Questions of what is interdisciplinarity have generated a small blizzard of books and articles (e.g., Chubin et al., 1986; Becher, 1989; Klein, 1990; Easton & Schelling, 1991). At this stage, our empirical (as opposed to theoretical) understanding of what it means to work in, and search for, information resources in an interdisciplinary field is minimal. Some basic descriptive work, perhaps using several operational empirical measures to discover the "lay of the land," will likely turn up results as novel and stimulating as the studies discussed earlier. Based on those findings, the next steps in the study of interdisciplinary information seeking could be planned more rationally.

Prospective possibilities in applied research

In addition to doing basic research, we in library and information science are also engaged in a profession with many practical questions to answer regarding the provision of services to meet information needs and uses. It seems reasonable to hypothesize that certain types of resources and services would be particularly useful for the interdisciplinary scholar:

- "One-stop searching" could readily be done in resources that are themselves multidisciplinary, such as the "Dialindex" database of index terms and hits on terms across databases provided by DIALOG Information Services, as well as DIALOG's "OneSearch" capability in which several databases can be searched simultaneously for topics of interest. Indeed, scholars in the Getty Online Searching Project were particularly taken with the OneSearch capability and found that it revealed work in other fields relevant to their own work of which they had been unaware previously (Bates et al., 1995). Likewise the "Permuterm" subject indexes—i.e., indexes of title words of articles—of the three citation databases produced by the Institute for Scientific Information (ISI)—*Arts & Humanities Citation Index*, *Social Sciences Citation Index*, and *Science Citation Index*—each function as subject indexes across a wide range of subject fields.

- Citation indexes themselves would be particularly useful for interdisciplinary research as well. The principle of ISI's citation indexes is that they list all the materials ever published that happen to be cited in a given time period, such as a year, in a carefully selected set of thousands of scholarly journals. The scholar may be surprised to discover that someone in another field has used his or her work or that the study of a favorite topic of interest is going on in another field one has never heard of.

  Making these links through citations instead of through subject terms is particularly valuable because the same theme or issue is often discussed in different vocabulary from one field to another (see Weisgerber, 1993, pp. 241–44, for a catalog of problems associated with subject indexing access. Smith [1974] also found difficulties with mapping subject terms from database to database). By following up citations to works of proven value, there is no need to know another field's vocabulary in order to locate the information.

- The provision of selective dissemination of information services would be particularly valuable to interdisciplinary scholars compared to those in conventional disciplines. This hypothesis coincides with the Packer and Soergel (1979) findings discussed earlier. It is by no means clear, however, that this hypothesis will be demonstrated to hold true in the humanities, where scholars like to do their own searching and browsing in the literature.

Practical testing of the above hypotheses could be done in a variety of ways. For example, bibliographic instruction classes could be offered specifically for people in interdisciplinary fields and which included the above sorts of sources. Plumbing people's reactions at the time and later, after some experience with these sources, could give a sense of how beneficial researchers found them to be. Though scholars are ordinarily loathe to admit to any deficiencies in their information-searching techniques, they might be more inclined to take a special class if it is offered as a way to learn new online sources.

Next, if, as assumed, it is more difficult for interdisciplinary scholars to do research in documentary resources, then might it not also be so for students? Some work has already been done in this area (SantaVicca, 1986; Bartolo & Smith, 1993), but much remains to be studied. Should students in such fields have more intensive—and different—training in library research and targeted to their special needs? An experiment could be conducted to test a bibliographic instruction package directed to students of interdisciplinary fields. We can surmise in the short term as to what kinds of training they need, but clearly the best long-term solution is to get the basic research data, discussed earlier, upon which to base course design.

To this point of the discussion, secondary sources—the kind that are the principal concern of libraries—have been the focus. But some primary archival sources in some interdisciplinary fields may be different also from those in conventional disciplines. Scholars in all the ethnic studies fields, as well as women's studies and gay and lesbian studies, may not have the usual range of documentary sources available to them. Because the people being studied in these fields were often outsiders and relatively powerless in the establishment structures of society, information must be gathered in unconventional ways, including through oral histories.

Conclusion

Altogether, the mix of research and library techniques needed by scholars and students in interdisciplinary fields may be unique to such fields. As such, these people constitute a significant and distinctive class of scholars, much deserving of research on their information needs and information-seeking behavior. Results from such studies would shed light as well on deeper questions regarding the life history of fields and disciplines and the inherent nature of interdisciplinary research.

REFERENCES

Bartolo, L.M., & Smith, T.D. (1993). Interdisciplinary work and the information search process: A comparison of manual and online searching. *College & Research Libraries, 54*(4), 344–353.

Bates, M.J. (1994). The design of databases and other information resources for humanities scholars: The Getty Online Searching Project report no. 4. *Online & CDROM Review 18*(6), 331–340.

Bates, M.J., Wilde, D.N., & Siegfried, S. (1993). An analysis of search terminology used by humanities scholars: The Getty Online Searching Project report no. 1. *The Library Quarterly, 63*(1), 1–39.

Bates, M.J., Wilde, D.N., & Siegfried, S. (1995). Research practices of humanities scholars in an online environment: The Getty Online Searching Project report no. 3. *Library & Information Science Research, 17*(1), 5–40.

Becher, T. (1989). Academic tribes and territories: Intellectual enquiry and the cultures of disciplines. Bristol, PA: Society for Research into Higher Education and Open University Press.

Chubin, D.F., Porter, A.L., Rossini, F.A., & Connolly, T. (1986). Interdisciplinary analysis and research: Theory and practice of problem-focused research and development. Mt. Airy, MD: Lomond.

Crane, D. (1972). *Invisible colleges: Diffusion of knowledge in scientific communities.* Chicago, IL: University of Chicago Press.

Easton, D., & Schelling, C. (Eds.). (1991). *Divided knowledges; across disciplines, across cultures.* Newbury Park, CA: SAGE.

Garvey, W.D. (1979). *Communication: The essence of science: Facilitating information exchange among librarians, scientists, engineers, and students.* New York: Pergamon Press.

Hogeweg-de-Haart, H.P. (1984). Characteristics of social science information: A selective review of the literature. Part II. *Social Science Information Studies, 4*(1), 15–30.

Hurd, J.M. (1992). Interdisciplinary research in the sciences: Implications for library organization. *College & Research Libraries, 53*(4), 283–297.

Klein, J.T. (1990). *Interdisciplinarity: History, theory, and practice.* Detroit, MI: Wayne State University Press.

Meadows, A.J. (1974). *Communication in science.* London: Butterworths.

Metz, P. (1983). *The landscape of literatures: Use of subject collections in a university library* (ACRL Publications in Librarianship No. 43). Chicago, IL: American Library Association.

Mote, L.J.B. (1962). Reasons for the variations in the information needs of scientists. *Journal of Documentation, 18*(4), 169–175.

Packer, K.H., & Soergel, D. (1979). The importance of SDI for current awareness in fields with severe scatter of information. *Journal of the American Society for Information Science, 30*(3), 125-135.

Pikoff, H. (1991). Improving access to new interdisciplinary materials. *Library Resources & Technical Services, 35*(2), 141-147.

Pinelli, T.E. (1991). The information-seeking habits and practices of engineers. *Science & Technology Libraries, 11*(1), 5-25.

SantaVicca, E.F. (1986). Teaching research skills in linguistics: An interdisciplinary model for the humanities and the social sciences. *Research Strategies, 4*(4), 168-176.

Smith, L.C. (1974). Systematic searching of abstracts and indexes in interdisciplinary areas. *Journal of the American Society for Information Science, 25*(6), 343-353.

Stoan, S.K. (1984). Research and library skills: An analysis and interpretation. *College & Research Libraries, 45*(2), 99-109.

Watson-Boone, R. (1994). The information needs and habits of humanities scholars. *RQ, 34*(2), 203-216.

Weisgerber, D.W. (1993). Interdisciplinary searching: Problems and suggested remedies (A report from the ICSTI Group on Interdisciplinary Searching). *Journal of Documentation, 49*(3), 231-254.

6

Internet Web-searching instruction in the elementary classroom: Building a foundation for information literacy

Objectives

The growing Internet accessibility for educational purposes has raised a range of issues regarding the means of integrating instruction in such information access with the students' other learning experiences, the nature of the skills needed by children in support of developing information literacy, and the role of the school library media specialist in this instruction.

This project was the focus of an experimental graduate course taught jointly by faculty from the Department of Education (Kafai, with Philip Ender) and the Department of Library and Information Science (Bates) in the Graduate School of Education and Information Studies at UCLA. The group decided as the class focus to examine "Education on the Internet" through both the reading of theory/research and practical experience working with teachers and elementary school children. The emphasis for the first course was on examining how teaching through use of the Internet could be achieved and determining what Education and Library and Information Science (LIS) graduate students should learn about the Internet and about education and LIS research literatures to be effective scholars, master teachers, or library media specialists in this new area of research and theory.

The "SNAPdragon" Project was created to investigate how children can interface with the Internet by asking them to build an annotated directory of websites for other children. The project's general goal was to

First published as Kafai, Y. & Bates, M. J. (1997). Internet Web-searching instruction in the elementary classroom: Building a foundation for information literacy. *School Library Media Quarterly*, 25(2), 103–111.

build children's information literacy skills. More specifically, the objective was to have children develop an understanding of what the Internet and Web searching are, gain some skills in searching (varying with their ages), and develop their critical-thinking skills by evaluating the information they gathered from various sites.

Furthermore, the researchers wanted to provide children with a context in which the search for and retrieval of information would no longer be an isolated experience, but rather connected to their classroom learning and to a larger social goal—to share their insights with other children. Instead of keeping the annotated search results confined to individual classrooms, a collaborative directory was implemented that could be accessed by other children through the World Wide Web. The construction of an information structure such as a directory was seen as another powerful way for children to gain better understanding of existing Web directories such as Yahoo, etc.

By observing students' efforts, the researchers could start to answer questions such as: Can children effectively use the search engines currently available? Can they find appropriate resources in a directed search? Can they evaluate and use the selected resources? The SNAPdragon Project was a first step and only a few classrooms were involved in the preliminary research. The insights gained in this small study, however, will help teachers and school library media specialists design better learning environments in regard to classroom management, the role of the school library media center in Internet instruction, children's information searching and information evaluation, and students' motivation and interest.

Background

The rush to connect schools to the Internet is in full swing. In the 1994 report *America's Children and the Information SuperHighway*, Lazarus and Lipper (1994) concluded that it is critical that all children have access to the Internet and, furthermore, that children's needs must be given a high priority as technology strategies are developed and implemented. The National Center for Education Statistics report *Advanced Telecommunications in U.S. Public Schools, K–12* (Heaviside et al., 1995) documents, however, that as of fall 1994 "thirty-five percent of public schools have access to the Internet but only three percent of all instructional rooms (classrooms, labs and media centers) in public schools are connected to the Internet." In elementary schools, the figure is thirty percent connectivity at the school level (Heaviside et al., 1995, p. 3). While many schools have begun to give students Internet access, and allow them to browse and search for information and build their own World Wide Web pages, it is still an open question in what ways Internet activities can effectively be used and integrated with other classroom learning.

It is evident, merely from the use of such terms as "browse" and "search for information," that capability with Internet use should draw upon the expertise of school library media specialists in some fashion. "Challenge 4" of *Information Power: Guidelines for School Library Media Programs* (American Association of School Librarians and Association for Educational Communications and Technology, 1988) is "To provide leadership and expertise in the use of information and instructional technologies" (1988, p. 10). The excitement generated by the World Wide Web and its search engines provides a golden opportunity for teachers and library media specialists to work more closely on the development of curriculum and on the integration of information literacy skills into that curriculum.

The projects to be described, in which students used Internet information sources for their classroom learning, represented examples of development of many key elements of information literacy, as discussed by Doyle (1994): recognizing the need for information; formulating questions based on the needs; identifying potential sources of information; developing successful search strategies; accessing the information; and evaluating, organizing, and integrating the information into an existing body of knowledge. There are other important formulations of these skills (Eisenberg & Berkowitz, 1988; American Library Association Presidential Committee on Information Literacy, 1989; Kuhlthau, 1993; California Media and Library Educators Association, 1994) as well; all involve the fundamental concept that development of information literacy enables the child to engage in activist, self-directed learning. As Mendrinos notes: "Resource-based learning and high technology foster a nondirective teaching style in which the student controls learning within the framework of the curriculum" (1994, p. 12).

There is as yet relatively little LIS research on children's information use and information-seeking. Walter (1994) provides an extensive survey of research to date on children's information-seeking. Solomon studied elementary school children's use of an online public access catalog. He found that even first-graders were able to use an OPAC and that difficulty with the variety of index terms was a significant problem for the children (Solomon, 1993). Likewise, Walter et al., found that children ages nine to twelve were able to use both browsing and keyword-type catalog interfaces, though here, too, children had some difficulty finding the right terms to retrieve their desired information (Walter, Borgman & Hirsh, 1996). Gallo and Horton report results of a study in which high school teachers were given unlimited access to the Internet. They found that teachers could benefit from ongoing training related to their computers and the Internet (Gallo & Horton, 1994).

In the education field, a considerable number of studies have examined the educational potential of Internet-based projects for language arts and social and natural sciences. Many projects use telecommunication activities for learning writing (Bruce & Peyton, 1990; Bruce & Rubin, 1991; Goldman & Newman, 1992; Riel, 1992). The results indicate that providing students with an audience other than their peers or their teacher has significant effects on improving writing performance. In other projects, students build together a networked database that allows them to annotate and link their contributions to research reports (Scardamalia et al., 1992).

More recent projects use the Internet to give students access to scientific databases such as weather information and provide them with communication facilities and analysis tools for data display (Gordin, Polman & Pea, 1994; Jackson et al., 1994). Studies that link instruction of information-searching strategies with specific subject learning are still rare. One notable exception is Linn's development of the Knowledge Integration Environment (1996), a hypercard stack with pointers on how to find and use scientific information on the Internet and to help students ages ten to fourteen ponder scientific questions.

The project

Overview

For the implementation of the SNAPdragon Project, the researchers took advantage of an existing consortium of West Los Angeles schools, called School Network Action Project (SNAP). SNAP was started by the schools and Apple Computer and was funded by a series of other business and industry partners to provide all the participating schools with servers and Internet access. At the beginning of the project in January 1996, most of the schools (but not all their classrooms) had been connected to the Internet. There had not been extensive use of this connectivity, however, due to a series of technical problems.

To begin the collaboration, the researchers contacted all the SNAP schools in November 1995 asking teachers and technology coordinators to send in applications indicating their interest. Schools were informed that the SNAPdragon Project would run concurrently with a UCLA graduate seminar in which students would not only examine and discuss the educational benefits of Internet activities, but would also be required to hold an internship in a local school. By January, more than twenty applications had been received, and teachers, UCLA graduate students, and instructors met once in January to get to know each other and to select the sites. For this project, just six classrooms participated because the researchers wanted to match each classroom with one UCLA graduate student or researcher. The classrooms were selected so that at least one classroom from each of the four schools or school districts involved in SNAP was included. Table 1 provides an overview of the grade levels, number of students, number of computers with Internet access in each classroom, and search topics.

Each classroom had a different setup, a different number of students, and a different search topic. These varying conditions for this initial effort proved to be very productive for understanding the ways in which web-searching instruction can be integrated with classroom instruction. For all the differences, it was hoped that the collaborative activity would provide enough "glue" to bring all the students and their teachers together.

The UCLA graduate students who interned at the SNAP school sites attended regular classes each week to receive instruction in the research and theory of both Education and LIS that related to the SNAPdragon experiment, and they were instructed in the practical aspects of searching the World Wide Web in classroom and laboratory instruction.

The SNAPdragon website, containing the students' directory of favorite websites, was set up and maintained at the UCLA Graduate School of Education and Information Studies by Ender, and can be accessed at http://www.gseis.ucla.edu/SNAP/snapdragon.html.

The UCLA course for graduate interns

The interns

To provide instruction, the graduate student interns first had to be introduced to Internet searching themselves. The UCLA course for the graduate students combined theory and practice. In fact, it was an interesting challenge for the three instructors to identify the mix of materials that would be most useful for the graduate students' general education, as well as preparation for their internships working with teachers and children. In this sense, the joint work of Ender (the computer specialist), Bates (the LIS specialist), and Kafai (the Education specialist) modeled the kind of cooperative work that the technical support person, the school library media specialist, and the teacher need to do together to create effective classroom learning and development of information literacy with the Internet.

TABLE 1. *Overview of Participating SNAP Classrooms*

SCHOOL NAME	GRADE	STUDENTS	INTERNET COMPUTERS	CLASSROOM SEARCH TOPIC	CURRICULUM INTEGRATION
Corinne A. Seeds UES	1/2	33	6	Airports/Iditarod	yes
	1/2	31	6	Ocean Animals	yes
	3/4	30	15	Black History/Poetry	yes
Open Charter School	3/4	64	1	City Building	yes
Westwood Charter School	5	9	1	National Parks	no
Hawthorne Elementary School	6	29	1	Ancient Egypt	yes

The first several sessions for the graduate students at UCLA consisted of part lecture/discussion and part instruction and laboratory practice in Internet use, especially World Wide Web use. To help students understand the network and the Web, Ender developed lectures, demonstrations, and laboratory practice sessions on the Internet, totaling about six hours, for the students. In the latter part of the course, the class was divided between classroom lecture/discussion and the time spent interning at the SNAP schools.

The academic portion of the course drew on two literatures. Kafai lectured and led discussions on the research literature of education concerning the use of computer-mediated communication in the classroom. Within this context, students reviewed the history of technology in education and examined theoretical foundations of learning over networks and using long-distance communication. Students studied a series of case studies that used the Internet in classrooms to enhance children's learning in science, language arts, and social sciences. In addition, students looked at social issues surrounding the access to the Internet.

Bates lectured on the research, theory, and practice of information studies, covering three major areas: (1) the concept of information itself and some of the underlying paradigm of the LIS field, in an effort to sensitize the students to some of the issues and outlook necessary to think like an information professional; (2) information needs and information-seeking behavior of children; and (3) practical online searching skills, drawing on what research has shown to be the most difficult areas for successful searching. In particular, students were shown how even some of the simplest search problems can be complicated by variety in vocabulary and differences in search engines.

The schools

All schools in the study had powerful models of Macintosh computers, from LCIIs to PowerMacs. Figures given above for numbers of computers are solely for machines with Internet access, not the number of all machines in the classroom or school. All classes searched on the Netscape browser.

- The Corinne A. Seeds University Elementary School, a laboratory school located on the UCLA campus, contained three internship sites—two combined first/second-grade classes and the computer laboratory being used for third/fourth-grade students. The school student body was ethnically and socioeconomically diverse; one of the first/second-grade classes was bilingual (English/Spanish). The two combination first/second-grade classrooms each had six networked Macintosh computers for classes of thirty-three and thirty-one students, respectively, each with one instructor. The combination third/fourth-grade classes had their Internet experiences as a part of a two-week-long computer class, which was held in a separate computer laboratory in the school.

- The Open Charter School is located in an ethnically and socioeconomically diverse section of the city of Los Angeles. As a charter school, it had enjoyed a high degree of academic autonomy over the years. In the 1980s it received support from Apple Computer to install computers in every classroom. The combined third- and fourth-grade class involved in this project had two teachers, sixty-four children, and one computer.

- The Westwood Charter School is a public West Los Angeles city school located in a middle-class, mainly single-family-dwelling neighborhood. An ethnically diverse group of nine students from a fifth-grade classroom participated. Students went to a laboratory separate from the classroom.

- The Hawthorne Elementary School is a middle-sized public school in the Beverly Hills Unified Public School District, with about 750 students in grades kindergarten through eighth. A sixth-grade class with twenty-nine students and one computer participated.

Elementary classroom instruction

The six classes included the grades from one to six and had a wide variety of instructional arrangements. This variety enabled the researchers to get a good sense, in this preliminary study, of the various issues involved in providing Internet training in the classroom. Under each classroom configuration, the curricular content and instructional arrangements are first described, then the searching training, and finally mastery by the children.

The graduate students interning in each classroom worked with the instructors (with oversight from the Graduate School of Education and Information Science faculty) to develop the Internet experience for each classroom. One of the interns was a senior librarian in the UCLA University Research Library with a graduate degree in education; another was an extension student with computer background; and the other four were graduate students in education.

Class #1: Six-computer classroom: Grades one/two

Curriculum and arrangements Students in this University Elementary School class ranged in age from six through eight. Some were still learning to read, while others were fluent readers. About one-third of the students had computers at home.

A rug surrounded by chairs was the area where students met as a class. There were several tables designated as work stations for small group activities as well as a reading corner. Students were introduced to the Internet by working in pairs (two pairs at a time) at one computer.

Students used the Internet for two of their class projects. They had been working on constructing a real-world-style community since the fall. When a field trip to an airport was anticipated, the decision was made to conduct a search on airports on the web. The second project concerned the Alaskan dog-sled race, the Iditarod. The teacher gave each student the biography of a "musher" (dog-sled driver) that she had obtained from the Internet. The students followed "their" mushers throughout the days-long race. The official Iditarod page included frequent updates of the race standings, which the teacher printed and reported to the class each day or so. She also posted a map of the route so that the mushers' progress could be tracked with flags. Even students without well-developed reading skills were able to find the Iditarod pages and recognize the status of their mushers.

Searching In two rounds of work on the airport project, the children were shown how to move around on the page and how to follow up links. They were coached to type in the URL, or coded address, of the Big Bear Airport, and then were given a list of other airports with their URLs.

It was anticipated that students could explore those airport pages in which they might have some personal interest individually. This did not turn out to be a realistic expectation, however. In the second round, bookmarks of various airports—different ones for each computer—were put on the computer in advance so that students could simply click on the bookmark, rather than having to type the URL. ("Bookmarking" is a capability that makes it possible to click on a Web page address and have it automatically recorded in the local computer, so it can be looked up later without having to type in the URL.)

Class #2: Second six-computer classroom: Grades one/two

Curriculum and arrangements This bilingual class had ten thirty-minute sessions using the World Wide Web. A school library media specialist was also present and available for help at each session. The children were studying "ocean life" over the course of the semester. Prior to the introduction and use of the Internet, the class discussed sea life, read about fish and ocean mammals, did some library research, and collected appropriate books to have available in the classroom throughout the duration of the project. Each student selected one ocean fish or mammal to learn more about. They were to use the Internet to find more information for their sea animal research reports.

Students found quite a bit of information on their topics. The amount of information, however, varied considerably from one species to another. There was far more age-appropriate information on dolphins, sharks, and whales than for seahorses, star fish, or eels, for example. It should come as no surprise that the website that excited the most enthusiasm and fascination on the part of the children was one that contained a photograph of a human leg that had been partially chewed by a shark.

Searching In this class, a different solution was tried regarding the Internet addresses of sites of interest on ocean life. Instead of bookmarking the sites, so children could simply click on the names of sites, the teacher and intern searched the Web in advance, located appropriate sites, then wrote the URLs on a poster-sized chart for the children's reference. The teacher felt it was important for the children to type the URLs themselves, in order to gain a broader familiarity with the keyboard as well as the Web browser's interface. This was a difficult and time-consuming task for the children, however, as they made many typing errors with the complicated URL address codes. An instructor needs to make a decision regarding how much of the Internet learning time should be devoted to mastering keyboard skills.

Class #3: Laboratory class: Grades three/four

Curriculum and arrangements In the Seeds laboratory school, each class in the third and fourth grade was attending a computer class in the computer laboratory one hour a day for two weeks at a time. Every two students had a PowerMac computer to work at in the fifteen-machine lab. During the first week, the students learned how to use word-processing and drawing programs. During the second week, they studied the World Wide Web. The graduate intern observed the second week of three series of third/fourth-grade classes.

The large number of computers for any given group of students was an advantage for this class. On the other hand, disadvantages were that movement back and forth between classroom and laboratory took up computer session time, and, more important, the laboratory arrangement tended to separate study topics in the lab from what the children were studying in their classroom. Coordination between lab instructor and classroom instructor was needed to bring these two sets of activities into harmony. The students studied poetry sites.

Searching In each new Internet class the teacher gave an introduction to the Internet, described the goals of the class, and had a question-and-answer period. The teacher provided a specific site most of the time for the students to visit and evaluate. Near the end, he opened the experience and encouraged advanced students to use the search engines to find other types of information.

What was quite noticeable in this case was the disparity between students who had prior access and experience with the Internet, and those who did not. The students with prior Internet experience were more knowledgeable about the features and tended to dominate the interaction at the computer. They often decided which sites to visit and how long to stay on a page before moving on. The students who were experts tended to be boys.

Class #4: One-computer class: Grades three/four

Curriculum and arrangements The Open Charter School grades three/four class, with sixty-four children, was involved in a year-long project of building a city of the future, called City Building Education™. Since the children were already organized into various "commissions" for building the city, the intern and the teacher structured the Internet search sessions around these commission themes: *Historical Commission*: museum websites; *Building and Safety Commission*: landmark websites; *Imagination Commission*: artists/composers/filmmakers websites; *Transportation Commission*: mass transit websites; *Environmental Commission*: environmental websites; *Social*

Services Commission: websites related to homelessness, unemployment, poverty, and disabilities; *Communication Commission*: websites related to e-mail and sharing information over the Internet; *Agricultural Commission*: websites related to food, gardens, and cooking.

Several times a week for a month, two hours of the school day were set aside for Internet time. The sessions were managed by having four of the commissions take half-hour turns sitting in a circle of chairs around the computer.

The search session was structured by the intern, who came to class equipped with addresses of websites (URLs), and who then looked up the websites as the children observed. This strategy was adopted because it seemed the most efficient way to describe how the Web worked to large groups of children.

As the sessions evolved, the students took turns working different "jobs" related to the search. There was a "mouse master," a "reader," and a "scribe" to record each commission's annotations. These jobs were rotated for each Web page search.

Searching The Internet sessions in this one-computer classroom were focused on critiquing the websites found (more in the "critical thinking skills" section). Websites were selected in advance by the intern, and entered for the students by the intern.

In the process, these sessions also introduced the students to basic concepts about the Internet: how it is a network of computers linked by a spider's web of telephone lines; how the data go through telephone lines from computer to computer; how browsing can be done through the use of scroll bars, hypertext links (links to other bodies of information embedded within the current text being examined), and bookmarks. It was judged that this was the most information that the students could grasp at this point in their education; search engines and techniques for selecting search terms would have to wait. The researchers concluded that children at this age require support in their search process, particularly with scanning text and using hypertext links—at least when the number of students per computer is so high.

Class #5: Laboratory class: Fifth grade

Curriculum and arrangements This laboratory class of nine fifth-grade students represented the one instance in our project where the Internet instruction was not integrated with the classroom lessons. These children had adequate typing and spelling skills, were all comfortable with computers, and some had computers at home.

The children met in the lab for two hours once a week for six weeks. Generally, the first part of each session was used for discussion, mini-lessons, and problem-solving. Because there was only one Internet-linked computer available, the children were divided into self-selected collaborative groups of three. The children selected the topic "national parks." The three groups took turns searching the Net for sites containing information about national parks. The children preferred sites with pictures and colorful graphics. Sites composed of text only or with more than one or two pages were left unexplored. In general, children rarely spent more than a few minutes at any one site.

The most popular site was the Hawaii Volcanoes National Park site. It contained a map of the caldera superimposed over a photographic image of the area. The colors were vivid and most of the names and locations on the map were "hot buttons" that linked the visitor to a brief description of the selected feature or area. These hot buttons encouraged the children to explore at a greater depth than if the information had been contained in a single site. (Clicking on what looks like a button on the screen provides a link to another section of the site, or to another website.)

Searching This group of nine fifth-graders meeting in the laboratory was able to learn and practice a lot of search skills. In the first two sessions they explored the Internet. They learned how to navigate, perform searches, use bookmarks, visit sites, and use hot buttons.

Halfway through the national parks project, they were asked to find six national parks as follows: two in Europe, two in the United States, one in either Africa or Australia, and an additional park not in the United States. This task was designed to encourage the children to perform more directed searches and to formulate alternative search arguments.

Finding European parks proved to be particularly difficult since the term "European" did not appear in the titles or descriptions of the parks located in Europe. The children had to be helped to come up with other terms, such as searching for parks in individual countries. In the process they learned some important lessons about how tricky searching using more general words can be.

Limited observation of these relatively computer-savvy fifth-graders suggests that children who are age ten or older are capable of finding resources on the Internet. Just as in the library media center, they may benefit from the assistance of an intermediary to help improve their results in negotiating the Internet. Their typing, spelling, vocabulary, and Boolean logic skills do come into play and can limit their ability to find appropriate resources. With direction, however, they are able to formulate search arguments and narrow or broaden a search depending on the previous search results, and they are capable of comprehending conceptual hierarchies when they have adequate base knowledge.

Class #6: One-computer class: Grade six

Curriculum and arrangements The sixth-grade class in the Beverly Hills school was studying ancient Egypt in its social science unit. The teacher and intern agreed to have the SNAPdragon activity be part of the students' project reports for that unit. In addition to reading in their textbook or consulting resources in the library media center, students used the World Wide Web for finding additional information on specific topics of their choice about ancient Egypt. In a first discussion, students expressed interest in topics such as weapons and arms, fashion, and animals, that they intended to pursue.

In this case, the teacher was unfamiliar with the Internet, while some of the students had unusually good computer experience. Most of the students had computers in their homes and had seen their parents or siblings using one. Eighteen of the twenty-nine students had experience using the Internet itself. Furthermore, there were two students who had used HTML in the class. (HTML is the formatting language used to input and make accessible the contents of Web pages.)

Because this was also the teacher's first contact with the Internet, the decision was made to take advantage of the large number of students with Internet experience in the class. Students were divided up into teams of five to six members. A team member who was considered to be an "Internet expert" then became the tutor for the team and guided the other students in their searches.

After the teacher and the intern jointly gave a general introduction for the class on the Internet and the SNAPdragon Project, they then met with the tutors and gave direction on how to introduce the World Wide Web to their team members and how to assign and rotate different roles, such as mouse master or reporter. For the remainder of the project, the teacher set up specific times at which each team could convene and conduct their searches.

Searching These computer-savvy sixth-graders were able to master the most sophisticated searching techniques of all the six classes studied. They were shown how to use different search engines, how to formulate and constrain their searches by using combination terms such as "ancient Egypt" and "weapons," and how to bookmark sites. The student teams were able to search on their own, under the guidance of the team's "tutor," independently of the other activities going on in the classroom.

Website content

The topics studied and searched by the students were mentioned above under "Curricular Content and Instructional Arrangements." Some general points are in order, however, regarding the Web content.

In general, many websites were not child-friendly. The use of big words and lots of text without pictures generated complaints by the students. In fact, text-only sites were often left unexplored. The researchers found that including the word "kids" in the searches usually turned up more colorful, interactive sites in plain English. These were the children's favorites.

Because of their familiarity with television, the children demanded high production values; they wanted quality audio, video, and heightened interactivity. For example, at a site found in the search for information on ancient Egypt, children could submit their name and have it returned in hieroglyphs.

In sum, the researchers found the following regarding website content:

1. Children prefer websites with high visual content and short, simple textual content.

2. Children are inspired to talk about their social views and surroundings when they view Internet sites featuring children's artwork and photographs from other places.

3. Children would like to see more animation and interactivity on the Internet.

4. Children have a low tolerance for long download times.

Critical thinking skills and interschool collaboration

Web searching taught children about a major new information source, and, for the older students, provided some active searching skills. But to complete the experience as a means of developing information literacy, the project was also designed to help the students develop critical thinking skills by evaluating the sites they found on the web, then creating a directory of their evaluations for all other students in participating classrooms.

The variety of quality and function of websites provided a rich field for learning. In viewing a site, children had to determine, first of all, whether its content related to their interests, then extract information for their projects, and, finally, write an evaluative directory entry for the site.

As with books, the children were quick to assume everything they found about their topic on the Internet was correct just because it was there. The children learned that the information they found on the Web could be submitted by adults or by children and that the information came from around the world. Eventually, they learned to distinguish sales and marketing sites from more neutrally informational sites.

In general, it was difficult for the younger children—through the fourth grade—to evaluate the sites or to write annotations. They could determine what they liked, but had trouble articulating why they liked it. When asked why they liked a site, the common answer was "it had lots of information," or "it had good information." Their awareness was helped by talking about whether the information was easy to read. If there were both pictures and text at the site, they were asked if the pictures helped their understanding. Their favorite sites were often those created by other children.

With younger children, it was necessary to develop the annotations with the child. Older children were also reluctant to write annotations; they did not initially see the point or value in doing so.

When the SNAPdragon site became "live," that is, when the children could find their own directory postings on the web, they were delighted. It gave them a great sense of pride to know that children and adults from around the world could read their comments and also benefit from the information provided in their favorite sites. Students were much more engaged and willing to write annotations on sites when they realized that other students could see them on the web.

In one case, a student wanted to write "This site sucks" as his annotation. After he realized how widely his annotation could be read, he decided to expand his commentary! These sessions also gave students a chance to practice reading and writing. Issues of vocabulary came up repeatedly because many websites included difficult words. (See figure 1 for example children's website annotations.)

The role of the library media specialist

As this was a first experimental effort, the researchers believe that the use of the SNAP schools, the development of the SNAPdragon website, and the development of curriculum for the graduate course were enough to tackle at once. Consequently, with the graduate interns acting, *de facto*, in the role of the school library media specialist, the researchers did not actively seek to involve the media specialists in the project schools for this project. The graduate student involvement, however, did provide insight into some of the kinds of roles the media specialist can assume in information literacy projects involving Web searching. There are clearly abundant opportunities

CHILD'S AGE: **5**	WEB SITE TITLE: "Herp Pictures" ANNOTATION: *I liked it because the pictures were very cool. My favorite picture was the corn snake eating the mouse. They should make all the pictures in color.*
CHILD'S AGE: **7**	WEB SITE TITLE: "Jason's Snakes and Reptiles" ANNOTATION: *I liked some of it. This page was not as interesting as Kyle's Herp page, there was not as much information. Jason is like me. He got his first snake when he was 6 and so did I. I think only kids who are really really really into snakes would like this page.*
CHILDREN'S AGES: **8–10**	WEB SITE TITLE: "Hands-on Children's Museum" ANNOTATION: *We like that you can do things. This site has mazes. Some of the mazes are too easy and too big for the page. It would be better if they would shrink the mazes. We think other kids would like this site because people like mazes.*
CHILDREN'S AGES: **10–11**	WEB SITE TITLE: "Banff National Park Main Index" ANNOTATION: *Format: Detailed information with text, pictures, and hot buttons. This site talks about animals that live there, what to do there, the weather, and what to bring. You can also read it in French or English. Comments: It has lots of cool pictures. Audience: Everyone. Interest: Great.*

FIG. 1. *Example children's website annotations*

for—and arguments for—school library media specialist involvement in Internet instruction in schools.

World Wide Web searching is an obvious extension of the many other kinds of information searching that fall within the range of the library media specialist's expertise. As professionals engaged in life-long continuing education, they are likely to have mastered this technology and its use well before most of the teachers in a school have. In line with the proactive teaching role recommended for media specialists by Kay Vandergrift (1994), Internet instruction is a natural venue for the specialist to approach teachers and engage with them in curriculum planning and instruction. Having a higher comfort level with computers and with the Internet, the library media specialist can provide the missing link between the teacher and the technical support person, as well as be the expert in information-searching techniques and information resource evaluation. The library media specialist's expertise in resource evaluation is particularly needed with Internet resources because the historical editorial controls provided by paper publishers are frequently missing in materials published on the Internet.

In some cases, the school library media center may be the first place in the school where one of the computers has Web access. It then becomes a natural extension of the library media specialist's role to introduce teachers to the possibilities of using the Internet in the classroom. In fact, in one case in this study, the school's vice-principal approached the intern, saying that the teachers had expressed an interest in having her conduct a "World Wide Web workshop" for them.

Further, the library media specialist can identify good websites for support of teaching just as has long been the case with identifying and purchasing materials supportive of curriculum. The library media specialist can provide moral support and additional help in the classroom when the teacher introduces the web. Finally, the specialist can be recognized as having a special expertise in the teaching enterprise: expertise in searching for information. This has always been true for library materials, but is not always recognized outside the walls of the library media center and inside the classroom.

Like all new arenas for human activity, the Web and Web searching will soon come to be seen as *someone*'s area of expertise. This is a golden opportunity for school library media specialists to fill that role in a school. But the stance must indeed be proactive. No one assigns the role—and someone else will surely occupy the area if library media specialists do not.

Discussion and conclusions

In March 1996, the SNAPdragon Project was brought to a temporary completion. In addition to the students' annotations, the current website featured digitized samples of drawings provided by the students. The researchers concluded our intervention with another meeting in March, to which all the participating teachers, some of the students, and other interested researchers and visitors came to share their experiences. While the SNAPdragon Project was not a systematic study of different classroom settings and students' information literacy skills, some valuable insights were gathered nonetheless.

All children, in first through sixth grade, were able to use websites to advantage in their learning. All children could learn to scroll through a site and use hypertext links to other sites. Older children could learn to use search engines and the rudiments of Boolean logic. Once students had experienced some frustration in searching, they were then receptive to learning more about, for example, differences between search engines.

Students were able to extract information for their school projects from the sites. But selecting good sites in the first place was sometimes difficult for them. Titles and descriptions returned by search engines were sometimes misleading and difficult for the children to evaluate. This problem was compounded by their reluctance to read or scan the list of results. It appeared that only titles were used to decide which site to visit. Since the system was often slow, picking the wrong site precluded visiting additional sites.

The Web searching process produced relatively few child-friendly sites. Visiting too many boring, uninvolving, or irrelevant sites can retard the value of the experience. This can be compensated for, in part, by selecting some good sites in advance for the students; otherwise, learning to pull good information from poor is a valuable part of a child's information literacy learning.

Writing evaluative annotations of sites was a challenge for all children; younger ones needed to be prompted and assisted. Interest and enthusiasm for contributing to the SNAPdragon website rose substantially when children realized that their annotations could be accessed by people around the world and would certainly be seen by the children at the other five test sites.

As noted in many policy reports and discussion, access to the Internet is an important issue, if only for the limited resources of computers, phone lines, and wiring. While providing all students with computers might not be possible, the researchers found that working with even one Internet-accessible computer turned out to be feasible, given certain classroom arrangements.

In general, the students' interest in Internet activities was high. It helped that the children saw "surfing the Net" as a "cool" thing to do. Their enthusiasm was further fueled by finding their own work represented on the web. This sense of having an Internet identity seemed to be of great value to the students.

While the project in its first installment was initiated and organized by adults, the researchers believe that having the students handle all aspects, from creating the site and collecting annotations to indexing the entries, will prove to be the best learning experience. In fact, one of the most valuable learning experiences for the members of the university course appeared when confronted with the task of categorizing the first SNAPdragon submissions. There was extensive debate on what category names to choose and how deeply to index the contents. In the end the Dewey Decimal Classification main categories were adopted.

In retrospect, the researchers wished that the children had had the opportunity to contend with the same issues. While the categorization of musical instruments, animals, and plants is a common activity in elementary classrooms, students usually do not deal with creating any kind of directory or index. Becoming information literate includes dealing, as end-users, with all the issues associated with organizing, accessing, and using information. The SNAPdragon Project challenged students to grow in these skills.

ACKNOWLEDGMENTS

Our thanks go to Philip Ender, our Graduate School of Education and Information Science colleague who set up the SNAPdragon website and directed laboratory instruction, and to the graduate interns and classroom teachers whose creative participation made this project possible: interns Phyllis D. Braxton, Diane Childs, Howard H. Lo, Marlene Martin, Kim Rose, and Louise Yarnell; and teachers Raul Alarcon, Sara Boulton, Jaime Calderon, Denise Cole, Faith Dennis, Janet Galeko, Dolores Patton, and Cathy Rodriguez. The researchers also wish to thank Virginia A. Walter for her very helpful input. This article builds upon an Apple Computer Advanced Technology Group Technical Report (Kafai et al., 1996).

REFERENCES

American Association of School Librarians and Association for Educational Communications and Technology. (1988). *Information power: Guidelines for school library media programs* (p. 10). Chicago, IL: ALA.

American Library Association Presidential Committee on Information Literacy. (1989). *Information literacy: Final report.* Chicago, IL: ALA American Association of School Librarians.

Bruce, B., & Peyton, J.K. (1990). A new writing environment and an old culture: A situated evaluation of computer networking to teach writing. *Interactive Learning Environments, 1*(3), 171–192.

Bruce, B., & Rubin, A. (1991). *Electronic quills: A situated evaluation of using computers for writing in classrooms.* Hillsdale, NJ: Lawrence Erlbaum.

California Media and Library Educators Association. (1994). *From library skills to information literacy: A handbook for the 21st century.* Castle Rock, CO: Hi Willow Research and Publishing.

Doyle, C. (1994). Information-literate use of telecommunications. *CMLEA Journal, 17*(2), 17–20.

Eisenberg, M.B., & Berkowitz, R.E. (1988). *Information problem-solving: The big six skills approach to library & information skills instruction.* Norwood, NJ: Ablex.

Gallo, M.A., & Horton, P.B. (1994). Assessing the effect on high school teachers of direct and unrestricted access to the internet: A case study of an east central Florida high school. *Educational Technology Research and Development, 42*(4), 17–39.

Goldman, S., & Newman, D. (1992). Electronic interactions: How students and teachers organize schooling over wires. *Interactive Learning Environments, 2*(1), 31–44.

Gordin, D.N., Polman, J.L., & Pea, R.D. (1994). The climate visualizer: Sense-making through scientific visualization. *Journal of Science Education and Technology, 3*(4), 203–226.

Heaviside, S. et al. (1995). *Advanced telecommunications in U.S. public schools, K–12.* (NCES 95-731). U.S. Dept. of Education, Office of Educational Research and Improvement, National Center for Education Statistics.

Jackson, D.F. et al. (1994). Implementing "real science" through microcomputers and telecommunications in project-based elementary classrooms. *Journal of Science Education and Technology, 3*(1), 17–26.

Kafai, Y. et al. (1996). *Building a foundation for information literacy: Creating an annotated WWW index by children for children* (Apple Technical Report No. 154). Cupertino, CA: Apple Computer.

Kuhlthau, C.C. (1993). *Seeking meaning: A process approach to library and information services.* Norwood, NJ: Ablex.

Lazarus, W., & Lipper, L. (1994). *America's children and the information superhighway.* Santa Monica, CA: The Children's Partnership.

Linn, M.C. (1996). Key to the information highway. *Communications of the ACM, 39*(4), 34–35.

Mendrinos, R. (1994). *Building information literacy using high technology: A guide for schools and libraries.* Englewood, CO: Libraries Unlimited.

Riel, M. (1992). A functional analysis of educational telecomputing: A case study of learning circles. *Interactive Learning Environments, 2*(1), 15–30.

Scardamalia, M. et al. (1992). Educational applications of a networked communal database. *Interactive Learning Environments, 2*(1), 45–71.

Solomon, P. (1993). Children's information retrieval behavior: A case analysis of an OPAC. *Journal of the American Society for Information Science, 44*(5), 245–264.

Vandergrift, K.E. (1994). *Power teaching: A primary role of the school library media specialist.* Chicago, IL: American Library Association.

Walter, V.A. (1994). The information needs of children. *Advances in Librarianship, 18*, 111–129.

Walter, V.A., Borgman, C.L., & Hirsh, S.G. (1996). The science library catalog: A springboard for information literacy. *School Library Media Quarterly, 24*(2), 105–110.

7

An exploratory profile
of personal home pages:
Content, design, metaphors

ABSTRACT

An exploratory sample of 114 personal home pages, drawn from a home page directory available on the World Wide Web (People Page Directory: http://www.peoplepage.com), was analyzed to detect patterns and trends in home page content and design. Covered in the analysis were types of informational content included in the home pages; internal organization and structure of the content, including type and number of hypertext links; miscellaneous content elements, such as "sign guestbook" and number of hits to the page; and physical design features such as photos, motion and audio elements. Metaphors used in the design of the pages and degree of self-revelation were also considered.

The home pages displayed a great variety of content and of specific types of formatting within broader formatting approaches. While some content elements were quite popular, none of them—not even name—was found on all home pages. Nor did the pages evidence reliance on any single dominant metaphor, such as home page as "home" in the sense of domicile. It appears that though certain features may be frequently found in it, the personal home page as a social institution is still very much under development.

First published as Bates, M. J., & Lu, S. (1997). An exploratory profile of personal home pages: Content, design, metaphors. *Online & CD-ROM Review, 21*(6), 331–340.

Introduction

Use of the Internet and the publishing and navigation tool known as the World Wide Web has grown explosively in recent years. Many companies, organizations and individuals have created a virtual presence on the Web by mounting a website which anyone else with Web access can visit, read and explore. The primary entry and access point for a website, generally called the home page, is the focus of this article.

Navigation tools such as Netscape Navigator enable people to access websites by entering the site's URL, or Universal Resource Locator; by searching on vocabulary terms in websites with the help of search engines such as Infoseek; or by searching in directories of names of people and companies.

Vast amounts of attention in the form of news reporting and discussion have been devoted to the Web in newspapers and journals; however, empirical research on this dramatic new communication and information medium is still in its early stages. In particular, while numerous articles have advised people how to create home pages (December & Randall, 1994; Falcigno & Green, 1995; Spear, 1995; van Brakel et al., 1995), no research analyzing the character and content of personal home pages or websites was found in preparation of this article. Just one article analyzing the content of corporate or organization websites was found—a study of library websites (Clyde, 1996).

Home pages are commonly developed and made available on the Web by companies, organizations and individuals. It is the purpose of this article to describe a study of a sampling of personal home pages; business and other organizational home pages were excluded.

The authors became interested in the question of the character of personal home pages because it appeared to us that the home page represents a new social form or device. People are representing themselves to the world through a new medium. How do they present themselves there? What kind of information do their home pages contain? Does this new social device of the home page draw on old social and document forms or create entirely new ones?

The objective here is to develop a preliminary profile of some personal home pages and thus provide an initial characterization of this new social form.

Questions the authors asked of the data included:

1. What was the purpose of the home pages: specifically, were there common patterns of social types of home pages?

2. Did the home pages draw on any pre-existing dominant metaphors or were they developing their own metaphors?

3. What kinds of information were most commonly included?

4. How was the information organized within the home page?

5. Were there any regularities in the hypertext links to other websites within the home pages?

To answer these questions, the home pages were analyzed for the general character of information provided, metaphorical references, specific elements of information, the organizational structure of the home page, and the number and type of hypertext links within the pages. In addition to the quantitative data, our qualitative assessment of the character of the pages will be presented in ensuing sections.

Methodology

To examine personal home pages, it would clearly be desirable to select a random sample of such pages from across the World Wide Web. That in turn, however, is a very difficult challenge. With the number of available websites growing explosively, and available directories always incomplete and overlapping, selecting a true random sample may be next to impossible. We experimented with another alternative—drawing names randomly from a telephone book and then searching for them on the Web. This, too, proved impractical and almost certainly not in fact representative: impractical because most of the names selected did not show up on the Web, and unrepresentative because there is no guarantee—in fact, it is quite unlikely—that the mix of people appearing in telephone books (or other name listings) parallels the mix of people appearing on the Web, which still represents a minority of the population.

However, since we did not know if studying home pages would prove to be either interesting or feasible in any case, we decided in the end to select a systematic sample from one of the available Web directories of home pages. Such a sample would obviously represent a self-selected group—those who submitted their sites for inclusion in that particular directory—but the sample would have the advantage of not being consciously or unconsciously biased in selection on our part. Using such a sample, we could then learn of the characteristics of personal home pages in at least an exploratory manner.

The People Page Directory (*http://www.peoplepage.com*), found through Netscape Navigator (2.0) Net Directory, contained "about 5000" entries, according to its founder and Webmaster, Rhese Hoylman, in June 1996 when the sample for this study was drawn. Entries available at that time in the directory had been submitted since a year earlier, June 1995. The first five entries under each letter were taken for the sample. As the letters D, K, Q, T, U, X, Y and Z each contained fewer than five entries, the size of the total sample was 114 home pages.

The directory was arranged by earliest submitted entries first, so this sampling method tends to draw on entries that were submitted toward the beginning date of the directory—that is, mid-1995—while randomizing the entries alphabetically within each letter. As home page owners can update their home pages at any time, however, the sampled home pages represented their current state as of June 1996. The sample was limited to the United States context; any site submitted from outside the country was passed over for the next listing.

Submission to the People Page Directory is voluntary and free. The following types of information are asked of people when they submit their listing: "real last name," "real first name," "alias/handle," e-mail address, home page address, password (so the submitter can revise the entry if desired), city, state/province, country, URL of favorite website, favorite newsgroup and favorite IRC (Internet Relay Chat) channel.

Drawing on the work of others, van Brakel et al. (1995) characterize home pages variously as:

- "a designed and designated entry-point for access to a local website" (December & Randall, 1994);

- ". . . a graphical door and screen that are full of information, in which links to related information are included" (Dougherty & Koman, 1994).

Operationally, in this study a home page was defined as the first screen of information that appears upon entering the URL address (drawn from the People Page Directory) of a website in a search on the World Wide Web. The page may be of varying lengths, compared to paper pages, but reaches its end when it cannot be scrolled down any further. The only exception to the "first screen" rule occurred occasionally when the first page was a referral from an older to a newer location, or was in some way quite evidently a sort of "see reference" page to what was clearly the main home page. There were only a handful of such instances and there was no ambiguity in interpreting them.

The home pages were then analyzed for their characteristics. A trial sample of home pages was first examined and a wide range of features identified as being of possible interest. These traits were then grouped into several classes:

- information about the website as a whole;
- purposes of home page;
- personal information content of pages;
- home page internal structure, including links;
- miscellaneous content elements/features;
- home page physical features.

Categories within each of these classes of information that had been discovered in the pre-sample were then tallied in the sample proper and are presented in the results section.

Results

The website as a whole

Among the 114 home pages, 40% (45 pages) are located on commercial servers (i.e., final characters of Web address are "com"), 36% on educational servers ("edu"), 19% on network servers ("net"), four percent on organizational servers ("org") and one on an unknown server. The text of 105, or 92%, of the home pages was written by the owners (the individuals submitting the home pages to the directory), with the remainder having been written by someone else.

Purpose and function of the home pages

In reviewing the home pages, several functions of the pages were identified. Some pages could possess more than one of these functions, and were so tallied, but few did. These functions were identified by the contents of the page and the "feel" we perceived compared to paper documents. For instance, if the information largely overlapped with typical contents of resumes, even if the word "resume" was not used, it was assumed that a principal purpose of the home page was to present the author's professional capability and experience.

TABLE 1. *Purposes of home pages*

PURPOSE	OCCURRENCE	PERCENTAGE
Present own professional capability and experience	51	44.7
Play with system capability	33	28.9
Announce products or upcoming performance	23	20.2
Political campaign	3	2.6
Looking for dates	3	2.6
Miscellaneous and unknown	5	4.4
TOTAL	118*	N/A

* *Some home pages have multiple purposes so the total is above 114.*

Table 1 displays the most common discerned purposes encountered.

Fully 45% (51 pages) presented professional capabilities or background. Among these, six pages made explicit mention of looking for work. For example, Carolyn Gibbs states: "Take a look at my resume . . . I"m available for hire June 1996!!' (*http://www.ced.berkeley.edu/~cgibbs*). Another 20% (23 pages) announce products or upcoming performances. So nearly two-thirds of the home pages present—and implicitly or explicitly advertise—the home page creator's professional capabilities or business.

Such information can be interpreted in a couple of ways. On the one hand, announcing one's work experience is a way of attracting possible interest on the part of employers, even if one is gainfully employed currently. And certainly, in those cases where people are explicitly looking for work, or explicitly advertising a product or upcoming performance, there is no question that the home page is directly serving a work-related purpose.

However, the extent of professional information provided varies across the sample home pages. In some cases, it appears that the author of the page is not interested in employment so much as in offering information for exchange with others as part of a conventional get acquainted ritual. Exchange of information about one's work is a very common and important component of such conversational interchanges for Americans—in fact, that piece of information is often the second proffered, after one's name. In these cases there is generally less detailed information and the organization of the information on the page has less resemblance to a conventional resume format.

In fact, even in those pages with the most resume-type organization, there are often substantial deviations from the standard format. The creators of the home pages appear to enjoy experimenting with the more flexible possibilities of Web documents and include photographs, icons and other format deviations from conventional resumes (e.g. Andy Dong's page, *http://hart.ME.Berkeley.EDU/~adong/adong.html*).

On the other hand, two areas generally considered delicate in American social life—politics and religion—are correspondingly scarce in the content of the home page sample. Just three pages mention religious beliefs and three discuss politics. One home page brings both of these hot topics together. Its title: "Jewish Dude With a Conservative Attitude: Alan's New Conservative Home Page" (*http://www.cris.com/~Alcanh/*).

The 33 home pages (29%) categorized as playing with system capabilities appeared to be presenting their home page largely for the fun of it, to share in the new phenomenon and present themselves to the virtual world. For example, one home page is titled: "Jeffrey and Patricia Gyurke present: Informative and fun things to explore!" (*http://www.pennet. com/jgyurke/*).

Another states: "Yes, It's . . . Meredith's Homepage." It continues: "Hello. This, as you might have already gathered, is my home page. I have actually only had my computer for two months and sixteen days, so you may have to bear with me as I struggle to figure out what all these funny little buttons do" (*http://www.geocities.com/Sunset Strip/1764/*). Still another states: "I have no idea why I'm creating this Web page except for the sole purpose of doing it. Oh well, I hope it works" (*http://studentweb.tulane. edu/~ahernan/*).

Miscellaneous purposes were to look for a missing person and create a focus for a family name and people having that name (one each).

Metaphors and social or document forms

We also examined the pages to determine whether any identifiable metaphors or pre-existing social or document forms seemed to guide the wording and organization of the pages. As noted in the previous section, the most commonly used basis for the design of the page appeared to be the resume—sometimes explicitly labeled, other times seeming to influence the presentation of the page without the use of the term. Here we examine whether explicit or implicit metaphors and social forms guided the home page creators, at least partially, in their development and presentation of the pages.

The phrase "home page" probably originated from the sense of "home" found in the phrases "home base" in climbing or "home plate" in baseball. The home page in a website, like the home base or home plate, is the starting point, and the point to come back to in order to get reoriented or start again. Once "home" was used in the name, however, some interpreted the word in the sense of primary domicile—which, after all, is closely related to, and probably the origin of, the meanings in the sports usages.

We found six home pages that used explicit or implicit references to home as domicile in describing the home page: "Aaron's Home Sweet Home Page" (*http://www. lookup.com/Homepages/70500/main.htm*), "Spartan's Haven. You are guest number __ to visit my house" (*http://www.clark. net/pub/spartan/*) and "Welcome to my humble abode" (*http://www.colum. edu/~phillips/*) are examples. One of the six presented a graphic that looked like a room with a sign on the room's wall: "Welcome to my home" (*http:// www.enter.net/~gquier/*).

Other terms implying location that were found one or more times among the home pages were the following: "quadrant," "world" (as in "maggy's world" (*http://pinky.interaccess.com/maggy/*)), "space," "spot," "domain" and "inferno." On the whole, however, there were far fewer references to home pages in this sense of a physical home than there were home pages built on the model of the resume.

There were hints of other pre-existing social forms in the language and format of the pages as well. In the physical world, American homes are sometimes labeled with small signs, often attached above the front doorway or hanging down from the porch roof, stating, "The Smiths," or "Welcome to the Smith Family Home," or the like. Because these signs usually have so little text, it is difficult to determine with confidence whether any of the sample home pages were developed with a similar function in mind. However, two or three of the home pages seemed to these authors to be evoking that same spirit. For example, one page has a title, "Welcome to Mike & Nancy Nalbone's Home Page!," and is accompanied by a photo of the couple smiling in a warm and inviting way (*http://pluto.njcc.com/~nalbone/*). Such "welcome" signs may be seen not only as physical signs but also as declarations of the family home as proud social unit, declaring itself to the world in a modern, democratized (and therefore much simplified) version of the heraldic shield.

Another form the home page might be seen to resemble is the business card or calling card. The small standard size of the card today limits the amount of text that can be placed on it. However, in the nineteenth century, calling cards were often more elaborate. When photography was a new innovation in the last century, one type of calling card, known by the French name *carte de visite*, included photographs as a special, impressive feature (see Mathews, 1974; Morgan, 1942, pp. 665–6). (Our thanks to Anne Gilliland-Swetland for this suggestion.) These cards measured from 5 x 8 centimeters up to 6 x 10 centimeters. Lena Marianne Arvola's home page evokes such a photographic calling card (*http://pearl.mhtc.net1-chase/index.html*).

With a frame measuring approximately 11 x 14 centimeters, in turn containing several smaller frames each outlining a class of information, it contains the usual business card information, a photograph and an image of her personalized automobile license plate. (Personalized plates may be seen as another form of modern heraldry!)

After a while the *cartes de visite* consisted primarily of the photos and less the usual calling card information. People would exchange the photos and then put them in an album. The twentieth century Web parallel to creating an album might be "bookmarking" a site so that it can be revisited again easily.

Since preparing home pages involves writing, it might be expected that metaphors of document forms might drive the development of home pages. Elements of the resume and calling card format have already been discussed. If there is a standardized format for the home page as document, however, we have been unable to identify it yet. Other than occasional mentions made of the home page creator as its "author," no clear, dominating sense of home page as type of document was recognized, other than ones already mentioned.

Since the creators of these home pages develop them themselves, for the most part, another possible way the creators might see their home pages is as an explicit "creation," a work of art. They may have done so privately, but other than one person who titled her home page "Mary's Fantabulous Web Oeuvre" (*http://grove.ufl.edu:80/~mebbahl1/index.html*) we did not detect explicit evidence within the pages that their creators viewed the website in this manner.

On the whole, while home page creators did draw partially on metaphorical senses for how they conceptualized their home pages, it would appear that for the most part they are remaining open to the development of the home page as its own new social form. Resume-like forms are popular but by no means overwhelmingly dominant, and considerable freedom was exercised in the internal structure and content of home pages. Remaining sections of this paper will detail other aspects of home page design.

How personal or self-revealing are the home pages?

One of the ways in which the authors of the pages differed considerably was in the degree to which they revealed themselves and took social risks. Making a home page available to the virtual community can both reveal and hide the person. The truth or completeness of the statements could not be determined from a reading of them, of course, but it was possible to note how extensive and self-revealing the provided information appeared to be.

Two of the sample proved to be Trojan horses in this directory of personal sites: they were company home pages, one of them selling website development. Another home page was submitted by an individual but contained nothing but the specifications of that individual's house for sale.

Three others were curious sorts of borderline cases as personal home pages. One was called the "Shoe Salesman's Home Page" (*http://funnelweb. utcc.utk.edu/~lyle/shoe.html*) and was dedicated to "my fellow shoe clerks around the world." It was clearly a site that was personally very meaningful and well thought through by the author, containing, among other things, frequently asked questions about shoes, links to shoe companies and even humor. However, the home page contained no personal information, not even the name, of the author, though a hypertext link was made available at the end to "me."

Another home page called "Yenzo's Climbing Corner" (*http://www2. coastalnet.com/~cn3111/index.html*) was, similarly, "dedicated to North Carolina Rock Climbing" and contained hypertext links to a variety of information on that subject, but no personal information. Those links, as with the shoe salesman home page, did however contain one that led to the page author, titled: "Read article from <u>Who is Yenzo?</u>" Finally, one other site gave the author's name but no other conventional personal information—only links to over 40 poems written by the page author. Poetry can, of course, be very revealing too, but generally in a different way.

Only 90 (79%) of the home pages provided the author's full name; 17 (15%) gave nicknames or aliases. One hundred and five (92%) gave electronic mail addresses and 18 (16%) provided telephone numbers.

Another important form of self-revelation and presentation of self is the photograph. Forty (35%) of the home pages contained photographs. Of these, 22 had photo(s) of the author, self only, while four had photos of self with other people and six had photos of self in a scene (some with pets or objects) more extensive than just the self alone. Thirteen home pages had other photos. (Any given home page could have more than one type of photo.)

Specific kinds of personal information

Typically, the home page authors provide a range of information that, however extensive, is moderately revealing—listing work, favorite websites, hobbies, etc. Table 2 lists the various kinds of information tallied, arranged by frequency of appearance of the type of information in the home pages.

An average of 5.9 items appear on the home pages out of a total of 32 types of items we tallied. Thus, in this sample the top six items listed in

TABLE 2. *Type of personal information present.*

ITEM NO.	TYPE OF PERSONAL INFORMATION	OCCURRENCES	PERCENTAGE
1	e-mail address	105	92.1
2	name	90	79.0
3	favorite websites	64	56.1
4	gender	44	38.6
5	photo	40	35.1
6	current work	37	32.5
7	educational background	36	31.6
8	hobbies, interests	35	30.7
9	address	22	19.3
10	past work	22	19.3
11	phone or fax number	18	15.8
12	alias or nickname	17	14.9
13	personal history	15	13.2
14	work capacity	15	13.2
15	resume (formally labeled)	13	11.4
16	age	12	10.5
17	favorite book, CD, food, etc.	12	10.5
18	publication list	11	9.7
19	geographical region	10	8.8
20	friends' home pages	8	7.0
21	family background	7	6.1
22	honor or award received	7	6.1
23	marriage status (explicitly stated)	7	6.1
24	cultural background	5	4.4
25	research areas	5	4.4
26	military service	4	3.5
27	religious beliefs	3	2.6
28	current Web project	2	1.8
29	personal seal	2	1.8
30	favorite people	1	0.9
31	list of courses taught	1	0.9
32	news groups sponsored by	1	0.9

Table 2 can be seen as the most likely to appear on personal home pages, though the frequency of the last of these is already down to less than one third of the sampled pages.

Home page structure, including links

We identified three gross types of internal structure within home pages. The first consisted of strictly a contents menu of links to other pages, called here "menu home page." In these cases there would be no or virtually no text on the page other than the menu listing of links. The second type of home page consisted entirely or almost entirely of straight running text, with no or few links. The third type of internal structure had many links and often contained a menu or contents list at the beginning of the page. Recall that in all these cases, the stated structure refers only to the first, or "home" page at the website, scrollable from top to bottom.

The "menu" type of home page was found in ten, or nine percent, of the home pages. There were 16, or 14%, of the second type of home page, the straight text. Finally, the great majority of the home pages—88, or 77%—were of the third type.

Links were defined in Netscape 2.0 as the blue underlined elements of home pages. No distinction was made in the general count between links within a page or website and links to other websites. All but five of the home pages, or 96%, contained one or more such links. Altogether, there were 2184 links found in the 114 home pages, for a mean of 19.2 links per home page. The median number of links per home page was 14 and the mode was 11. The highest number of links found on a single home page was 215. Table 3, "Distribution of home page links," displays the link frequencies.

Content types of links were examined as well. Nearly all home pages—107, or 94%—contained links to other home pages. In addition 41, or 36%, contained links to search engines and 42 (37%) contained links to shareware.

Miscellaneous content elements/features

In the pilot test we identified a number of other miscellaneous features of the home pages that may be a part of the developing home page culture and character. These were then counted in the sample proper. Table 4, "Miscellaneous elements/features," lists the features in order of frequency.

Several of the most popular features draw upon characteristics specific to the interactive and ever-changing environment of the Web. Number of hits

TABLE 3. *Distribution of home page links.*

NUMBER OF LINKS	OCCURRENCES	PERCENTAGE
0	5	4.4
1–5	12	10.5
6–10	23	20.2
11–15	23	20.2
16–20	17	14.9
21–25	13	11.4
26–30	5	4.4
31–35	5	4.4
36–40	1	0.9
41–45	3	2.6
46–50	1	0.9
>50	6	5.3
TOTAL	114	100

TABLE 4. *Miscellaneous elements/features.*

ITEMS POSTED	OCCURRENCE	PERCENTAGE
Number of hits to home page	60	52.6
Last update date	49	43.0
"Under construction" and its variants	41	36.0
Free speech blue ribbon	25	21.9
Sign guestbook	20	17.5
Copyright notice	15	13.2
Icon "new"	15	13.2
Disclaimer	5	4.4
Clock or calendar	4	3.5
Directories where indexed	3	2.6
Member of HTML Writers Guild	2	1.8
Time of creation	2	1.8
Awards for website	1	0.9

to the page, latest update date, clock or calendar, and "under construction" all reflect the distinctive character of the network environment. These four would be meaningless, a demonstration of inadequacy or impossible to do if they were to appear in a book or business card.

Here however they are a potential source of pride for the home page creator. Number of hits to the page may show the popularity of a page but it also shows that the creator of the page knows how to add such a feature to the page. Latest update date, clock or calendar, and "under construction" also highlight the mutability of Web records and imply a home page owner actively engaged in the Web through an ever-changing website. Though "time of creation" appears in the paper world as publication date, it is understood by visitors to Web home pages that such a time can change frequently without requiring the issuance of a whole new page or site, so in this way reinforces the sense of rapid changeability associated with the Web.

The phrase "under construction," which appears in no fewer than 41 home pages (36%), may serve another function as well, given how new the Web is, with the social norms and expectations still under formation. If one puts up a home page and is a little uncertain about how it will be received, adding the "under construction" rubric can imply that an actually-finished home page is not yet in its finished state, while one tests the waters to see if the home page gains acceptance. If one concludes that one's page is not fashionable or has some other flaw, one can change it with no loss of face—after all, it was still "under construction" up to the time it was changed. The 15 cases where the icon "New" was used presumably represent instances where the home page creator wants to signal changes that have been made recently in the page.

The "sign guestbook" feature is a particularly interesting one for our exploration of the social character of home pages. On the Web it represents another "cool" feature that a home page maker can add to his or her site. It also gives the page creator an opportunity to receive feedback from people visiting the site.

Socially, outside of the Web, signing a guestbook is something one does both in homes as well as in public places such as churches, museums, restaurants and funeral homes. The custom is generally to sign one's name and address with brief comments appropriate to the location. Guestbooks are very easily provided in the real, as opposed to virtual, world. A guestbook is simply placed in a prominent place and visitors have the option to sign and make comments, or not. While this may be technically somewhat harder to achieve in the world of the Web, the social arrangements are remarkably similar. The visitor has the option to sign or not, and the opportunity to provide a little feedback. Twenty of the home pages in this sample, or 17.5%, had this option. As only some people provide guestbooks in their real homes too, it would be interesting to see how this rate in the virtual world corresponds with the availability of guestbooks in real homes in our society.

While the above features highlight what is new about the Web as a communication medium, the remaining features in this section are evidence of social forms and issues being transferred from the paper to the electronic environment. ("Sign guestbook," along with being a technical feature that could be added to home pages, was also a social device carried over from the paper world.) The large number of home pages with the "free speech" blue ribbon symbol present reflects the controversies currently brewing in our society about how to handle intellectual freedom issues in the context of a new communication medium with its own distinctive parameters of access and availability.

Copyright notices and listings of directories where the home page is indexed are features carried over from the paper world. While much of the talk in the early days of electronic access centered around the freedom from constraints that network access was thought to have made possible on the Internet, it is not surprising that people want to maintain ownership of their intellectual property—at least, that is, until and unless our society undergoes a sea change in its attitudes toward intellectual products. Likewise, the model of professional associations in the print world is carried over in the "HTML Writers Guild" and the award for the website continues the pattern of awards for the development of intellectual products in the paper world.

Physical features of home pages

Home pages may have textual, visual (including both still and motion) and audio components. Table 5, "Visual and audio features of home pages," lists the frequencies of various features in the study sample.

Among 114 home pages, 44 (39%) have a standard white or grey background; 18 (16%) have a plain colored background other than white or grey, and 52 (46%) have some kind of patterned background such as flowers, logos etc. (regardless of color). There are also 90 home pages (79%) that use icons and/or artwork to represent or illustrate the contents of the pages. Also, as mentioned earlier, 40 (35%) of the 114 home pages contain photographs.

Some motion feature or features appear in 38, or 33% of all the home pages. Of these, in 33 the motion appears directly on the screen while five

TABLE 5. *Visual and audio features of home pages.*

FEATURES	OCCURRENCES	PERCENTAGE
Icons or artwork	90	78.9
Background		
Patterned designs—any color	52	45.6
Colors other than white or grey	18	15.8
White or grey	44	38.6
Motion picture	38	33.3
Click to pull up	5	4.4
On screen	33	28.9
Sound (click to pull up the feature)	6	5.3

must be clicked on to pull up the motion feature. (Motion includes scrolling text, blinking text, as well as full-fledged moving images.)

Sound features are relatively new on the Web and correspondingly showed up less frequently in the sample. Six home pages (five percent) contained an audio feature: in all cases, one had to click to summon the sound.

Summary and conclusions

Personal home pages in this sample of 114 pages appeared to serve a number of functions for their creators. Fifty-one pages (45%) displayed professional capabilities and experience (with or without explicit mention of "resume"), and another 23 pages (20%) announced products or upcoming performances. Thus, though these were all personal home pages, they were also personal *business* home pages too.

In American society, however, presentation of one's business background serves an important social function as well. When two people first meet, they generally give each other their names, then their occupations. So, publishing this kind of information on a personal home page serves to announce oneself both to potential social and business contacts.

Another large group (33, or 29%) appeared simply to be enjoying the capability of presenting a home page to the world and displayed no specific purpose other than this. A few home pages were serving miscellaneous other functions: Six of those presenting resume information stated explicitly that they were looking for work. A smattering of others were seeking dates, engaged in political activities, looking for an adopted person's birth parents, etc.

We had expected that the popular usage of the phrase "home page" might elicit a number of references to the personal home page as a "home" in the conventional sense of domicile ("home sweet home," "my humble abode," and the like), but only a half-dozen such cases were found.

On the whole, the creators of the home pages seem to be open to them as a new social form and the pages were relatively free of efforts to carry over old metaphors or forms.

A wide range of types of information was provided on the home pages. Of the content types that were tallied, an average of 5.9 items appeared in each home page. The ten most popular items, in descending order—from 92% to 19%—were e-mail address, name, favorite websites, gender, photo, current work, educational background, hobbies or interests, mailing address, and previous work experience.

The great majority of home pages, 88 (77%), had an internal structure of text, many links, and often contained a menu or contents list at the head of the page. Of the remaining, 10 (9%) of the home pages consisted solely of menus leading to other pages with content and the final 16 (14%) consisted entirely or almost entirely of straight running text, with no or few links. Ninety-six percent of the sample contained links of some sort—to other locations on the page, to other pages or to other websites. The median number of links per page was 14 with the highest number being 215. Forty-one, or 36%, contained links to search engines and 42 (37%) contained links to shareware.

The home pages were observed to contain several features that would not exist or would be different in character in a non-electronic environment. Number of hits to the home page, latest update date and the rubric "under construction," or variants thereof, all appeared on more than a third of the home pages. Intellectual freedom issues from the paper world were addressed here, too, with 25 instances of the free speech blue ribbon and 15 copyright notices. In 20 cases a "sign guestbook" feature enabled visitors to the site to respond to the site in a manner very similar to signing a guestbook and commenting when visiting a real home or museum.

Regarding the home pages' physical appearance, 70 pages (61%) used a colored or patterned background (other than white or grey) and 90 pages (79%) used icons or artwork to represent or illustrate the contents of the pages. One or more motion features appeared in a third of the home pages; just five percent contained audio elements.

Overall, the home pages reviewed displayed a great variety of content and of specific types of formatting within broader formatting approaches.

While some content elements were quite popular, none of them—not even name (90%)—was found on all home pages. Evidently, the creators of these pages felt free to structure them as they wanted and no standardized or required fashionable approach was identified in the sample.

Nor did the pages evidence reliance on any single standard metaphor, such as home page as "home" in the sense of domicile. The closest pattern in the paper world that a substantial minority of the pages resembled was that of the resume, but even those home pages were quite freely and variously structured. In sum, based on this small exploratory sample, it appears that the form and content of personal home pages on the World Wide Web are still quite open and various. Though certain popular features may be found in it, the public social form known as the "personal home page" has not yet developed a fully standardized character and social role, recognized by all. The home page as a social institution is still very much under development.

NOTE

Shaojun Lu was an accomplished scholar in China, having published over 40 journal articles and two books. He was an Associate Professor in the School of Library and Information Science at Wuhan University. He won the Chinese National Scientific and Technological Information System Research Award. He then came to the United States and earned a Ph.D. degree in Information Studies at the University of California at Los Angeles in 1998, with Marcia J. Bates as his doctoral advisor. His career as a tenure-track assistant professor at the State University of New York at Oswego was cut short by his untimely death on March 1, 2000.

REFERENCES

Clyde, L. (1996). The library as information provider: The home page. *The Electronic Library, 14*(6), 549–558.

December, J., & Randall, N. (1994). *The World Wide Web Unleashed.* Indianapolis: SAMS Publishing.

Dougherty, D., & Koman, R. (1994). *The Basic Handbook For Microsoft Windows.* Sebastopol, CA: O'Reilly & Associates.

Falcigno, K., & Green, T. (1995). Home page, sweet home page: Creating a web presence. *Database, 18*(2), 20–28.

Mathews, O. (1974). *The album of carte-de-visite and cabinet portrait photographs 1854–1914.* London: Reedminster Publications.

Morgan, W.D. (Ed.) (1942). *The complete photographer: A complete guide to amateur and professional photography* (Vol. 2). New York: National Educational Alliance.

Spear, B.J. (1995). Preparing pages for the World Wide Web. *Online & CD-ROM Review, 19*(6), 325–327.

van Brakel, P.A., Roeloffze, C., & Van Heerden, A. (1995). Some guidelines for creating World Wide Web home page files. *The Electronic Library, 13*(4), 383–387.

8

Undergraduates' personal academic information management and the consideration of time and task-urgency

ABSTRACT

Young undergraduate college students are often described as "digital natives," presumed to prefer living and working in completely digital information environments. In reality, their world is part-paper/part-digital, in constant transition among successive forms of digital storage and communication devices. Studying for a degree is the daily work of these young people, and effective management of paper and digital academic materials and resources contributes crucially to their success in life. Students must also constantly manage their work against deadlines to meet their course and university requirements. This study, following the "Personal Information Management" (PIM) paradigm, examines student academic information management under these various constraints and pressures. A total of 41 18- to 22-year-old students were interviewed and observed regarding the content, structure, and uses of their immediate working environment within their dormitory rooms. Students exhibited remarkable creativity and variety in the mixture of automated and manual resources and devices used to support their academic work. The demands of a year-long procession of assignments, papers, projects, and examinations increase the importance of time management activities and influence much of their behavior. Results provide insights on student use of various kinds of information technology and their overall planning and management of information associated with their studies.

First published as Mizrachi, D. & Bates, M. J. (2013). Undergraduates' personal academic information management and the consideration of time and task-urgency. *Journal of the American Society for Information Science and Technology, 64*(8), 1590–1607.

Introduction

In an age of extraordinarily rapid turnover in information technologies, university students are on the front lines in mastering and using these new technologies while carrying on with more familiar information management habits and techniques. Understanding how students approach their complex academic information worlds is of primary importance today as academic libraries and educational institutions face the challenge of pioneering new and relevant services in a variety of virtual and print formats under increasing budget constraints.

This article discusses findings from a study of the personal academic information management behaviors of typical undergraduates, ages 18 to 22. This demographic group of students is often described as "digital natives," those individuals who have grown up in a digital, high-tech world. Using ethnographic methods, the study looks at how extensively these students actually integrate digital tools and information into their academic information worlds, their preferences in tools and organizational schemes, and how and under what circumstances they choose to use high- or low-tech tools. The fundamental research question addressed was this: How do undergraduate students manage their academic information ecologies in their dormitory rooms? Findings demonstrate a complexity of behaviors driven by individual personalities and affections as well as by time pressures and constraints, allowing a much richer understanding of our college students than the generic stereotype of the always online and plugged-in technophile.

Historically, information behavior was considered largely in terms of the mental world of the individual—what influenced the choices and actions of the individual person seeking information. Increasingly, however, we are coming to recognize the importance of personally created external structures to our effective utilization of information. The information environment created by an individual is essentially a scaffold, simplifying work with information-intensive tasks by providing external reminders and by physically structuring the information in a way that supports internal mental manipulation and use of it in work or study.

In short, in information-intensive tasks, the individual works within his or her own personally created *information ecology*. Understanding that ecology is essential to a full understanding of information seeking and use. To use another analogy, which is not as far fetched as it may at first appear, spiders live by capturing and eating insects. They do so by spinning a web that ensnares and stores the insects. It would be unimaginable to try to understand spiders as a species without also studying the creation and use of webs by these spiders. Biologists describe the spider-plus-web as the "extended phenotype," that is, the animal combined with the structures it creates in its environment to support living (Dawkins, 1999). To speak of the student's "information ecology" is not merely to use a metaphor. The student working among his or her academic information resources is, in truth, working in an ecology he or she created. Failing to design that ecology well may even be associated with academic failure. The student-plus-academic information ecology is a *combined package that must be understood as a whole*, just as the spider cannot fully be understood without seeing it in relation to the webs it spins.

The study described herein represents a distinctive convergence of theoretical paradigm, study subjects, and research design. The study builds on the paradigm known as "Personal Information Management" or PIM (Jones, 2008). This literature concerns the study of the ways in which people collect, organize, and use the information they need in their immediate work or study environments. The vast literature of information seeking and use addresses many aspects of information behavior, but the most immediately and highly used context of information use—one's desk and local environment—is one of the least explored in the research literature.

Although there is a growing body of PIM literature, most of that literature addresses business and other work environments. We are unaware of any study that addresses this core personal information management behavior of college students. Studying students at this historical moment is of particular interest also because of the rapidly shifting forms of information and communication technologies (ICT) available to them. Implications of this research are of interest to many communities—researchers in information science, PIM, information technology development, education, student counseling, and the world of new technology startups among others.

The study employs ethnographic/naturalistic methods. Ethnographic methods are characterized by fieldwork or observations of phenomena in their natural environments, an approach known as *naturalism* as opposed to designed experiments and laboratory studies. These methods are used to produce detailed and accurate descriptions of a society, culture, or phenomenon. They are particularly well suited to studying students in their work environments, for instance, in their dormitory rooms. Writing specifically about using naturalistic approaches for the study of Personal Information Management, Naumer and Fisher (2007) state: "Naturalistic inquiry techniques can be a powerful means for better understanding contextual factors that affect an individual's PIM style" (p. 77).

In sum, this study investigates how undergraduate students manage their personal academic information ecologies in their dormitory rooms: the content, structure, and organization of those environments, how students apply and use information tools therein, and whether distinct models of information behavior can be discerned. Much is learned about the variety of techniques and tools, both paper and digital, that students use for PIM as well as about their methods of organization and archiving patterns. Among the findings from this study are the importance of time and task-urgency in the students' organization and management systems and how they are primary factors in the flow of their information work. This observation appears to be unique within the relevant literature and has immediate implications for information work flow models.

Review of related work

Literatures relevant to this study include Personal Information Management, both in the management literature and in the information science literature, time in information management, student information seeking, and student "millennials" in relation to information technology.

Personal information management (PIM)

In Malone's (1983) groundbreaking study of the organization of people's desks and offices at their place of employment, he states: "I use the term *desk organization* loosely to include not only the desks, but also the tables, shelves, file cabinets, and other information repositories in people's offices" (p. 100). Participants gave Malone a tour of their office during which they explained "what information was where and why it was there" (p. 100). Two major units of desk organization are identified as "files" and "piles." Both "are ways of collecting groups of elements into larger units . . . files are units where the elements are explicitly titled and arranged in some systematic order . . . piles . . . are the individual elements that are not necessarily titled, and they are not, in general, arranged in any particular order" (pp. 105–106). Malone also describes the two most important functions of desk organization uncovered in his study—a way to find things, and a way to remind the owner of tasks that need to be done, which he calls finding and reminding functions.

Studies in numerous other disciplines outside of information science have followed up on Malone's approach including environmental psychology (Lansdale, Parker, Austin et al., 2011), industrial ergonomics (Lottridge, Chignell, & Straus, 2011), human-computer interaction (Song & Ling, 2011), and design (Wodehouse & Ion, 2010).

Jones is the most active proponent of PIM (2006, 2008). He states that PIM "refers to both the practice and study of the activities a person performs to acquire or create, store, organize, maintain, retrieve, use, and distribute the information needed to compete tasks ... and fulfill various roles and responsibilities" (Jones, 2006, p. 453).

Lansdale (1988) considers the psychological processes involved in the management of personal information, specifically classification and memory. In stressing his point that many of the issues involved in the automation of information management are essentially psychological in nature—particularly recall, recognition and categorization—he creates a theoretical framework for developing user-oriented information management systems.

A parallel line of research can be found in information science that studies the individual's office information organization and management. It began with Soper (1976) and continued with Case (1986, 1991) and Kwasnik (1989). Hartel continued this work with an examination of the arrangement of informational materials in the home by cooking hobbyists (Hartel, 2007). These authors addressed information organizational behaviors, behaviors of specific populations, and how people make classificatory choices when organizing their information. Despite these earlier studies, examining the information world created by individuals is still a relatively underdeveloped part of information behavior research.

Time in information management

"Time is one of the main contextual factors of information seeking" according to Savolainen (2006, p. 110) addressing the question of temporal context as conceptualized in information seeking studies. He notes that "[E]ven though the research abounds in expressions implying temporal contexts ... the temporal factors have rarely been discussed in information studies" (p. 111).

Time as a factor in information management was identified by Kwasnik (1989) in her study of how people organize documents in their own offices. She noted how people distinguished the placing of materials in their offices by the frequency ("very seldom used") or urgency ("must deal with immediately") (p. 208) of their use. In a later publication she stresses that these classificatory decisions are based less on a document's attributes than on the context in which the person finds himself when making this decision—his or her goals, purposes, knowledge, history, etc. (Kwasnik, 1991).

Balter (1997) studied e-mail organization strategies and recognizes that "anti-organization" behaviors, that is, failure to organize, compete with organization behaviors in the same individual when that person is feeling the effects of information overload (i.e., amount of incoming e-mail to process) and time pressure. Undergraduates demonstrate this type of behavior in waves throughout their academic term as assignments and deadlines press upon them. But the general PIM literature does not treat the time factor or its effects with such emphasis or centrality. In the PIM literature, time is considered an element that can be managed through effective personal information behaviors and systems. Time management is an element of task management—scheduling and calendaring tasks in a project, but it is not discussed as a key factor guiding or interfering with an individual's information organization and management. This article draws attention to the time element in a way not typically seen in the PIM literature.

College student information seeking

College students are the subjects of numerous studies of information-seeking behavior (e.g., Gabridge, Gaskell, & Stout, 2008; Kuhlthau, 1991; Weiler, 2005; Whitmire, 2004), Internet-use behavior (e.g., Agosto, 2002; McMillan & Morrison, 2006), library behavior (e.g., Keefer, 1993; Mellon, 1986), research behavior (e.g., Kracker, 2002; Kracker & Wang, 2002; Valentine, 1993; Walters, 2009), information literacy (e.g., Head, 2008; Seamans, 2002), and behavior with technology (e.g., McMillan & Morrison, 2006; Mennecke, Valacich, & Wheeler, 2000; Pena-Shaff, Martin, & Gay, 2001; Weisskirch & Milburn, 2003). For all that has been studied and written about them, however, it is a population whose behaviors within their own academic information worlds have yet to be explored. This section reviews a few papers illustrative of the findings on student information seeking.

Holliday and Li (2004) discuss several studies that explore students' attitudes towards the general research process. They cite a study by Valentine that found that there was often a gap between what their instructors thought of as good academic resources, and the students' ability and lackadaisical efforts to find them. Valentine's study also points to students' chaotic manner of finding information, their heavy reliance on the sources most familiar to them—usually the web, and their preference for convenience and speed (Valentine, 2001, as cited by Holliday & Li, 2004). Other studies indicate students' use of ineffective search strategies generated by their inability to think of and employ a number of alternative terms, synonyms, broader and narrower terms while searching, resulting in poor quality information retrievals. Holliday and Li point out that while a great deal is known regarding students' attitudes and search habits, very few studies attempt to explore their "deeper cognitive and affective behavior in the more holistic context of their research process" (2004, p. 356).

Lee looked at undergraduate information-seeking behavior and asked a question related to aspects addressed in this study: "Do existing [library and information] structures continue to make sense and help users locate needed information in a timely fashion? In view of technological advances, should we find new ways to structure resources to further facilitate information seeking?" (2008, p. 211). She interviewed fifteen students of diverse backgrounds and asked them to describe their research process. One notation she makes is of particular interest for this study:

> Most participants possessed a small collection of their own information sources, too. Some had a subscription [or regular access] to a magazine or a newspaper . . . that was sometimes used for coursework. From time to time, the students consulted the textbooks from current or previous classes and/or other books they had for personal interests. The students across disciplines reported this personal collection habit. Few, however, had saved article printouts from previous classes. One student labeled herself a pack rat and admitted saving everything for later use. Others simply discarded article printouts as soon as they finished the paper or project in hand. (p. 214)

This demonstrates that a personal academic collection culture does exist among undergraduates, although Lee seemed to focus on traditional print items to the exclusion of digital items. This current study uses a broader range of academic information, and looks at the environment and ecologies in which the students interact with it.

Librarians at the University of Rochester in New York hired anthropologist Nancy Fried Foster to lead a study of how students at their institution actually go about writing their research papers (Foster & Gibbons, 2007). Among the many findings from their extensive study, the researchers learned that the physical design of the library and its facilities is not especially compatible with the way students prefer to use their physical study space. The authors also discuss the technologies available to students and what students actually use. They observe, for example, that even though students have laptops, they did not bring them to class. "That is when we discovered how itinerant students were during the day, carrying what they needed for long stretches . . . it was simply not practical for most to include a laptop along with all the other things they brought to classes . . . laptops came out when students planned to be in one place for a while to do their work." (pp. 46–47). This current study has been informed by the methods used in the Rochester study.

Undergraduates today

Digital Natives, also known as the Millennials, the Net-Generation, Net-Gens, and Generation Y, are usually described as young people born between 1982–2000, the age bracket of most undergraduates today. Several institutions support research into the academic, technological, and general lifestyles of these students. Examples of annual national surveys and other studies can be found at websites such as UCLA's Higher Education Research Institute (HERI) (UCLA Graduate School of Education and Information Studies, 2012), Indiana University's projects at the Survey Research Center (Indiana University Center for Postsecondary Research, 2012), and the University of Michigan's College Student Experiences Questionnaire Assessment Program (University of Michigan, 2012). Most of the authors reviewed below base their findings on national surveys and studies.

In 2002, the Pew Internet and American Life Project released a major report on the use of the Internet by college students and how they have incorporated it into their education and social lifestyles (Jones, 2002). The report covers use of Internet features such as e-mail, instant messaging (IM), recreational online browsing, and downloadable music files. It found that as a group, college students are early adopters of the Internet incorporating new uses of its features before other population groups. Purposes for Internet use among students fell into two broad categories: educational and social. In their academic environments they reported using the Internet to contact professors, conduct research, work on collaborative projects with other students, and receive messages from academically oriented e-mail services. In their social lives they use the Internet for social communications, for entertainment, to stay in touch, and forward messages to friends and family. The study concluded that for college students, the Internet is "integrated into their daily communication habits and has become a technology as ordinary as the telephone or television" (Jones, 2002, p. 2). This report is still cited extensively as a benchmark of students' behaviors with technology in the early 21st century.

In the years since its publication, use of new communication technologies and features has proliferated among college students. In recognition of the speed with which the technological landscape evolves, a second study was undertaken over three academic terms between Fall 2005–Fall 2006 to investigate students' use of the Internet and to compare results to the 2002 study (Jones, Johnson-Yale, Millermaier, & Perez, 2009, p. 1). This report acknowledges the impact of social networking sites, especially Facebook, on the students' Internet use and behaviors, but reports that in many ways, their behaviors changed little since the earlier study. The report discusses the rise of blogging habits among undergraduates, but is too early to detail the impact of the surge of smart-phone usage which allows easy access to the Internet and other online applications.

Oblinger (2003; Oblinger & Hawkins, 2005) not only discusses the characteristics of today's college students, she stresses that these students are markedly different from previous generational groups. Millennials, as Oblinger calls them, tend to be visual learners, preferring to acquire their knowledge from a television or computer screen to text-heavy print materials. Having grown up with Sesame Street and cable music television stations like MTV with their short clips and fast changing action, they seem to have little patience for the slower, more traditional pedagogical methods of higher education. Multitasking is the norm.

They also prefer hands-on methods when learning. Concepts should be introduced at the students' point of need when they perceive the imme-diate worth or application. Most of their scholarly motivation reflects an academic climate that emphasizes earning good grades (an extrinsic form of motivation) rather than an altruistic pursuit of knowledge for its own pleasure. They are used to a high degree of instant gratification, especially with information on the web, and are very concerned with saving time.

Research design and methods

Within the broad topic of how students manage their academic information ecologies, the following specific questions are addressed in this article:

1. What are the contents of these ecologies?

2. How are these environments structured and organized?

3. How do students apply and use information tools within this ecology?

4. Can distinct patterns of information behavior be discerned?

Academic information is defined in this study as the information collected and generated by students for the purpose of facilitating or fulfilling their needs for coursework, scholarly research, and institutional requirements. As students collect academic information for their particular needs it becomes their *personal* academic information, which they shape into an actual physical milieu in their dormitory rooms and school backpacks. They create these information environments through their inclusion of physical and digital tools and carriers for actions, such as studying, reading, writing, sorting, piling, reminding, and so on. The dynamic properties within the environment and students' cognitive and physical interactions with the information constitute a personal academic information ecology.

The students sampled were limited to those living in campus dormitories. The relatively uniform conditions found in dormitory facilities should help minimize factors emanating from variations of family, social, economic, spatial circumstances, and commuting conditions that exist among students living in other types of housing. Dorm living is a broadly shared experience among college students throughout the United States, and there is an identifiable dormitory culture as discussed by sociologists, anthropologists, and scholars of higher education (e.g., Blum, 2009; Goffman, 1961; Moffatt, 1989; Nathan, 2005).

Approximately 9,400 undergraduates live in the University of California at Los Angeles (UCLA) campus residence halls out of a total undergraduate population of more than 26,000 during the academic year, defined here as three 10-week quarters (www.orl.ucla.edu). Student dormitories are located in the northwest section of campus, between 0.6 and 1.0 miles from most classrooms on the east side of campus. UCLA authorities are very chary of issuing permission to do research with undergraduate dormitory residents. It is a common request, and few opportunities are provided. The authorities felt that this study was particularly apropos to the students' own needs and so agreed to it. Students were then recruited through advertising within the dorms.

The ethnographic approach, developed by anthropologists and sociologists, has, as a central tenet, the creation of an understanding of a phenomenon as experienced by and through the eyes of its participants. Pollner described how ethnography can be used as a tool to discover "the extraordinary organization of the ordinary" (1987, p. xvii). Because this study sought to uncover the students' organic information systems, that is, the behaviors and systems they develop in their own living spaces, ethnographic methods seemed most appropriate, as they would allow students to describe their physical and digital study worlds as they saw them and interacted with them.

The ethnographic approach concentrates on qualitative depth of interaction with the study subjects, rather than breadth or statistical representativeness of categories. However, all students shared the basic requirements of living in a UCLA dorm and being between 18 and 22 years old and enrolled in a baccalaureate program at UCLA. Eight students lived in single occupancy rooms, and the rest shared their rooms with one or two roommates. The original intent was to recruit 18 to 24 students, but interest was high, and a total of 41 were studied. The final set consisted of 28 women and 13 men, with a mixed racial/ethnic background reflective of the campus (and the Southern California community) as a whole. The numbers of students in their first through fourth years were 11, 20, 4, and 6, respectively. Twenty-two students were in the sciences, 11 in the social sciences, 7 in the arts/humanities, and one was "don't know."

Using multiple methods to test the same question, sometimes known as triangulation, is known to strengthen the validity of the findings through a cross-examination of answers. Three methods for gathering data were employed: 1) guided tours by the students of their academic environments, supported by video and photographic inventories, 2) semistructured interviews following an interview protocol, and 3) free-write descriptions by the students themselves of their information environment and behaviors.

By sequencing these elements in this manner, the students had maximum freedom to identify elements of importance to them in the environment, and to shape their descriptions as desired, with minimal influence from the investigator. Only after they identified elements of interest would the investigator then pursue further questions. Sample portions of actual tours can be viewed at: http://youtube/ b4sVSMkwvFl ("Lynn"), http://youtube/4z7QkyqGnl4 ("Oscar"), and http://youtu.be/3BViz6Lyumc ("Olivia"). The tour, which was video- and audio-recorded, usually lasted between three to nine minutes during which the student showed the contents and basic organizational structure of her or his environment. The rest of the time with the student was audio-recorded. These interviews generally lasted between 20 and 45 minutes. Specific probing questions arising from the tour and questions on other topics from the interview protocol followed (see the interview protocol at Mizrachi, 2011, pp. 263–267). Photographs were taken of items and areas in the environment that seemed particularly noteworthy based on the student's emphasis on them, or the interviewer's interpretation of their uniqueness or typicality.

After the student and researcher completed the semistructured interview and any other relevant discussions about the environment and student behaviors, the researcher then asked the student to write about "How I organize or manage the information I need for school in my residence hall room," for up to 10 minutes using any means preferred. Most wrote short essays, some used an outline or bullet format, and some preferred to sketch their environments.

Several students commented on how much fun the interview was, how interesting the topic was, or that they had never thought of their behaviors in such a way. In general it appeared that the students enjoyed the opportunity to share and talk about themselves. Student names used in this text are pseudonyms.

Using the qualitative methods of Glaser and Strauss's Grounded Theory approach (Glaser & Strauss, 1967), transcripts of each interview were coded and more than 100 codes listed, some more specific than others depending on the details provided by a particular student. Concept categories included the following: contents of the environment, structure/organization, use/application of tools, information behaviors and flow, evolution/development of the environment, and social/cultural influences. Tables of the concepts and categories were created, enabling efficient visual analysis. Data from each student's experience were thus compared and contrasted through repeated ventures into the data, and general behavioral tendencies and variations were then drawn. It is these behavioral tendencies and patterns that are described in the next section.

Findings

In this section, the nature of the information ecologies created by students in their dormitory rooms is first examined. Here, students store their academic resources and, usually, do their most intensive studying. Then we turn to the dynamic processes of acquiring and transmitting academic information. First we examine the paper and electronic tools and channels used by the students, then turn to the specific means students use to acquire, organize, and manage their information resources. In the subsequent Discussion section, we draw out several major themes that appeared in the analysis of these data.

Academic information environments

As one first-year student stated:

> In order to stay organized for school, I try to keep things in a
> certain place on my desk or in my drawers all the time so that
> I will always know where to find it. For example, I keep all my
> binders and notebook paper in my bottom drawer so whenever
> I need to restock or find use for it I know where to access it.
> As for my books for classes, they all sit on my desk. Also on

my desk are pens, pencils, index cards, and [sticky] notes—
essential to being a student [here]. On my laptop, I try to keep
subfolders for different courses I am taking at the time so that
I can easily find documents I've typed for the class. (Debbie)

To open the interviews, students were asked where they keep their
academic "stuff." They always began at their desk area, which they indicated was the focal point for their information environment. Each desk
contains a shallow keyboard tray on the left side, three drawers reaching
to the floor on the right, a chair, and a two-tiered bookshelf, which some
students remove and relocate on the floor nearby. Many students also attach
a desk-extension, like a table-leaf, which increases the depth of their desk
by approximately ten inches. Figure 1 shows typical examples of students'
desk organization.

Students post academic information on their walls (which are lined
with bulletin-board material in some rooms), and side surfaces of dressers,
closets, bookshelves, and doors, especially those furnishings and areas
that are closest to the students' desks. Figure 2 shows multiple calendars
posted on a student's wall.

Shelves and drawers in closets, dressers, and bed frames are used as
storage areas for various types of academic information, and piles of information carriers and repositories can usually be found on top of furnishings
with convenient flat surfaces, such as dressers, tables, mini-refrigerators,
televisions, and window sills. Occasionally, piles of academic information
can be found on the floor or bed, especially before major deadlines or
exams. Most students who report using their bed as an additional study
space do so for what they call light study tasks such as reviewing or light
reading, but prefer to sit at their desks for tasks requiring more focus. Many
use space under their beds for storing academic materials. Closets in the
rooms usually extend to the ceiling to maximize space, but it is difficult
for some students to access and the inconvenience becomes a barrier to
fully utilizing this space.

Four types of information were identified in the students' academic
environments: course-related, institutional, extracurricular, and supplementary. This study focuses specifically on the first two types. These
types of information came in both paper and electronic forms. (Because
most of the latter is digital today, the terms *digital* and *electronic* will be
used interchangeably.)

Physical information contents of the rooms include notebooks, binders,
folders, boxes, planners, calendars, books, and course readers, singly and in
files and piles. Externally produced materials include textbooks, personal

FIG. 1. *Photos of desk organization.*

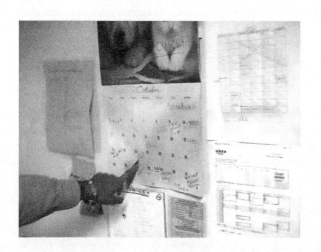

FIG. 2. *Multiple calendars and schedules on wall.*

books, reference books, library books, newspapers, magazines, course readers, handouts distributed in class (power points, readings, syllabi), fliers, announcements, and calendars. Self-produced materials include class notes, assignments (homework, papers, drafts), exams, note-cards, lists, reminders, and print-outs from digital sources.

Digital contents of the students' academic information environments are more numerous, open-ended, and challenging to list than physical contents. Types of digital contents found and used can be divided into seven categories: social networking sites, general communication sites and applications (public e-mail, instant messaging, texting, etc.), academic communication sites (institutional e-mail, student portals, course Web pages, etc.), electronic publications (e-journals and articles, e-zines, etc.), software applications, academic websites (created specifically for academic, educational, or reference purposes such as "dictionary.com," and "sparknotes.com"), and general Internet sites.

Transport tools (backpacks, book bags, etc.), allow students to re-create an academic environment in the library, study lounge, or other space for the same types of tasks they perform in their dorm rooms. These carriers are also used as an organizational tool and for storing some components of the environment such as stationery supplies and materials of immediate or near-immediate use.

From the descriptions of the students' academic information environments above, a visualization can be constructed which shows the different environmental spheres as concentric circles focused around the desk area, room, campus spaces, and off-campus spaces. The transport tools penetrate and move through all of these spheres. Figure 3 (overleaf) illustrates the construction of students' academic information environment.

Use of tools and channels

Students in this study demonstrate a broad variety of behaviors and preferences in the use and application of information tools for their academic tasks. For example, Jackie states "[My laptop is the] basis for everything... I do everything on my computer and take it with me everywhere," while Charles always keeps his computer in his room and prefers using traditional paper tools for many of his needs. Ursula uses many of the features in her cell phone: "Much of my academic information is also in my phone. I record a lot of things in my phone. Sometimes I even take notes under the memo pad of my phone," but Nancy rarely uses her supplemental phone functions: "It takes longer to write or text in my phone than write in my paper planner."

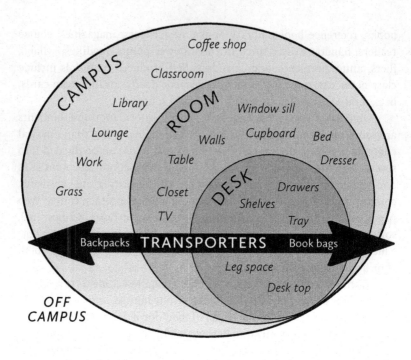

FIG. 3. *Academic information spaces.*

This section describes how students use specific tools within their academic information environment and for their academic tasks. The tools most commonly used by students in this study and discussed below are their computers, including software, Internet and social networking sites, format preferences for reading, and cell phones and their various functions.

Computers All of the students in this study own a laptop, which they consider the key element in their life as a student: "Like most people my age, my computer is kind of my central device for academic and social networking" (Yolanda). "I would probably say that academic information-wise, all of it centers around my MacBook. I honestly don't know how people in the past were able to go through school without a computer" (Zoey).

Interviews with the students took place in October and November 2009, before the public release of the Apple iPad and other more recent innovations. All of the students at the time of this study own at least one laptop. One student also uses a desktop computer. Almost half of the students reported that they regularly leave their computers in their rooms and do *not* bring them to class. Six reasons were identified for doing so:

1) security concerns (theft or damage to their computer); 2) professors' attitudes against computers in the classroom; 3) technical reasons; 4) the size and bulk of their computers; 5) open computers provide too many distractions to focus properly in class; and 6) individual learning styles and preferences to write notes by hand on paper.

Many students take notes on their computers for certain kinds of classes, especially large lecture classes in the social sciences and humanities fields, but find digital note-taking is not practical for other kinds of classes such as small discussion-based groups, and science and mathematics classes. The latter frequently use formulas, graphs, and other graphic forms of information that cannot be easily represented on a laptop.

Software and Internet All the students in this study use a word processing program as well as other standard programs in the Microsoft Office suite such as PowerPoint, Excel, or their equivalents. The next most commonly mentioned type of software among participants is a digital Post-it or note-pad feature, which they use for list-making and reminders. Digital clocks, calendars, alarms, and color-coding features are also used. Several students mentioned using iTunes, Adobe Acrobat, Google docs, and different photo applications such as Photoshop.

On the Internet, students overwhelmingly access Google, Wikipedia, and Dictionary.com for quick information needs, beginning their research assignments, and for spelling, thesaurus, and fact checks. Other commonly mentioned sites include those recommended by their instructors and classmates, Google Scholar, the Library webpages (catalogs, databases and e-resources), news sites, and e-mail. For more details about these students' online behaviors, see Mizrachi (2010).

As an example of bookmarked sites typical among the students, Janice, a freshman, has her student portal page (my.ucla.edu, an institutional information site to which students can log on for personalized information pertaining to all aspects of their academic progress and career), Facebook, the Library catalog, "Sparknotes" (a site offering study guides and discussion forums on various academic subjects), a job search site, and her e-mail. Other academically related Web pages commonly found bookmarked include quick reference sites, course websites, and other sites specific to the institution or their future profession.

Course websites and features Online course websites are an essential tool for all students in this study and are accessed regularly for communication and announcements from their instructors and classmates. Different instructors use various features and integrate different kinds of online requirements, so the student experience is often conditioned to some degree by faculty expectations. The most commonly mentioned uses by students in this study are for accessing announcements, homework assignments, readings, lecture notes, and PowerPoint slides. Usually the latter two sources are accessed, downloaded, and often printed before the corresponding lecture, and students follow along, or, more commonly, take their class notes on them either electronically or by hand. Ten of the students report participating in online discussion forums through their course website. Some post questions, read classmates' questions, and use the answers and discussions as a review or study guide for their exams.

Several students report accessing audiocasts and podcasts of class lectures through their course Web pages. They use the podcasts as "make-ups" for when they miss a class, and as supplementary sessions. Students usually view or listen to these broadcasts on their laptops, but some listen to the audiocasts on their iPods or MP3 players. Eric explains "I don't [audio] record lectures but lectures are usually podcasted. I can easily download them. . . . I usually just use the standard download utility and then use iTunes to manage my music, and broadcasts, and whatnot. And I usually just put them on my iPod or listen to them straight away on my computer speakers."

Social networking All students in this study have a Facebook account that they use primarily for social purposes. Other sites and social communication tools mentioned by students include Zynga (browser-based games that can be played alone and as an application on social networking websites), Tumblr (a blogging platform), Twitter (a social networking/microblogging system), Skype (a software application that allows users to make voice calls, chats, and video conferencing over the Internet), and ooVoo (an audio/video instant messaging client for Windows).

Most of the students in this study recall using Facebook on at least one occasion for an academic purpose during their undergraduate years. Most common uses are posting or chatting about homework questions with classmate "friends," and organizing study groups: "I create an event then invite people" (Iris). Vivi worked on a group project with her class-mates through Facebook. They gathered together in the same room, each with their own laptop, and posted their working document into a single Facebook thread. "We thought it more efficient for our lab report. Each worked on a different section. This way we could talk about it, share ideas easily, but still work on our own parts. It was easier than e-mail." Elaine often takes pictures of her professor's notes on the classroom whiteboard with her camera and then posts them on Facebook to share with her classmate "friends." No student reported "friending" a professor, though a couple had become "friends" with TAs, and one became a fan of a UCLA librarian's Facebook page.

Format preferences for reading

> In an ideal world I would prefer to have [my readings in print] because it is definitely easier to have it in front of you because you can highlight it and stuff. But I definitely prefer when [classes] have online readings because you don't have to buy a textbook. And it's more convenient, you can just click on it. Yeah, it saves you money and then also it's nice when you don't have papers all over the place. . . . But I definitely do get more out of [the reading] when it's on paper. (William)

Students in this study show a mixture of habits and preferences when they need to read academic information for an academic task. Most state a definite preference for reading in print rather than online because reading online 1) causes eyestrain, 2) offers too many distractions, 3) print is more portable and easier to use, and, most commonly mentioned, 4) students can interact with the text much better in print than online. Highlighting and taking notes on the print copy is important to them and many state that being physically involved with the reading is how they learn best. In actuality, however, many of the students do most of their reading online because they don't want to waste paper, don't have their own printer, paper and/or ink are expensive, or it is just more convenient.

Studies are beginning to show a relationship between the type of reading format and the cognitive process of information absorption. "There is a close relationship between the media we use to read—books or digital technology—and the way we read and think. . . . Digital technology is often preferable for searching and scanning short snippets . . . slow reading of books is still essential for nurturing literacy and the capacity for extended linear thought" (Miedema 2009, pp. 19–20).

Cell phones All of the students in this study have cell phones, which they keep close at hand and easily accessible at all times. Debbie keeps hers on a chain with her student identification card and room key, which she calls the "three essentials of a UCLA student." It is important to note that while some students own a current smart phone model, many others have older or simpler models that offer only a minimum of features. The five

FIG. 4. *Electronic and paper sticky notes.*

most common uses cited by the students are calling, texting, alarm clock/ reminder, calendar, and notes/memo.

The great majority of students use texting "a lot!" but some dislike it and limit it or do not use it. Alarm clock and reminder functions are also highly used by the students in this study for both academically related purposes and personal tasks. They are set not just for waking up in the morning, but also to help them remember meetings and other appointments.

Some, like Yolanda and Steve, use their calendar applications as their primary scheduler and planning tool, which they coordinate with their e-mail accounts. Several others however, note that they only use the calendar feature on occasion or rarely, stating they prefer using paper calendars and planners.

Though twenty of the forty-one participants in this study say they use the notepad or memo function on their phone, several of them qualified their use as only sometimes or rarely. For writing quick notes to themselves, there is a wide variety of responses: typing it in a text, writing it in a paper planner or scratch paper, or even, as eight students mentioned, writing it on their hands. See Figures 4 and 5.

Acquisition, manipulation, organization, and archiving of academic information

Acquisition Course material enters the students' domain through multiple actors, and contains multiple elements. Instructors distribute print handouts, use course webpages and email to disseminate PowerPoint slides, readings, assignments, communications and announcements; they

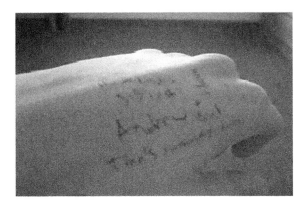

FIG. 5. *Information written on a student's hand.*

assign course readers, lecture supplements, and textbooks, present lectures and lead discussions in class, and provide consultation and guidance in office hours, all of which generates course material information with which the students must engage and interact. Teaching assistants, tutors, classmates and outside consultants such as librarians and knowledgeable acquaintances can also contribute to this corpus through verbal discussions, communications, sharing and recommendations of relevant sources. The students themselves generate course material when they interact with the information to produce notes and study aids, work on their homework and practice exams, conduct research, or find supplementary sources and information which they consult and record to expand upon their understanding of the topic or complete an assignment. Academic information is thus collected and imbibed through both conscious action and passive reception in a multitude of ways and formats.

Jones uses the act of highlighting a passage in a document for further understanding and use as an example of the interwoven nature of information management and information use, one of the main themes in his book on PIM (Jones, 2008, pp. 59–60). From the moment students anticipate an encounter with coursework information, they begin engaging in preliminary management decisions. Even before leaving their rooms for classes on the other side of campus, they must consciously decide how they will record their notes, and bring along the paper or electronic means to do so in their backpacks. If they have printed out slides or lecture notes from the course Web page, should they transport them in a folder containing all information from that course, or just the information relevant to that day, week, or particular unit of study?

Most students in this study use separate spiral notebooks for each class to capture their raw notes when taking them by hand. Others use loose leaf pages or scratch paper. Some later copy their notes into digital form or into another notebook to make them neater and more organized for review or reinforcement later. Lynn says "I'm taking four classes so I have four different notebooks." Hans also has one notebook for each class, but class notes for those sequential courses taken over two or three quarters, such as chemistry and math, are kept chronologically in the same notebook for easy reference.

Many instructors require course readers or lecture supplements for their classes, and it is common for students to take their class notes directly onto these paper-based tools. This was especially common in science classes such as chemistry. Instructors often post PowerPoint slides or lecture notes ahead of time on the course webpage, which students then print out and take their notes on. A few will pull the slides up online in class and take their notes digitally. Students who took notes electronically did so using Microsoft Word, Notebook View, or Google Docs, an Internet-based word processor. Students using minicomputers transfer notes they take in class to their regular laptops by using a Universal Serial Bus (USB or "flash drive") or e-mailing them as attachments.

One implicit theme in student comments is that their choices in recording lecture material is in part stimulated by the way the instructor uses PowerPoint. In some cases, the PowerPoint contains essentially the whole lecture; in other cases the PowerPoint slides just list what are essentially titles of topics covered, with little content, whereas other cases fall in between, where much of the lecture is on the slides, but students add supplementary information that the instructor provides in class. This raises the question of what the optimal design and use of PowerPoint slides might actually be. How can professors best use PowerPoint to help students learn? Despite the very pervasive use of this software in society and in education, and despite hundreds of articles written on it, a search of the *Web of Science* revealed only a smattering of empirical studies to test the best use of PowerPoint, with no dominant research theme (e.g., Griffin, Mitchell, & Thompson, 2009; Savoy, Proctor, & Salvendy, 2009). Much more needs to be learned.

Other forms of course materials in print format include those they acquire through purchase or loan: textbooks, course readers, reserve material from the library, library books, and notes borrowed from friends and acquaintances. Most students in this study seek ways to minimize costs by using strategies such as purchasing used books, purchasing books through discount online venders, finding materials through the Facebook "Marketplace" application, photocopying whenever possible, or borrowing them from the library or an acquaintance. Course material in digital format with which the students interact include: e-mails, class discussion board postings, online readings from the course webpage, online reserve material, e-books, e-journals, scholarly and public webpages, pod-casts, and audio-casts.

Manipulation and organization Students develop and employ strategies to assist their cognitive absorption and understanding of the information. They must effectively integrate the information with other course material and organize it all in a system that allows easy access for quick reference and referral. Though some actions and strategies can be applied in both print and online formats, students in this study use a greater variety of strategies when they interact with their paper-based material.

After class, in their information environments in their dorms or elsewhere, most students continue to interact with their raw notes in their original notebooks. Some students copy their notes into a second notebook both to reinforce their understanding of the material and to make its appearance neater and more organized, thus making future reference and review easier. Nancy even adds her own references to the textbook or other sources in her copied notes.

Xena uses one spiral notebook for all her classes but upon returning home she tears out the pages, groups them together by class, and places them into a pile on her desk. At a later time she files them into separate class binders in chronological order. Charles and Elaine both prefer to take their raw notes on scratch paper that they have saved over time or found in recycling bins. Elaine files them directly into course binders in her room, but Charles, a fourth year bioengineering student, copies them into a spiral notebook.

Manipulation may involve making alterations to appearance, format or location of the information. Cognitive and physical interactions with academic information include reviewing, reading, writing, copying, sorting, piling, filing, discarding, deleting, archiving, placing (purposefully setting information within the environment for accessibility, visibility, and reminding), shifting (e.g., moving information carriers from one pile, file, or side of the desk to another etc.), and prioritizing (by urgency, or importance). These actions occur throughout the various stages of the student's work flow, not necessarily in a linear manner, and depend upon temporal factors as well as individual personality and habits.

Organizing physical materials Students tend to place the work they intend to do first on top of their desks within comfortable reach of where they sit. Three general behavioral patterns present themselves: keeping coursework and materials in their backpack until ready for immediate use, pulling out all materials at once and piling them in consistent locations on or around the desk until use, or less systematic behaviors that vary in consistency. Contents of the piles are most commonly found in either chronological order (usually the most recent items on top, older items further below) or urgency, with items relevant to the tasks that are most urgent on top. In general, students create a piling or filing system for their coursework that enables them to find the physical information they need when they need to interact with it by grouping current information together by course and maintaining those groupings by chronology and urgency. Often a pile will also serve as a reminder or motivator for work yet to be done. Working their way through a pile provides satisfaction and serves as a visual reminder of accomplishment. Highlighting and other uses of color coding are common strategies for interaction, as are creating note cards, and among chemistry students, building physical models of information they need to internalize.

Nonurgent materials Strategies for keeping nonurgent but still relevant materials among the students in this study include: filing material into folders or binders which are kept in the immediate environment; creating separate piles that are organized by course topic and placed in specific locations within the environment such as a bookshelf or drawer; and "stashing" the information in a convenient location. Contents of these stashes are in no particular order and may or may not have further uses.

Archiving/retention/disposal Students in this study show an overall tendency to retain used course material after the completion of the course for various reasons with a variety of thoroughness and sophistication. Some only retain their digital materials, but most students do retain selections of their physical books, readings, notes and projects, and a few claim to keep everything. Reasons given for retention are the following: 1) keep for future reference and referral, 2) share or pass material on to other students, 3) the course material was especially interesting, 4) they were especially proud of achievements in the class, and sometimes 5) just keep for sentimental reasons or habit. It is also not unusual for students to retain course material from high school and even earlier.

Organizing digital materials Most discussions of academic digital material organizational schemes and interactions centered on Word documents or the equivalent, and the course readings and PowerPoints students had downloaded, but a few also touched on e-mail management. Several digital organizational schemes are present among the students in this study, and a small minority does not systematically organize their digital course material but instead relies on search features. The most common organizational method found was a hierarchical system of folders in the My Documents program (or its equivalent) headed by a folder titled "college" (or its equivalent), year, quarter, and class. Variations of this method are less hierarchical and use fewer folder categories; for example, filing the documents in the appropriate class folder within the appropriate year but not by quarter. A second common method is simply to keep current work on the desktop and upon completion either delete it or file it straight into My Documents (or its equivalent). In their study of students' organizational strategies of personal online academic information, Hardof-Jaffe, Hershkovitz, Abu-Kishk, Bergman, and Nachmias (2009) also found that "[t]he folder hierarchy is the standard mechanism for organizing personal information in digital environments" (p. 3). They found four patterns of folder creation but the design of this study is so different that it is not possible to directly compare their results.

Within the online environment, students create ways to manipulate their academic information to assist them in their learning and studying tasks. Some students execute these manipulations entirely online, and others use a combination of both virtual and physical strategies. Students' discussions of how they study and process their online materials do not reveal as many varieties or as much sophistication as the strategies used when the course material is in print and physical formats. Most strategies appear to be modified transferences of practices developed in print rather than completely novel innovations.

E-mail organization E-mail is the primary tool for academic communication. All of the students who discussed e-mail behaviors use multiple e-mail accounts. Even though they all receive an official UCLA e-mail account, most prefer to maintain a previous account as their principal site. Many manage their multiple accounts by forwarding incoming messages to a single address, and they often leave their e-mail open whenever they are on their computer or use an online or phone application to notify them of a new message. Of the 70 students who first contacted this researcher in answer to the recruitment fliers, 25 used their UCLA accounts, 23 used Gmail, nine used Yahoo!, five used Hotmail, and one each used sbcglobal, live.com, and a work e-mail. E-mail folders organized by subject matter are often employed as management strategies or students search by key word.

Digital archives Parallel archival preferences can be found among students for retaining both their physical and digital course materials. Individual personalities appear to drive students' practice of minimal retention, selected retention, or comprehensive retention.

Institutional information

This study reveals only a limited number of organization and management systems specifically for interacting and maintaining institutional information, unlike the wide variety of methods found with course materials. These methods are the same types used for archiving course materials. Most of the students keep the physical documents and materials that they feel important enough to save for further reference or referral in a consistent place so that they know where to find it when it is needed. This may be piled on a designated spot on a desk or closet shelf; piled with similar material in a desk drawer; filed in a vertical file container; or filed in a designated binder, and some types may be posted on a wall or bulletin board. Institutional information received electronically—almost exclusively by e-mail, is usually filed in a "college" or similar folder, in document format, or an e-mail account.

Ancillary strategies and tools

Ancillary strategies in the academic information ecology are those purposeful actions that support a student's information management and organizational goals. They are not the primary outcomes of information organization and management, but an integral and conscious part of the process. Students in this study discussed three strategies that they use to help them manage the information relevant to their tasks and roles as students: planning, noting, and reminding.

Planning is the formulation of a scheme or method to accomplish an academic task. It can include deconstructing a project or goal into smaller components and mini-goals and prioritizing those components. It can also include scheduling component tasks—meshing them into a manageable timeframe by assigning dates and times.

Reminding actions are those whose outcomes cause the student to remember or think of a specific task.

Noting is the recording of "information scraps"—"short, self-contained personal notes that fall outside of traditional filing schemes" (Bernstein, Van Kleek, Karger, & Schraefel, 2008). Though it may result in reminding, noting differs from a reminding action because its primary outcome is a record for referral or reference.

For each of these strategies, students use enabling actions such as jotting, list-making, outlining, ordering, sorting, color coding, highlighting, posting, and placing. Various tools used for executing these actions include paper planners, paper and electronic calendars, paper and electronic post-its, Word documents, electronic spreadsheets, note-paper, the student's hand, scratch paper, memo and text functions on the phone, alarms, and whiteboards. See examples in Figures 2, 4, and 5. Iris and Kathy discussed how they increased the efficiency of their ancillary strategies after their freshman years by expending more effort on their noting, planning, and reminding behaviors.

Sophistication of organizational systems show a pattern of development as students progress through their academic careers and the number of documents they interact with and maintain grows. This is true with both their physical and digital formats. In part, it may be the natural consequence of a growing and dynamic collection. Obviously the new freshmen are dealing with much less material than the upper classmen, and many appear to be developing their schemes as they go along. Quantities of material may also depend on the characteristics of the students' classes or major. Several examples of second year students making conscious efforts at improving their organizational systems were noted; upper division students have successfully made the transition to college and learned how to balance their independence with their responsibilities. Observing the environments of students in all stages of college and hearing them discuss their organization methods brings this into sharp focus.

Discussion

In this section, three emergent themes arising from the study are discussed: 1) variety of information behaviors and hybrid use of tools, 2) information organization and archival methods, 3) temporal arc of student information management.

Variety of information behaviors and hybrid use of tools

Individuality of behaviors Individuality of adult personal information management behaviors and practices is well documented in the PIM literature. "People vary greatly in their approaches to keeping and organizing information. Even people in the same work situation show tremendous variation" (Jones, 2008, p. 127). According to Gwizdka and Chignell: ". . . [E]ven people who have quite similar profiles with respect to job and demographics can exhibit huge observable differences in PIM-related behaviors, their choices of strategy, and their preferences in tools. These differences apply both with respect to paper-based information management and to the management of electronic information" (2007, p. 207). Gwizdka and Chignell note there are so many variables affecting individual behaviors, both external to the person and internal, that explaining causality may not be possible at this point in the research. However, they do conclude that "Individual differences are contextually dependent, and they respond to changing situations and task demands dynamically" (p. 217).

This current study of undergraduates' information practices clearly shows that a broad spectrum of individual information behaviors and preferences also exists among students. It is unfortunate then, that this demographic group is so easily stereotyped in popular media as well as by academic institutions. Carlson writes about the "Millennials" in the Chronicle of Higher Education: "They are smart but impatient. They expect results immediately. They carry an arsenal of electronic devices—the more portable the better" (Carlson, 2005). UCLA Magazine published an article in July 2010 titled "R U Talking 2 Me?" that discusses the impact of new technologies on communication, culture and education. The first sentence begins: "In a world where it's obsolete to note that laptops are the new spiralbound notebooks . . ." (Hewitt, 2010).

Findings from among the students in this study show that these sorts of assumptions are overgeneralized and inaccurate for this population. Individuality of behaviors among undergraduates should be as recognized and respected as it is among adults. Laptops have not replaced spiral notebooks for all note-taking purposes, for example, and preference for reading important academic material in print format is still found among most of the students. Although some use their phone features or computer applications for noting important information and dates, many others prefer a paper planner, post-its, or even his or her hand! Furthermore, high-technology behaviors and preferences are not necessarily consistent under varying contexts and circumstances even within individuals. We saw, for example, that Jackie takes her computer everywhere with her, but is highly dependent on her paper planner, and for certain classes takes notes in her spiral notebook.

Learning styles and information styles The recognition of the spectrum of individual behaviors is important for educators and educational institutions when policies are being considered that try to unify or narrow the students' PIM choices. Barreau (2008) writes: "Past studies suggest PIM behaviors are highly personal, idiosyncratic, and contextual and there is evidence that at least some behaviors persist over time" (p. 2). Administrators and educators are very familiar with theories of learning styles (individual approaches or ways of learning), and the need for varieties of pedagogical methods to address these differences in learning styles so that each individual can best fulfill her or his potential. It becomes apparent that there are individual *information styles* too. These appear to be based in endogenous factors within each individual, and may or may not be tied to learning styles. But to attempt to implement institutional programs based on the assumption that all students need or even want to use the newest technology (e.g., iPads for all students) is inherently unfair to those students whose information styles and preferences may differ.

The students in this study often appear to give great thought to the tools they use for their ancillary strategies as well as other information tasks. Even when they see their peers do similar information tasks differently, they express confidence that they are using the appropriate tool *for them*, and it seems presumptuous to try to convince students otherwise. Students who are pressured or socialized into adopting expected behaviors may never even have the opportunity to discover which methods work best for them, and this in itself may act as a barrier to fulfilling their potential.

Hybridity of tools and styles Beagrie (2005) refers to personal digital collections as extensions of physical artifacts used as external memory and reference aids and recognizes a shift in collection format "from physical to hybrid to digital" (p. 1). Whether or when this shift to a total digital world will materialize is not within the scope of this study. But current behavioral tendencies of the student participants here show a hybrid use of high-tech and traditional formats, tools, and collections rather than a reflexive rush towards total embracement of the newest gadgets and applications. Standard information tools for all students include both physical—books, notebooks, binders, paper and stationery, as well as digital—laptop computers, cell phones, and their respective applications. Students' choice of tools and formats to use for their various tasks and under various circumstances appears to be driven by cognitive styles, learning styles, information styles, and personality traits.

It is possible that digital native students do not even recognize the distinction between the different formats as sharply as older digital immigrants do. Growing up in a digital world allows for an attitude that considers technical gadgets a natural part of life. They are simply part of a repository of "stuff" students use for many things including academics. Comparatively, the clothes in their closet are "stuff" they wear for different occasions and different circumstances, even though they consist of different "formats," for example, shirts, tank tops, sweaters, and so on. What they choose to wear and when depends primarily on the context or the occasion as well as the students' personalities and tastes. The extent of a student's array of "stuff" may be constrained by outside factors such as socio-economic status or cultural practice, but the variety of behaviors possible within those limitations is still immense and reflects individual personalities, tastes and styles.

Student information organization

Principles of information organization As noted earlier, the student's desk is the focal point of the academic information ecology. Here, students engage in studying, reviewing, reading, writing, sorting, and all the other information management activities. Students need to know where the items or tools are when they need them and be able to access them with the least amount of effort, preferably at a glance.

Time is extremely valuable for these students; besides classes and academic obligations, they fill their days with jobs, volunteer activities, social activities, leisure, and just "chilling." They also feel the pressures of completing both their academics and tasks of everyday life within a physically confining space, which they typically share with one or two roommates. As they arrange their areas, students express consideration of specific attributes of items, such as height, bulk, color, format, use, and convenience.

From this study it is possible to identify four broader principles that guide their organizational schemes beyond item characteristics in a more encompassing manner: accessibility, visibility, urgency, and work flow. Table 1 shows the four principles and the primary conditions of which they are a function.

In the PIM literature, much study is devoted to finding and re-finding strategies. Students in this study place items in their desk area that need to be found and re-found quickly (urgency) and easily (accessibility, visibility). Students tend to place the items of most frequent use and importance in plain view for convenience and reminding purposes. Even those who keep material they use daily in a desk drawer because they like a clear desk area know that the drawer is the item's location and they can see their important material by simply opening the drawer.

TABLE 1. *Information management principles.*

PRINCIPLE	FUNCTION OF:
Accessibility	Time, space, least effort
Visibility	Space, reminding, least effort
Urgency	Time, reminding
Work flow	Time, information load, personality, cognitive style (combine to create an individual system)

The more ephemeral types of information, such as reminders, are placed in close proximity to their desks, as it is important to students to be able to see and/or amend their notes concerning tasks, due dates, and activities in a quick glance from their academic center. See Figures 2, 4, and 5. Materials that are not immediate or urgent are stored further from the ecological center as space and their assigned values allow.

Work flow is a mini-system that students create for engaging in a task within their academic environment. Some students demonstrate consistent preferences for how they like to organize their things while they work, whereas others are more varied in behavior. For some, things to do are kept on the left side of the desk and moved to the right as they are completed, for example. Time influences the work flow significantly—the amount of time engaged in a task, time left until the deadline, time of day (or night) the work is being performed, and so on, as does the information load involved in the task or the load with which the student is coping at that point in general. These factors combine with the individual's personality and cognitive style to influence the student's work flow system, which in turn guides how that student organizes and manages his or her academic information.

Beyond convenience and expediency there is a deeper need that these organizational practices also address: the human need to feel a sense of control and ownership over one's environment. Through the act of creating a working space that will be theirs exclusively for the next 9 months, by filling it with their possessions, arranging and maintaining it to the satisfaction of their tastes and individual personalities, students claim ownership of their environment. During an academic term, especially a 10-week quarter, students often find themselves feeling stressed and even overwhelmed by the sheer volume of information entering their domains over which they are expected to attain a degree of mastery. Effectively interacting with their academic information through these management processes helps many students relieve this stress and feel a sense of accomplishment. This renewed sense of control then helps the student maintain the confidence to meet further challenges as they arise.

Archival practices Referring to the importance and urgency of the materials held in one's office, the PIM literature labels materials hot, warm, or cold (Sellen & Harper, 2002, pp. 169–170), with the "hot" items being the most current and pressing. This echoes the archival and records management literatures' concept of the document life cycle passing through active, semiactive, and inactive stages (SAA online glossary, accessed July 5, 2012), except that these latter fields more often refer to the institution or department's resources, rather than solely the resources associated with one individual's work flow.

Students' academic information flow is similar to the above in many respects, both in physical and digital formats. Items at the core of their environment include the hot information used that day—class notes, assignments in progress, etc. Warm information may be found in a pile on the desk, in the backpack, or digitally accessible on the laptop. These are the items relevant to a task that the student works on regularly or plans on doing soon. Most students retain at least some course material and institutional information beyond the term or year it was produced or used. Usually it is stored in a box at home or in a less accessible space in their dorm room. This, of course, is their cold information.

The very nature of being an undergraduate student implies a state of temporariness with an identifiable beginning and end. Being an undergraduate is not someone's life's work but rather a phase. The life-cycle of their academic information therefore differs from personal documents in an office or records in an institution. Except perhaps for students aiming for academic or research careers, being an undergraduate is more comparable to working on a major project (with many subprojects) that lasts 4 or 5 years and then ends. Thus, the life-cycle of their academic information in their dormitory rooms is probably best visualized from the perspective of project management.

Temporal arc of student information management

As noted above, time wields a major influence over the principles guiding students' information organization and management behaviors. There are many different aspects to time—time of day, time of year, time remaining until an event, time passed, timing, timeframes for projects, the multiple components and measurements of time, and so on, and each of these aspects influences students and how they manage their information. This can be seen by the detail and precision with which so many of the students in this study schedule and plan their time (see Figures 2 and 4). It is their way of coping with the challenge of coordinating and managing all of their affairs, including their academics, into four different calendars, and the demands and impositions these sometimes competing calendars place upon the student. The four calendars are society's general annual calendar, the institutional calendar, course calendars, and the individual's calendar.

In the PIM literature and other studies of personal collections, participants are adults who establish their work-space environments with the understanding of a semblance of permanence. A person usually moves into an office area, takes advantage of the facilities provided for information management, perhaps adds a few personal touches, and establishes him or herself for the duration of their employment or relationship with the company or institution. Moves do occur, but usually not on a regular basis. When managing their information, workers may group a set of documents together into a physical folder for example, which they file away in their work space, and theoretically at least, they will be able to re-find it again 4 months or 4 years later.

Students living in residential hall facilities do not share that sense of permanence. They move into their room in fall knowing full well that they are expected to move out completely at the end of the academic year in spring. And then they must re-establish themselves in another room again the following September. Students taking summer quarter classes are assigned entirely different rooms during those 6 to 8 weeks than they occupied in the previous term or can expect to occupy in fall. They create their academic information environments in their rooms with the expectation of impermanence. It is only a matter of time, 9 months at most, until they must break down their environment and move on. This time-related imposition impacts students' information management decisions, especially their retention and archival behaviors, because for the sake of convenience and practicality, they know they must travel light. The students are circumscribed in this manner by the temporal arc of the institutional/academic calendar.

Within the academic year are various impositions of the institutional calendar that affect the students' information management behaviors: The 10-week quarter system, final exam weeks, breaks and holidays, registration deadlines, payment deadlines, deadline for declaring a major, and so on.

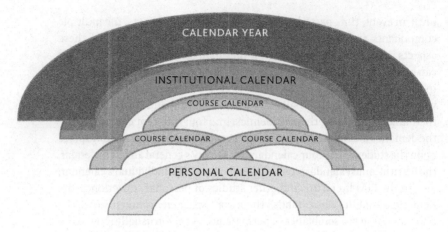

FIG. 6. *Temporal arcs.*

The institutional calendar is imposed upon the student. Other than exercising the choice of enrolling and attending or not, the student has no control over that calendar.

Students are further obliged to meet the demands of the schedules and deadlines of each of their instructors and courses—meeting days and times, assignment due dates, exams, office hours, and so on, all of which must fit into the framework of the institutional calendar. In theory, students have some control over their course schedules in that they choose and schedule their own classes, but, in practice, they must ensure that they are fulfilling their compulsory courses, prerequisites, and general education requirements, which often limits their choices in any given term.

The fourth calendar is that of each individual student, that is, his or her own schedule of classes, activities, study time, work time, meal time, nap time, social gatherings, sleep, and so on, that he or she creates in association with the three imposed temporal arcs. As illustrated earlier, most students work hard at planning and scheduling times for the activities of their academic and extra-curricular obligations. As assignments, projects, exams, or institutional deadlines approach, students' academic information environments reflect the upswing in the amount and intensity of information interaction. Papers and other materials are left around their space more haphazardly as less time is available to maintain systematic management. After tasks, projects and deadlines are met and completed, attempts are then made to "straighten up" the environment through management activities such as sorting, prioritizing, shifting, discarding, deleting, archiving, and re-organizing piles and files to return to or improve upon the previous sense of order. The model in Figure 6 illustrates the imposition of the annual, institutional, and course calendars upon the students' personal time schedules.

Conclusions

Contrary to the stereotypes of today's college students perpetrated by massive surveys, high-tech companies, the media and even institutions of higher education, students in this study demonstrate an individualistic approach to their information management behaviors. Their organizational schemes are driven by accessibility, visibility, urgency, and work flow factors which vary by context and are impacted by the multiple time factors, deadlines and calendars inherent in academia. Students employ a hybrid of electronic and traditional information tools and develop their own personal information styles just like the professional adults discussed throughout the PIM literature. Bernstein and his co-authors include in their definition of information "scraps" the idea that scraps occur because appropriate management tools are not available or being used (Bernstein, Van Kleek, Karger, & Schraefel, 2008, p. 3). Rather than viewing this as strictly a technological gap, we should also consider personal choice, information styles, and context. Perhaps jotting a note on one's hand, or using a paper calendar *is* the right strategy or tool for that particular student and his or her purposes at that time. Different information styles may be more the result of cognitive and affective differences than a direct reflection of high-tech opportunities or socialization. Further research should explore the possible relationships of technological choices with information and learning styles. Some students stated they remember things better, or they learn better when they write information by hand rather than texting or taking notes electronically. Most students admitted that they absorb information better when they read in print than online. How do the kinesthetic differences in these actions affect their cognitive processes?

What becomes evident upon close study of these students' information ecologies is that they are managing a very complex and high-pressure informational milieu. Further, this study was conducted at a time of rapid turnover in information technology modalities, where the students are juggling and combining old and new forms on a daily basis. But the complexity is not limited to the variety of information and communication technologies used. The students are also under relentless time pressure to produce assignments, prepare for tests, write papers, and conduct all the leadership and other extracurricular activities associated with their college experience. Much of the apparatus supporting their work as students consists of planning devices, reminders, texts-to-self and a variety of other means to meet these pressures. Instead of working on a single project for weeks or months, as is often the case in the work world, students often conduct several projects a week, if we take into account the quizzes, assignments, lab experiments, and so on that they must routinely complete on a tight schedule.

When we also take into account the fact that students in this age range may be living away from home for the first time, may be exploring relationships and sexuality, are working on developing an adult identity, and may be discovering new and exciting intellectual and career pursuits, it is impressive that they still manage to study and learn at all!

But putting the other elements aside and just considering the students' academic pursuits, this study has demonstrated that *academic information organization and management* is a surprisingly demanding challenge and a nontrivial element of student academic lives. In all the research and writing about the "Freshman experience," about undergraduate learning styles, and about challenges in general for the person seeking to succeed in college, we should certainly add a consciousness of the information collection and management demands of the college experience.

REFERENCES

Agosto, D. (2002). Bounded rationality and satisficing in young people's web-based decision making. *Journal of the American Society for Information Science and Technology, 53*(1), 16–27.

Balter, O. (1997). Strategies for organizing email. In H. Thimbely, B. O'Connail, & P.J. Thomas (Eds.), *Proceedings of the 12th Conference of the British Computer Society Human Interaction Specialist Group—People and Computers XII* (pp. 21–38). Bristol, UK: Springer.

Barreau, D. (2008). From novice to expert: Personal information management in learning contexts. CHI 2008, Florence, Italy. Retrieved from http://pim2008.ethz. ch/papers/pim2008-barreau.pdf

Beagrie, N. (2005). Plenty of room at the bottom? Personal digital libraries and collections. *D-Lib Magazine, 11*(6). Retrieved from http://www.dlib.org/dlib/june05/ beagrie/06beagrie.html

Bernstein, M., Van Kleek, M., Karger, D., & Schraefel, M.C. (2008). Information scraps: How and why information eludes our personal information management tool. *ACM Transactions on Information Systems, 26*(4). Retrieved from http://portal.acm. org/citation.cfm?id=1402256.1402263

Blum, S.D. (2009). *My word! Plagiarism and college culture.* Ithaca, N.Y.: Cornell University Press.

Carlson, S. (2005). The net generation goes to college. *Chronicle of Higher Education, 52*(7), Retrieved from http://chronicle.com/weekly/v52/i07/07a03401.htm

Case, D.O. (1986). Collection and organization of written information by social scientists and humanists: A review and exploratory study. *Journal of Information Science, 12*(3), 7–104.

Case, D.O. (1991). The collection and use of information by some American historians: A study of motives and methods. *The Library Quarterly, 6*(1), 61–82.

Dawkins, R. (1999). *The extended phenotype: The long reach of the gene.* Oxford: Oxford University Press.

Foster, N.F., & Gibbons, S. (Eds.). (2007). *Studying students: The undergraduate research project at the University of Rochester.* Chicago, IL: Association of College & Research Libraries.

Gabridge, T., Gaskell, M., & Stout, A. (2008). Information seeking through students' eyes: The MIT photo diary study. *College & Research Libraries, 69*(6), 510–522.

Glaser, B.G., & Strauss, A.L. (1967). *The discovery of grounded theory strategies for qualitative research.* Chicago, IL: Aldine.

Goffman, E. (1961). *Asylums: Essays on the social situation of mental patients and other inmates.* Chicago, IL: Aldine.

Griffin, D.K., Mitchell, D., & Thompson, S.J. (2009). Podcasting by synchronising PowerPoint and voice: What are the pedagogical benefits? *Computers and Education, 53*(2), 532–539.

Gwizdka, J., & Chignell, M. (2007). Individual differences. In W. Jones & J. Teevan (Eds.), *Personal information management.* (pp. 206–220). Seattle, WA: University of Washington Press.

Hardof-Jaffe, S., Hershkovitz, A., Abu-Kishk, H., Bergman, O., & Nachmias, R. (2009). Students' organization strategies of personal. *Journal of Digital Information, 10*(5). Retrieved from https://journals.tdl.org/jodi/article/view/438/541

Hartel, J. (2007). *Information activities, resources, and spaces in the hobby of gourmet cooking* (unpublished doctoral dissertation). University of California, Los Angeles.

Head, A.J. (2008). Information literacy from the trenches: How do humanities and social science majors conduct academic research? *College and Research Libraries, 69*(5), 427–446.

Hewitt, A. (2010). "R u talking 2 me?" *UCLA Magazine*, July: 23–25, 48.

Holliday, W., & Li, Q. (2004). Understanding the millennials: Updating our knowledge. *Reference Service Review, 32*(4), 356–366.

Indiana University Center for Postsecondary Research. Retrieved from http://cpr.iub.edu/index.cfm

Jones, S. (2002). The Internet goes to college: How students are living in the future with today's technology. *Pew Internet & American Life Project.* Retrieved from http://www.pewInternet.org/reports/

Jones, S., Johnson-Yale, C., Millermaier, S., & Perez, F.S. (2009). Everyday life, online: U.S. college students' use of the Internet. *First Monday, 14*(10). Retrieved from http://www.uic.edu/htbin/cgiwrap/bin/ojs/index.php/fm/article/view/2649/2301

Jones, W. (2006). Personal information management. *The Annual Review of Information Science and Technology, 41,* 453–503.

Jones, W. (2008). *Keeping found things found: The study and practice of personal information management.* Burlington, MA: Morgan Kaufmann.

Keefer, J. (1993). The hungry rats syndrome: Library anxiety, and the academic reference process. *RQ, 32*(3), 333–339.

Kracker, J. (2002). Research anxiety and students' perceptions of research: an experiment. Part I. Effect of teaching Kuhlthau's ISP model. *Journal of the American Society for Information Science and Technology, 53*(4), 282–294.

Kracker, J., & Wang P. (2002). Research anxiety and students' perceptions of research: an experiment. Part II. Content analysis of their writings on two experiences. *Journal of the American Society for Information Science and Technology, 53*(4), 295–307.

Kuhlthau, C.C. (1991). Inside the search process: Information seeking from the user's perspective. *Journal of the American Society for Information Science, 42*(5), 361–371.

Kwasnik, B.H. (1989). How personal document's intended use or purpose affects its classification in an office. In N.J. Belkin & C.J. Van Rijsbergen (Eds.). *Proceedings of the SIGIR '89* (pp. 207–210). New York: ACM Press.

Kwasnik, B.H. (1991). The importance of factors that are not document attributes in the organisation of personal documents. *Journal of Documentation, 47*(4), 389–398.

Lansdale, M. (1988). The psychology of personal information management. *Applied Ergonomics, 19*(1), 55–66.

Lansdale, M., Parkin, J., Austin, S., & Baguley, T. (2011). Designing for interaction in research environments: A case study. *Journal of Environmental Psychology, 31*(4), 407–420.

Lee, H. (2008). Information structures and undergraduate students. *Journal of Academic Librarianship, 34*(3), 211–219.

Lottridge, D., Chignell, M., & Straus, S.E. (2011). Requirements analysis for customization using subgroup differences and large sample user testing: A case study of information retrieval on handheld devices in healthcare. *International Journal of Industrial Ergonomics, 41*(3), 208–218.

Malone, T.W. (1983). How do people organize their desks? Implications for the design of office information systems. *ACM Transactions on Office Information Systems, 1*(1), 99–112.

McMillan, S.J., & Morrison, M. (2006). Coming of age with the Internet: A qualitative exploration of how the Internet has become an integral part of young people's lives. *New Media & Society, 8*(1), 73–95.

Mellon, C. (1986). Library anxiety: A grounded theory and its development. *College & Research Libraries, 47*, 160–165.

Mennecke, B.E., Valacich, J.S., & Wheeler, B.C. (2000). The effects of media and task on user performance: A test of the task-media fit hypothesis. *Group Decision and Negotiation, 9*(6), 507–529.

Miedema, J. (2009). *Slow reading.* Duluth, MN: Litwin Books.

Mizrachi, D. (2010). Undergraduates' academic information and library behaviors: Preliminary results. *Reference Services Review, 38*(4), 571–580.

Mizrachi, D. (2011). *How do they manage it? An exploratory study of undergraduate students in their personal academic ecologies* (Doctoral dissertation). University of California, Los Angeles. Retrieved from Dissertations & Theses @ University of California (Publication No. AAT 3501911).

Moffatt, M. (1989). *Coming of age in New Jersey: College and American culture.* New Brunswick: Rutgers University Press.

Nathan, R. (2005). *My freshman year: What a professor learned by becoming a student.* Ithaca, N.Y: Cornell University Press.

Naumer, C.M., & Fisher, K.E. (2007). Naturalistic approaches for understanding PIM. In W. Jones & J. Teevan (Eds). *Personal information management* (pp. 76–88). Seattle, WA: University of Washington Press.

Oblinger, D.G. (2003). Boomers, gen-xers, and millennials: Understanding the "new students." *EDUCAUSE Review, 38*(4), 37–47.

Oblinger, D.G., & Hawkins, B.L. (2005). The myth about students: "We understand our students." *EDUCAUSE Review, 40*(5), 12–13.

Pena-Shaff, J., Martin, W., & Gay, G. (2001). An epistemological framework for analyzing student interactions in computer-mediated communication environments. *Journal of Interactive Learning Research, 12*(1), 41–68.

Pollner, M. (1987). *Mundane reason: Reality in everyday and sociological discourse.* New York: Cambridge University Press.

SAA Online Glossary. Retrieved from http://www.archivists.org/glossary/term_details. asp?DefinitionKey=247

Savolainen, R. (2006). Time as a context of information seeking. *Library & Information Science Research, 28*(1), 110–127.

Savoy, A., Proctor, R.W., & Salvendy, G. (2009). Information retention from PowerPoint (TM) and traditional lectures. *Computers & Education, 52*(4), 858–867.

Seamans, N.H. (2002). Student perceptions of information literacy: Insights for librarians. *Reference Services Review, 30*(2), 112–123.

Sellen, A.J., & Harper, R.H.R. (2002). *The myth of the paperless office.* Cambridge, MA: MIT Press.

Song, G., & Ling, C. (2011). Users' attitude and strategies in information management with multiple computers. *International Journal of Human-Computer Interaction, 27*(8), 762–792.

Soper, M.E. (1976). Characteristics and use of personal collections. *The Library Quarterly, 46*(4), 397–415.

UCLA Graduate School of Education & Information Studies. *Higher Education Research Institute.* Retrieved from http://http://heri.ucla.edu/index.php

University of Michigan. *Monitoring the future.* Retrieved from http://monitoringthe future.org/

Valentine, B. (1993). Undergraduate research behaviour: Using focus groups to generate theory. *Journal of Academic Librarianship, 19*(5), 300–4.

Valentine, B. (2001). The legitimate effort in research papers: Student commitment versus faculty expectations. *The Journal of Academic Librarianship, 27*(2), 107–15.

Walters, W.H. (2009). Google Scholar search performance: Comparative recall and precision. *Portal: Libraries and the Academy, 9*(1), 5–24.

Weiler, A. (2005). Information-seeking behavior in generation Y students: Motivation, critical thinking, and learning theory. *Journal of Academic Librarianship, 31*(1), 46–53.

Weisskirch, R.S., & Milburn, S.S. (2003). Virtual discussion: Understanding college students' electronic bulletin board use. *The Internet and Higher Education, 6*(3), 215–225.

Whitmire, E. (2004). The relationship between undergraduates' epistemological reflection, reflective judgment and their information seeking behavior. *Information Processing & Management, 40*(1), 97–111.

Wodehouse, A.J., & Ion, W.J. (2010). Information use in conceptual design: Existing taxonomies and new approaches. *International Journal of Design, 4*(3), 53–65.

TWO

User-centered design
of information systems

Another information system fails—Why?

It seems as though we hear every month of yet another multimillion-dollar information technology failure in the California state government. In the latest case, a system to link welfare networks was abandoned after the expenditure of $18 million. It is time we learned the lessons of why these systems fail. To date, many managerial, oversight and technical problems have been identified, but two very important elements are underplayed or missing altogether in the discussion.

The first missing element is a deep understanding of the human factor in technology implementation and use. Information technology often is looked upon as something you go out and buy and install, like bringing home a new lamp and plugging it in. But, in fact, to function effectively, information technology has to be fully and successfully integrated into the activities of the people who use it.

A new automated information system, especially one built around the core activities of an agency, will change almost every activity of the agency and will inevitably alter power positions and job descriptions of everyone along the way. A manager's power may be increased because the new information system enables the integration of two departments under one command, or it may be weakened because fewer workers are now needed. That manager will not be passive about these changes.

First published as Bates, M. J. (1999, July 15). Another information system fails—Why? [Op-Ed piece]. *Los Angeles Times*, p. B9.

Even the lowliest clerk may dig in and sabotage the project because it necessitates a move from an office with a window to one without a window. High-level managers commissioning new systems ignore these factors at their peril—yet they often do ignore them.

The other big piece missing from the discussion is information expertise—an understanding of how people search for and use information, and how best to organize information within the computer to facilitate retrieval. For example, a system that holds the names of 50,000 people will not be too problematic when retrieving duplicate names; with a system of 5 million names, the duplication problem explodes and can halt the entire system unless sophisticated solutions are employed. More generally, information retrieval systems of all kinds are notoriously size-sensitive and do not scale up well without significant design changes.

In most real-world information systems, simple, conventional database structures are not adequate for handling the messiness of the information.

Imagine a child welfare agency's information system: At any given moment, a child may be under several governmental jurisdictions, may be at one stage of a lengthy, multistage process determining the disposition of the child's case and may be under a complicated arrangement set up by the court for visitation by a parent or guardian.

The design of a system to organize such information so that it is retrievable and useful for the various agencies and individuals who need to access that file is a major task in and of itself. It requires expertise not only in computer systems, but also in information organization and retrieval techniques. Each type of information in that child's file may need to be indexed according to different principles of categorization, with different search capabilities made available for the file users for each type of information.

For example, one type of information may lend itself best to a classification using just a few categories; another type may best be searched using a thesaurus of technical vocabulary in use in that particular agency. Information-related design skills do not replace computer systems analysis; rather, people with these skills should be working with the systems analysts—and their expertise should be given equal weight with that of the analysts.

The technology is highly visible; the information, and the social meaning of the information technology, are not so visible. Usually, in the design of such systems, great attention is paid to buying the computers and programming them, while the human and information-related factors are shortchanged or ignored altogether.

2

The design of browsing and berrypicking techniques for the online search interface

ABSTRACT

First, a new model of searching in online and other information systems, called "berrypicking," is discussed. This model, it is argued, is much closer to the real behavior of information searchers than the traditional model of information retrieval is, and, consequently, will guide our thinking better in the design of effective interfaces. Second, the research literature of manual information seeking behavior is drawn on for suggestions of capabilities that users might like to have in online systems. Third, based on the new model and the research on information seeking, suggestions are made for how new search capabilities could be incorporated into the design of search interfaces. Particular attention is given to the nature and types of browsing that can be facilitated.

Introduction

As more and more different types of databases are brought online, the universe of information available to search online is beginning to resemble the vast array of sources available in manual print environments. From an original emphasis on bibliographic databases, which are the online equivalent of abstracting and indexing (A & I) services, databanks have expanded to the full text of journals and other documents, as well as

First published as Bates, M. J. (1989). The design of browsing and berrypicking techniques for the online search interface. *Online Review, 13*(5), 407-424.

directories, encyclopedias, and other reference sources traditionally available in libraries. Soon there really will be something approaching whole libraries accessible by computer.

As more types of resource are brought online, however, the searcher has a more complex search environment to consider, both in terms of types of sources to use and search techniques to employ with these sources (Williams, 1986; Hawkins, Levy, & Montgomery, 1988). We need to expand our understanding of these resources and the search techniques to use in them, and at the same time, expand our view of how the search interface should be designed to assist searchers with their new, complex tasks.

In this article the following is done:

- A new model of searching in online and other information systems, called "berrypicking," is discussed. This model, it is argued, is much closer to the real behavior of information searchers than the traditional model of information retrieval is, and, consequently, will guide our thinking better in the design of effective interfaces.

- The research literature of manual information seeking behavior is drawn on for suggestions of capabilities that users might like to have in online systems.

- Based on the new model and the research on information seeking, suggestions are made for how these capabilities could be incorporated into the design of search interfaces. Particular attention is given to the nature and types of browsing that can be facilitated.

A "berrypicking" model of information retrieval

The classic model of information retrieval (IR) used in information science research for over 25 years can be characterized as follows (compare Robertson [1977], especially p. 129):

This model has been very productive and has promoted our understanding of information retrieval in many ways. However, as Kuhn (1970) noted, major models that are as central to a field as this one is, eventually begin to show inadequacies as testing leads to greater and greater understanding of the processes being studied. The limitations of the original model's representation of the phenomenon of interest become more and more evident.

It is only fitting, then, that in recent years the above classic model has come under attack in various ways (Ellis, 1984a; 1984b; Bates, 1985, 1986). Oddy (1977) and Belkin et al (1982) have asked why it is necessary for the searcher to find a way to represent the information need in a query understandable by the system. Why cannot the system make it possible for the searcher to express the need directly as they would ordinarily, instead of in an artificial query representation for the system's consumption?

At the other end of the model, that of document representation, powerful developments in computing make possible free text and full text searching so that the traditional document representation (controlled vocabulary) takes on a different role and, for some purposes, is less important in much information retrieval practice.

Here I want to challenge the model as a whole—to the effect that it represents some searches, but not all, perhaps not even the majority, and that with respect to those it does represent, it frequently does so inadequately. As a formal model for testing, it has taught us much; as a realistic representation of actual searches, it has many limitations. As a consequence, as long as this model dominates information science thinking, it will limit our creativity in developing IR systems that really meet user needs and preferences.

The model I am about to propose differs from the traditional one in four areas:

1. Nature of the query.

2. Nature of the overall search process.

3. Range of search techniques used.

4. Information "domain" or territory where the search is conducted.

The first two areas will be dealt with in this section and the second two in the next section.

Let us return for a closer look at the classic model. Fundamental to it is the idea of a single query presented by the user, matched to the database contents, yielding a single output set. One of Gerard Salton's (1968) contributions to research in this area was the idea of iterative feedback to improve output. He developed a system that would modify the query formulation based on user feedback to the first preliminary output set. The formulation would be successively improved through the use of feedback on user document preferences until recall and precision were optimized.

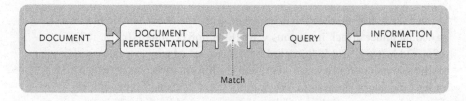

FIG. 1. *The classic information retrieval model*

But Salton's iterative feedback is still well within the original classic model as presented in Figure 1—because the presumption is that the information need leading to the query is the same, unchanged, throughout, no matter what the user might learn from the documents in the preliminary retrieved set. In fact, if a user in a Salton experiment were to change the query after seeing some documents, it would be "unfair," a violation of the basic design of the experiment. The point of the feedback is to improve the representation of a static need, not to provide information that enables a change in the need itself.

So throughout the process of information retrieval evaluation under the classic model, the query is treated as a single unitary, one-time conception of the problem. Though this assumption is useful for simplifying IR system research, real-life searches frequently do not work this way.

In real-life searches in manual sources, end users may begin with just one feature of a broader topic, or just one relevant reference, and move through a variety of sources. Each new piece of information they encounter gives them new ideas and directions to follow and, consequently, a new conception of the query. At each stage they are not just modifying the search terms used in order to get a better match for a single query. Rather the query itself (as well as the search terms used) is continually shifting, in part or whole. This type of search is here called an evolving search.

Furthermore, at each stage, with each different conception of the query, the user may identify useful information and references. In other words, the query is satisfied not by a single final retrieved set, but by a series of selections of individual references and bits of information at each stage of the ever-modifying search. A bit-at-a-time retrieval of this sort is here called *berrypicking.* This term is used by analogy to picking huckleberries or blueberries in the forest. The berries are scattered on the bushes; they do not come in bunches. One must pick them one at a time. One could do berrypicking of information without the search need itself changing (evolving), but in this article the attention is given to searches that combine both of these features.

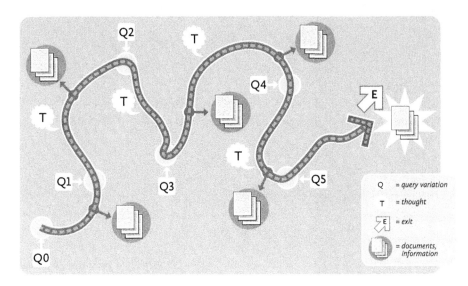

FIG. 2. *A berrypicking, evolving search*

Figure 2 represents a berrypicking, evolving search. In Figure 3 (overleaf) we see the size of the picture shrunk in order to show the context within which the search takes place.

The focus of the classic model in Figure 1 is the match between the document and query representations. The focus of the model in Figures 2 and 3 is the sequence of searcher behaviors. The continuity represented by the line of the arrow is the continuity of a single human being moving through many actions toward a general goal of a satisfactory completion of research related to an information need. The changes in direction of the arrow illustrate the changes of an evolving search as the individual follows up various leads and shifts in thinking. The diagram also shows documents and information being produced from the search at many points along the way.

In the case of a straightforward single-match search of the classic sort, we can think of the arrow as being very short and straight, with a single query and a single information output set. Thus, we can see that this model differs from the classic one in the first two respects mentioned above: (1) The nature of the query is an evolving one, rather than single and unchanging, and (2) the nature of the search process is such that it follows a berrypicking pattern, instead of leading to a single best retrieved set.

There is ample evidence of the popularity of searches of the evolving/berrypicking sort. Reviews of research by Line (1974), Hogeweg-de-Haart

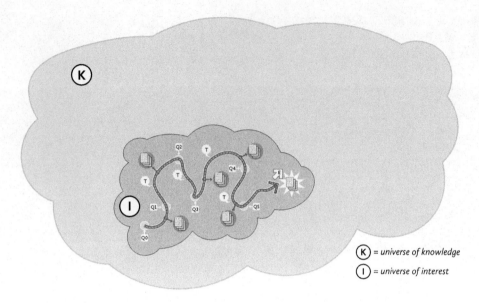

FIG. 3. *Context of berrypicking search*

(1984), Stone (1982), and Stoan (1984) attest to the popularity of this approach in a variety of environments, particularly in the social sciences and humanities. A recent landmark study by Ellis (1989) on social scientists supports and amplifies the results of earlier studies. Kuhlthau's work (1988) with high school students suggests that there is a great deal of exploratory searching that goes on, both before and after a topic for a paper is selected. While the research reviewed here refers largely to the academic environment, I would suggest that many searches by people in many contexts other than academic can also be better characterized by the berrypicking/evolving model than by the classic IR model. The sources consulted may differ, but the process is similar.

How and where users search for information now

It was argued in the previous section that information seekers in manual environments use a berrypicking/evolving search mode. In this section we will examine in more detail some of the search techniques used and information sources consulted by users in manual environments.

We might be tempted to say that the path taken in Figures 2 and 3 is simply a series of mini-matches of the classic sort. That is, that at each point where searchers identify documents of interest, they are making a match as represented in Figure 1, and that Figure 2 is simply a representation of searching at a higher level of generality. To make that assumption, however, would be to misrepresent what is being proposed here. Figure 2 is different in essential character, not just in level of generality. Specifically, in a real search there are many different ways people encounter information of interest to them. We will discuss several of them below. Only one of those ways is the kind represented by the classic model.

Users employ a number of strategies. With the help particularly of Stoan (1984) and Ellis (1989) I will describe just six of them, which are widely used:

1. *Footnote chasing* (or "backward chaining" [Ellis, 1989]). This technique involves following up footnotes found in books and articles of interest, and therefore moving backward in successive leaps through reference lists. Note that with this technique, as with other citation methods, the searcher avoids the problem of subject description altogether. This method is extremely popular with researchers in the social sciences and humanities. See, for example, Stenstrom and McBride (1979).

2. *Citation searching* (or "forward chaining" [Ellis, 1989]). One begins with a citation, finds out who cites it by looking it up in a citation index, and thus leaps forward.

3. *Journal run* Once, by whatever means, one identifies a central journal in an area, one then locates the run of volumes of the journal and searches straight through relevant volume years. Such a technique, by definition, guarantees complete recall within that journal, and, if the journal is central enough to the searcher's interests, this technique also has tolerably good precision. In effect, this approach exploits Bradford's Law: the core journals in a subject area are going to have very high rates of relevant materials in that area.

4. *Area scanning* Browsing the materials that are physically collocated with materials located earlier in a search is a widely used and effective technique. Studies dating all the

way back to the 1940s confirm the popularity of the technique in catalog use. Frarey (1953), in reviewing three of those early studies, found that use of the subject catalog is divided about equally between selecting books on a subject on the one hand, and finding the shelf location of a category in the classification in order to make book selections in the stacks on the other hand. The latter is, of course, the sort of area scanning described here. Recent work by Hancock (1987) again confirms the importance of this approach.

5. *Subject searches in bibliographies and abstracting and indexing (A & I) services* Many bibliographies and most A & I services are arranged by subject. Both classified arrangements and subject indexes are popular. These forms of subject description (classifications and indexing languages) constitute the most common forms of "document representation" that are familiar from the classic model of information retrieval discussed earlier.

6. *Author searching* We customarily think of searching by author as an approach that contrasts with searching by subject. In the literature of catalog use research, "known-item" searches are frequently contrasted with "subject" searches, for example. But author searching can be an effective part of subject searching as well, when a searcher uses an author name to see if the author has done any other work on the same topic (Ellis, 1989).

Until now most of the emphasis in online databanks and other automated IR systems—theoretical, experimental, and operational—has been on use of just one of the above techniques, namely, searching abstracting and indexing services. It is assumed that to do an automated information search one is searching on a bibliographic database, a list of references with or without abstracts, that is just like an abstracting and indexing service, except that it is online. In experiments, the "document representations" in the classic IR model may involve very sophisticated methods, but most come down to some form of representation of the contents of documents that is usually much shorter, and different from, the documents themselves. In short, most IR research, until a recent flurry of interest in full text databases, has been research on databases of document surrogates.

Real searches, by contrast, use all the above techniques and more, in endless variation. It is part of the nature of berrypicking that people adapt the strategy to the particular need at the moment; as the need shifts in part or whole, the strategy often shifts as well—at least for effective searchers. So, to return to an earlier point, the berrypicking model does not represent a number of mini-matches of the classic sort, i.e., between search term and A & I service (database) term. Rather, the evolving/berrypicking search also involves the third and fourth features mentioned earlier: (3) the search techniques change throughout, and (4) the sources searched change in both form and content.

We have generally assumed in library/information science that the fifth technique in the list above, the A & I search, is clearly superior to the others. That is an important reason for the primacy given to the bibliographic search in our research and practice. However, Stenstrom and McBride found, when they asked the social science faculty where they got the references for journal articles they used, that over 87% of them said they got the references from abstracting journals only occasionally, rarely, or never (Stenstrom & McBride, 1979, p. 429). They relied far more heavily on footnote chasing: 69% (p. 429). Both Stoan (1984) and Ellis (1989) provide evidence and are very persuasive on the power and effectiveness of these other techniques for academic researchers and students at the very least.

Some of the other search techniques described above are possible on some systems—see, for example, Palay and Fox (1981), Croft and Thompson (1987), Cove and Walsh (1988), Noerr and Noerr (1985). See also Hildreth's masterly review of intelligent interfaces for bibliographic retrieval systems (Hildreth, 1989). Nowhere, to my knowledge, however, are all of these techniques easily applied by a searcher within a single system.

A model containing a unified perspective, incorporating the full range of searcher behaviors in the information seeking process, may make it easier to design many more such features for information retrieval systems. Ellis (1989) has presented the results of his own research on social scientists and, on that basis, argues for the implementation of most of the above techniques, as well as others not discussed here. The particular mix of different capabilities that should ultimately be made available is a question deserving much more attention in the future.

Citation searching is also available, of course, in online systems in the Institute for Scientific Information databases. This searching method is now widely accepted in library/information science as another valuable database approach. Not all readers may be aware, however, of how hard Eugene Garfield had to work in the 1960s and 1970s to persuade librarians of the value of citation searching. I vividly recall observing an otherwise very capable reference instructor telling a class in the late 1960s that a citation index was a waste of money, that it was just a vanity publication for professors—its only value being for them to look up and see who was citing their own work. My point here is that we have yet to fully accept all six of these techniques as valid, effective approaches to information. Even citation indexing, now widely used, was not received easily into the thinking of library/information science.

From the standpoint of general effectiveness in searching, it is clear, on reflection, however, that, other things being equal, the searcher with the widest range of search strategies available is the searcher with the greatest retrieval power. We in information science feel that information searchers should take more advantage of A & I services in online or manual form. We, in our turn, should recognize that these other techniques used so commonly by researchers must have some real value for them, and that there may be times when they are preferable (see Stoan, 1984). With each of the six retrieval techniques described above, it is possible to think of instances when that technique is clearly superior to the others as a route to the desired information.

I would argue on two grounds that these techniques should all be available in at least some future automated IR systems, and that our model of information retrieval should include berrypicking through use of these and other techniques:

1. The more different strategies searchers can use an information store, the more retrieval effectiveness and efficiency is possible.

2. There are many experienced searchers who use these techniques already—in a berrypicking mode—with great satisfaction. These approaches represent well established patterns that are handed down from scholars to their students and which work well for them in many cases. If we want to meet users' needs, we should enable them to search in familiar ways that are effective for them.

To summarize the argument to this point, this model of searching differs from the trawditional one not only in that it reflects evolving, berry-picking searches, but also searches in a much wider variety of sources, and using a much wider variety of search techniques than has been typically represented in information retrieval models to date. With this broader picture of information retrieval in mind, many new design possibilities open up. In the next section, some of those possibilities will be examined, with particular attention to the role of browsing in the broader search process.

Search capabilities for a berrypicking search interface

Browsing.
The view of searching as frequently being an evolving/berrypicking process, and one which uses a variety of types of information sources and search techniques, changes our sense of what browsing capabilities should be like in online systems, and how the database and the search interface should be designed. Concepts of browsing in IR systems are becoming more and more sophisticated. See Noerr and Noerr (1985), Wade and Willett (1988), Cove and Walsh (1988), Hildreth (1982), Bawden (1986), Ingwersen and Wormell (1987). But there is still a lingering tendency in information science to see browsing *in contrast* to directed searching, to see it as a casual, don't-know-what-I-want behavior that one engages in separately from "regular" searching.

However, as Ellis notes (1989), browsing is an important part of standard information searching; he calls it "semi-directed or semi-structured searching" when used this way. He recommends that browsing of a variety of types of information, e.g., contents pages, lists of cited works, subject terms, should be made available in automated systems. He further argues that since the user is doing the browsing, and we therefore do not have to design a cognitive model of user browsing into the system, that providing browsing features should be relatively simple.

Relatively simpler perhaps, but making effective provision for browsing capabilities involves its own complexities. The techniques above combine browsing and conventional use of the information access apparatus in a variety of specific configurations. With all of the six techniques above, as well as with other features that might be designed for browsing, it will be desirable to set up combinations of features that incorporate browsing in different ways in each case.

The nature of browsing associated with each of the techniques listed above is examined in more detail below. Key design features recommended for automated IR systems will be stated for each technique.

So that there is no confusion, however, I want to emphasize that browsing and berrypicking are not the same behavior. There will be a great deal of discussion of browsing in the remainder of this article, but only because browsing has received less attention in our field than other kinds of searching. Berrypicking involves the use of a wide variety of techniques, some of which are very standard and others which involve a considerable amount of browsing. One of the points emphasized in this model is precisely that people use a wide variety of techniques.

Each of the six techniques is discussed below, followed by some general points about database and interface design for berrypicking and browsing.

Footnote chasing

In footnote chasing one might want both to be able to browse through the article or book that generates the references as well as through the list of references—in fact, to move back and forth easily between the two parts of the document. The body of information browsed in footnote chasing has a coherence and meaning that clusters around the idiosyncratic purposes of the author of the article or book. Browsing in the footnotes or endnotes will be minimal if the searcher only looks up individual references found in the text, and sticks to them. Browsing of the references can be more extensive if the searcher scans the list, independently of an originating textual reference.

KEY DESIGN FEATURES Users can get the following easily, preferably by direct manipulation, e.g., with mouse and pull-down menus:

1. Overview of document contents a chapter or section headings.

2. Full text of documents and references.

3. Ability to jump back and forth between text and references.

Citation searching

In citation searching, one might want either to browse the set of references that cite a given starter reference, or read any of the citing articles. No single human has created this grouping of citations; rather they come together because they all happen to cite the originating reference. They may otherwise be quite unrelated. Such a collection of references is likely to be stimulating to creativity, as the citing articles may not be on the "same" topic in the conventional sense, yet nonetheless create a grouping that has at least one key thread of similarity that may go along unconventional lines. (See also Bawden [1986].) Because of this unconventional grouping, the user might well want to expand the search indefinitely in any direction, that is, upon finding a citing article, learn which articles cite it, and so on.

KEY DESIGN FEATURES Users should have the ability to:

1. Scan lists of citing references.

2. Make simple single step jumps to (a) full text of citing articles, and (b) full list of references in citing article.

3. Make jumps in any direction ad infinitum, i.e., the user should not have to "return to go" and re-enter a starting article for each jump in any direction.

Journal run

Looking through journals manually, the searcher flips through issues, scanning large chunks of the text of the articles, as well as the contents lists and abstracts. Here the grouping of articles is the subject area represented by the coverage of the journal. When the journal has a very broad subject coverage, such as that of *Science* or *American Psychologist,* it is unlikely to meet a searcher's need for information on a topic of the normal degree of specificity associated with a research project. To put if differently, browsing such general journals is probably useful more for general monitoring of the environment, rather than contributing to a well defined need.

In cases where the journal coverage is a more specific subject area, however, reviewing the contents lists or articles in that journal may be an excellent way to see quickly a large number of articles exactly in the heart of an area that interests one. The grouping of articles that results from their joint publication in a journal can be expected to be coherent and well thought out, since the focus of journals is generally well defined by editors for prospective authors.

KEY DESIGN FEATURES

1. Easy specification of journal title and starting date in journal run search.

2. Easy jumps between contents lists and articles and back again.

3. Capability of requesting, if wanted, standard section headings in scholarly articles, such as "Methodology," or "Conclusions," so the searcher is shown these sections directly.

Area scanning

This technique is most commonly used with books arranged by a library classification scheme on the shelves of a library. With area scanning, one may either follow the exact arrangement of the classification scheme by reading linearly along the shelves, or alternatively, and, I suspect, more commonly, deliberately not follow that order. In practice, one of the most useful aspects of area scanning is that one can visually scan in a random manner over the shelves in a subject area of interest.

The effect of this latter method is to "jump the rails" of the classification scheme, to skip to other parts of the scheme that are near the starting point, without having to look at every single intervening book and category. This technique represents a deliberate breaking up of the conventional classified order, while enabling the searcher to remain in the same general initial subject area. Thus the search domain may consist of a variety of specific areas within one larger area.

Area scanning is the quintessential form of browsing in manual environments. As noted earlier, the research shows that it has remained very popular over many years among users. It is reasonable to presume that it meets some real needs. More research into why this approach is popular is desirable. However, here are a couple of guesses:

(1) The searcher is exposed to a variety of related areas, some of which, because of the jumping around, may be related in unexpected ways—thus producing serendipitous discoveries.

(2) The searcher can look directly at the full text of the materials. By flipping through the pages and reading a passage here and there, the searcher gets a quick gestalt sense of the "feel" or character of the author and his or her approach. Whatever that feel is, it is almost never accessible through any classification or subject description.

KEY DESIGN FEATURES

1. A library's listing of its books on the shelves arranged by the order of the classification scheme is called a shelf list. Thus, for area scanning linearly along the shelves, a capability of browsing the shelf list can be provided.

2. For "jumping the rails" of the classification scheme, browsing at several levels of generality within the classification scheme itself can be provided, i.e., giving the searcher the option of browsing a list of the most general categories in the scheme, or a list of the general categories plus their subdivisions, and so on, down to the full detail of the scheme.

3. At any point, with either of the first two capabilities listed in this section, the searcher should be able to ask for "snapshots" of full text of books (more discussion later).

Subject searching in bibliographies and A & I services

In discussions of "browsing" in online databases, the term usually refers to reading short lists of alphabetically arranged subject terms or reading citations and their associated abstracts. In fact, in such activities there is little sense of the random visual movement usually associated with browsing. Indeed, the lists of terms printed out are short, and the printing of citations is costly, so searchers often keep it to a minimum. When the cost of printing out abstracts falls, and/or CD-ROM database use becomes more widespread, true browsing may be easier to do.

It may help the discussion here if we compare the manual form of A & I services, and consider how they are used for browsing. We may be able to do more, of course, with the online form, but let us first see if the text lends itself to browsing in principle. A very common pattern in manual forms of A & I services is to arrange the abstracts by a classified order, and attach a subject index using more specific subject terms. When an online searcher searches by controlled vocabulary, or by free text on the titles and abstracts, all the entries associated with the more specific subject terms are brought together in one location, so they become easy to examine. In the manual form, usually only the abstract numbers are brought together in the index. So grouping entries by these specific terms is a useful function of online services, though the browsing potential is limited for the reasons given above.

Since the A & I services generally arrange the abstracts by a classified order, it is possible in the manual form to browse through the abstracts in a classified section. This is generally impractical in online databases unless the search is also limited to certain dates or issues of the service, because the online database usually combines many years of the service in one, and each classification category therefore contains very large numbers of items (see Bates, 1984). However, in a database in which cost per reference is not a factor, then some sort of browsing in the classified sections might be possible, particularly if brief forms of the reference were printed out, so many could be seen on the screen at once.

KEY DESIGN FEATURES The user should have the capability of:

1. Rapid browsing of many references without cost, and/or ability to ask to see every nth reference in a large set (see further discussion in Bates, 1976, p. 21ff).

2. Browsing the classification used in an A & I service, as well as abstracts within each classification, either all or every nth one.

Author searching

Author searching makes sense as a form of *subject* searching in that authors tend to write on similar things from one article or book to another. Thus, if one item pays off, maybe another by the same person will too. While bibliographies and catalogs have brought together in one place the references to an author's work since time immemorial, it would be a novel contribution of online systems if they made it possible to see grouped in one place the full text of an author's works. Library stacks do it for books, but there is currently no way to bring together other forms of publication, or to combine book texts with those other forms. When the day comes that full text online becomes very cheap, this grouping of an author's work in one place will be possible. The question in the meantime is, can we design the interface to make it easy to "flip through" the pages of the author's work?

KEY DESIGN FEATURES When author searching, the user should have the capability of calling up:

1. Bibliographies of authors' work,

2. "Snapshots" of the text of works (see discussion later), and

3. Features that enable footnote chasing and citation searching.

Each of these approaches can be seen as a different way to identify and exploit particular regions in the total information store that are more likely than other regions to contain information of interest for the search at hand. To put it differently, these are different ways of identifying berry patches in the forest, and then going berrypicking within them.

Database and interface design

Suggestions for implementing specific design features have been made above. In this section some across-the-board proposals are made for the design of databases and interfaces for browsing and berrypicking:

- To reproduce the above search capabilities, databases will need to contain very large bodies of full text, as well as different types of text (narrative, statistical, bibliographic references, etc.). At the same time the structure of the databases will need to be such that the searcher can move quickly from one form of information to another, in other words, not have to follow a complicated routine to withdraw from one database and enter another.

- Several authors have pointed out the value of helping the user of a system develop a mental model or "metaphor" of the system to guide them (Norman, 1988; Carroll & Thomas, 1982; Elkerton & Williges, 1984). Various models have been used in the design of interfaces for information systems, for example, Weyer (1982) used the book, which approach was also supported by Elkerton & Williges (1984) in their research, and Borgman (1986) used the card catalog. In teaching students general information searching, Huston (1989) has suggested using the model of community-based information networks as a basis for explaining the online literature reviewing process. Hannabuss (1989), on the other hand, has argued for a view of information seeking as a form of conversation, especially with reference to the pattern of turn taking in conversation, and those parts of conversation that involve question asking and answering.

Now that so many different types of information are going online, including much full text, a good place to start as a model of information searching for a berrypicking interface might be the physical library itself. It is the actual physical layout of a library that people are most familiar with, rather than the complex intellectual relationships we develop among catalog entries, books, periodical indexes, journals, etc. Creating a virtual physical layout on the screen may make it easier for the searcher to think of moving among familiar categories of resources in an information retrieval system, in the same manner in which they move among resources in the actual library. This may be particularly useful at the beginning of a search, when the user could see a physical representation of an imaginary library on the screen. The searcher might then be reminded of whole classes of resource which they might otherwise forget.

Many years ago, the psychologist George Miller (1968) pointed out how very physical our memories are, and how easily we remember things by their physical location. Jones and Dumais (1986) challenge the idea that spatial metaphors help information system users recall where something was filed. However, I am suggesting the idea primarily as an orientation device, a way to give users a familiar basis from which to move forward. (See also Bennett, 1971; Bolt, 1978; Woods, 1984; Michel, 1986; and Hildreth's discussion of the General Research Corporation's "Laserguide" CD-ROM online catalog, [1989, pp. 90–94].)

There are many complex issues involved in adapting such a model in an interface, which cannot be dealt with here. Suffice to say that the transfer will not be simple, and may ultimately be modified somewhat away from the more literal image of the library as testing proceeds and as users gain greater familiarity with computer interfaces generally.

Browsing in a manual environment is a physical activity, involving body or eye movements of a fairly random character. Thus to be effective in an online environment, a browsing capability should also allow for random movement, at least of the eyes. An aspect of browsing that has been commented upon is the juxtaposition, in time or space, of different ideas or documents that stimulate the thinking of the information searcher (Foskett, 1983, p. 53). To reproduce this in an online environment, it will be necessary to make rapid movement across large amounts of text possible.

The physical metaphor of the library that was suggested above may facilitate such searching particularly well. For example, if the interface can produce a picture on the screen that looks like the books on a shelf, the searcher can transfer a familiar experience to the automated system. So that if a mouse or similar device makes it possible to, in effect, move among the books, a familiar physical experience is reproduced and the searcher can take advantage of well-developed browsing skills. Until the full texts of books are online, the searcher may examine extensive subject information about the book, such as contents lists, index entries, and the like (Atherton, 1978).

Once such a form of movement is possible online, it should be transferable to other kinds of information environments where such movement was more difficult in manual situations. For example, the searcher might move among categories of a classification scheme used in an A & I service, or follow up leads of related terms in a high-powered online thesaurus. (See also Bates, 1986.)

As noted earlier, the value of flipping through the pages of a book may be due, at least in part, to being able to read passages of a writer's work to get a feel for his or her approach and determine whether it appeals. In large full text databases it will be desirable to be able to do this as well. It would be easy to program a command that would produce a series of randomly selected passages, or "snapshots," each two or three paragraphs in length. Such passages should be truly randomly selected—just as happens when we flip through an article or book—because it is precisely what is not indexed that we want to sample.

Incidentally, in a recent study, based on a random sample drawn from three different types of libraries, I learned that both reference books and "regular" books use a surprisingly limited and robust set of patterns of organization within the book. These patterns have endured in very stable form over hundreds of years and in many Western cultures (1986). The overwhelming majority of contents lists, for example, are two pages or less in length. Plans to use snapshots of text for browsing purposes, therefore, should not produce nasty surprises in terms of displaying segments of complex or unusual file structures. (I am speaking of the structure of the book as a whole, not of what may appear internally to a diagram or illustration.)

The searcher should be able, with a single command, to call for a search mode and screen that is set up for one of the six techniques above (or others). That is, it should not be necessary to issue a string of commands to get the information needed on screen to begin. Each whole technique should be built in as a package that the searcher can call upon when desired. Movement through screens should resemble movement through a real-life source using a given strategy (again the physical metaphor). For example, for the searcher doing a journal run, it should be possible to type in a journal title and year, preceded by some phrase such as "journal scan." The contents page of the first issue of that year then appears on the screen. The searcher can then by, say, highlighting a title, easily ask to see the article full text. Another command or highlight sends parts or all of the article to be printed. And so on.

Hypertext approaches appear tailor-made for berrypicking searching (Conklin, 1987). Being able to jump instantly to full bibliographic citations from references in the text, for example, is a technique that hypertext handles well.

Berrypicking frequently requires the capability of seeing substantial qualities of information on the screen at once. Screens used should be high definition for easy reading and scanning.

The interface design should make it easy to highlight or otherwise flag information and references to be sent to a temporary store. Such a store can then be printed out when the searcher is ready to leave off searching. The necessity otherwise of either writing information down by hand or printing out information in bits and pieces interspersed between search commands would be tiresome and would reduce search effectiveness.

Conclusions

As the sizes and variety of databases grow and the power of search interfaces increases, users will more and more expect to be able to search automated information stores in ways that are comfortable and familiar to them. We need first to have a realistic model of how people go about looking for information now, and second, to find ways to devise databases and search interfaces that enable searchers to operate in ways that feel natural.

A model of searching called "berrypicking" has been proposed here, which, in contrast to the classic model of information retrieval, says that:

- Typical search queries are not static, but rather evolve.

- Searchers commonly gather information in bits and pieces instead of in one grand best retrieved set.

- Searchers use a wide variety of search techniques, which extend beyond those commonly associated with bibliographic databases.

- Searchers use a wide variety of sources other than bibliographic databases.

Drawing on the research of Ellis (1989), Stoan (1984), and others, a half-dozen typical search techniques used in manual sources have been described (footnote chasing, citation searching, journal run, area scanning, A & I searches, author searches). The specific behaviors associated with these techniques, in particular, browsing behaviors, have been analyzed. Methods have been proposed for the implementation of these techniques in database design and search interface design in online systems.

In conclusion, as Rouse and Rouse note, after an extensive survey of the literature of information seeking behavior:

> Because information needs change in time and depend on the particular information seeker, systems should be sufficiently flexible to allow the user to adapt the information seeking process to his own current needs. Examples of such flexibility include the design of interactive dialogues and aiding techniques that do not reflect rigid assumptions about the user's goals and style. (Rouse & Rouse, 1984, p. 135)

REFERENCES

Atherton, P. (1978). *Books are for use: Final report of the Subject Access Project to the Council on Library Resources* (ED 156 131). NY: Syracuse University School of Information Studies.

Bates, M.J. (1976). Rigorous systematic bibliography. *RQ, 16*(1) 7–26.

Bates, M.J. (1984). The fallacy of the perfect thirty-item online search. *RQ, 24*(1), 43–50.

Bates, M.J. (1986). An exploratory paradigm for online information retrieval. In B.C. Brookes (Ed.), *Intelligent information systems for the information society. Proceedings of the Sixth International Research Forum in Information Science (IRFIS 6), Frascati, Italy* (pp. 91–99). Netherlands: North-Holland.

Bates, M.J. (1986). Subject access in online catalogs: A design model, *Journal of the American Society for Information Science, 37*(6) 357–376.

Bates, M.J. (1986). What is a reference book? A theoretical and empirical analysis. *RQ, 26*(1) 37–57.

Bawden, D. (1986). Information systems and the stimulation of creativity. *Journal of Information Science, 12*(5) 203–216.

Belkin, N.J., Oddy, R.N., & Brooks, H.M. (1982). ASK for information retrieval: Part 1: Background and theory. *Journal of Documentation, 38*(2) 61–71.

Bennett, J.L. (1971). Spatial concepts as an organizing principle for interactive bibliographic search. In D.E. Walker (Ed.), *Interactive Bibliographic Search: The User/Computer Interface* (pp. 67–82). Montvale, NJ: AFIPS Press.

Bolt, R.A. (1978). *Spatial data management system*. Marine Architecture Group (NTIS #AD-777 878/OGA). Cambridge, MA: MIT Press.

Borgman, C.L. (1986). The user's mental model of an information retrieval system: An experiment on a prototype online catalog. *International Journal of Man-Machine Studies, 24*(1) 47–64.

Carroll, J.M., & Thomas, J.C. (1982). Metaphor and the cognitive representation of computer systems. *IEEE Transactions on Systems, Man, and Cybernetics, 12*(2), 107–116.

Conklin, J. (1987). *A survey of hypertext*. Microelectronics and Computer Technology Corporation. (MCC Technical Report #STP-356-86, Rev. 2). Austin, TX.

Cove, J.F., & Walsh, B.C. (1988). Online text retrieval via browsing. *Information Processing & Management, 24*(1) 31–37.

Croft, W.B., & Thompson, R.H. (1987). I³R: A new approach to the design of document retrieval systems. *Journal of the American Society for Information Science, 38*(6) 389–404.

Elkerton, J., & Williges, R.C. (1984). Information retrieval strategies in a file-search environment. *Human Factors, 26*(2) 171–184.

Ellis, D. (1984a). The effectiveness of information retrieval systems: The need for improved explanatory frameworks. *Social Science Information Studies, 4*(4) 261–272.

Ellis, D. (1984b). Theory and explanation in information retrieval research. *Journal of Information Science, 8*(1) 25–38.

Ellis, D. (1989). A behavioural approach to information retrieval system design. *Journal of Documentation, 45*(3) 171–212.

Foskett, D.J. (1983). *Pathways for communication*. London: Bingley.

Frarey, C.J. (1953). Studies of use of the subject catalog: Summary and evaluation, In M.F. Tauber (Ed.), *The Subject Analysis of Library Materials* (pp. 147–166). New York: Columbia University, School of Library Service.

Hancock, M. (1987). Subject searching behavior at the library catalogue and at the shelves: Implications for online interactive catalogues. *Journal of Documentation, 43*(4) 303–321.

Hannabuss, S. (1989). Dialogue and the search for information. *ASLIB Proceedings, 41*(3) 85–98.

Hawkins, D.T., Levy, L.R., & Montgomery, K.L. (1988). Knowledge gateways: The building blocks. *Information Processing & Management, 24*(4) 459–468.

Hildreth, C.R. (1982). Online browsing support capabilities. *Proceedings of the ASIS Annual Meeting, 19*, 127–132.

Hildreth, C.R. (1989). *Intelligent interfaces and retrieval methods for subject searching in bibliographic retrieval systems*. Washington, DC: Library of Congress Cataloging Distribution Service.

Hogeweg-de-Haart, H.P. (1984). Characteristics of social science information: A selective review of the literature. Part II. *Social Science Information Studies, 4*(1), 15–30.

Huston, M.M. (1989). Search theory and instruction for end users of online bibliographic information retrieval systems: A literature review. *Research Strategies, 7*(1) 14–32.

Ingwersen, P., & Wormell, I. (1986). Improved subject access. Browsing and scanning mechanisms in modern online IR. *Proceedings of the 9ᵗʰ annual International Conference on Research and Development in Information Retrieval,* Pisa, Italy (pp. 68–75). New York: Association for Computing Machinery.

Jones, W.P., & Dumais, S.T. (1986). The spatial metaphor for user interfaces: Experimental tests of reference by location versus name. *ACM Transactions on Office Information Systems, 4*(1) 42–63.

Kuhlthau, C.C. (1988). Developing a model of the library search process: Cognitive and affective aspects. *RQ, 28*(2) 232–242.

Kuhn, T.S. (1970). *The structure of scientific revolutions* (2ⁿᵈ ed.). Chicago, IL: University of Chicago Press.

Line, M.B. (1974). Information requirements in the social sciences, In *Access to the Literature of the Social Sciences and Humanities,* proceedings of the Conference on Access of Knowledge and Information in the Social Sciences and Humanities, Queens College, City University of New York (pp. 146–158). New York: Queens College Press.

Michel, D. (1986). *When does it make sense to use graphic representations in interactive bibliographic retrieval systems?* (Manuscript). Los Angeles: University of California Graduate School of Library and Information Science.

Miller, G.A. (1968). Psychology and information. *American Documentation, 19*(3) 286–289.

Noerr, P.L., & Bivins Noerr, K.T. (1985). Browse and navigate: An advance in database access methods. *Information Processing & Management, 21*(3) 205–213.

Norman, D.A. (1988). *The psychology of everyday things.* New York: Basic Books.

Oddy, R.N. (1977). Information retrieval through man-machine-dialogue. *Journal of Documentation, 33*(1) 1–14.

Palay, A.J., & Fox, M.S. (1981). Browsing through databases. In R.N. Oddy et al. (Eds.), *Information Retrieval Research* (pp. 310–324). London: Butterworths.

Robertson, S.E. (1977). Theories and models in information retrieval. *Journal of Documentation, 33*(2) 126–148.

Rouse, W.B., & Rouse, S.H. (1984). Human information seeking and design of information systems. *Information Processing & Management, 20*(1–2) 129–138.

Salton, G. (1968). *Automatic information organization and retrieval.* New York: McGraw-Hill.

Stenstrom, P., & McBride, R.B. (1979). Serial use by social science faculty: A survey. *College & Research Libraries, 40*(5) 426–431.

Stoan, S.K. (1984). Research and library skills: An analysis and interpretation. *College & Research Libraries, 45*(2) 99–109.

Stone, S. (1982). Humanities scholars: Information needs and uses. *Journal of Documentation, 38*(4) 292–312.

Wade, S.J., & Willett, P. (1988). INSTRUCT: A teaching package for experimental methods in information retrieval. Part III. Browsing, clustering and query expansion. *Program, 22*(1) 44–61.

Weyer, S.A. (1982). The design of a dynamic book for information search. *International Journal of Man-Machine Studies, 17*(1) 87–107.

Williams, M.E. (1986). Transparent information systems through gateways. Front ends, intermediaries, and interfaces. *Journal of the American Society for Information Science, 37*(4) 204–214.

Woods, D.D. (1984). Visual momentum: A concept to improve the cognitive coupling of person and computer. *International Journal of Man-Machine Studies, 21*(3) 229–24Z4.

3

Where should the person stop and the information search interface start?

ABSTRACT

Many users of online and other automated information systems want
to take advantage of the speed and power of automated retrieval, while
still controlling and directing the steps of the search themselves. They
do not want the system to take over and carry out the search entirely for
them. Yet the objective of much of current theory and experimentation
in information retrieval systems and interfaces is to design systems in
which the user has either no or only reactive involvement with the search
process. It is argued here that the advanced information retrieval research
community is missing an opportunity to design systems that are in better
harmony with the actual preferences of many users—sophisticated systems that provide an optimal combination of searcher control and system
retrieval power. The user may be provided effective means of directing the
search if capabilities specific to the information retrieval process, that is,
strategic behaviors normally associated with information searching, are
incorporated into the interface. There are many questions concerning (1)
the degree of user vs. system involvement in the search, and (2) the size,
or chunking, of activities; that is, how much and what type of activity the
user should be able to direct the system to do at once. These two dimensions are analyzed and a number of configurations of system capability
that combine user and system control are presented and discussed. In the

First published as Bates, M. J. (1990). Where should the person stop and the information
search interface start? *Information Processing & Management, 26*(5), 575-591.

process, the concept of the information search stratagem is introduced, and particular attention is paid to the provision of strategic, as opposed to purely procedural capabilities for the searcher. Finally, certain types of user-system relationship are selected as deserving particular attention in future information retrieval system design, and arguments are made to support the recommendations.

Introduction

Much of the advanced research and development of automated information retrieval systems to date has been done with the implicit or explicit goal of eventually automating every part of the process. New theoretical and technological developments have made possible impressive system designs—internal design features allowing many aspects of the search and retrieval to be handled automatically, often including modeling of the user and more or less natural language interfaces (Morehead, Pejtersen, & Rouse, 1984; Brooks, Daniels, & Belkin, 1985; Daniels, 1986; Fidel, 1986; Croft & Thompson, 1987; Fox, 1987; Pollitt, 1987; Vickery, Brooks, & Robinson, 1987; Salton & Buckley, 1988; Fuhr, 1989). An unspoken assumption seems to be that if a part of the information search process is not automated, it is only because we have not yet figured out how to automate it.

Some systems are designed to assist users to do their own searching (Meadow et al., 1977, 1989), and some permit browsing (Palay & Fox, 1981; Noerr & Noerr, 1985; Cove & Walsh, 1988), but much experimental research seems to be moving toward an ultimate ideal of the system that takes a request in natural language, goes off and searches the information store, and returns to the user the ideal best retrieved set of documents or information.

In other cases, the user is brought more into the search process, but in a reactive way. The implicit assumption in much information retrieval (IR) system design is that the system (and behind that, the system designer) knows best. The user provides information and responds when called on, but the system controls the pace and direction of the search.

Effective systems, in which everything is done for the user, will doubtless be produced, will be very useful for many searchers, and may not be far over the horizon. But—and this is a very important qualification—not all searchers want that kind of response from an information system. There are times when many people want to do their own searching, that is, to *direct* their own searching. They may still want the power and speed of an automated information retrieval system, but only to do certain things.

There is considerable empirical research available that supports the idea that at least some people want to control their own searches or do other things that typical automated systems do not allow and often do not even aspire to make possible (see Stenstrom & McBride, 1979; Stoan, 1984; Stone, 1982; Hogeweg-de-Haart, 1984; Ellis, 1989), also discussion and review of research in Bates (1989). Many want a sense of control over the search; they want to know what is going on during the search, and what information is being included and rejected and why.

One of the reasons why there is so much effort to design systems to do the searching for the user is that current systems are difficult to use. It is argued here that that difficulty is related to the fact that current systems are often not designed around the actual behaviors that people find compatible in information searching in manual environments. The interfaces are not designed around search behaviors that promote the strategic goals of an information search, and that make using good search strategy easy and natural. Currently, the exercise of good strategy is usually achieved in spite of, or is superimposed on, information system designs.

Consequently, the goal has been formed in much IR research to have the system do the searching for us, but that is not the only alternative. It should also be possible to design search interfaces that harmonize with and make easy the prosecution of good search strategy, systems that make it easy for novices to move quickly into good searching because the system promotes it.

One can use the analogy of automatic shifts and automatic cameras (Bates, 1989). Side by side with these highly automated forms of technology there is a very strong demand for stick shift automobiles and cameras with hand settings. These latter forms may incorporate many wonderful new automated parts, which their buyers are happy to have, but certain aspects of the operation of both stick shift automobiles and manual cameras remain in the control of their users. Similarly, we may find that many users of sophisticated information systems are happy to take advantage of computer power, but insist on retaining a heavy component of user power as well. Therefore, in this article we do not ask the usual question, "How can we automate everything in an information retrieval system?" Rather, we ask, "Which things shall we automate and which not?"

Once such a question is raised, the matter of design quickly becomes more complicated than that question sounds. If we design an information retrieval system and interface intended to be controlled during the search process by the user, then we may want to design *whole new capabilities* that are not relevant when the entire process is taken out of the searcher's hands.

So, let us reword that last question more precisely: "What capabilities should we design for the system to do, and what capabilities should we enable the searcher to exercise?"

In recent years, there has been an explosion of writing on the design of the human-computer interface, and a number of authors have given attention to developing general models of the nature of the interface and design principles to use in creating the interface (e.g., Cuff, 1980; Bannon et al., 1983; Norman, 1983, 1984; Borgman, 1984; Shneiderman, 1987; Farooq & Dominick, 1988; Helander, 1988; Kammarsgaard, 1988; Taylor, 1988a, 1988b). It is assumed in this discussion that good general design principles of the sort suggested by the above-referenced authors will underlie any interface developed for an information retrieval (IR) system.

In addition to general design principles, however, there are design issues specific to the information search process that should be considered as well in attempting to create an optimal interface for information retrieval systems. These information-search-specific features are the focus here. Thus, for example, suggestions to be made in this article are largely independent of one of the most common distinctions made among interface designs, namely, whether activities are carried out through use of menu, prompt, command, or direct manipulation modes. On the other hand, we will give a great deal of attention to facilitating elements of behavior that are specific to information searching.

Another commonly discussed issue regarding interfaces will be largely ignored here as well, namely, design for novices vs. advanced users. Design features to be proposed can be adapted up or down for users with greater or lesser experience; my concern at this point is the prior one of identifying the features in the first place.

Some of what will be discussed in this article involves capabilities that, to be workable, have to be incorporated in the internal design of the system, that is, into the searching and file organization, as well as into the interface. My primary interest is in what the user experiences when searching, and that, of course, entails the interface. I do not, however, mean to imply that only interface design is involved in the suggestions to be made.

In this article, various ways of dividing the labor of an information search between person and system will be considered. We will look at a number of different configurations composed of the two dimensions of degree of system involvement in the searching, and types of search activity carried out by the person or by the system. The merits of the various possibilities are considered and recommendations made for future research and development.

TABLE 1. *Levels of system involvement*

LEVEL	DEFINITION
0	No system involvement All search activities human generated and executed.
1	Displays possible activities System lists search activities when asked. Said activities may or may not also be executable by system (higher levels).
2	Executes activities on command System executes specific actions at human command.
3	Monitors search and recommends System monitors search process and recommends search activities:
a	Only when searcher asks for suggestions.
b	Always when it identifies a need.
4	Executes automatically System executes actions automatically and then:
a	Informs the searcher.
b	Does not inform the searcher.

How can the labor be divided between system and user?

Levels of system involvement

Table 1 lists five levels of system involvement (SI) in searching. By implication, the amount of the user's involvement is the complement of that
of the system—that is, the more the system involvement, the less the user
has to do in the actual search process.

In Table 1, the general terms "search activity" or "action" are used to
cover several types of search thinking or behavior that the user or system
might engage in. Those activities will be discussed in the next section.

At Level 0 the designated search activities are human generated and
executed; they are not suggested or carried out by the system. At Level 1 the
system may list available or recommended search actions when asked. It
may also explain how to carry out search activities, or instruct the user in
search strategies. System ability to list these activities, however, in no way
necessarily entails system capability to *carry out* the activities. The latter
capability may be in the hands of the searcher only, the system, or both.

At Level 2 the system can actually carry out search actions on command of the searcher. It still responds passively to the searcher, however,
having no capability to analyze searches or develop strategies. At Level 3,
the system shows some artificial intelligence for the first time. Using more
or less sophisticated techniques, the system can now monitor a search
dynamically, analyze it, and recommend search activities, either when a

TABLE 2. *Levels of search activities*

LEVEL	NAME	DEFINITION
1	Move	An identifiable thought or action that is a part of information searching.
2	Tactic	One or a handful of moves made to further a search.
3	Stratagem	A larger, more complex set of thoughts and/or actions than the tactic; a stratagem consists of multiple tactics and/or moves, all designed to exploit the file structure of a particular search domain thought to contain desired information.
4	Strategy	A plan, which may contain moves, tactics, and/or stratagems, for an entire information search.

searcher asks for help (3a), or at any time it detects problems (3b). Finally, at Level 4 the system receives the user's query and executes the entire search for the user, either informing the user of decisions made along the way (4a), or not (4b).

It should be noted that these levels are not necessarily descriptive of entire systems. That is, any given IR system may contain subsystems or features drawn from various levels.

Type of search activity

Our second problem is to decide how to chunk search behavior. In Table 2, four levels or types of search activities (SA) are described.

The "move," or identifiable thought or action that is a part of information searching, is the basic unit of analysis of search behavior considered in this model, in much the same way that "field" is the basic unit of analysis in the literature of file organization. It is the smallest unit used in our discussion of searching, just as "field" is for file organization. The term may be operationalized in different ways in particular instances, depending on the needs of the moment. For example, in using "field" in catalog design, the "imprint," i.e., place of publication, publisher, and date, may be defined as a single field for some purposes, and in other cases the individual components may be considered fields.

In like manner, in observing search behavior, we may want to define "enter search formulation" as a move, or pick on some smaller actions as moves, such as "enter term A," "enter AND operator," etc. "Move," like "field," is a basic-unit, workhorse term, and is to be applied to small, discrete thoughts or actions associated with information searching.

"Move" is a neutral term, and can be applied to any sort of activity associated with searching. Moves can be a part of orderly, well-planned searches or random, formless efforts by people who do not know what they are doing. (Compare Fidel's use of the term "moves" specific to online searching in current systems, which is "changes in query formulation, . . . made to resolve three problem situations," viz., when retrieved sets are too large, too small, or off target [Fidel, 1985, p. 61].)

"Tactic" represents the first level at which strategic considerations are primary. A tactic is a move or moves made with the purpose of improving or speeding the search in some way. A tactic is carried out either in anticipation of problems, or in response to them, even if the "problem" is simply taking longer than one would like to find something.

Table 3 includes definitions for some example tactics representing the range of categories of tactics suggested by the author to date. For example, the tactic SUPER is to move upward hierarchically to a broader term. SUPER is strategic because the searcher does it to improve the search in some way. To SUPER may increase the recall, since broader terms often describe larger sets of documents. Or the searcher may use SUPER because she now realizes that an initial term used covered only part of the concept she wanted to express. (The reader is referred to Bates [1979a, 1979b] for fuller lists of tactics. Other techniques specific to searching in operational database retrieval systems are discussed in Harter [1985] and Fidel [1985].)

A "stratagem" is a complex of a number of moves and/or tactics, and generally involves both a particular identified information search domain anticipated to be productive by the searcher, and a mode of tackling the particular file organization of that domain. A stratagem is larger than a tactic because it generally involves a repetitive sequence of activities designed to exploit both a particular information domain and a mode of searching selected to be particularly effective in that domain.

A domain might be a series of volumes of a journal, a citation index, an online directory of addresses, or any number of other bodies of information characterized by common features and organizational structure. A shrewdly chosen line of attack on that organizational structure can lead to very effective retrieval. Choice of a stratagem and its associated information domain is often part of designing a strategy for a search. Strategies frequently involve the search of several information domains, with different stratagems for each domain. Table 4 lists and defines some example stratagems.

For example, the "Journal Run" stratagem involves identifying a promising journal and scanning through it for articles of interest. The search

TABLE 3. *Selected example search tactics (See Bates, 1979a, 1979b for other tactics.)*

MONITORING TACTICS	
CHECK	To review the original request and compare it to the current search topic to see that it is the same.
RECORD	To keep track of trails followed and of desirable trails not followed or not completed.
FILE STRUCTURE TACTICS	
SELECT	To break down complex search queries into subproblems and work on one problem at a time.
SURVEY	To review, at each decision point of the search, the available options before selection.
CUT	When selecting among several ways to search a given query, to choose the option that cuts out the largest part of the search domain at once.
STRETCH	To use a source for other than its intended purposes.
SEARCH FORMULATION TACTICS	
SPECIFY	To search on terms that are as specific as the information desired.
EXHAUST	To include most or all elements of the query in the initial search formulation; to add one or more of the query elements to an already-prepared search formulation.
REDUCE	To minimize the number of elements of the query in the initial search formulation; to subtract one or more of the query elements from an already-prepared search formulation.
PARALLEL	To make the search formulation broad (or broader) by including synonyms or otherwise conceptually parallel terms.
PINPOINT	To make the search formulation precise by minimizing (or reducing) the number of parallel terms, retaining the more perfectly descriptive terms.
TERM TACTICS	
SUPER	To move upward hierarchically to a broader (superordinate) term.
SUB	To move downward hierarchically to a more specific (subordinate) term.
RELATE	To move sideways hierarchically to a coordinate term.
REARRANGE	To reverse or rearrange the words in search terms in any or all reasonable orders.
CONTRARY	To search for the term logically opposite from that describing the desired information.
RESPELL	To search under a different spelling.
RESPACE	To try spacing variants.
IDEA TACTICS	
RESCUE	In an otherwise unproductive approach, to check for possibly productive paths still untried.
BREACH	To breach the boundaries of one's region of search, to revise one's concept of the limits of the intellectual or physical territory in which one searches to respond to a query.
FOCUS	To look at the query more narrowly, in one or both of two senses: (1) to move from the whole query to a part of it or (2) to move from a broader to a narrower conceptualization of the query.

TABLE 4. *Example stratagems*

STRATAGEM	DEFINITION
Journal run	Having identified a journal central to one's topic of interest, one reads or browses through issues or volumes of the journal.
Citation search	Using a citation index or database, one starts with a citation and determines what other works have cited it.
Area scan	After locating a subject area of interest in a classification scheme, one browses materials in the same general area.
Footnote chase	One follows up footnotes or references, moving backward in time to other related materials.
Index or catalog subject search	One looks up subject indexing terms or free text terms in a catalog or abstracting and indexing service (online or offline) and locates all references on one's topic of interest.
Author subject search	Having found an author writing on a topic of interest, one looks up that author in catalogs, bibliographies, or indexes to see if he or she has written any other materials on the same subject.

domain is the run of volume years examined and the search technique is to locate the journal and scan through contents lists and relevant articles within the issues. A searcher would ordinarily engage in this stratagem after having noticed that many articles of interest for the topic at hand are published in the journal.

Stratagems are discussed in more detai in (Bates, 1989), though not under that name. Research evidence is reviewed there supporting the importance of these techniques to searchers. All of the example stratagems in Table 4 are currently implementable manually, and some online. It is argued in (Bates, 1989) that all should be available online, and means of implementing them online are discussed.

The military sense of stratagem is a "maneuver designed to deceive or surprise an enemy" (*American Heritage Dictionary of the English Language*, 1969, p. 1273). There is no implication of deception in the usage of the term here, however. A stratagem may, in some cases, constitute the entire search; more often, an entire search involves many moves, tactics, and stratagems.

A "strategy" is a plan for an entire search, and may contain all of the previously mentioned types of search activity. A strategy for an entire search is difficult to state in any but the simplest searches, because most real-life searches are influenced by the information gathered along the way in the search. Searchers alter the search formulation and the next steps to be taken in light of information discovered in the search process (Bates, 1989). However, here is an example search strategy for a fairly simple search:

To write a five-page report on the history of the Universal Decimal Classification scheme:

- Search the online catalog by subject or title for a basic text on library classification and cataloging.

- Locate the text and read basic information about the history of the scheme.

- Note references in the text to books and articles giving more detail on the scheme.

- Look up call numbers of referenced books and journals in the catalog.

- Locate items.

If desired, this strategy could be described in even more detail by listing the individual moves needed to accomplish each step in this description. For example, each move needed to look up and locate the text in the stacks could be described.

Now that the search activity levels have been defined, more needs to be said about the relationships among these types. Search activities have been arrayed top to bottom in Table 2 from small to large amounts of activity that would commonly be associated with each. Tactics may involve one or more moves, a stratagem may include tactics and moves, and strategies may include all three.

However, it should be noted that these four types of activity are not just different sizes of the same thing. It is not the case that one can necessarily put some moves together to make a tactic, some tactics together to make a stratagem, and some stratagems together to make a strategy. Sometimes a tactic is a single move, sometimes several. A stratagem may employ tactics or not; and so on. Each of these is an "emergent" phenomenon; each higher level of search activity is conceptually different, that is, has different properties, from the lower levels, as well as (usually) being more extensive in some sense, just as water is something different from and more than merely the addition together of hydrogen and oxygen.

Furthermore, no claim is made that tactics and stratagems exhaust the kinds of more global activities that a searcher would engage in beyond moves. Any particular search may include other behaviors and cognitions. Thus, a search composed entirely of tactics, or entirely of stratagems, would not be common nor would it be an objective to be desired. At this point, all other activities that searchers engage in besides tactics and stratagems, for

TABLE 5. *System involvement by search activity*

SYSTEM INVOLVEMENT LEVEL		SEARCH ACTIVITY LEVEL			
		MOVES 1	TACTICS 2	STRATAGEMS 3	STRATEGIES 4
No system involvement	0	0-1	0-2	0-3	0-4
Displays possible activities	1	1-1	1-2	1-3	1-4
Executes actions on command	2	2-1	2-2	2-3	2-4
Monitors search and recommends	3	3-1	3-2	3-3	3-4
Executes automatically	4	4-1	4-2	4-3	4-4

want of a more complete model, must be described in terms of the moves of which they are composed. Currently, the description of a strategy may include various combinations of all three lower types of search activity.

System involvement and search activities combined

Now we are in a position to combine the two dimensions, levels of system involvement (SI), and types of search activities (SA), into a single table. See Table 5. The table creates twenty combinations (plus subcategories at levels 3 SI and 4 SI) of system involvement and search activity level. To put it differently, the categories represent twenty different ways in which the user and the system can share the activities of information searching.

From here on, the twenty possible configurations will be labeled with a two-part number: The first part represents the level of system involvement and the second part represents the level of search activity. These number combinations are all listed in Table 5; for example, "0-2" represents no system involvement associated with tactics.

Each cell of the table should be seen as representing a possible con-figuration of combined human-system search activity. That activity may be realized through many different possible specific designs and specific capabilities. For example, the ability of the system to carry out a tactic at the searcher's command (cell 2-2) may be manifested through many different types of interface designs (menu, direct manipulation, etc.), and there are many different particular tactics that designers may choose to implement. So each cell represents a whole class of capabilities and designs, not just one.

On the other hand, each configuration represented in the table need not define a whole system. These combinations are ways of thinking about human-system relationships in an information retrieval system.

In a system of any complexity there may be many different combinations of that relationship implemented in different parts of the system. For example, one system may have excellent methods of implementing tactics and strategies in the interface while making no provision for stratagems. Or a system may monitor (Level 3 SI) one function of the search interface, but have no monitoring capability regarding several other functions, and so on. A designer who chooses to use any of these configurations may combine it in countless ways in a full system design. The purpose here is to present these possible configurations.

Note that the fundamental focus in the table, as well as throughout this article, is on *human direction of activities*. Thus while every cell represents some combination of human and machine activity, that combination is assumed, wherever possible, to be directed by the searcher. So, for example, looking at Level 1 SI and scanning left to right across the table, we can say that this level is concerned with designing configurations in which the searcher can direct the system to display possible moves the searcher can carry out (cell 1–1), direct the system to display possible tactics the searcher can carry out (1–2), etc.

As we go from top to bottom in the table the system has greater power in searching; likewise, moving from left to right in the table, the system can carry out search activities that are larger. In systematically examining the various combinations of system involvement and search activity, we hope to gain a fuller understanding of, and a new way of thinking about, the powers that can be put into the hands of the user of an IR system.

In the remainder of this section, each row of Table 5 is considered in turn.

Level 0 system involvement

At the 0 SI level there is no system involvement in the designated search activity. Said activity must be carried out by people, either at the system terminal or completely manually. So, for example, with a system that permitted moves, but had no strategic capabilities (i.e., no tactics, stratagems, or strategies—a configuration common in online systems today), the searcher would have to break down every strategic intent into a series of moves that the system could understand.

To illustrate this example, the searcher may decide to use the tactic CONTRARY when searching on the term "literacy." This tactic is to search for the term logically opposite from that describing the desired information. So, where there is no system involvement at the tactics level (0–2), the searcher must think up the tactic, that is, get the idea to search for the logical opposite of "literacy," then actually think of the logical opposite, "illiteracy," and finally, search on the term "illiteracy." The first two moves are mental, and the last, to search on the term "illiteracy" may involve one or several further moves on or offline, such as verifying the term in a thesaurus, then entering it as both a controlled vocabulary and free text term in an online search.

So, in this example, many moves were involved, and they made it possible to carry out a tactic in an online search, but there was no system involvement with the tactic *as a unit*. The system did not talk about CONTRARY in its interactions with the user—not as a possible search behavior (Level 1 SI), not as a command the searcher could use (Level 2 SI), not as a recommended action (Level 3 SI), and not as a unit automatically carried out (Level 4 SI).

Level 1 system involvement

At Level 1 the searcher can ask for information about searching. Little of the information currently offered searchers online is strategic in nature; most of it is at the move level. Help screens instruct people in how to word commands and the like, but seldom offer advice on higher level search activities. When we are thinking about possible information that can be provided the user who requests it in an IR system, recommendations about search strategy, including the use of stratagems and tactics, should be included in our thinking as well, whether or not the system has the capacity to carry out these techniques itself.

Recommendations associated with Level 1 can be put in even broader terms: *Information should be provided by the system at the level of the human process engaged in, rather than just in terms of explaining the system to the user.* It is not the job of the user to conform to the system; rather it is the job of the system to help the user achieve his/her goals through the system. The user should be the reference point. Explaining the mechanics of a command is all right for the person who requests an explanation, but information should also be available to assist the searcher in using that command as a part of the search process as understood and thought about normally by human beings. That system assistance then suggests links between the human conceptual process and system capabilities that aid the user in carrying out his/her desired activity.

This is an important point. We want to look here at various possible combinations of human and searcher effort. One way for the system to help is to provide information that promotes the searcher's thinking process, even if actions at that level are not available directly to the searcher in that system. For example, if the searcher asks for help on tactics, the system

TABLE 6. *Suggested tactics in response to searcher requests**

SEARCHER COMMAND	SYSTEM RESPONSE LIST
Too many hits	SPECIFY
	EXHAUST
	PINPOINT
	BLOCK
	SUB
Too few hits	NEIGHBOR
	TRACE
	PARALLEL
	FIX
	SUPER
	RELATE
	VARY
No hits	RESPACE
	RESPELL
	REARRANGE
	CONTRARY
	SUPER
	RELATE
	NEIGHBOR
	TRACE
Need other terms or Wrong terms	NEIGHBOR
	TRACE
	SUPER
	SUB
	RELATE
Revise terms	RESPACE
	RESPELL
	FIX
	REVERSE
	CONTRARY
	SUPER
	SUB
	RELATE
Revise search formulation	SPECIFY
	EXHAUST
	REDUCE
	PARALLEL
	PINPOINT
	BLOCK

*Definitions of most of above tactics in Table 3; others in Bates [1979a].

may suggest CONTRARY, even if there is no CONTRARY command. It is still of value to the searcher to have this tactic suggested, because it might be one that he or she would not have thought of otherwise, and the searcher can then figure out how to effectuate this particular activity using the existing system. So this particular form of system involvement, though elementary, can make a material difference in the quality and satisfactoriness of the search.

Note that at this level the system is not monitoring the search—it is not figuring out what the searcher should be doing. Rather it is passively responding to the request of the searcher for more information. In the following paragraphs, each cell in Level 1 SI is considered in succession:

1-1 This level corresponds most closely to current help screens in IR systems. The searcher uses a command such as "help" or "explain" along with a command or feature and is told how to use that capability. In most current operational systems, such as online catalogs and databank search services, e.g., DIALOG, the level of search activity available to searchers is almost all at the "move" level. This holds true whether the system operates with a menu or command approach. An example command would be "Help Subject," with the system responding with instructions such as, "To search by subject enter 'Find subj' followed by the subject you want to search." (To choose to search by subject is a strategic decision, but in most cases that decision has been made by the time the searcher asks for the help. The response to the query is purely procedural, i.e., at the move level.)

1-2 In this category, in response to requests from the searcher, the system provides information on tactics the searcher can use. This is the first level at which the information is *strategic* rather than purely procedural. Here the searcher wants to know about techniques that can be used to make a better search.

The left-hand column of Table 6, "Suggested tactics in response to searcher requests," lists some request phrases that the searcher might enter, and the right-hand column lists suggested tactics. A "Help Help" command could list the possible request phrases. Only the tactics' names are listed in Table 6, but in the actual response the tactics could be defined and examples given, either automatically or in response to a command or mouse click by the searcher.

Definitions of tactics given in Table 3 were originally developed to facilitate the searching of knowledgeable, generally professional searchers. Choice of tactics to propose to users and wording of definitions could be simplified for casual end users.

INFORMATION SEARCH STRATEGIES

Select most appropriate strategy for your need:

1. Locating information for research term paper.
2. Locating information for book report.
3. Locating materials on professor's reading list.
4. Verify or complete a reference for a bibliography.
5. Locate section in book stacks on your topic of interest.

FIG. 1. *Help screen partial list of strategies*

1–3 As in level 1–2, in response to requests from the searcher, the system responds with lists and descriptions of stratagems. Each stratagem could be defined and suggestions made for when best to use each one.

1–4 Here the system would describe an entire search strategy for a user who requested it. As noted earlier, since searches often change in mid-stream depending on what searchers have already found, this approach might have limited value for more sophisticated searchers. However, in cases where a type of need is very common and a certain sequence of steps can be identified as usually being useful in that case, such an approach could be of considerable value.

For example, it might be quite helpful to undergraduate students in a college or university to be able to select one of a set of common search strategies and be told how to carry it out. A partial list of strategies that could be listed in a college or university online catalog help screen appears in Figure 1: When the student selects one of these strategies, the system displays a general purpose list of steps that are likely to be productive in the stated situation.

Level 2 system involvement

At Level 2 the system executes search activities at the searcher's command. This level is of particular interest because it represents the possibility of designing system configurations in which the searcher enters, as a single command, instructions to do various types of search activities, many of which are themselves strategic units. In most current information retrieval systems, the user must assemble a variety of atomistic moves, in the right order and with correct spelling and formatting of a series of commands, to produce what he or she may be thinking of as a single unit. If for example the searcher can input a command to carry out a particular tactic that would ordinarily involve a half-dozen mental and online moves, it may be much easier and faster for that searcher to do a good search on an automated system.

In this section we consider ways in which systems might be designed to enable the searcher to enter a single command that would accomplish an entire move, tactic, stratagem, or strategy. Each cell in this row of Level 2 SI is considered in succession below:

2–1 This is the level at which most online systems work most of the time. Most of the things a user can do are at the level of moves. For the most part the search capabilities available to the users are neutral; that is, they are not linked to strategic considerations in optimizing a search.

2–2 With search capabilities in this category the searcher can tell the system to carry out a tactic. Here for the first time the searcher does not have to do all the thinking and search formulating in carrying out a tactic. At this point the system itself starts to have the ability to carry out strategic activities (not just describe or instruct in them, as at Level 1 SI).

To return to an example used earlier, if the user inputs "CONTRARY literacy" the system could look in its thesaurus for the logically opposite term to "literacy," OR it in with "literacy," and search on it too. Artificial intelligence techniques are not needed—only proper indications in the stored thesaurus.

Other term tactics would be relatively easy to program. SUPER, SUB, and RELATE could all revise search formulations automatically to include broader, narrower, or related terms listed as such in a thesaurus resident in the IR system. Implementation of such a capability might be along these lines: The searcher highlights the component in a search formulation that is to be altered, types in or hits some function key that indicates, e.g., SUB, and the thesaurus automatically substitutes an ORed set ("hedge") of narrower terms for the indicated term.

REARRANGE can be handled with a straightforward permutation algorithm, and RESPELL and RESPACE can be carried out with the help of dictionaries and algorithms that look for terms that vary by only one or two characters or spaces.

Search formulation tactics, in particular, EXHAUST, REDUCE, PARALLEL, PINPOINT, and BLOCK, could be implemented by allowing the searcher to edit search formulations on screen, similar to editing in word processing. Postings set sizes and example brief citations could be displayed after each modification to enable the searcher to assess the effectiveness of the tactic in improving the search.

These last five tactics all involve manipulating the search formulation by adding or subtracting ANDed and ORed terms. Inherent in the Boolean logic, as is well known, is the fact that each additional AND element will produce an output set that is the same size or smaller than the previous set, and each additional term ORed with a preexisting term in the search formulation will produce an output set that is the same size or larger. So dropping or adding OR and AND elements can increase or decrease output sets as desired by the searcher. Ability to implement these tactics quickly, without laborious re-entering of terms, could make fast, powerful improvement in search formulations and results possible. (See also discussion in Bates [1979a, 1987].)

2-3 At this level the searcher can call up stratagems from the system. Stratagems involve a search domain and a method of searching the domain. The searcher calls up the stratagem and the system asks for any information it needs to implement it. The purpose here is to make it possible for the searcher to do quickly and easily what he or she would normally do in carrying out a stratagem manually.

The Journal Run was used earlier as an example of a stratagem. It might be implemented by allowing the searcher to input (or select through a menu) the phrase "Journal Run." The system then asks for the journal title and years to be reviewed, and whether the searcher wants to see contents lists or the full text of the journal articles first. Since people doing a Journal Run in a manual environment often browse through articles and read short sections of the article here and there, the system might also offer "snapshots" or randomly selected passages from the articles (see Bates, 1989).

Thus, in response to the request for a stratagem, the system makes available to the searcher a package of capabilities specific to that stratagem, with the interaction at the interface designed to be as well fitted as possible to the search needs associated with that particular stratagem. The specific configuration of the interface interactions and the specific combination of capabilities for the searcher will be different in the case of each stratagem. Elsewhere I have suggested key design features associated with each of six stratagems (though not under the name of "stratagem") (Bates, 1989).

2-4 Here the searcher can call up an entire search strategy. This might be achievable in cases where the search is relatively straightforward and requires a routine series of actions. An excellent example of that is Rita Bergman's "scripts" (1981) for common types of searches in the chemistry literature, such as the search for a Registry Number. After asking for the search, the user is shown a prompt screen, which asks for the relevant information needed by the system to carry out that search type.

Another variant of allowing the searcher to select whole strategies is the following: The searcher is shown a full array of search devices—moves, tactics, stratagems, and strategies. He/she may then select any desired combination, rather like punching in programming on a video cassette recorder. The system then executes just what the searcher has asked for in the chosen sequence.

Level 3 system involvement

This is the level at which the configurations begin to show artificial intelligence, in monitoring and reacting to the search dynamically. Not surprisingly, it is more difficult on the whole to implement capabilities at this level than at the previous levels.

Levels 3a and 3b refer, respectively, to suggesting help only when the user asks for it, or always when the system identifies a need. Since people do not always know when they need help, or when help would make a difference, a compromise might be for a message such as "Help Available" to appear in the corner of the screen when the system identifies a problem. If the user ignores it, the message goes away after a minute. Thus the user is informed but not forced to respond to or deal with a screen that overrides the current search.

3-1 At this level the system monitors searcher moves and suggests improvements, either when the searcher asks, or at any time. The easiest problem to identify is incorrectly spelled or non-existent commands. Poor choice of moves, on the other hand, is a strategic problem that is difficult to identify at the level of moves, except where a move is illegal or impossible at a certain point in a search.

In the IIDA project Charles Meadow (1977) experimented with identifying some common problems at the move level and giving feedback to searchers. For example, the searcher might get a message if commands were repeated too often or if "thrashing" was observed.

3-2 At this level recommendations are made when some tactic would be beneficial or when current tactical behavior is observed to be inadequate. Tactics can be recommended when the system observes problems. Here are some examples: When a very large or very small number of postings, or no postings at all results from a search formulation, the system can suggest that the searcher use one or more tactics from a list of tactics helpful at those points (see Table 6).

The use of all very broad terms in the search formulation can lead to a message suggesting SPECIFY; a very lengthy complicated search formulation can lead to the suggestion of SELECT.

3-3 Monitoring of searches to suggest stratagems is an approach with some interesting possibilities. Most stratagems involve identifying a domain of information that potentially has a lot of information of the type desired. For example, in a manual library environment the searcher may notice that a lot of the articles of interest in a new area appear in one particular journal. Thus, to go to that journal and look through issue after issue for relevant articles is a good stratagem at that point in the search. Suppose the searcher does that, and notices two or three articles by the same individual that are exactly in the topic of interest. The searcher may then do an author search to find everything else the author has written on that topic. Having identified those articles by that author, our searcher now scans through the references at the end of the articles to find other articles, authors, or journals of interest; and so on.

In this example, the searcher uses three stratagems in a row—journal run, author subject search, and footnote chasing. A system that is monitoring user searches might also be able to identify points where certain stratagems look like smart things to do. Suppose the searcher described above enters a standard Boolean search in a bibliographic database. The search formulation produces a retrieved set of 100 items. The system tallies the frequencies of journals and authors in that set. Where the number of publications in the retrieved set from any one journal exceeds a certain threshold, then the journal run stratagem is suggested. In like manner, where the number of publications by any one author in the retrieved set exceeds another threshold, the author subject search is suggested.

3–4 At this level the system would be monitoring the search in order to suggest whole strategies. If the system recognized that an individual was inputting the necessary elements for a certain type of search for which a strategy was already available, e.g., a Registry number search in chemistry, it might suggest that the user call up the strategy instead.

Level 4 system involvement

At this level the system conducts the given activity automatically for the user. At level 4a, the user is informed of what the system is doing as it goes along; at Level 4b, the user is informed only of the final result. Since no system is yet available that can read minds, useful activities at this level presuppose that the searcher has in some way communicated a need to the system. From that point however, the system conducts its activities automatically.

Level 4a would involve describing system activities to the searcher—whatever their internal system design—in ways that are meaningful and useful to the searcher. The need for a user to know what has been done for him or her, even when the results are satisfactory, has often been ignored or underestimated by human intermediaries and IR system designers alike. People frequently need to make their own assessment of whether all likely sources of information, including search terms used, have been examined, in order to determine whether their search has been adequate or should be extended to other domains. Thus, even Level 4a gives the user some control of a type not often available in more advanced IR systems.

At level 4a SI we may imagine that the system reports its activities as moves, or tactics, or stratagems, or strategies, or some combination thereof. That is, the various cells at level 4a represent different ways of reporting to the user what the system is doing automatically. Design configurations that might be tested would answer questions such as: Do people want to learn what the system is doing in a move-by-move way (Level 4a–1), or in higher-level strategic terms (Levels 4a–2, 4a–3, 4a–4)?

For the general user, it would seem to make more sense to show searchers what is happening in strategic terms, such as "expanding the search by using broader terms," than to say merely, "replacing term A with term B." Professional searchers however, may want to see more of the search at the move level, so that they know exactly what is being altered and how.

Level 4b, where the system carries out whole searches automatically, is the level which resembles the objective being sought by much IR research today. Here the user would describe a need and the system would determine a strategy and carry it out automatically. In this case the user's involvement in directing the search is minimal.

Recommendations

Having engaged in the two-way analysis of levels of system involvement in searching by types of searching activities, we are now in a position to return to the question posed at the beginning of this article: Where should the person stop and the information search interface start? Table 7 summarizes the current implementation status of the various categories of user-system searching capabilities, as well as the recommended directions for future research.

Operational information retrieval systems, particularly online catalogs and database search services, are currently implemented largely at the move level (1–1 and 2–1). Strategic behavior in information searching must overwhelmingly be exercised by the human searcher (0–2, 0–3, 0–4). Little or no strategic advice, let alone actual operational capability of a strategic nature, is provided by systems to the user.

TABLE 7. *Implementation status and recommendations*

		SEARCH ACTIVITY LEVEL			
SYSTEM INVOLVEMENT LEVEL		MOVES 1	TACTICS 2	STRATAGEMS 3	STRATEGIES 4
No system involvement	0	*Search activities carried out by searcher*			
Displays possible activities	1	*Most operational IR systems now*	*Area of recommended development*		*Hold for later*
Executes actions on command	2				
Monitors search and recommends 3	a b	*Bypass*			
Executes automatically 4	a b		*Hold for later*		
		Common current objective of IR experimental design			

The goal of many experimental information retrieval systems, on the other hand, is to leap over most of the possible mixtures of human and system involvement to a completely automatic search for the user (Level 4b SI). Exciting as these possibilities are, I believe that there are equally exciting areas of development that are being overlooked.

I recommend that more research and development attention be paid to the central area of Table 7 (1–2, 1–3, 2–2, 2–3, 3–2, 3–3). It will be argued in various ways in the remainder of this section that we can expect a high payoff for the development of these capabilities. Furthermore, as these capabilities are tried, we may learn more about how to develop the remaining categories in the table, in particular, how to provide assistance with strategies for whole searches (1–4, 2–4, 3–4), and how to improve the all-automatic searches (Level 4 SI), where so much energy is going now.

It is recommended that we bypass level 3–1 for the most part, wherein the system monitors a search and suggests moves. Meadow's excellent study found that this combination required sophisticated design and was difficult to do (Meadow et al., 1977). Many actions at the move level do not track well with human thinking about searching. It is often hard to tell from search moves what search strategies or tactics are intended by the searcher. If we choose to invest the considerable effort that would be required to do such sophisticated monitoring, and I think it *is* desirable to be able to give users such feedback, let us first try to develop the monitoring in terms of search activities that are strategic, that is, that correspond better with human thinking about searching. It may actually prove to be easier to determine the searcher's intent, and thus provide good monitoring and advice, when the searcher's allowable actions are in strategic, rather than move-level units.

Research efforts may thus pay off more if they are invested at the tactics level and above, 3–2 and 3–3, rather than at the 3–1 (move) level. Also, computer systems have improved greatly since Meadow's efforts in the mid-1970s; we might find it easier to develop search monitoring in association with IR systems that give users strategic search capabilities directly as tactic and stratagem commands rather than through the combination of many moves that are subject to many interpretations.

In addition to the above general points, I make the following arguments for the recommendation to develop the center area of Table 7:

1. Research has demonstrated that people are familiar with, and want, capabilities at strategic levels. Strategy development and modification, particularly with subject searching, has been frequently identified as the most, or one of the most difficult of all phases of searching (Standera, 1978; Fenichel, 1980–81; Matthews, Lawrence, & Ferguson, 1983; Markey, 1984; Borgman, Case, & Meadow, 1989; Hildreth, 1989).

The response of the information science research community so far has been mainly to try to eliminate the stage of strategy development altogether for users. But other research shows that at least some users take it for granted that they should control their information searching, and rarely delegate the task (Stone, 1982; Hogeweg-de-Haart, 1984; Stoan, 1984; Ellis, 1989). We still do not know how widespread these attitudes are, but then we have tended not to ask the question either, since so much research is geared toward producing the perfect automatic Level 4b search.

There is also evidence that many queries begin in a very unclear state (Taylor, 1968; Kuhlthau, 1988). It is just not possible to clarify the query without some interaction and experimenting. Donald Norman makes some cogent points in this regard:

> Third-person interaction [command mode] is well suited for situations in which the job is laborious or repetitive, as well as those in which you can trust the system (or other person) to do the job for you properly. Sometimes it is nice to have a chauffeur. But if the job is critical, novel, or ill-specified, or if you do not yet know exactly what is to be done, then you need direct, first-person interaction. Now direct control is essential; an intermediary gets in the way. (Norman, 1988, p. 184)

It is certainly the case that many information searches are "critical, novel, or ill-specified." Thus, the possibility of designing a "stick shift" information search interface and system deserves considerably more exploration.

2. Closely related to these points about the desire and need to have control of search strategies and behaviors are issues about control generally in an automated interface. Human beings have a variety of social and emotional, as well as intellectual, needs. Things they interact with in their environment, even supposedly neutral machines, tend to get incorporated into the human social world and to play roles determined by people that may not be the ones originally intended. Designers who do not acknowledge these needs and behaviors may find their products misapplied or rejected.

Most people have a strong desire for a sense of effectiveness in and mastery of their environment, particularly with respect to things that affect them in a close and personal way. Control of tools or powerful machinery can touch deep issues of personal power and freedom. For example, in the United States, where cities are spread out over large areas, learning to drive and acquiring a driver's license is a veritable rite of passage for many American teenagers. Ability to drive marks a transition to freedom, mobility, and power over one's circumstances that provides at one blow many of the perquisites of adulthood. I think it is therefore no accident that many American citizens are resistant to the use of public transportation or car pools, even in those cases where they are convenient and cheaper than cars.

As computers are experienced more and more as commonplace personal utilities, I think we can expect to see the same urge for control over computer systems, including information retrieval systems, that we see with cars. To quote the refrain of a popular television commercial of a few years ago, "Mother, I'd rather do it myself!" Experiences with many hand-holding menu-driven systems are showing that after a modest amount of experience, users frequently want the capability of controlling the processing more directly themselves. In seeking to provide the convenience of a wholly automatic Level 4b information search to users, we in information science may unwittingly be robbing people of the power and freedom of choice that they want to keep.

3. Donald Norman makes another critical point relative to the issues discussed in this article:

> When I use a direct manipulation system—whether for text
> editing, drawing pictures, or creating and playing games—I
> do think of myself not as using a computer but as doing the
> particular task. The computer is, in effect, invisible. The
> point cannot be overstressed: make the computer system
> invisible. This principle can be applied with any form of
> system interaction, direct or indirect. (Norman, 1988, p. 185)

Information retrieval systems designed at the move level (0–1 through 4–1) are definitely not systems in which the computer is invisible. Moves allowable in many current IR systems, including some advanced experimental ones, are conceptualized in terms of the mechanics of operating the system (system focus), rather than in terms of the search steps that usually characterize human thinking about finding information (human focus). With most current systems, the searcher must translate, or break down, every desired search action into moves, largely meaningless strategically, which can then be understood by the system. Users might get the feeling that the computer system is invisible if they could carry out actions that track better with their normal thinking about searching. Systems designed with tactics and strategies available to users in various forms should be a step closer to that goal.

4. As noted earlier, the goal of much theoretical information science research has been to produce the perfect Level 4b automatic search. But most of this research is based on the idea of retrieving information from a database of document surrogates (usually bibliographic citations with or without abstracts), or occasionally full text documents. As I note in (Bates, 1989) however, we are already moving into an era in which a much wider range of information sources is being put online. In using those different types of sources in manual print environments, searchers are now using a wide variety of stratagems. We may expect them to want to use the same stratagems in advanced new information retrieval systems as well. Yet neither the stratagems nor the full variety of types of databases are generally even considered for inclusion in many of the experimental IR systems now under development. Thus users may soon be demanding search capabilities and databases which are not even planned for these otherwise very sophisticated systems.

It is very difficult to design IR systems that produce good automatic searches for users, and so it has made sense that research so far has been restricted largely to one type of database at a time. However, with operational databanks already expanding beyond the type of sources available in many experimental systems, the latter, no matter how clever the system architectures that are being developed, are at risk of falling behind the practical demands of systems already in use.

5. The final argument for developing the center cells of Table 7 is that to do so may prove interesting philosophically, psychologically, and in terms of IR theory. We may learn a lot more about how people think about and carry out information searches in trying to make search capabilities available at various levels. We may also learn a lot more about what sorts

of intellectual symbiosis are possible and workable between humans and computers.

If we use, rather than ignore, the special traits of humans in the design of human-computer interfaces for information systems, we may find our abilities enhanced in unpredictable and creative ways. Those of us who use word processing systems have long since noted that our writing patterns and fluency have changed considerably since we abandoned the typewriter. A really good information retrieval system that allows us to exercise strategic search choices quickly and easily may, in like manner, lead us to explore knowledge and research our information needs in far more powerful and creatively stimulating ways than we ever imagined in the days of the manual library or the simple online bibliographic database.

ACKNOWLEDGEMENTS

I wish to thank Vanessa Birdsey, Christine Borgman, Donald Case, Carol Fenichel, Raya Fidel, and Dee Michel for their comments on this manuscript. In particular, my thanks go to Dee Michel for drawing my attention to a "levels" approach to search behavior through his development of a different set of levels of search activity.

REFERENCES

American Heritage Dictionary of the English language. (1969). Boston: Houghton Mifflin.

Bannon, L. et al. (1983). Evaluation and analysis of users' activity organization. In *Proceedings CHI '83 Human Factors in Computing Systems.* New York: Association for Computing Machinery, 54-57.

Bates, M.J. (1979a). Information search tactics. *Journal of the American Society for Information Science, 30*(4), 205-214.

Bates, M.J. (1979b). Idea tactics. *Journal of the American Society for Information Science, 30*(5), 280-289.

Bates, M.J. (1987). How to use information search tactics online. *Online, 11*(3), 47-54.

Bates, M.J. (1989a). The design of browsing and berrypicking techniques for the online search interface. *Online Review, 13*(5), 407-424.

Bergman, R.F. (1981). Beyond SDI: On-line retrieval scripts in the chemical substances information network. *Proceedings of the 44th ASIS annual meeting, 18,* 276-278.

Borgman, C.L. (1984). Psychological research in human-computer interaction. *Annual Review of Information Science and Technology, 19*:35-64.

Borgman, C.L., Case, D.O., & Meadow, C.T. (1989). The design and evaluation of a front-end user interface for energy researchers. *Journal of the American Society for Information Science, 40*(2), 99-109.

Brooks, H.M., Daniels, P.J., & Belkin, N.J. (1985). Problem descriptions and user models: Developing an intelligent interface for document retrieval systems. In *Advances in*

Intelligent Retrieval: Informatics 8 (pp. 191–214), Proceedings of a conference jointly sponsored by ASLIB, the ASLIB Informatics Group, and the Information Retrieval Specialist Group of the British Computer Society, Oxford. London: ASLIB.

Cove, J.F., & Walsh, B.C. (1988). Online text retrieval via browsing. *Information Processing & Management, 24*(1), 31–37.

Croft, W.B., & Thompson, R.H. (1987). I³R: A new approach to the design of document retrieval systems. *Journal of the American Society for Information Science, 38*(6), 389–404.

Cuff, R.N. (1980). On casual users. *International Journal of Man-Machine Studies, 12*(2), 163–187.

Daniels, P.J. (1986). Cognitive models in information retrieval—An evaluative review. *Journal of Documentation, 42*(4), 272–304.

Ellis, D. (1989). A behavioural approach to information retrieval system design. *Journal of Documentation, 45*(3), 171–212.

Farooq, M.U., & Dominick, W.D. (1988). A survey of formal tools and models for developing user interfaces. *International Journal of Man-Machine Studies, 29*(5), 479–496.

Fenichel, C.H. (1980). The process of searching online bibliographic databases: A review of research. *Library Research, 2*(2), 107–127.

Fidel, R. (1985). Moves in online searching. *Online Review, 9*(1), 61–74.

Fidel, R. (1986). Towards expert systems for the selection of search keys. *Journal of the American Society for Information Science, 37*(1), 37–44.

Fox, E.A. (1987). Development of the CODER system: A testbed for artificial intelligence methods in information retrieval. *Information Processing & Management, 23*(4), 341–366.

Fuhr, N. (1989). Models for retrieval with probabilistic indexing. *Information Processing & Management, 25*(1), 55–72.

Harter, S.P., & Peters, A.R. (1985). Heuristics for online information retrieval: A typology and preliminary listing. *Online Review, 9*(5), 407–424.

Helander, M. (Ed.). (1988). *Handbook of human-computer interaction.* Amsterdam: North-Holland.

Hildreth, C.R. (1989). *Intelligent interfaces and retrieval methods for subject searching in bibliographic retrieval systems.* Washington, DC: Library of Congress Cataloging Distribution Service.

Hogeweg-de-Haart, H.P. (1984). Characteristics of social science information: A selective review of the literature. Part II. *Social Science Information Studies, 4*(1), 15–30.

Kammarsgaard, J. (1988). Four different perspectives on human-computer interaction. *International Journal of Man-Machine Studies, 28*(4), 343–362.

Kuhlthau, C.C. (1988). Developing a model of the library search process: Cognitive and affective aspects. *RQ, 28*(2), 232–242.

Markey, K. (1984). *Subject searching in library catalogs: Before and after the introduction of online catalogs.* Dublin, OH: OCLC Online Computer Library Center.

Matthews, J.R., Lawrence, G.S., & Ferguson, D.K. (Eds.). (1983). *Using online catalogs: A nationwide survey: A report of a study sponsored by the Council on Library Resources.* New York: Neal-Schuman.

Meadow, C.T., & Epstein, B.E. (1977). Individualized instruction for data access. In *On-line information: Proceedings of the 1st international on-line information meeting, London, England* (pp. 179–194). Oxford, England: Learned Information.

Meadow, C.T. et al. (1989). Online access to knowledge: System design. *Journal of the American Society for Information Science, 40*(2), 86–98.

Morehead, D.R., Pejtersen, A.M., & Rouse, W.B. (1984). The value of information and computer-aided information seeking: Problem formulation and application to fiction retrieval. *Information Processing & Management, 20*(5–6), 583–601.

Noerr, P.L., & Noerr, K.T.B. (1985). Browse and navigate: An advance in database access methods. *Information Processing & Management, 21*(3), 205–213.

Norman, D.A. (1983). Design principles for human-computer interfaces. In *Proceedings CHI '83 Human Factors in Computing Systems* (pp. 1–10). New York: Association for Computing Machinery.

Norman, D.A. (1984). Stages and levels in human-machine interaction. *International Journal of Man-Machine Studies, 21*(4), 365–375.

Norman, D.A. (1988). *The psychology of everyday things*. New York: Basic Books.

Palay, A.J., & Fox, M.S. (1981). Browsing through databases. In R.N. Oddy et al. (Eds.), *Information Retrieval Research* (pp. 310–324). London: Butterworths.

Pollitt, S. (1987). CANSEARCH: An expert systems approach to document retrieval. *Information Processing & Management, 23*(2), 119–138.

Salton, G., & Buckley, C. (1988). Term weighting approaches in automatic text retrieval. *Information Processing & Management, 24*(5), 513–523.

Shneiderman, B. (1987). *Designing the user interface: Strategies for effective human-computer interaction*. Reading, MA: Addison-Wesley.

Standera, O.R. (1978). Some thoughts on online systems: The searcher's part and plight. In *The Information Age in Perspective,* Proceedings of the American Society for Information Science 41st Annual Meeting (Vol. 15, pp. 322–325).

Stenstrom, P., & McBride, R.B. (1979). Serial use by social science faculty: A survey. *College & Research Libraries, 40*(5) 426–431.

Stoan, S.K. (1984). Research and library skills: An analysis and interpretation. *College & Research Libraries, 45*(2), 99–109.

Stone, S. (1982). Humanities scholars: Information needs and uses. *Journal of Documentation, 38*(4), 292–312.

Taylor, M.M. (1988a). Layered protocols for computer-human dialogue. I: Principles. *International Journal of Man-Machine Studies, 28*(2–3), 175–218.

Taylor, M.M. (1988b). Layered protocols for computer-human dialogue. II: Some practical issues. *International Journal of Man-Machine Studies, 28*(2–3), 219–257.

Taylor, R.S. (1968). Question-negotiation and information seeking in libraries. *College & Research Libraries, 29*(3), 178–194.

Vickery, A., Brooks, H., & Robinson, B. (1987). A reference and referral system using expert system techniques. *Journal of Documentation, 43*(1), 1–23.

4

Design for a subject search interface and online thesaurus for a very large records management database

ABSTRACT

A design for a subject search interface and online thesaurus is described which embodies several novel features:

- A subject search interface designed to feel simple enough to be used successfully by end users with only a high school education, and which is linked to an online thesaurus in such a way as to allow easy selection of desired terms and automatic creation of Boolean statements.

- A novel type of thesaurus designed specifically for the online environment and to be used online in real time by end users with little or no knowledge of online searching. The thesaurus contains groupings of related terms called clusters, and is intended to maximize recall.

- Integration of the thesaurus and search interface into a single system, thus eliminating the necessity of moving in and out of the thesaurus in order to identify search terms, and eliminating the necessity of re-entering search terms that have been identified, as is often the case in existing systems.

First published as Bates, M. J. (1990). Design for a subject search interface and online thesaurus for a very large records management database. *Proceedings of the 53rd ASIS Annual Meeting, 27,* 20–28.

- Design of this system for a multi-million item records management database. This system has been designed for the Los Angeles Department of Water and Power, for use by its 10,000 person staff, and is in the process of development now. Records management is an area of information retrieval system design that has been relatively neglected in information science. Design for such an environment has some interesting properties, which are dealt with in this article.

Introduction

The design of automated information retrieval systems for records management has been a relatively neglected area in the literature of information science research and development. Records management systems deserve more attention, however, as the problems are similar to those confronted in other areas of information science, while at the same time offering some unique challenges in their own right.

Several years ago the Los Angeles Department of Water and Power (DWP) made the decision to develop a single, unified automated records management system for their offices. With over 10,000 employees and 28 divisions, the DWP is a very large operation. Manual records management had been previously handled within divisions, or, frequently, within even smaller administrative units. Many different approaches were taken to handling records: there was no single universal system in use. Thus, the development of a unified automated system represented an enormous administrative and operational change, as well as a shift to automation.

A handful of divisions had elected to develop their own vocabularies, index records with them, and put the resulting files online with a system developed for the DWP known as FASTRACK, but in general, prior to the current effort, records management at the DWP was manual and fragmented into many local systems within the Department. Development of a single automated system out of such a large, heterogeneous operation has required a multi-million dollar investment in system design, computer programming, and analysis of existing records and filing systems. The principal contractor has been Stone & Webster Engineering Corporation, and a major subcontractor to Stone & Webster is California System Design, Inc. (CSDI).

The automated records management system being developed is known as EZRA. It is based, with extensive modifications, on TextDBMS, a full text storage and retrieval software product, mounted in DWP's IBM 3090 mainframe environment.

EZRA has a relatively sophisticated, attractive, and user-friendly interface. Users of the system are expected to include everyone who would normally have need to call on the Department's files, from clerks and secretaries to top management. The interface is designed for both data entry and retrieval.

Contents of the database are extremely heterogeneous; over 150 record types have been identified, and include many types of vital records, correspondence, internal reports, and even purchase orders. The ultimate size of the database is not known, but is expected to reach several million items, at a minimum.

Management at the DWP has been particularly desirous that they should have effective means for high recall in the database, in order to allow ready retrieval of information for litigation support and other situations where location of all records relevant to a given matter is essential. Consequently, a high priority of the management has been to have some kind of thesaurus for the system, in order to promote consistency of indexing and effectiveness of retrieval. (The EZRA system would not itself function as a litigation support system, which is a type of information retrieval system with very different requirements from general records management systems, but could be used to find readily all documents that needed to be put into a separate litigation support system for individual cases.)

The sub-problem of thesaurus development for EZRA was problematic in several respects, and had a long history itself within the larger history of the design and development of the EZRA records management system. In January 1989, when the design of EZRA was largely complete, I was asked by California System Design to succeed an earlier outside consultant on the thesaurus, and make suggestions regarding the design and development of the thesaurus for EZRA. I did my own system-analytic review of DWP's requirements for a thesaurus and online subject search capability, of the relevant records management procedures at the DWP, and of existing controlled vocabularies already in use at the DWP.

I presented a system design for a subject search interface and for an online thesaurus to be incorporated in the design of EZRA. The DWP tentatively approved the design for these two components in summer of 1989. Prior to giving final approval, DWP management asked that two things be done: the thesaurus development process be prototyped to pin down development costs, and detailed software design be done to insure that the interface could in fact successfully be incorporated into the existing EZRA design.

In the summer and fall of 1989, Michael Williams and Nancy O'Boyle of CSDI did the software design for the proposed search interface, and Patricia Haines, working under my direction, prototyped the thesaurus development process. The DWP liked the results, which were presented in December 1989. The project was funded and final development and implementation began in summer of 1990.

I have argued elsewhere (Bates, 1986, 1989) that most thesauri in use in online systems were developed for manual systems and are not fully adapted to the needs of the online environment. The intention in this case was to take advantage of the online context to design a thesaurus fully adapted to that environment and, it is hoped, one that will meet online search needs better. The search interface was also adapted to the needs of a situation like that of the DWP's, with a large number of end user searchers relatively naive in search techniques. The thesaurus design and the interface design were thus developed as an integral whole, each part intended to maximize the performance of the other part. Thus, both elements will be described and discussed together in the next section.

Features of the search interface and online thesaurus

Constraints and characteristics of the DWP environment

To make understandable the choices made in the design of the interface and thesaurus, more needs to be said about the records management environment and the needs of the DWP in particular. Designing for this environment was quite challenging, containing both unusual opportunities, as well as some powerful constraints. The following requirements were identified:

- Indexing and data entry at the DWP are decentralized and might ultimately take place in ten or more locations. Indexers could not be presumed to have more than high school educations, let alone advanced training in indexing or information science theory.

- Searching would be done by potentially nearly every employee of the DWP, not just by a small cadre of highly trained individuals. Searchers would include everyone from clerks up to top management, and both frequent, experienced users, and novice, occasional users.

- DWP staff wanted to use the DWP's own familiar internal terminology for indexing and retrieval, rather than completely novel terminology drawn from outside sources.

- Since design of the EZRA system was nearly complete, the proposed subject component had to be able to fit into the existing system without extensive changes. Also, even if the new thesaurus/subject search component could be added to the existing system with little or no perturbation of already developed code, the system must itself be simple in design, due to the high cost of original programming for mainframe systems.

Other features specific to the records management environment added other constraints and opportunities. The long history of records management being handled separately within individual divisions or sub-divisions of the DWP had led to a wide variety in practices and procedures and, consequently, resistance to being brought under a single design. Real differences in needs between divisions further complicated the situation. The needs of engineering, public relations, customer service, and management staff, among others, are intrinsically varied and naturally led to different preferences in record handling.

A distinguishing feature of records management as a type of information management is the importance of *record type.* Legal and operational requirements of record use necessitate the development of retention schedules, which determine how long records of a given type are to be maintained, and in what form (hard copy, microfilm, etc.). The types of descriptive elements, including subject terms, applied to records are also specific to record type. During the process of conversion to the single automated system, each division or section of the DWP developed its own set of "indexing criteria" for each record type, that is, decided which of some 35 fields would be used in record description (cataloging) in the case of each record type. Divisions made different choices in this regard. So, for example, one division might choose to use the controlled vocabulary field for the record type "proposals," and another might not, considering the title field alone to be sufficiently subject indicative for their needs.

Because of this division to division variation, searching had to be designed so that it could be done against all fields bearing subject information, not just against the controlled vocabulary field. Those five fields (not all implemented in EZRA yet) are controlled term, title, contents/description, abstract, and full text. (The contents/description field has been used to date for whatever subject description a division wished to enter, pending the development of the thesaurus.) Thus the use of controlled vocabulary alone could not be presumed to be sufficient for high-recall searching. The system had to be designed so that free text terms could also be searched in other fields in order to guarantee high recall.

Free text searching in a multi-million item database could lead to serious problems, however, given the other constraints mentioned earlier, namely searchers with little or no understanding of the complexities of subject searching in large databases. Fortunately, the emphasis on record type in records management systems also constituted an opportunity. People searching in a records management database frequently want a particular record type. A Boolean AND between record type and subject terms can cut down substantially on retrievals, and reduce some false drop potential. Serious problems remain, however, in enabling searchers unsophisticated in search techniques to achieve high recall—with tolerable precision—in a multi-million item database. In the next section is discussed the response that was developed to this set of constraints and requirements at the DWP.

Interface design and thesaurus module

The DWP's EZRA Records Management System (RMS) interface is designed to offer five different search types to the user. One of these search types provides holdings information (which files have been input, which ones have been removed because of expiration of retention period). The other four types represent search capabilities of increasing complexity. The simplest two provide prompt screens asking for the more common search criteria likely to be used in a search of an RMS, such as date range, record type, originating and receiving individual or organization, etc. It is the other two search types that will contain the thesaurus search capability. One of these, the "free form," is indeed free form and is intended for use by sophisticated searchers who understand Boolean logic. It is a search mode that permits some of the most powerful search capabilities found in online database systems and in TextDBMS, such as Boolean logic, proximity searching, field specification, relational operators, wild card searches, etc.

It is the thesaurus component of the remaining search type that will be the topic of this article, as this search type is the one most likely to be used by the less experienced searcher, and so represents the greatest design challenge. This type is called a "Standard Search" in EZRA.

Figure 1 shows the initial screen a searcher sees upon having selected a Standard Search. In this case the searcher may select any among all 29 searchable fields. (It should be recalled, however, that number of fields applied to any one record varies by record type and by choice of indexing criteria within each division or section of the DWP.) The user types an "x" by all fields of interest for the search.

Once all desired fields have been x'd, then secondary screens appear for each field, asking the searcher to input specific terms for each field. For

```
RMIS0310                      RECORDS MANAGEMENT SYSTEM                    11/11/88
User ID                            STANDARD SEARCH                        00:00:00


 __ Abstract              __ Document Number          __ Record Type Code
 __ Accession Number      __ Document Title           __ Record Type Name
 __ Anywhere              __ Document/Form Name        __ Reference Doc. ID
 __ Contents or Description __ Dollar Amount           __ Section/Zone
 __ Contract ID Number    __ Equipment ID             __ Storage Media
 __ Controlled Term       __ Full Text                __ Vendor Code
 __ Document Date         __ Microfilm Location        __ Vendor Name
 __ Document Distribution __ Originator/Organ.         __ PS File Index Code
 __ Document Identification __ Plant/Facility Code      __ RRA Number
                         __ Recipient/Organ.          __ RRC Box Number


                  TYPE "X" NEXT TO YOUR CHOICE(S) AND PRESS ENTER

     ===============================================================================

 PF1: Help        Enter: Proceed                 PF3: Return       PF12: More PFkeys

 PF13:Mainmenu    Clear:Redisplay                PF24:Signoff      PF12:More PFkeys
```

FIG. 1. *Initial standard search screen*

example, if "document date" is x'd, a screen appears giving the option of specifying a particular date or of giving a date range.

The searcher fills in such specific search information on prompt screens for each field x'd on the initial Standard Search screen. Multiple terms entered within a given field are OR'd together. For example, if several vendor codes are listed, the system automatically OR's them together. Then the OR'd set from each field is ANDed with the results of every other field search, including the thesaurus.

When the thesaurus component is complete, there will be a separate slot for it at the bottom of the screen in Figure 1. Since the thesaurus, designed for high recall, generates large numbers of OR'd terms (as we shall shortly see), it is processed last. The OR'd set from the thesaurus is searched against the results of the other fields rather than against the whole file, to keep down processing. Results are also processed against either all five subject bearing fields (default) or against fields designated by the searcher in the next screen shown after this initial Standard Search screen. In that next screen the searcher also enters a subject term of interest. At that point the thesaurus module kicks in.

To see how the thesaurus module works, let us suppose the searcher enters the term "Ground wire." A screen like that in Figure 2 will appear. This screen contains terms used by various divisions of the DWP, relevant

```
Your Search Word(s): Ground wire
Subject: Ground wires

    TYPE 'X' NEXT TO YOUR CHOICES AND PRESS ENTER,
    OR TYPE 'X' HERE ___ TO HAVE SYSTEM SEARCH FOR YOU

      __No Terms from this Subject (See Related Subjects Below.)

    DWP TERMS: __Ground wires    __Electrical Grounding

    DIVISION TERMS:

      IPP/SEP/PDC:    __Grounding    __Overhead ground wires
      __Equipment Grounding    __Fence grounding
      Bd. WP Comm.:  __Ground wire

    POWER SYSTEM CODE:

      File Folder:    __Ground wire contract agreement with General Telephone
      under Code Name: Communication system—General telephone service

      Code Name:    __Generation—General—Boulder Canyon Project—Power Plant
      Equipment—Contract for Installation of High Voltage Conductors and
      Ground Wires

    RELATED SUBJECTS: Use subjects you like as search words for new subject
    searches. See also:

    Wire accessories.    Wire carriers.    Wire procedures.
    Wire schedules.      Wire sketches.    Wire transfers.    Wires.
```

FIG. 2. *First example screen in response to subject search term request.*
NOTE: *This example has been assembled for illustration purposes only, and does not represent an analytically developed cluster.*

categories from the "Power System File Code," a hierarchical classification long used for management files, and terms drawn from external vocabularies, such as that of the Electric Power Research Institute. "DWP" terms are ones drawn from external vocabularies or ones that are otherwise of general applicability. This arrangement enables different divisions to use their own preferred vocabulary, if they wish. The hope is that all terms will eventually become "DWP" terms, as the various divisions become accustomed to using a common system.

The contents of this screen are *not* created dynamically, but rather are pre-existing units in the thesaurus called "clusters." A cluster consists of terms that are synonymous, or minor variants, for DWP purposes, of a core concept. (Note: Larson [1989] also uses the term "cluster," but for a different entity.) This screen is called up because the user's search term (word or phrase) matched somewhere in this pre-existing set of closely related terms. (The matching algorithm will be described shortly.) By x'ing slots on the screen the searcher then has a full range of options in use of these terms to search:

1. If the searcher x's individual slots, then an OR'd set is created out of those terms automatically, and AND'd with the results of searches reported out of other fields.

2. If the searcher x's the slot to "have system search for you," then all slotted terms in the cluster are automatically OR'd together and searched as in (1).

3. If the searcher x's "No terms from this Subject," then this cluster is ignored.

The design of the thesaurus and interface is such that it is possible for a term to match on more than one cluster—the thesaurus will be designed to keep that number to five or fewer—so the searcher may be shown more than one such cluster in succession. After the searcher makes these choices in the one or more clusters shown, all terms selected by whatever means are OR'd together.

The reasoning behind the automatic OR'ing of terms x'd in all clusters is the following: It is assumed that when a user's single search term (word or phrase) matches on more than one cluster, the clusters must be closely related core concepts and so terms found in them should be OR'd as variants on essentially the same concept, rather than ANDed as markedly distinct concepts. For example, the searcher's term "Material count" might match with both a cluster on material inventory and one on material control. All terms that the searcher likes and x's from these two clusters are OR'd together for the search.

In the cases where a term matches on more than one cluster because the term has two or more distinct meanings, we presume that searchers will not approve a search on any but the desired meaning. This is one of the advantages of showing terms to the searcher, rather than automatically generating a broader search.

The search term "Ground wire" in Figure 2 matches with what is known as a "regular cluster," that is, the match is with a fairly specific concept that is not so broad that it is likely to retrieve many thousands of records. Novice or occasional users may, however, use broader, more common terms that match with very large numbers of records on heterogeneous topics, most of which would not be of use to them. Also, even a searcher who is

```
Your Search Word(s): Wire

Subject: Wires

YOUR SEARCH WORD(S) ARE PART OF MANY SUBJECT TERMS.
TYPE 'X' BY UP TO 5 SUBJECTS, THEN PRESS ENTER,
OR TYPE 'X' HERE_____ TO SEARCH ON "WIRES" ANYWAY

  __No terms from this subject.

  __Actuator wires   __Ground wires   __Jumper wires   __Pilot wires

  __Power wires   __Scrap wires   __Shield wires   __Signal wires

  __Wire accessories   __Wire carriers   __Wire diagrams

  __Wire ducts   __Wire manufacturers   __Wire markings

  __Wire mileage   __Wire procedures   __Wire schedules

  __Wire sketches   __Wire spools   __Wire transfers
```

FIG. 3. *System response to the input of a high frequency term.*
NOTE: *This example has been assembled for illustration purposes only, and does not represent an analytically developed cluster.*

more sophisticated may want to use a general term because she/he does not know a good specific term, or has tried more specific terms and failed to find anything.

To deal with these various broad-term cases, the thesaurus and interface make use of "high frequency clusters." To illustrate these, suppose that the searcher had used the word "Wire" instead of "Ground wire" in the previous example search. In an electrical utility, "wire" may be a very common word. Figure 3 shows a high frequency cluster for "Wire."

To the searcher, this screen looks very similar to the screens for regular clusters. But here all terms are actually cross-references. Terms in such high frequency clusters consist only of the labels ("cluster titles") for regular clusters. Once the searcher x's desired terms, the next screens shown will be the corresponding regular clusters, from which the searcher selects the actual specific search terms that will be used in the set of OR'd terms. If the searcher nonetheless wants to search on the broad term anyway, that option is also available ("... OR TYPE 'X' HERE TO SEARCH ON 'WIRES' ANYWAY"). The searcher need not understand the full inner structure of thesaurus and matching algorithm; she/he need only "x" desired terms on whatever screens appear.

The term "cluster title" is used to distinguish the cluster's label from the terms within the clusters. (The term "Subject" is used on the screen for system users.) Cluster titles are selected to be the most representative term for the cluster, the one most expressive of the core concept for the cluster. Such terms also appear within the clusters and so may be selected for searching by users.

As noted earlier, cross references are always only cluster titles. This promotes consistency in cross referencing and keeps down the number of terms needed for cross references. The intention is that the abundance of terms provided to the searcher should be within clusters, and the searcher should be guided to find good clusters. Thus any term a searcher selects in a high frequency cluster will lead directly to a regular cluster.

To summarize the search process from the user's point of view, the typical search can be characterized as follows:

1. The user x's all fields of interest on the Standard Search screen, plus the slot for "Thesaurus" when that is desired.

2. After the user has filled in screens for all other search fields, a final screen asks the user to state the desired search term and to "x" off which of the five subject-bearing fields the search formulation is to be run against.

3. The system searches for a match of some kind between the search term and the thesaurus clusters.

4. The searcher is shown one or more screens containing the clusters of terms around the concept represented by the user's search term. If the system has found no match whatsoever with the search term, the user is asked to enter a new term.

5. The searcher x's off all desired search terms on the screens as they are presented. If the search term was fairly specific, then the screens shown the searcher are regular clusters, and x'd terms go directly into the set of search terms to be OR'd together. If the search term is broad, then it matches with a high frequency cluster, which contains only cross-references to cluster titles. The user x's one or more cluster titles of interest on the high frequency screen, is then shown the corresponding regular clusters, and x's off the desired search terms in the usual manner.

6. When all relevant screens have been viewed, the system OR's together all selected thesaurus terms, AND's them with the product of the other fields searched, and shows the searcher all records meeting the complete search formulation. For example, the logic of a search might appear as follows:

[Date range] AND [Originating organization]
AND [Record type] AND
[Hedge of OR'd subject terms from thesaurus search]

The search algorithm

Now, with an understanding of regular and high frequency clusters, it is appropriate to describe the matching algorithm that incorporates both types of cluster. The objective in running a match between the searcher's term and a thesaurus is, of course, to identify terms that will retrieve relevant records. Questions of match with type of cluster and with single words vs. whole term or phrase must be solved, and solved in a reasonably economical way. The algorithm shown in Figure 4 is the solution being used in this case.

Here's how the algorithm proceeds: The user's entire search term—word or phrase—is first run against cluster titles. An exact match with an entire regular cluster title (plurals are to be ignored) leads to a display of the matching cluster. The searcher then x's all desired terms within the displayed regular cluster. An exact match with a high frequency cluster title leads to the display of that high frequency cluster; the user then picks desired regular cluster titles, and the full regular clusters are in turn displayed, as above.

Only when a *cluster title* search fails, does the system then search on the terms *within the bodies* of clusters. Here too, the match is on the full search term, not with individual words within terms. Successful searches here bring regular clusters to the screen, as above. If this search comes up with no matches in the bodies of the regular clusters, then *individual words* within the search term, as opposed to the whole search phrase, are matched against the high frequency cluster titles, most of which are of single word length. If all these options fail, then the searcher is asked to input a new term.

Note that relatively uncommon single-word terms will appear only in the bodies of regular clusters, and will not be made high frequency clusters. During the process of creating the thesaurus, the frequency of terms (single or multiple-word) within clusters will be monitored to keep them, in most cases, in five or fewer regular clusters. It is presumed, in any case, that a given term will not logically fall within very many term clusters, if each is built around a distinct concept, even assuming some overlap in meaning of concepts.

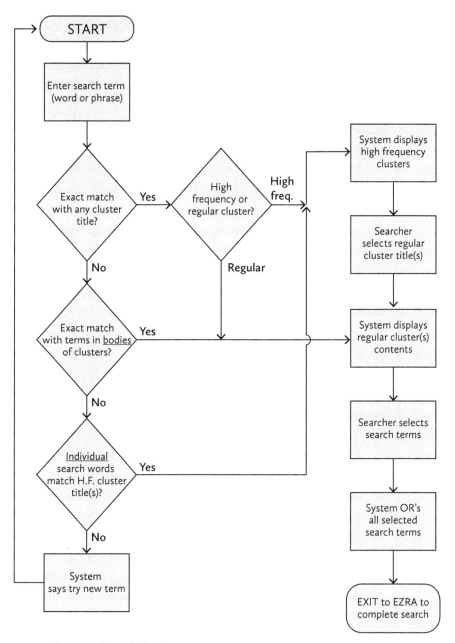

FIG. 4. *Cluster match search algorithm*

Thesaurus characteristics

Discussion of the thesaurus up to this point has been integrated with consideration of the interface. There are, however, several considerations about the design of the thesaurus that are specific to it. Thesaurus design will not begin de novo. During the period when records management was overwhelmingly done manually at the DWP, a handful of the divisions of the Department developed their own vocabularies and had them mounted on a less sophisticated automated records management system designed for the DWP called FASTRACK. The largest of these vocabularies, with over 9,000 terms in it, will form the skeleton around which the clusters will be developed.

These controlled vocabularies are unusual. They have some kinds of vocabulary control, and lack others. Attention has been paid to collocating phrases of different lengths, such as "Services," "Consulting services," and "Computer consulting services," yet no references have been made between related, or even partially synonymous terms, such as "Earthquake" and "Seismic...." Features of these pre-existing vocabularies have been taken advantage of in the design of this system.

Elsewhere I have presented extensive evidence to the effect that even in controlled vocabulary environments there is an enormous range of terms used by both searchers and indexers for any one topic (Bates, 1986, 1989). Furthermore, even the most popular term is likely to be used by only a minority of searchers. Consequently, it would appear to be somewhat illusory to attempt to achieve maximum recall by using only controlled terms—that is, in the conventional sense of "control" through selection of one and only one term to stand for a concept in indexing and searching.

Online searchers have long since resorted to a widespread preference for searching on uncontrolled phrases against both natural language and controlled term fields as a way to maximize recall. In fact, in online searching, the distinction between controlled and uncontrolled terms blurs, because of the effectiveness of proximity searching on multiword phrases against both controlled and uncontrolled term fields of the record. So the philosophy of control in this thesaurus is that vocabulary control shall consist of grouping term variants around a concept, and making it easy for searchers to select and search on those variations without having to key them in, rather than eliminating the variation.

Recognizing that online searchers want both controlled and uncontrolled terms, Sara Knapp (1984) designed the BRS "TERM" database some years ago, which consisted of clusters of related terms. Under each term title, she listed the terms used for a concept by several different thesauri, and added natural language terms as well. Knapp's TERM database was the inspiration for the thesaurus component of this system.

BRS has since dropped TERM, which is unfortunate. The idea was good. BRS did not update it regularly, and the records were expensive for searchers to print. Searchers had to go through a cumbersome process of entering a separate database to identify terms, then return to the home database and re-enter by hand all the relevant terms found in TERM. In short, the TERM database was not integrated with an easy-to-use search interface, as is planned here. In the system being developed here, searchers need only "x" desired terms, and will not have to leave a search and enter and return from a separate database in order to use the thesaurus. Nor will there be a cost associated with use of the thesaurus.

Use for indexing and data entry

To promote ease of programming, ease of use, and, ultimately, consistency in term use between indexing and searching (to the extent that is possible), the data entry and end user searching components of this system have been designed to be as similar as possible. Indexers will search on candidate terms in the thesaurus to find relevant clusters in the same way as end users will search for good search terms. Once an indexer finds a cluster describing a topic in a record being subject indexed, the indexer's chosen terms need not be re-keyed. Instead, the indexer simply x's all terms to be applied to a record from a cluster and, in the data entry mode, those terms are then automatically inserted into the "controlled term" field of the record being indexed.

The vocabulary will be instantly receptive to new terms because indexers will be permitted to use terms they do not find in the clusters, if they feel there is no current term in the clusters that meets their need. Any such term that does not have a match in the clusters will automatically be flagged by the system. At frequent intervals an "indexing administrator," who has training in indexing and vocabulary control, will call up all such flagged terms and vet them.

The objective is to be generous in adding such new terms to clusters, in line with the reasoning stated earlier that there is a great deal of inherent variety in terms used by searchers and indexers both. The clusters are to capture that variety and control it by grouping related terms together. However, terms which are ungrammatical, or represent a misunderstanding of the concept, will be eliminated and replaced with more appropriate ones. The indexing administrator, who will understand the design principles of the thesaurus in a way that many indexers will not, will also maintain the integrity of the thesaurus, by insuring that stray concepts do not appear within inappropriate clusters, and the like.

Discussion

The multi-stage search algorithm against term clusters introduces economies in the search process, helps unskilled indexers locate and assign good terms easily, and helps the end-user searcher do a high-recall search in a very large database without, it is to be hoped, overwhelming numbers of retrievals. Nor is sophistication with Boolean logic necessary.

In particular, the system makes it easy to find and search on large numbers of term variants. Searchers and indexers do not need to look in a print thesaurus, nor need they make complicated moves into and out of a separate thesaurus. Neither indexers nor searchers need retype selected terms.

It has long been a staple of psychological research that recognition of terms is much easier than recall—in the psychological sense of recall from memory. A moment's reflection about online searching supports this psychological research result. Most of us can identify good terms from a list of related ones far faster and in greater numbers than we can think up such terms on our own. On the whole, the design of information retrieval systems has seriously underutilized this powerful feature of human psychology. It is the objective of this system to take full advantage of this trait.

Also, as mentioned earlier, there is now extensive evidence to the effect that people generate enormous variety in the description of any given topic. This variety even extends to indexing done by skilled indexers within controlled vocabularies. This is a remarkably robust result, having been found in indexer consistency studies, searcher consistency research, and in fields outside information science altogether.

It is thus unrealistic to think that controlled vocabulary alone will lead to consistency in indexing and searching in any environment, but especially in one such as the Los Angeles Department of Water and Power where both indexers and searchers are relatively untrained and heterogeneous in background. Instead of unsuccessfully pursuing the dream of the one best subject term for a topic, this design is set up to provide as much as possible of that natural human variety to users of the system, so that they can capture this variety easily in their own searching or indexing.

Finally, a fundamental design question lurking behind the choices made in the design of this particular system has to do with optimal combinations of human and system activity in information retrieval systems (cf. Bates [1990]). Which parts of the search are best done by humans and which best done by machines?

This question arises in several ways in this system. Current experimental efforts in information retrieval system design to expand searches automatically are still expensive, difficult, and not wholly reliable. Language is devilishly complex, and people and their searches vary along almost countless dimensions, which are very hard to capture in any system. Programs to parse language and model the user are promising but still difficult to make really effective.

Searchers often require some interaction with a system in order to fully recognize their own information needs. Matthews and Lawrence (1984) found that online catalogs that forced people through something like a thesaurus led ultimately to greater satisfaction with their searches on the part of users than systems that did not make users explore terms.

Arguably, a system that combines human strengths—such as knowing one's own needs best, and knowing language better than any parser—with computer strengths, particularly rapid calculation and retrieval, may be a very satisfying, even excellent design. Perhaps we need not try to make the computer perform exactly and fully the way humans do in order to get a powerful system. Whether the system described here proves to be such a satisfying system remains to be seen. But it does represent an attempt to move in that direction.

REFERENCES

Bates, M.J. (1986). Subject access in online catalogs: A design model. *Journal of the American Society for Information Science, 37*(6), 357–376.

Bates, M.J. (1989). Rethinking subject cataloging in the online environment. *Library Resources & Technical Services, 33*(4), 400–412.

Bates, M.J. (1990). Where should the person stop and the information search interface start? *Information Processing & Management, 26*(5), 575–591.

Knapp, S.D. (1984). Creating BRS/TERM, a vocabulary database for searchers. *Database, 7*, 70–75.

Larson, R.R. (1989). Managing information overload in online catalog searching. *Proceedings of the 52nd ASIS Annual Meeting, 26*, 129–135.

Matthews, J.R., & Lawrence, G.S. (1984). Further analysis of the CLR online catalog project. *Information Technology and Libraries, 3*(4), 354–376.

5

The design of databases and other information resources for humanities scholars: The Getty Online Searching Project report no. 4

ABSTRACT

Based on the results of a two-year study of online searching by humanities scholars, conducted by the Getty Art History Information Program, implications are drawn for the design of information products for the humanities. Scientists and humanities scholars not only have different kinds of information needs, they also relate to their own literatures in fundamentally different ways. As a result, humanities researchers need information products that do not arise out of the conventional assumptions and framework that have produced the familiar databases and other information products in the sciences and industry. These characteristic differences of humanities scholars are first discussed; then design implications are considered in the following areas: design and content of databases, indexing vocabulary in humanities resources, and interfaces and command languages.

Introduction

The Getty Art History Information Program conducted a study of the online searching behavior of humanities scholars during 1989 and 1990.

First published as Bates, M. J. (1994). The design of databases and other information resources for humanities scholars: The Getty Online Searching Project report no. 4. *Online & CD-ROM Review, 18*(6), 331–340.

In cooperation with the Getty Center for the History of Art and the Humanities in Santa Monica, California,[1] Visiting Scholars at the Center were given the opportunity to do unlimited online searching of databases through DIALOG at a workstation in the Getty Center Library. Participants were given one day's training by DIALOG staff, then had 24-hours-a-day access to the workstation to do fully subsidized searching on their own for the rest of their year at the Center. With the scholars' permission, data were gathered on their experiences by means of complete transaction logs of their searching, and through extensive personal interviews with them.[2] Altogether a total of 27 scholars across the two years participated in the study.

This enormous body of data has provided an unusually detailed look at the behavior and attitudes of humanities scholars toward end-user online searching. Results of this research are being published in several journals, in order to reach the various audiences that are interested in the topics of the articles (Bates et al., 1993; Bates, 1996; Bates et al., 1995; Siegfried et al., 1993). Articles are numbered to make for greater ease in identifying and distinguishing them. It is the purpose of this, fourth, article in the series to extract from the Getty data implications for the design of humanities information resources, particularly including databases and other online resources.

This article draws on the study results but consists substantially of my own opinions, speculations and judgments. Any errors in judgment or interpretation are entirely mine, and not the fault of my Getty colleagues; nor does the content of this article in any way represent the official position of the Getty Art History Information Program. I have benefited greatly from the association with my Getty colleagues; we felt, however, that this article should bear my name only, as it contains so much that is only my view.

To understand humanities scholars' use of online systems properly, it is first necessary to understand the role of literature searching in the scholarly life of humanists. Attitudes expressed and comments made by the scholars revealed patterns in how they relate to and use their literature that are significantly different from our understanding of how scientists

---

1   The J. Paul Getty Trust is a private operating foundation. Two of its six programs are the Getty Art History Information Program and the Getty Center for the History of Art and the Humanities. These two entities collaborated on the project.

2   Marilyn Schmitt conceived the Getty Online Searching Project: she designed the study together with Susan Siegfried and Deborah N. Wilde. Siegfried and Wilde carried out the collaborative project plan and oversaw the gathering of data throughout the project. Marcia J. Bates designed the interview schedule for the second year's data, analyzed the data for both years, formulated conclusions, and contributed insights from the discipline of information science. Jeanette Clough and Katherine Smith transcribed the DIALOG search statements and Smith transcribed the interviews, for subsequent analysis. Vanessa Birdsey coded the search data into categories developed by Bates.

relate to and use their literature. As scientists have been studied more exhaustively, and as much of information science theory has been developed to meet scientists' needs, it is now appropriate to analyze the differences between scientists and humanities scholars, and to draw implications for changes and extensions in information science theory and practice. We need to understand these distinctive attitudes in order to provide information services and products that will support humanities scholars effectively in their research.

In the second section, this relationship of the scholar to the literature is discussed. Implications of this research and of the factors mentioned in the second section for three aspects of information products and services— design and content of databases, indexing vocabulary of databases, and interfaces and command languages—are discussed in the third section. The fourth section contains a summary and conclusions.

Relation of the scholar to the literature of a field

In this section we will discuss some differences between humanities scholars and scientists in their relation to the literatures of their fields. Much of the thinking in library and information science regarding databases and online searching has been conditioned by the characteristics and needs of the sciences. I believe that the unique characteristics and needs of the humanities have been too little understood and attended to—hence the deliberate use of contrast here between these domains of research.

So many different specific methodologies are comprised within both domains that anything said must necessarily be a generalization with many exceptions. I believe that a pattern of difference remains between the sciences and humanities, however, that has important implications for the thinking on the topic of this article. Thus I generalize—in the spirit of the old line that says: "all generalizations are false, including this one."

Humanities scholars relate to the literature of their field differently to scientists. In the sciences, the objects of study are generally natural and social phenomena. To conduct research, the scientist usually observes these phenomena directly or by means of tools such as microscopes, chemical analysis, etc. Upon completion of the research, the scientist publishes a description of the work and its results. No one confuses the resulting publication for the research, however—in other words, the map is not the territory. The discovery, the scientific advance, is understood to have taken place in the laboratory or in the field, not in the article written to describe that discovery.

In the humanities (defined broadly here to include literature, the arts, philosophy, religion and history), by contrast, the situation is more complicated. The objects of study in the humanities are frequently thoughts and ideas partly or entirely found in *writings*. These writings may be published or unpublished. Thus, both the objects of the study and the text describing the research may be writings found in libraries.

Further, there are important senses in which the "discovery" or unique contribution of the humanities scholar may be seen to *inhere in the writing* in a way that is much less frequently found in the sciences. I will attempt to develop these points in the following paragraphs.

In the humanities, so-called "primary materials" include the writings that are the direct objects of study, parallel to the natural phenomena studied by the scientist. Such materials may include diaries, manuscripts and letters, as well as the published works that are to be objects of study, such as the works of a poet or philosopher. In the arts, such primary materials may include such things as paintings and musical scores.

"Secondary materials" are the works of others *about* primary materials or other secondary materials. "Tertiary materials" are the bibliographies, databases and other works organizing primary and secondary materials. One of the important steps students in the humanities make is to move from studying secondary works (often found by means of tertiary sources) to studying primary materials, and coming up with their own understanding of them. Students of Thomas Mann initially read works of criticism of Mann to understand his writings; later they will select some theme to write on and use primary materials to research and develop that theme. (This holds true in the arts as well, where the scholar will study diaries, contracts, exhibition catalogs, or other library and archival materials in addition to studying the artwork, music, dance or other performance that engendered the research interest.)

In the humanities, therefore, in contrast to much of the sciences, the locus of discovery may be in writings. That discovery is then reported on in other writings. Consequently, humanities scholars tend to have a very intimate relationship to the world of writings and publications as well as to their storehouses—namely, libraries and archives. The statement that "the library is the laboratory of the scholar" holds much truth in it. For the scientist, the laboratory or the field is where the action of research takes place, while the library is where the results are archived. For the humanities scholar, those two functions of research and archiving largely take place in the same place, wherever the information is kept.

This pattern of difference has consequences for research methods as well. For the humanist, ability to conduct documentary research is a vital part of the knowledge of research methods gained in undergraduate and graduate school. One cannot write a history, or a biography, or a critique of a work of art, without knowing these techniques. This knowledge is gained from a mentor and becomes a part of the knowledge that identifies the scholar as competent in the field. In short, the ability to do research through primary and secondary materials in libraries and archives is an integral part of the research paradigm identifying a given humanistic field. One cannot do research and gain the doctorate in the humanities without knowing these techniques.

By contrast, for the scientist, knowledge of research methodology largely concerns techniques carried out in the field or laboratory: that is, experimental or statistical techniques. In the sciences, these are the techniques learned from a mentor. For scientists, ability to use documentary resources is a small and peripheral bit of knowledge picked up along the way. Such knowledge is not at the heart of their professional sense of self, the way it is for scholars.

These differences have major practical consequences for designers and marketers of databases. There is a powerful bad news/good news contrast here. Because use of documentary resources is so intimately integrated into the humanist's sense of professional self, so much at the heart of humanistic research methodology, any marketed innovation in information searching that does not blend well with these strong pre-existing biases in use of information on the part of scholars will likely fail.

While the scientist may have only a passing knowledge of information searching, and so be reasonably pliable when it comes to learning new techniques, the humanities scholar may be more resistant. This situation may come about not because scholars are naturally any more or less stubborn, difficult, etc. but rather because change in the area of information searching cuts deeper into the heart of their research paradigm than is the case for scientists. Change in this area automatically has more ramifications and requires more adjustments. That is the bad news.

The good news is that if information innovations can be introduced that blend well with humanities research methods, the likelihood of regular, frequent use by the scholar of these innovations is great—far greater than is generally the case for the scientist, whose use of information resources is relatively more sporadic and infrequent.

Improvements in information access will reach into the daily activities of the humanities scholar in the same way that a major new laboratory tool or a new experimental research technique might for the scientist. Once the database vendors or producers tap into this heartland of humanities research, their services may become vitally important to scholars—as important as any other major new methodological innovation is in any field. The rate of use may then rise dramatically.

The scientist and the scholar relate differently to the literatures in their fields in other senses as well. The humanities value the unique vision of the scholar: the *particular* way in which the evidence is marshalled in the book or article; the *particular* insights developed and elaborated; the *particular* graceful wording achieved by the individual. By contrast, the uniqueness of the discovery in the scientist's book or article is largely in the laboratory event or other event that happened outside the writing and which is then reported in the writing—not generally in the wording or perspective brought to the writing itself by the scientist.

As noted above, there are plenty of exceptions to this generalization. Every scientific field can point to classic articles or brilliantly unique formulations of insights, just as certain more mundane or trivial kinds of research in the humanities can be done fairly much as well by one person as by another. But a pattern of difference remains.

Consider this test of my point: in a scientific laboratory a junior graduate student may be assigned the task of writing up the results of a research project for publication. The project may have been conceived by a senior professor in the laboratory and five people have worked on it, including the student. How often could a senior scholar in the humanities assign to a research assistant the task of writing his or her latest work? In most cases, it would be inconceivable.

This is what was meant earlier when I said that in many senses the "discovery" in the humanities inheres in the writing. A biography of a famous writer, for example, is judged on how the author marshalled the evidence, and the insights that the author had and expressed in the writing. For the most part, there is no separate discovery, apart from the writing, that the author of the biography can point to and say, "this is what I discovered."

Though sometimes new original sources come to light, as in the discovery of the Dead Sea Scrolls, and sometimes people do discover things that are reported on, say, directly to the media, rather than through scholarly writings—as in the recent discovery of the true identity of the author of "The Story of O"—overall, recognition and esteem come to the humanities scholar for the *completed text* analyzing and assessing the object of the study. The particular mix of insights and expressions of ideas in the text about the object of study is what the scholar is rewarded and recognized for.

Consider, by contrast, the discovery in physics, a few years ago, of the "J" particle. Two laboratories competed to find it, one each on the West and

East coasts. They both found it, and so close together in time that the two labs agreed to share credit for it. Such courtesies do not always happen; witness the recent competition and hostilities between American and French laboratories regarding the discovery of the HIV virus.

In either of these scientific examples, however, other scientists are not going to judge which laboratory deserves credit for the discovery based on how well the reporting article was written—unless the quality of the writing is so execrable that the bare facts of the research do not succeed in being communicated; whereas, in the humanities, two scholars writing on the same subject at the same time will indeed be compared and judged on the nature of the insights expressed in the writing, the marshalling of the evidence in the writing, and the grace of their writing.

This is not to say that publications are unimportant for the scientist—quite the contrary. But the role publications play for the sciences is significantly different to the one they play for the humanities. As has been long discussed in the sociology of science, publication of results is accepted as the means of marking priority of discovery (Ziman, 1968). In fact, publication is so well established as a mechanism for according recognition for a discovery that it is usually less important who *makes* the discovery first than who *publishes* the discovery first. So, publication is woven intimately into the social structure of science. Publication is highly meaningful to scientists, but in a way that is nonetheless different from its role in the culture of humanists.

For the scientist the importance of the publication lies in establishing priority of discovery. Once that has been done, the published work has an archival function: it represents and stores for history what was discovered when and by whom, but this archive loses its value for current scientific debate quickly, as new discoveries supersede the results printed.

By contrast, while work in the humanities can also be superseded or fall out of fashion, that uniqueness of vision that the author brings to bear on the subject may be of interest far longer. The particular insight brought to a subject by the author can itself constitute a kind of "discovery" because many topics of interest in the humanities are revisited again and again, each time bringing the perspective of a new scholar or a new age—the insights in a particular work may be of interest again and again.

"Knowing the literature" for the scientist may, in practice, consist more of knowing who is doing what in which laboratory, and who has recently discovered what in those laboratories, than it does of being familiar with the actual publications that result from the laboratory work. Indeed, it has long been documented that the scientists on the cutting edge of a research field know—through an "invisible collage" of researchers who they meet at conferences and through telephone contact (and nowadays, electronic mail)—everything important that has been discovered in their field months and years before it reaches formal publication (Garvey, 1979; Meadows, 1974).

While the humanities researcher may know that a colleague is working on a biography of so-and-so, and may even know a few of the things that the colleague has discovered about the biography, real knowledge of that colleague's research does not come until the actual publication and reading of the biography: until, that is, a scholar experiences the writer's distinctive perspective on and shaping of the research material.

There are important practical consequences for our discussion here of the uniqueness of insight that scholarly writers bring to bear on their research subject. It means that those who claim knowledge of a research area in the humanities must be familiar with a large number of *particular writings,* and must have read those writings in order to absorb the insights. One cannot just know the discoveries, as in the sciences: one must know specific written works.

Striking results that emerged in this project were the interview comments by a half-dozen of the scholars to the effect that *of course* they expected to know all the literature in their research area. (These comments were made spontaneously. No interview question had been designed to probe this question.)

One of the six scholars who commented said the following:

"Just by being around you've actually seen most of
them. Because it's a very small field. And one reads journals—and you actually know what's been brought out
by whom, and what's important anyway. You obviously
miss the odd book here and the exhibitions out in the
sticks somewhere. But the most important books, the
most important items you would have in your head . . ."

Another noted that he did not see database searching as being of much use for scholars working on specialized books since they would be aware of most, if not all, of the recent literature on their topic. Still another observed that if a search is done by a specialist in the field then the relationship between what the computer yields and what the searcher knows is approximately one to ten—for every ten titles, there may be one that is new to the searcher.

For these scholars, finding just one or two previously unknown items was a pleasant surprise and was considered a successful search. This contrasts with the usual assumption in information retrieval theory that people making requests will know none-to-few of the items retrieved in a search of a topic of interest to them.

The sum total of these differences between the domains of science and the humanities is that advanced humanities scholars, much more than scientists, consider it an essential part of their intellectual patrimony to know a large body of particular writings. The scientist must know the research results, but much less so the particular writings coming from the research. (As Wiberley and Jones [1989, p. 639] note: "While scientists spend much of their time with collaborators working with laboratory equipment . . . humanists spend most of their time alone, reading.")

We might then ask, how do scholars find out about the things to read in the first place? Might they not then need databases? Several recent studies on scholars suggest that the sorts of databases found in online vendor services are little used for this purpose. Scholars most frequently find references for additional reading in other books and articles they read, in book reviews, and in conversation or correspondence with colleagues.

In Guest's study (1987, p. 163), in fact, these three sources ranked first, second and third, respectively, while abstracts and indexes ranked seventh. Tibbo (1993, p. 117) found in her study of 25 historians that 84% used footnotes and bibliographies of recent monographs, while only 24% used abstracts and indexes. It is precisely these abstracts and indexes that are most commonly mounted as online databases. If scholars already know most of the literature through their other normal contacts and sources in the field, then of what value is database searching for such people? Clearly, database searching will have a different role in the scholar's research life than it might for others.

In the Getty Online Searching Project, scholars who used DIALOG databases commented frequently on their value for interdisciplinary searching—searching in areas that they normally would not see (Bates et al., 1995). They were particularly fond of DIALOG's "OneSearch" feature, which allowed them to search over several of many databases at once. So the biggest surprises for them came from retrievals in fields outside their usual range of research. Apparently, in these cases, since they already knew the literature well in their own area of expertise, the online database search functioned not as a primary research tool but rather as a means of identifying publications relevant to their interests that are outside their usual area of research, as well as a way to capture the odd occasional work they had not yet encountered in their primary area.

Though these results may seem initially discouraging, I think they are the key to understanding how to make information products that scholars *will* use. Some of these ways will be discussed in the following sections.

Implications for design of databases and information systems

Design of databases

Specialized bibliographies My first suggestion is a hunch—an idea between the lines, as it were—picked up from an analysis of the scholars' comments. They were not asked directly about this matter because we did not know in advance that it might be of importance. What I noticed is that the "database," as it is conventionally conceived of in online services, did not seem to be a particularly meaningful concept for the scholars. They did not fall into talking about databases the way we commonly do in information science, despite their full day's training in DIALOG or the fact that most had had many previous opportunities to use the databases in their print index forms.

They could talk comfortably about types of literature that they felt were missing in the databases, and had many suggestions for additional types of information they wanted to see, but suggestions about additional desired *databases*, or bodies of information the size of a typical online database, were scarce.

Based on the discussion in the previous section, I suggest that there are at least two reasons for these reactions. First, humanities scholars seldom use the print form of these abstracting and indexing services either. The up-to-date currency provided by the frequent appearance of A&I services is of far more concern in the sciences than in the humanities.

Second, the kind of bibliographic resource that is more likely to be of value to the humanities scholar is the more specialized bibliography in a narrower field—sometimes "one-shot," sometimes recurrent. One-shot bibliographies are particularly valuable if they are annotated and/or organized in a way useful for the scholar. These bibliographies are likely to have numbers of references in the hundreds *or* thousands, not the hundreds *of* thousands. So the size of the standard online database may feel unnaturally large for scholars, and its content may not be the kind of resource they would most often use.

As noted in the preceding section, scholars get references most frequently from sources that are neither abstracts and indexes nor specialized or one-shot bibliographies. But the latter sort of resource is consistently more popular among humanities scholars than abstracting and indexing services are. Tibbo found that 36% of her historians consulted specialized bibliographies, while 24% used abstracts and indexes (Tibbo, 1993, p. 117).

Specialized bibliographies ranked fifth for Guest's 34 humanities scholars, compared to the abstracts and indexes, mentioned earlier, at seventh

(Guest, 1987, pp. 162–3). Wiberley and Jones studied eleven humanities scholars intensively and found that seven of the eleven used some form of formal bibliography, either for current awareness or for a current research project (Wiberley & Jones, 1989, p. 640). None of the types of bibliography used were abstracting and indexing services. Wiberley and Jones review still other research (1989, p. 642) that further confirms this pattern of preferring bibliographic sources that are specific and specialized to a much narrower field than abstracting and indexing services are typically.

All these results may contribute to explaining why, though the Getty scholars had the better part of an academic year to search and could do all their searching for free, only eight of the 27 scholars searched more than two hours total during all that time (Siegfried et al., 1993, p. 277).

Now it may be that the sorts of bibliographies preferred by scholars are so narrow and specialized that there is no practical commercial product possible. I suggest, however, that careful market analysis and product design may identify specialized and one-shot bibliographies that could be very popular and make both scholars and producers happy.

For one thing, most of these studies have looked at scholars' use of resources in libraries. The standard bibliography or reference tool, that is so central to research in a particular area that the scholar *buys* it and keeps it in the office, may prove to be a popular seller on CD-ROM, when it offers keyword searching and quick look-up capability on the office computer.

The up-to-the-minute currency value of frequently-published periodical indexes (and their corresponding databases) is much more important for the sciences than it is for the humanities. On the other hand, the publication of a one-time bibliography, brought together and annotated by an expert in the topic area of the bibliography, may be of immense value for the humanities scholar because of the expertise embedded in the organization of the bibliography and the commentary in the annotations. The experienced scholar who prepared the bibliography brings a direction and focus to the project that is born of years of experience with the subject matter. The best of such one-shot bibliographies tend to have a scholarly value and coherence that is missing from the sequentially published scientific indexes and abstracts. In the latter case, each abstract is a small informational unit unto itself; in the case of the scholarly bibliography, the whole is greater than the sum of the parts.

Database vendors have probably been loath to put such one-time scholarly bibliographies online or in CD-ROM format for fear that (1) they are going out of date from the moment they are produced and (2) once a scholar does a search or two on them, that scholar will have no need to return, having gotten all the retrievals that might be of interest. I think neither of these suppositions is accurate.

With regard to the first concern, it is well documented that the rate of decay of the value of humanities literature is much slower than that of the sciences (Fussler & Simon, 1961). Further, because of the cyclical, non-cumulative nature of humanities research, important writings may be returned to again and again by users of the literature. (Students of English still read Shakespeare: students of physics seldom read Newton.) Decay of value just does not work in the same way in the humanities as it does in the sciences.

With regard to the second concern—that scholars will use a bibliographic resource once or twice, never to return—I think there is an absolutely crucial difference between the use of the scholarly bibliography and the use of the scientific index. The scholar may return to the same body of information again and again, each time from a slightly different angle, each time with a richer background of understanding of the subject. An expert on the Italian Renaissance painter Piero della Francesca may write on him and his work for the expert's entire life: a biographical article one year, a piece on how the painter's work was financed the next, and a book on the religious symbolism of his paintings in the context of the Italian culture of the Renaissance over the next several years.

The expert's information resources on the painter and on art history generally constitute what one of the scholars in the Online Project called his "scholarly capital." This body of knowledge—sometimes stored in the head, other times stored in the home and office—will be returned to countless times during the expert's scholarly career.

In the sciences, return use of a bibliographic database depends on continued additions to the database of new publications as they appear. In the humanities, however, return use may depend instead on the importance and centrality of a body of bibliographic "scholarly capital" in a scholar's research.

Suppose, then, that small CD-ROM databases, containing numbers of references just in the hundreds or thousands and developed from scholarly bibliographies, were to be published by information industry producers. The demand will be smaller than for large scientific databases, but the cost will be smaller, too. As CD-ROM readers become more common in scholars' offices, it should be possible to sell such databases at prices that are even within the scope of the graduate-student and professors' salaries! Precisely because they are far smaller, they are more affordable. And because they represent the type and size of database with which the scholar is most familiar and comfortable, and will use again and again, they may be widely bought and used. Ability to do keyword searching, as well as search on ANDed combinations of terms, may give the CD-ROM version an advantage relative to the print version for the scholar.

Subfiles In the previous section, I said I had a hunch that the size of databases did not accord well with what scholars were used to in the manual environment. My suggestion was that database producers find a way to replicate the size—that is, the number of references—of many of the sources with which scholars are used to working. In most cases this would mean creating databases that are much smaller than the ones customarily available from vendors—databases with just 1,000 to 25,000, items, many at the lower end of this range. In that section, specialized and one-shot bibliographies were discussed; in this one, we look at subfiles.

There are many conveniences and economies of scale in the design of large databases as they are now conceived. Database producers and vendors have good reasons not to want to give these up. However, such benefits need not be forsworn in order to serve scholars better with small sized groupings of resources. From a single large database, the database producer can hive off sub-databases and sell them at affordable prices and in various data formats. The result may be an enlarged rather than diminished market.

Extensive data were provided in Getty Report No. 1 (Bates et al., 1993) to the effect that certain subject features, such as geographical area and historical period, were enormously important in the searching done by the humanities scholars in the Project. People identify their research interests by these aspects—Colonial American history, Renaissance Italian art, German Romantic literature, etc.—throughout the arts and humanities. These subject areas, I believe, form the natural groupings or regions of scholarship in the humanities. Often existing databases already have classification codes that would allow these sub-databases to be extracted easily by automatic algorithm.

They could be sold individually in CD-ROM form, made available through online vendors or on library catalogs, on or off the Internet. For example, once in a library catalog's version of a humanities database, the searcher might see a 30-item list of the sort of broad area categories described above. In a 300,000-item database, each such category would average 10,000 items in it. The searcher could opt to search the whole database or search just within a category subfile.

This has more benefits for the humanities student or scholar than may immediately be evident. One of the problems noted in the Getty Report No. 1 (Bates et al., 1993) was the frequency with which scholars wanted to be able to use very broad terms to describe their research topic. Because the research topic had several elements to it, when these several broad elements were combined they produced a research topic that was extremely specific.

But the individual elements were so broad that they would likely not even have been indexed because they would have been considered pointlessly broad by the indexers. For example, one of the queries in the Getty study was "image of the tree in literature, art, and science of medieval and Renaissance Europe." *Knowing that users could search on a database as small as 10,000 items within the larger database, the indexers could feel comfortable indexing such broad terms as "literature," "art" and "science."* Humanities scholars could thus search on database sizes that are (1) more *familiar* and comfortable in size, (2) specific to their research area of interest and (3) amenable to indexing by the broad terms on which they want to be able to search.

Now, I have noted earlier that the Getty scholars found online searching mostly useful for interdisciplinary research and only secondarily for research in their own area of expertise. I suggest that such use might indeed be the preferable purpose for *going online* to a database vendor and searching one or several mega-databases.

The smaller subfiles, on the other hand, that each represent the narrower subject area of interest to humanities scholars should be available in their offices on CD-ROM, or on the library's catalog via network from the office. It is the smaller, specialized databases, maximally convenient to the scholar's work, that will sell for the repeat—sometimes several times a day—uses.

Indexing vocabulary in databases

In this study, scholars were asked to type in their queries in their own natural language at the beginning of each search. Because they contained no DIALOG commands, these query statements were meaningless to DIALOG but the queries were captured for later analysis. Both these natural language statements (NLSs) and the actual search terms used in the subsequent database searches were analyzed. Much of the content of the Getty Report No. 1 (Bates et al., 1993) in this series is devoted to describing the classes of vocabulary used by the scholars in this study.

A brief summary of that analysis will be given here to support the suggestions to be made in this section. In both the natural language statements and search terms, significant numbers of uses were found of term types that are unusual in the sciences. Roughly half the NLSs included one or more names of individuals; a quarter contained geographical terms; a quarter contained discipline terms; and a sixth contained language representing dates or time periods (p. 17). By "discipline term" is meant a word or phrase that represents a discipline such as "history" or "philosophy." Overall, 84% of the Getty queries contained language representing one or more of the above categories (p. 16).

These several classes of terms were almost non-existent in a set of science queries that were compared to those from the humanities scholars. Queries in the science set, drawn from Saracevic and Kantor's study (1988) for the National Science Foundation (NSF), overwhelmingly contained what in the Getty study were called "other common" terms: that is, lower case subject terms (as distinct from upper case, proper nouns, adjectives, etc.) that did not fall into any of the categories listed above (individuals, geographical term, date term, etc.).

For example, two of the NSF study queries were these: "the relationship and communication processes between middle-aged children and their parents" (p. 195) and "occurrences, causes, treatment, and prevention of retrolental fibroplasia" (p. 195). These queries used solely "other common" terms.

In the Getty study, however, only 57% of the Getty natural language statements contained even one "other common" term; in other words, fully 43% did not contain any terms that fall in that category. One hundred percent of the NSF queries contained "other common" terms and only 18% contained language from one or more of the other categories besides "other common" (pp. 16–17).

Most of the time in information science, when we speak of thesauri and search terms, we mean the "other common" terms. Principles of thesaurus design emphasize these sorts of terms. However, as we have seen, for humanities scholars it is all the other sorts of terms that are of equal, if not greater, importance for information seeking. Perhaps this tilt toward "other common" terms in thesaurus theory and development arose because much of the impetus for the development of thesauri came after World War II, when science and technology libraries and indexing services needed more detailed and technically accurate indexing than previous systems had made possible.

The time has come for more attention to be paid to the unique needs of humanities scholars with respect to indexing vocabulary. Finding the best way to represent these other sorts of subject elements—names of individuals, geographical, date and discipline—is not obvious or easy, particularly in the online context.

The Getty Art History Information Program is currently developing some thesauri that focus on the above-noted common types of terms in the humanities. *The Getty Union List of Artist Names* is a database of several hundred thousand artists' names, drawn from nine Getty projects, that clusters together the often voluminous name variations referring to a single artist, both during the artist's lifetime and afterward.

Geographical names are problematic because geographical jurisdictions and names change frequently through time. The Getty's *Thesaurus of Geographical Names (TGN)*, a hierarchical database of place names, makes possible complete and consistent retrieval of geographical materials.

Historical dates and date ranges are frequently treated as secondary and relatively unimportant subject features of the indexing of databases' records—this despite the great importance of dates in the humanities. Several years of experimenting were necessary for the publishers of *Historical Abstracts* to find ways of coding dates that allowed for flexible retrieval on dates: that is, that allowed searches to meet either high precision or high recall requirements. Good handling of dates for effective online retrieval is not obvious and is not yet widely understood (see discussion in Bates [1992]).

Because discipline terms are very broad, they are normally seen as poor candidates for use in either indexing or retrieval—recall the discussion earlier about the query "the image of the tree in the literature, art and science . . ." Yet their frequent use indicates that these terms are often meaningful for humanities scholars. Their appearance indicated not only use as academic disciplines but also as objects of study. For example, one query stated: "checking for articles on Nietzsche and music."

The sample of discipline term uses in this study was too small to lead to confident identification of all the senses in which discipline terms are used, but there are clearly different ways in which they are used by scholars. Perhaps it would be possible to introduce these discipline terms into database indexing and retrieval by providing a special classification of them that indicated the special senses in which they are used by humanists. Their application then would provide more specific retrieval. Discipline term use by humanists needs additional study.

These major categories of terms—geographical, historical, discipline, and names of individuals and works—lend themselves well to faceted indexing. Indeed, two of the original master facets proposed by the developer of faceted indexing, S.R. Ranganathan, were "space" and "time." After starting with Library of Congress subject headings and after much trial and error, as well as detailed conceptual analysis, the developers of the *Art and Architecture Thesaurus* settled on a faceted approach as most useful for indexing in that field. Database producers in other areas of the humanities may find a faceted approach preferable too.

Overall, much more attention should be paid to the unique vocabulary needs of the humanities. Much remains to be learned and experimented with before thesauri in the humanities do the best possible job of meeting researchers' needs.

Interfaces and command language

Complaints about problems with Boolean logic and the subtleties of command language syntax in all the major vendors are well known and oft-repeated. I will not recapitulate them here. I do have one major point to make, however, based on the Getty scholars' online searching. Whatever we might say about the problems with these aspects of searching for the general user, these problems are even more severe for the humanities scholar.

Error rates and patterns are discussed in Getty Report No. 2 (Siegfried et al., 1993). The scholars had a total of one day's training in DIALOG before they began their online searching. Almost all their searching was done on their own. Considering these factors they had tolerable, though hardly ideal, error rates. Amount of searching was measured by number of search statements entered. Searching errors were marked as being either certain (the error, in its nature, was guaranteed to cause a failure) or probable (very poor strategy or grossly inefficient approach; there are common superior ways of doing this, but a searcher could conceivably have some reason for doing this).

Those ten scholars in the first year of the project (1989) whose total searching experience during the year went on for more than 50 statements had combined (i.e., probable plus certain) error rates of 5–12%, and the corresponding group in 1990, which consisted of nine scholars, had a combined error rate range of 8–33%. (Possible causes of the differences in error rates between the two years are considered in Report No. 2.)

In my observation, there are two broad classes of reasons for these problems. The first is that the very talents that make humanities scholars the good scholars they are often interfere with or substitute for the abilities that make one a good user of Boolean logic and a formal, logically oriented command syntax. Ability to see broad trends, sensitivity to metaphor, ability to recognize the significance of a series of seemingly unconnected historical events—these are all talents that clash with the mathematical precision and analytical logic required of one in using database syntax.

Let me illustrate with just one example of a searcher's error in this project. One of the DIALOG illustrations of the use of the "N" proximity operator appeared in the following way: (nN). The lower case "n" stood for the number of intervening words, and the upper case "N" stood for itself—to indicate a particular proximity operation. This is essentially an algebraic use of the lower case "n." One searcher, in creating a proximity phrase, input these characters in exactly this way, without converting the small "n" into a number.

If one is not oriented to algebra, or forgets one's high school algebra, this method of presenting this system capability may be confusing. After all, one could argue, why should a humanities scholar have to remember high school algebra, when scientists are not required in their later lives to remember the poems they memorized in their high school English classes? Systems need to be usable easily for the non-scientific mind. (A recent DIALOG manual does not contain this algebraic use and explains proximity "N" another way.)

I have taught online searching in one course or another for over 15 years. I have been repeatedly struck by the range of talents in my classes for this kind of task. Natural ability (or ability conditioned by earlier educational experience) has a wider range, in my experience, with regard to online searching, than it has for any other topic I have taught. Online searching is not like other subjects in that respect. I recall one student, in particular, who was one of the most brilliant ever to come through our program—but she was brilliant as a humanities thinker. Her online performance was lower than that of most of the class on the first day of class, and remained one of the lowest throughout the entire course.

To see such intelligence thwarted by a task that seems to some of us relatively simple conceptually, if not in practice, made me realize that online searching demands precisely what the engineers who designed it find easy, and does not take advantage of precisely those talents that humanities researchers have in abundance—and which are often lacking in engineers.

The second class of reasons for problems with online searching concerns problems with the vocabulary in the databases. As noted in the previous section, there are a variety of types of vocabulary in common use in the humanities that get short shrift in thesaurus development. Complications and gaps in the handling of dates, geographical areas and discipline terms make successful searches more unlikely even for the most skilled online searcher. One scholar in the study commented that he searched on people's names more than he otherwise would because he found searching on other types of terms more difficult.

Further, the need to *combine* these various types of terms can lead to problems as well. The humanities queries in this study frequently combined instances of several of these distinctive categories of terms, as in the "image of the tree" example mentioned earlier.

Proper representation of such queries using Boolean logic and proximity terms is quite difficult even for experienced searchers. Whereas science queries often used all terms of one type—here called "other common"—the humanities queries required sophisticated combinations of several different types. If even one of those types of terms is poorly designed in a particular database's thesaurus, then the ANDing of one of those terms with the rest of the query will likely lead to null or inadequate sets.

It is, further, a sad irony that effective online searching in this area requires high skill in the very sort of ability that, as noted above, humanities scholars find so difficult. I would therefore argue that here, above all, information system interfaces be developed that do not require an understanding of Boolean logic.

Fortunately, the very nature of humanities vocabulary may lend itself better to an interface design that is not obviously Boolean to the searcher. It is not only indexing that lends itself well to faceting, but also the description of queries. Through use of facets, a helpful interface could be designed for humanities information systems that displayed fill-in blanks for each major facet area and encouraged the user to fill in each of the blanks. No Boolean combination would be needed on the part of the searcher. Term types labels for the fill-in blanks, such as "Historical period" and "Geographical area, "would be easily understandable.

Then the system would do its own Boolean combination of the facets internally. A variety of combinations could be tested to find the best set of retrievals for the particular query. Internal measures could evaluate quality of retrievals by, for example, measuring the frequency of appearance of terms of each facet in selected records. The result of all these internal machinations could then be presented to the user. All the user has to know is what is wanted, not how to get it.

Humanities scholars can do—and did succeed in doing—adequate online searching with a day's training. But because of the complexities of vocabulary in the humanities, and the resultant complexity of queries, other solutions for online searching may be desirable for them in the long run. I have suggested, in a general way, how an interface and indexing language might be designed to make the process easier for the scholar.

Summary and conclusions

Humanities scholars related to their disciplinary literatures in ways significantly different to scientists. These differences have consequences—to date, insufficiently understood—for habits and methods of literature searching by humanities scholars. Assumptions based on the needs and practices of scientists will mislead in designing resources for the humanities.

Special, targeted, approaches should be used to meet the information needs of humanities scholars.

Means of automating specialized and one-shot bibliographies—which are used more by scholars than are conventional abstracts and indexes—as well as producing database subfiles as independent products have been discussed. Special problems of humanities indexing vocabulary have been described and ways of coping with these problems have been proposed. Finally, a simple approach for dealing with the complexity of humanities search queries has been proposed through the design of a faceted, fill-in interface.

Much remains to be tested and experimented with to optimize information resources for scholars. However, research from the Getty Online Searching Project and other studies of humanities scholars is beginning to point the way toward making information systems and resources better adapted to the particular needs and working styles of these heretofore relatively neglected users.

REFERENCES

Bates, M.J. (1992). Implications of the subject subdivisions conference: The shift in online catalog design. In M.O. Conway (Ed.), *The future of subdivisions in the Library of Congress Subject Headings system* (pp. 92–98). Report from the 1991 Subject Subdivisions Conference sponsored by the Library of Congress. Washington, DC: Library of Congress Cataloging Distribution Service.

Bates, M.J. (1996). Document familiarity in relation to relevance, information retrieval theory, and Bradford's Law: The Getty Online Searching Project report no. 5. *Information Processing & Management, 32*(6), 697–707.

Bates, M.J., Wilde, D.N., & Siegfried, S. (1993). An analysis of search terminology used by humanities scholars: The Getty Online Searching Project report no. 1. *The Library Quarterly, 63*(1), 1–39.

Bates, M.J., Wilde, D.N., & Siegfried, S. (1995). Research practices of humanities scholars in an online environment: The Getty Online Searching Project report no. 3. *Library & Information Science Research, 17*(1), 5–40.

Fussler, H.H., & Simon, J.L. (1961). *Patterns in the use of books in large research libraries.* Chicago, IL: University of Chicago Library.

Garvey, W.D. (1979). *Communication: The essence of science: Facilitating information exchange among librarians, scientists, engineers, and students.* New York: Pergamon Press.

Guest, S.S. (1987). The use of bibliographical tools by humanities faculty at the State University of New York at Albany. *Reference Librarian, 7*(18), 157–172.

Meadows, A.J. (1974). *Communication in science.* London: Butterworths.

Saracevic, T., & Kantor, P. (1988). A study of information seeking and retrieving. II. Users, questions, and effectiveness. *Journal of the American Society for Information Science, 39*(3), 177–196.

Siegfried, S., Bates, M.J., & Wilde, D.N. (1993). A profile of end-user searching behavior by humanities scholars: The Getty Online Searching Project report no. 2. *Journal of the American Society for Information Science, 44*(5), 273–291.

Tibbo, H.R. (1993). *Abstracting, information retrieval, and the humanities.* Chicago, IL: American Library Association.

Wiberley, S.E., Jr., & Jones, W.G. (1989). Patterns of information seeking in the humanities. *College & Research Libraries, 50*(6), 638–645.

Ziman, J.M. (1968). *Public knowledge: An essay concerning the social dimension of science.* London: Cambridge University Press.

6

Document familiarity, relevance, and Bradford's Law: The Getty Online Searching Project report no. 5

ABSTRACT

The Getty Online Searching Project studied the end-user searching behavior of 27 humanities scholars over a 2-year period. Surprising results were that a number of scholars anticipated—and found—that they were already familiar with a very high percentage of the records their searches retrieved. Previous familiarity with documents has been mentioned in discussion of relevance and information retrieval (IR) theory, but it has generally not been considered a significant factor. However, these experiences indicate that high document familiarity can be a significant factor in searching. Some implications are drawn regarding the impact of high document familiarity on relevance and IR theory. Finally, some speculations are made regarding high document familiarity and Bradford's Law.

Introduction

Over a 2-year period (1989–90), online searching by 27 humanities scholars was studied in the Getty Online Searching Project. Visiting scholars at the Getty Center for the History of Art and the Humanities in Santa Monica, California, were studied in a project designed and carried out

First published as Bates, M. J. (1996). Document familiarity in relation to relevance, information retrieval theory, and Bradford's Law: The Getty Online Searching Project Report no. 5. *Information Processing & Management, 32*(6), 697–707.

by the Getty Art History Information Program.[1] With the permission of the scholars, complete transaction logs were captured and analyzed, and extensive interviews were conducted with the scholars. In exchange for their co-operation, the scholars received unlimited free (i.e., subsidized by the Getty) online searching (as end-users) of about 60 DIALOG® databases in the arts, humanities, and social sciences. Each scholar was at the Getty Center for a year, so the 27 participants represented 2 years of visitors.

Extensive additional information on the study, its participants, and its results is provided in the previous four reports in this series (Bates et al., 1993, 1995; Siegfried et al., 1993; Bates, 1994).

One of the results of this study, concerning previous document familiarity, was quite unexpected—so unexpected that no question had been formulated for it in the interviews. This result has intriguing and potentially significant implications for various aspects of information science theory. Those implications are developed in this article. Many people participated in the conduct of this study, and the results discussed here would not have come about without their efforts.[2] However, as the discussion and speculations here are solely in information science, Bates, as the only information scientist in the project, is the sole author of this article.

The relationships of humanities scholars and scientists to their literatures

In both the humanities and sciences, it can be said that "being current" means knowing the latest research on one's topic of interest. But, in operational terms, knowing the latest research happens in quite different ways in the two research domains, because of inherent differences in those domains.

In science, if one is doing cutting-edge research, keeping up means, for the most part, knowing what people that are working on the same problems as oneself are doing at other universities and laboratories.

---

1   The J. Paul Getty Trust is a private operating foundation. Two of its programs are the Getty Art History Information Program and the Getty Center for the History of Art and the Humanities. These two entities collaborated on the project.

2   Marilyn Schmitt conceived the Getty Online Searching Project; she designed the study together with Susan Siegfried and Deborah N. Wilde. Siegfried and Wilde carried out the collaborative project plan and oversaw the gathering of data throughout the project. Marcia J. Bates designed the interview schedule for the second year's data, analyzed the data for both years, formulated conclusions, and contributed insights from the discipline of information science. Jeanette Clough and Katherine Smith transcribed the DIALOG search statements, and Smith transcribed the interviews, for subsequent analysis. Vanessa Birdsey coded the search data into categories developed by Bates.

Consequently, as has long been documented in research on scientific communication (Meadows, 1974; Garvey, 1979), researchers learn of the latest results directly by talking with or corresponding with (or, nowadays, e-mailing to) an "invisible college" of researchers at the competing sites. Such communication precedes publication of research results often by a year or more. Keeping up with and out-racing the competition in science would not be possible without the direct communication that long precedes the publication of results.

Consequently, an example scientist, Dr. Jones, may feel quite current in his field because he knows that there are only four labs in the country working on his problem. He communicates with people from those labs at conferences and through e-mail and knows just about exactly how far along each is in finding a solution to the same problem he is working on. By the time the results of recent studies at other labs reach print, he has known about these results for a year or more.

Sometimes, he looks up some articles by key people at other labs to put the references in a paper he is writing or to check some data or information on a technique. But this scientist is likely to leave unread much of the text in the articles that are looked up and never see many of the articles published on his subject altogether in his field. Why look up the articles, if one knows, from personal contacts, the essence of what has been found out on your subject? Under these circumstances, it can certainly be said that Dr. Jones "knows his field," and even, in some sense, "knows the literature" of his field, but, as will be seen, he knows it in a very different way from the way humanities scholars know their literatures.

In the humanities, being current in one's field means being familiar with a great number of actual, particular publications. The humanities value the unique vision of the scholar—the *particular* way in which the evidence is marshaled, the *particular* insights developed and expressed, the *particular* graceful wording produced by the author. The genius of a humanities scholar is expressed in the written result and cannot be fully known to others until the scholar's writings are actually published.

In the humanities, in a certain sense, *the "discoveries" of research inhere in the writing* of the ultimate published text. Research is done in libraries or archives, which is then written about in the resulting paper or book, just as the scientist does research in the laboratory that is reported in the resulting article, but there is a crucial difference between the two groups of researchers.

In science, the discovery lies in the event(s) that took place in the laboratory or out in the field; the discovery does not lie in the writing up of the research. The map is not the territory; the original contribution is *reported* in the research article, it is not *contained* in, it does not happen in, the research article.

In the humanities, the "discovery" is not just in what is found in the papers and manuscripts in the archives, it is also how the scholar analyzes, extracts, and develops insights about the material, then pulls that all together into a seamless whole of exposition and meaning in the published result.

Consider an example humanities scholar Dr. Smith, who knows that a colleague is working on a biography of a certain famous writer. She may even know a few of the things that her colleague has discovered in researching the writer's life—say, that the writer turned out to have had a previously unknown girlfriend at the age of 18.

Dr. Smith may wonder what impact this life event had on the writer's work. But she will not know what implications and conclusions her colleague draws regarding this discovery, will not know how the discovery is integrated into the author's thinking about the writer overall, and will not be able to assess whether the biography as a whole is good and insightful *until she actually reads the text of the biography.* Not until Dr. Smith reads the full, elaborated text of the biography will she understand the insights and perspective her colleague brings to her subject. The *same facts* may show up in another biography by a different author, but may be used in an entirely different and more, or less, insightful way.

A scientist might assign to the most junior research assistant in the laboratory the task of writing up the most recent experiment, on which as many as 10 or 15 people worked. In most cases, however, it would be inconceivable for a humanities scholar to assign to an assistant the task of writing up his or her latest book. Only that one individual, with his or her unique insights, can write the book. In the science lab it would usually make little difference which of three or four research assistants wrote up that study. In the humanities, on the other hand, the evaluation of the resulting document would be based almost entirely on what perspectives and insights the individual writing the document brought to that write-up.

If two scientific laboratories make the same discovery at the same time, their work will not be comparatively evaluated on the basis of which lab wrote the better article of the work. Such a thing sounds absurd, does it not? Rather, the work will be evaluated on the quality of what happened in the laboratory. Quality of writing or insight in the resulting article would be noticed in the sciences only if it were so bad that essential laboratory results were not made clear.

In the humanities, on the other hand, if two people research and publish biographies or critical analyses of the work of a famous artist or writer at the same time, the resulting works will be compared and evaluated based on the marshaling of evidence, the quality of insights, etc., that each author brings to bear in the published text of the books. What is new, what constitutes the unique contribution of researchers to the scholarship of their fields is the combination of the research and the analysis and expression in the completed texts that are published—usually not in something discovered apart from the writing of the work. It is in this sense that the discovery inheres in the writing in the humanities in a way that it generally does not in the sciences.

The important consequence of this situation is that *the scholar who claims to be current and knowledgeable in a field must have read closely and be intimately familiar with a large number of particular works. For this reason, prior familiarity may prove to be a much larger factor in information retrieval in the humanities than in the sciences.*

Many generalizations have been made here, to which plenty of exceptions can be found. There are some elementary research publications in the humanities that could as easily have been produced by one person as by another, and there are classic, unique texts in the sciences, but a pattern of difference remains that is significant and substantial.

The sharp (and, perhaps, somewhat overdrawn) contrast between the humanities and sciences is made here to point out that some of the assumptions made in information retrieval (IR) theory and research that are largely based on information needs and behaviors of scientists may not be applicable when studying researchers in the humanities.

The consequence of the above characteristic differences between scientific and humanistic fields is that, to keep up, the scientist must know the research results but much less the particular writings coming from the research. Humanities scholars, on the other hand, cannot fully know the latest research unless they have read and analyzed the unique insights brought to bear by the authors of humanities texts, i.e., until they have become intimately familiar with a large number of particular published works.

Therefore, the consequence for the humanities scholar is that a search in a database on one's chief topic of research interest is likely to yield a high number of hits that are already very well known to the scholar. The next section presents the data from the Getty study that are relevant to that point.

Document familiarity in the Getty study and other cases

Six of the 27 scholars interviewed made comments suggesting that they expected to know most or all of the literature they found in their searches. Such comments had not been anticipated, so no question was devised for the interview, and all the comments were spontaneous. It is not known how many more would have added to or contradicted these ideas.

However, these comments are remarkable because they contradicted outright a conventional, but little examined, assumption in IR research to the effect that users are generally unfamiliar with most or all of the documents in a retrieved set. In later sections, the role of document familiarity in IR system evaluation is discussed, but the data from the Getty study pertaining to document familiarity is reviewed first. Below, code numbers for scholars are keyed to be consistent throughout all articles on the Getty study—see the other articles for further results relating to the various scholars mentioned here (Bates et al., 1993, 1995; Siegfried et al., 1993; Bates, 1994).

One scholar (15) observed in passing that, if a search is done by a specialist in the field, then the relationship between what the computer yields and what the searcher knows is approximately one to ten—for every 10 items, there may be one that is new to the searcher. Scholar 8 commented on one of his searches that he did not know one third of the titles, but a lot of them were not critical to his interests. Another (18) noted

> Just by being around you've actually seen most of them.
> Because it's a very small field. And one reads jour-
> nals—and you actually know what's been brought out
> by whom, and what's important anyway. You obviously
> miss the odd book here and the exhibitions out in the
> sticks somewhere. But the most important books, the
> most important items you would have in your head . . .

Scholar 4 said he found one or two articles he had not known about, and so considered his search useful. When probed further, scholar 4 said that he knows his subject area well because he has been working in it for years; consequently, for him the relationship between the time spent on his search and the yield was good.

Likewise, scholar 5 commented that she found it "amusing to find something on a topic you think you know." From the tenor of this comment it is clear that the scholar took it for granted that she knew the literature of her subject, and that to find even one unfamiliar item was a surprise. Scholar 6 makes this expectation of previous familiarity even more explicit:

> I loved the idea that I could find [new] things
> on _____, on whom I am supposed to be some-
> thing of an expert, that I didn't even know existed.

Notice to what degree these comments alter usual thinking about retrieved sets. These scholars expected to know most retrieved records; they frequently did in fact know most of the records; and finally, most striking of all, they were pleasantly surprised when they actually found just one or two unfamiliar items of use out of large sets.

Let us note again the contrast made earlier between scientists' and humanities scholars' familiarity with the publications of their fields. At the moment the scientist (again, in general, not always) goes to research a question on his research interest, *he knows the research but few of the particular articles that have been published.* In this case, it makes sense, in traditional IR theory, to assume that document familiarity in online searching is a minor factor. Most retrievals will, in fact, be unfamiliar to the researcher, even if he knows many of the authors or topics of research addressed in the papers.

However, it is quite another matter when the humanities searcher knows 90% of the citations intimately, feels most of the remaining 10% are irrelevant, and considers a 200-item search to be a great success if it produces just one or two novel references! That is really a different situation from the one routinely assumed in IR research—and that different circumstance is the focus of this article.

Having reviewed the above results, one might still ask "How *do* humanities scholars learn of research then, if they do not find it in databases?" In an earlier paper in this series (Bates, 1994), literature was reviewed that suggested that scholars usually get references for the material they study in other ways besides searching online databases or the manual indexes those databases are derived from. Scholars pick up references for their reading in a variety of ways and from a variety of sources. They note references at the ends of articles and books they read, they hear things from colleagues or at conferences, they look up specialized bibliographies in narrow fields that may appear recurrently in journals (Wiberley & Jones, 1989), they use specialized "one-shot" bibliographies, and so on.

How then, should one think about what scholars do in using an online database? It would appear that online searching may not have the same role in scholarly research as it has in scientific research. This article returns to this question in a later section.

So on the basis of the suggestive Getty data (as well as, perhaps, personal reflections about other circumstances where the humanities pattern may hold true), it may be suspected that there are a substantial number of search situations where high document familiarity is a major factor in evaluating and selecting documents from a retrieved set. Document familiarity is now considered in relation to various elements of IR theory.

Document familiarity and relevance

The topic of relevance has generated an enormous literature of both analytical and empirical research. This literature has, in turn, been the object
of several major reviews (Saracevic, 1970, 1975; Schamber et al., 1990). From
the early days there was an awareness that relevance is a tricky concept,
and relevance judgments can be influenced by the judge's understanding
of the concept. Variability of relevance judgments based on the user's
understanding of the term was demonstrated definitively in a landmark
study in which 14 different concepts of relevance were tested, labeled "use
orientations" (Cuadra & Katter, 1967).

Early on, a common distinction began taking shape between (1)
relevance based on matches between subject content of the document
and of the query (or "topicality," Schamber et al., 1990) and (2) relevance
as based on the usefulness of a document to the user-judge in a particular
situation. Schamber et al. (1990) found the distinction in the literature as
early as 1959 in Vickery (1959a,b), who distinguished between "relevance
to a subject" and "user relevance."

The second kind of relevance has been variously called "utility" (Cooper,
1973), "situational relevance" (Wilson, 1973), and "pertinence" (Kemp, 1974;
Howard, 1994). There are important differences among these definitions;
however, they all fall generally in the second class of definitions.

In recent years, there has been an efflorescence of analysis (Schamber
et al., 1990; Harter, 1992) and research on relevance as experienced by the
user. Park (1993) and Barry (1994) have done particularly detailed empirical
studies of the various factors that user-judges take into account when
determining relevance of a document to their information needs.

For present purposes, the two broad types of relevance are called
"content relevance" and "utility relevance." In *content relevance,* a document
is said to be relevant to a query if the meaning of what is wanted in the
query finds a match in the topical content, or meaning, of the retrieved
document. In practice, these matches are usually determined by whether
some sort of subject term(s) in the document record, whether full text,
descriptors, or classification categories, match with subject term(s) of the
same meaning in the query.

The success of the match may be evaluated by the end-user or by the
experimenter. If the latter case, the experimenter is assuming that he or
she understands the user's needs as expressed in the query sufficiently to
recognize good matches and false drops. In general, with content relevance,
though there are variations in definition, it is assumed that both the query
and the documents have meaning that can be generally recognized, and the
relevance determined, often without the original requester being present.

On the other hand, *utility relevance* is usually more closely tied to an actual user's needs, though, with enough information, some experimenters may assume they can evaluate here for the user as well (cf. empirical data in Janes, 1994). In utility relevance, users evaluate the retrieved document based on whether they believe that it will actually have value for meeting their information needs in the present situation. A utility-relevant document, as defined here, may be content-relevant also, but is not required to be. For example, a retrieved record may be a false drop by content relevance measures, but the user may happen to find the supposedly irrelevant record to be of use in the present situation.

For a variety of reasons, a document with content relevance may prove to have no utility relevance for a user. The searcher may have seen it before; it may be in a remote library that cannot be accessed in the needed timeframe; it may be written in language too simple or complex for the user; it may be lengthy when the user wants a brief summary, and so on. It may even be on the right subject and meet all other ancillary criteria, such as the ones enumerated in the examples in the previous sentence, and still be rejected as having no utility relevance. This can come about because the requester got all the needed information from earlier examined documents in the retrieved set, and now this nth document is thus rendered superfluous.

This last situation, where reactions to later records in a set are influenced by exposure to earlier records in the set, has been examined by several researchers. Regazzi (1988) and Eisenberg and Barry (1988) detected order effects in relevance evaluations. Tiamiyu and Ajiferuke (1988) developed a model of the total relevance of a set of documents, arguing that inter-document dependencies need to be taken into account in any complete model of IR evaluation.

The above studies looked at the effects of seeing one retrieved document on the user's evaluation of subsequent documents in the retrieved set. However, the present scholars represented a different situation: they knew the documents before they even looked at the first record in the retrieved set.

It has been recognized that novelty can be a factor in a user's judgment of relevance. Barry identified three kinds of novelty in her study: content novelty (document provided information that was new to the user), source novelty (sources of the documents, such as authors, journals, publishers, were novel to the user), and stimulus document novelty (the document itself was new to the user) (Barry, 1994, p. 155). She analyzed the comments of users as they evaluated records retrieved. Just 1.1% of the comments were with respect to the novelty of the documents (stimulus document novelty) (p. 156). Note, however, that her analysis identified comments on document novelty, not familiarity.

A fundamental assumption of most IR testing appears to be that the user will be unfamiliar with most or all records retrieved. The purpose of an information search is to find out something about a subject one needs to learn about, so the assumption goes; therefore, encountering familiar records will be a small to non-existent problem in evaluating the retrieved set.

Yet the comments made by the aforementioned scholars in the Getty study suggest that previous familiarity may be a huge factor in their online searching. If so, then document familiarity must be incorporated in some way into thinking about IR and relevance. A full model of IR, one with "ecological validity," i.e., one that fairly represents the actual circumstances and environment of real searching, must somehow take into consideration searches whose retrieval sets have high percentages of records familiar to the searcher. A new model is not proposed here, but the document familiarity problem and some of its implications for consideration by the field are developed.

It seems reasonable to consider document familiarity to be a significant factor in utility relevance in at least some cases. For many of the humanities scholars, in fact, this one element of the relevance evaluation may be presumed to swamp all other considerations. If nine out of ten, or 99 out of 100, retrieved records are familiar and therefore rejected on utility relevance grounds, there is not going to be much room for other factors to have impact on the searcher's judgments. In such cases, in experiments seeking even reasonable verisimilitude, leaving document familiarity out of the calculations is to leave out most of what affects the outcome.

Document familiarity and IR

Earlier it was reported that research on humanities scholars has shown that they gather information from a variety of sources, a bit at a time, here and there. This pattern of searching resembles what has been called elsewhere a "berrypicking" mode—gathering items one or a few at a time, here and there, based on an ever-shifting query, ever-shifting search methods, and ever-shifting sources, like picking huckleberries in the forest—rather than making major one-time queries to large databases (Bates, 1989). Supposing that "berrypicking" is an appropriate label for the style of searching engaged in by humanities scholars, then what role can or should online database searching play—and, therefore, how can it be viewed in the theory of IR?

If the scholars have previously identified most of the references of interest and value to them in berrypicking mode before going online, then the online search of one or several large databases may be understood in the terms used by one of the scholars. Scholar 12 called online searching the "industrialization of scholarship" (Bates et al., 1995, p. 20). He seemed quite uncomfortable with this style of information seeking, but unwittingly, he may have described it quite accurately for our purposes.

If the Getty scholars are thought of as having previously roamed the forest picking berries (references and information) here and there, then the online search is indeed rather like some large machine that thunders across the forest floor systematically skimming off all the berries that remain scattered here and there on the bushes. Rather than being a primary search tool for these humanities scholars, the online search serves to pick up in a systematic swath anything that the regular berrypicking search modes failed to catch. (For the remainder of this article, and for the purposes of the questions being analyzed here, the discussion is based on the classic IR assumption that the online query remains stable—does not mutate into a different query—during a single online search.)

Results from the Getty study suggested another use for online searching for the scholars as well. Five of the scholars commented on the value of online searching to explore interdisciplinary topics or topics in neighboring areas (scholars 14, 15, 18, 20, and 24; see greater detail in Bates et al., 1995). DIALOG's OneSearch feature was popular, too, as a way to search several databases easily for a topic. As one of the scholars (15) explained:

> DIALOG, or something like DIALOG, will become more and more useful, and needed even . . . because the human-ities are moving in a direction that almost makes bib-liographic research of the old kind impossible, because the old kind has always been one discipline, one bibliography. Now that we are combining things [such as] architecture and film, or the image of medicine in the fine arts . . . These are [topics] that are truly interdisciplinary . . .

Scholar 15 was very enthusiastic about online searching, and he was rather ahead of many of his fellows in understanding the possibilities. It is doubted that scholars will soon give up their favored ways of searching, but online searching may well supplement old methods, particularly in the two ways discussed in this section—to scoop up the few missed items in one's specialization area, and, as noted by four others besides scholar 15, to help explore in previously unknown areas, especially in other disciplines.

If these two types of uses predominate for humanities users, then there is an ironic consequence of these searches for these users: the chances are that, in most cases, they will find more unfamiliar utility-relevant records on their topic of interest in databases that are remote or marginal to their interests than they will in databases that are central to their interests.

Measuring retrieval success

Based on the discussion in the preceding section, what the humanities scholar will find in a database that covers materials central to his or her interests is a huge number of already familiar records, along with the occasional document in the area of interest that is also unfamiliar. A standard content-relevant measure of retrieval success on the documents in the retrieved set will be almost completely useless for evaluating the success of such a search. In fact, 100% recall (proportion of relevant documents retrieved) and 100% precision (proportion of retrieved documents that are relevant), where relevance is content relevance, could yield not a single document of real (utility-relevant) interest to the searcher.

One way to deal with this situation is to start with the same premise the humanities scholars did—take for granted that most or all the retrieved records would be already familiar. The "true" retrieved set in this case would be all records in the retrieved set that are unfamiliar to the requester. Thus, the requester would identify the records that are familiar and unfamiliar, as well as relevant by whatever measure being used. Recall and precision measures could then be applied to this smaller set of unfamiliar documents (though recall would be as difficult as or more difficult than it ever is to measure).

There are at least two weaknesses with this approach.

1. It does not deal with those cases where the searcher sees a familiar document and is reminded to use it by seeing it. In this case a familiar record might be seen as a utility-relevant "hit," but it would not figure in the calculation of a method that ignored familiar records.

2. When the "true" set size is zero, i.e., all documents initially retrieved are familiar, this result might be of use to the searcher—to know that the system has no records to add to the scholar's own previously identified set (Stielow & Tibbo, 1988)—but the evaluation method has no way of recognizing and measuring this condition.

Overall, however, this approach of expecting, and taking seriously, document familiarity in those cases where it can be expected to be a significant factor should provide more internally valid research results than simply applying standard measures that ignore document familiarity. This suggestion is just a start on providing a truer measure for the user in a high document familiarity situation.

Document familiarity and Bradford's Law

This discussion ends with some speculation on the relationship between high document familiarity and Bradford's Law. Samuel Bradford originally proposed his model of the statistical behavior of information based on his empirical study of the number of relevant (content-relevant) articles that appeared in journals in two subject areas, applied geophysics and lubrication (Bradford, 1948). Though there has been much refinement of Bradford's Law in subsequent years (Brookes, 1977; Chen & Leimkuhler, 1986; Egghe, 1986; Lockett, 1989), his original formulation will be used here for its simplicity.

Bradford found that it was possible to group the journals into categories by descending numbers of articles per year on the topic that appeared in them, and that there was a pattern to the number of journals in each category. He says it well:

> [I]f scientific journals are arranged in order of decreasing productivity of articles on a given subject, they may be divided into a nucleus of periodicals more particularly devoted to the subject and several groups or zones containing the same number of articles as the nucleus, when the numbers of periodicals in the nucleus and succeeding zones will be as $1:n:n^2 \ldots$ (1948, p. 116)

In principle, there could be any number of zones, with the number of articles in each zone being the total number of articles divided by the number of zones. In his empirical data, however, he identified only three zones, and it simplifies things also for present purposes to look at three zones.

Bradford found in his empirical data that the value of n was roughly 5. Thus, for example, if three journals produced one-third of the references (in a three-zone example), then $5 \times 3 = 15$ journals produced the second third of the references, and $5^2 = 25 \times 3 = 75$ journals produced the third third of the references. Thus, a core of just a few journals is very dense with articles, a surrounding ring contains a substantially larger number of journals producing the same total of articles among them, and, finally, the outer ring has a comparatively extremely large number of journals, which jointly produce only the same number of content-relevant articles as each of the nucleus and the first ring.

This "Law of Scattering," or, as it was later called, "Bradford's Law," showed that articles on a topic are neither perfectly concentrated in core sources, as might be wished, nor are they perfectly randomly scattered, as might be feared. Instead, they follow a fairly consistent pattern in their scattering.

Suppose content-relevant articles in the humanities follow the above pattern, then what happens to utility relevance when document familiarity is a major factor? A sort of rough converse of Bradford's Law can be imagined.

Suppose articles and journals on the topic of interest of humanities scholar Dr. Smith are grouped by content relevance into the three zones, one-third of the articles in each zone. For present purposes, utility relevance can be simplified to consist solely of content relevance plus document unfamiliarity—i.e., to be utility-relevant to Dr. Smith, a document must be both content-relevant and unfamiliar. Based on the comments of the Getty scholars, almost all of the articles in the nucleus, a substantial number in the second zone and only a few in the third zone may be expected to be familiar. This parallels the experience of the Getty scholars who found that databases remote from their regular interests—the interdisciplinary users of searching—produced interesting new material.

In this example, while the number of content-relevant articles is the same in each zone, only a very few of the articles in the nucleus will be utility-relevant, because so many articles there are familiar. As there are fewer familiar articles in the next zone, there will be a higher percentage of utility-relevant articles there; finally, because very few articles are familiar in the outer zone, the highest number of utility-relevant articles will be found in the outer zone. Thus, while content-relevant articles number the same in each zone, the farther out one goes, the more utility-relevant articles per zone there are. This gives us a sense of converse relationship, with utility-relevant articles more likely to appear within that set of content-relevant articles that are dispersed among large numbers of journals in the outer ring(s).

However, since in the simplified example, utility relevance requires both content relevance and unfamiliarity, the utility-relevant articles are limited by the number of content-relevant ones in every ring. Since the per-journal frequency of content-relevant articles diminishes the farther out each ring is, there is a possibility that the number of utility-relevant articles *per journal* is actually flat across all rings.

This situation could be summarized as follows.

- The number of content-relevant articles per zone is the same across all zones. The number of content-relevant articles per journal decreases from the nucleus outward.

- The number of utility-relevant articles per zone increases from the nucleus outward (due to the impact of document familiarity). The number of utility-relevant articles per journal is (probably) flat across all zones.

Bradford found an average of less than one content-relevant article per year per journal in his outermost ring. If the present scholars found the same, and the inner rings, because of the high document familiarity, also averaged the same low per-journal rate of utility-relevant articles, then this condition of flat dispersal of all utility-relevant articles across all rings might obtain—i.e., only the occasional article in the center is unfamiliar among the many content-relevant, so the per-journal rate close in may be similar to the per-journal rate in the outer rings.

Suppose that this pattern proved to be the case, so that the per-journal rate of utility-relevant articles for the humanities searcher was the same throughout the region of journals that at least occasionally contain content-relevant articles on the scholar's area of interest. This figure would necessarily be low by all that has been discussed so far. If so, then the technique of browsing the dozens or even hundreds of appropriate journals would be an inefficient one, because one might find a utility-relevant article only every year or two in any given journal. Thus, the image used earlier of online searching as the machine rolling across the forest floor scooping up the occasional leftover "berries" of articles might be a quite accurate description of the strengths and limitations of online searching in this case for humanities scholars.

For the humanities scholar, most of the useful material is found using methods that do not include manual or online searching of conventional humanities databases. In other words, they get most of their berries other ways. If one thinks of the forest containing some patches where there are lots and lots of berries, and other parts with only a scattered few, then the scholars somehow find and pick the berries in the rich patches before they even get to online searching. What the online searching does for them is to systematically cull all the remaining berries—the few they missed in the rich patches, and the scattered ones in the less abundant patches that they had heretofore ignored.

Finally, it might also be asked if Bradford's Law, and its potential utility-relevance converse, apply to references in databases in a manner similar to their application with articles in journals. Might there be one, five, and 25 databases occupying zones 1, 2, and 3 for a humanities scholar, each zone containing the same number of content-relevant articles? Might the per-database number of utility-relevant articles then be approximately the same across all zones?

It remains to be seen what pattern of distribution utility-relevant articles fall into when IR system evaluation fully incorporates document familiarity.

Summary and conclusions

Comments by humanities scholars in the Getty Online Searching Project stimulated analysis and speculation about the different relationships scholars have to their literatures in comparison to those for scientists. Scholars feel that knowledge of their field consists in knowing many particular publications in their research area; for the scientist, being up-to-date consists more in knowing who is doing what in which laboratory than it does in knowing particular publications.

As a consequence of these differences, some humanities scholars were found to take it for granted that they would know all the significant literature in their subject specialty. Some considered a search successful if it produced only one or two items the scholar had not seen before.

How can this view of searching be reconciled with conventional assumptions regarding relevance and IR theory? Historically, previous familiarity with some of the retrieved records has been recognized as a possibility, but it was assumed to be a minor factor. However, a search for these humanities scholars could produce a high number of content-relevant records, most of which are familiar to the scholar—in which case only a handful (or none) are utility-relevant, if document familiarity is a factor in judgments of utility relevance.

If IR system evaluation is to retain ecological validity in the context of searches by humanities scholars (and in some other similar cases as well), then means must be found to deal with evaluation in situations where previous familiarity with documents is a major and not a trivial factor.

Finally, questions are raised about the impact of document familiarity on the operation of Bradford's Law. If articles and journals of interest to a humanities scholar are grouped in Bradford zones from a nucleus outward with equal numbers of content-relevant articles in each zone, then might there be a kind of rough converse of Bradford's Law with respect to utility relevance, where that measure includes document unfamiliarity? If articles in the core journals of interest are mostly familiar, then the scholar might actually find more content-relevant unfamiliar—i.e., utility-relevant—articles in the outer zone(s) than in the inner ones.

REFERENCES

Barry, C.L. (1994). User-defined relevance criteria: An exploratory study. *Journal of the American Society for Information Science, 45*(3), 149-159.

Bates, M.J. (1989). The design of browsing and berrypicking techniques for the online search interface. *Online Review, 13*(5), 407-424.

Bates, M.J. (1994). The design of databases and other information resources for humanities scholars: The Getty Online Searching Project report no. 4. *Online & CDROM Review 18*(6), 331-340.

Bates, M.J., Wilde, D.N., & Siegfried, S. (1993). An analysis of search terminology used by humanities scholars: The Getty Online Searching Project report no. 1. *The Library Quarterly, 63*(1), 1-39.

Bates, M.J., Wilde, D.N., & Siegfried, S. (1995). Research practices of humanities scholars in an online environment: The Getty Online Searching Project report no. 3. *Library & Information Science Research, 17*(1), 5-40.

Bradford, S.C. (1948). *Documentation.* London: Crosby Lockwood.

Brookes, B.C. (1977). Theory of the Bradford Law. *Journal of Documentation, 33*(3), 180-209.

Chen, Y.S., & Leimkuhler, F.F. (1986). A relationship between Lotka's Law, Bradford's Law, and Zipf's Law. *Journal of the American Society for Information Science, 37*(5), 307-314.

Cooper, W.S. (1973). On selecting a measure of retrieval effectiveness. *Journal of the American Society for Information Science, 24*(2), 87-100.

Cuadra, C.A., & Katter, R.V. (1967). Opening the black box of "relevance." *Journal of Documentation, 23*(4), 291-303.

Egghe, L. (1986). The dual of Bradford's Law. *Journal of the American Society for Information Science, 37*(4), 246-255.

Eisenberg, M., & Barry, C. (1988). Order effects: A study of the possible influence of presentation order on user judgements of document relevance. *Journal of the American Society for Information Science, 39*(5), 293-300.

Garvey, W.D. (1979). *Communication: The essence of science: Facilitating information exchange among librarians, scientists, engineers, and students.* New York: Pergamon Press.

Harter, S.P. (1992). Psychological relevance and information science. *Journal of the American Society for Information Science, 43*(9), 602-615.

Howard, D.L. (1994). Pertinence as reflected in personal constructs. *Journal of the American Society for Information Science, 45*(3), 172-185.

Janes, J.W. (1994). Other people's judgments: A comparison of users' and others' judgments of document relevance, topicality, and utility. *Journal of the American Society for Information Science, 45*(3), 160-171.

Kemp, D.A. (1974). Relevance, pertinence, and information system development. *Information Storage & Retrieval, 10*(2), 37-47.

Lockett, M.W. (1989). The Bradford distribution: A review of the literature, 1934-1987. *Library & Information Science Research, 11*(1), 21-36.

Meadows, A.J. (1974). *Communication in science.* London: Butterworths.

Park, T.K. (1993). The nature of relevance in information retrieval: An empirical study. *The Library Quarterly, 63*(3), 318–351.

Regazzi, J.J. (1988). Performance measures for information retrieval systems—An experimental approach. *Journal of the American Society for Information Science, 39*(4), 235–251.

Saracevic, T. (1970). The concept of "relevance" in information science: A historical review. In T. Saracevic (Ed.), *Introduction to information science* (pp. 111–151). New York: R.R.Bowker.

Saracevic, T. (1975). Relevance: A review of and a framework for the thinking on the notion in information science. *Journal of the American Society for Information Science, 26*(6), 321–343.

Schamber, L., Eisenberg, M.B., & Nilan, M.S. (1990). A re-examination of relevance: Toward a dynamic, situational definition. *Information Processing & Management, 26*(6), 755–776.

Siegfried, S., Bates, M.J., & Wilde, D.N. (1993). A profile of end-user searching behavior by humanities scholars: The Getty Online Searching Project report no. 2. *Journal of the American Society for Information Science, 44*(5), 273–291.

Stielow, F., & Tibbo, H. (1988). The negative search, online reference, and the humanities: A critical essay in library literature. *RQ, 27*(3), 358–365.

Tiamiyu, M.A., & Ajiferuke, I.Y. (1988). A total relevance and document interaction effects model for the evaluation of information retrieval processes. *Information Processing & Management, 24*(4), 391–404.

Vickery, B.C. (1959a). The structure of information retrieval systems. In *Proceedings of the International Conference on Scientific Information* (Vol. 2, pp. 1275–1289). Washington, DC: National Academy of Sciences, National Research Council.

Vickery, B.C. (1959b). Subject analysis for information retrieval. *Proceedings of the International Conference on Scientific Information* (Vol. 2, pp. 855–865). Washington, DC: National Academy of Sciences, National Research Council.

Wiberley, S. E., Jr., & Jones, W. G. (1989). Patterns of information seeking in the humanities. *College & Research Libraries, 50*(6), 638–645.

Wilson, P. (1973). Situational relevance. *Information Storage & Retrieval, 9*(8), 457–471.

7

Indexing and access for digital libraries and the Internet: Human, database, and domain factors

ABSTRACT

Discussion in the research community and among the general public regarding content indexing (especially subject indexing) and access to digital resources, especially on the Internet, has underutilized research on a variety of factors that are important in the design of such access mechanisms. Some of these factors and issues are reviewed and implications drawn for information system design in the era of electronic access. Specifically the following are discussed: *Human factors:* Subject searching vs. indexing, multiple terms of access, folk classification, basic-level terms, and folk access; *Database factors:* Bradford's Law, vocabulary scalability, the Resnikoff-Dolby 30:1 Rule; *Domain factors:* Role of domain in indexing.

Introduction

Objectives

In the current era of digital resources and the Internet, system design for information retrieval has burst onto the stage of the public consciousness in a way never seen before. Almost overnight, people who had never thought about information retrieval are now musing on how to get the best results

First published as Bates, M. J. (1998). Indexing and access for digital libraries and the Internet: Human, database, and domain factors. *Journal of the American Society for Information Science, 49*(13), 1185–1205.

from their query on a World Wide Web search engine, or from a remote library catalog or digital library resource. At the same time, and under the same stimulus, experts in a variety of fields cognate to information science—such as cognitive science, computational linguistics, and artificial intelligence—are taking up information retrieval questions from their perspectives.

In the meantime, those of us in information science, where information retrieval from recorded sources (as distinct from mental information retrieval) has long been a core, if not *the* core, concern, are faced with a unique mix of challenges. Information science has long been a field understaffed with researchers. Where some fields have 10 researchers working on any given question, we have often had one researcher for 10 questions. A promising research result from an information science study may languish for years before a second person takes up the question and builds on the earlier work. (This is not universal in the field; some questions are well studied.) As a consequence of this understaffing, we know a lot about many elements of information retrieval, but often in a fragmented and underdeveloped way.

At the same time, what we do know is of great value. Years of experience, not only with research but also with application in dozens of information-industry companies, have given information scientists a deep understanding about information retrieval that is missing in the larger world of science and information technology.

So at this particular historical juncture in the development of information retrieval research and practice, I believe there are a number of both research results and experience-based bits of knowledge that information scientists need to be reminded of, and non-information scientists need to be informed of—information scientists because the fragmentation and understaffing in our field has made it difficult to see and build on all the relevant elements at any one time, and people outside of information science because these results are unknown to them, or at least unknown to them in the information retrieval implications.

My purpose here is to draw attention to that learning and those research results associated with indexing and access to information, which have been relatively under-utilized by those both inside and outside of information science. These are results that seem to me to have great potential and/or importance in information system design, and for further research.

Making such a selection is, of course, a matter of judgment. I believe that the material below offers the possibility of enriching design and, when studied further, enriching our understanding of human interactions with information in automated environments.

Fully automated subject access

Before beginning to review that knowledge, we must first address a prior issue. Many people in our society, including many in the Internet and digital resources environments, assume that subject access to digital resources is a problem that has been solved, or is about to be solved, with a few more small modifications of current full-text indexing systems. Therefore, why worry about the various factors addressed in this article?

There are at least two reasons. First, the human, domain, and other factors would still operate in a fully automated environment, and need to be dealt with to optimize the effectiveness of information retrieval (IR) systems. Whatever information systems we develop, human beings still will come in the same basic model; products of human activity, such as databases, still will have the same statistical properties, and so on. As should become evident, failure to work with these factors will almost certainly diminish the resulting product.

Second, it may take longer than we think to develop fully automated systems. At conferences, researchers present their new system and say, "We are 70% there with our prototype system. Just a little more work, and we will have it solved." This happens because, indeed, it is not difficult to get that first 70% in retrieval systems—especially with small prototype systems.

The last 30%, however, is infinitely more difficult. Researchers have been making the latter discovery as well for at least the last 30 years. (Many of the retrieval formulas that have recently been tried were first used in the 1950s and 1960s. See, e.g., Luhn, 1957; Stevens, 1965.) Information retrieval has looked deceptively simple to generations of newcomers to the field. But IR involves language and cognitive processing, and is therefore as difficult to automate as language translation and other language processes based on real-world knowledge, which researchers have been trying to automate virtually since the invention of the computer. Information retrieval also poses serious scalability problems; small prototype systems are often *not* like their larger cousins. Further, user needs vary not just from one time to another, but from one subject domain to another. Optimal indexing and retrieval mechanisms may vary substantially from field to field.

We can do an enormous number of powerful things with computers, but effective, completely automated indexing and access to textual and text-linked databases eludes us still, just as 100% perfect automatic translation does, among other things. Meanwhile, a lot of other IR capabilities go undeveloped, in deference to the collective assumption that we will soon find a way to make it possible for computers to do everything needed in information retrieval.

The human side of the IR process needs attention too. The really sophisticated use of computers will require designs shaped much more in relation to how human minds and information needs actually function, not to how formal, analytical models might assume they do. Attention to these points will be productive for effective IR, no matter how soon, or whether, we find a way to develop good, fully automated, IR.

Human factors

Subject searching vs. indexing

It is commonly assumed that indexing and searching are mirror images of each other. In indexing, the contents are described or represented, or, in full-text searching, indicative words or phrases are matched or otherwise identified. On the searching side, the user formulates a statement of the query. Then these two representations, of document and of query, are matched to retrieve the results.

But, in fact, this is only superficially a symmetrical relationship. *The user's experience is phenomenologically different from the indexer's experience.* The user's task is to describe something that, by definition, he or she does not know (cf. Belkin, 1982). (Knowledge specifically of what is wanted would lead to a "known-item" search.) The user, in effect, describes the fringes of a gap in knowledge, and can only guess what the "filler" for the gap would look like. Or, the user describes a broader, more general *topic area* than the specific question of interest, and says, in effect, "Get me some stuff that falls in this general area and I'll pick what looks good to me." Usually, the user has no tools available to help with that problem of describing the fringes of the gap, or the broader subject area.

In many cases, the problem for the user is even more difficult than indicated above. In years of studies, Kuhlthau (1993) has documented that the very process of coming to know what one wants in the first place is seldom straightforward. In a search of any complexity, as for a student term paper, one does not so much "pick a topic," as is usually assumed, but rather discovers, develops, and shapes it over time through exploration in materials in an area of interest. One may use an information system at any point in this gradually developing process. The need may evolve and shift at each stage of developing knowledge of the subject. (See also my own model of the evolving and changing information need—Bates, 1989a.) Use of an information system early in a project will naturally come out of a much less well-specified and articulated information need—yet the searcher must nonetheless find a way to get the information system to respond helpfully.

The indexer, on the other hand, has the record in hand. It is all there in front of him or her. There is no gap. Here, ideally, the challenge for the indexer is to try to anticipate what terms people with information gaps of various descriptions might search for in those cases where the record in hand would, in fact, go part way in satisfying the user's information need. This can be seen to be a very peculiar challenge, when one thinks about it. What kinds of information needs would people have that might lead them to want some information that this record would, in fact, provide?

As Harter (1992) points out, discovering that a particular article is relevant to one's concerns, and therefore a good find, does not necessarily mean that the article is "about" the same subject as one's originating interest. As he notes, regarding his own article on the concept of psychological relevance: "The present article [on psychological relevance] may be found relevant, by some readers, to the topics of designing and evaluating information retrieval systems, and to bibliometrics; I hope that it will. However, this article is not *about* these topics" (p. 603, emphasis in the original). Conceivably, infinitely many queries could be satisfied by the record in hand. Imagining even the more likely ones is a major challenge. (See extensive discussions in Ellis, 1996; Green & Bean, 1995; O'Connor, 1996; Soergel, 1985; and Wilson, 1968.)

But in fact, historically, and often still today, catalogers and indexers do not index on the basis of these infinitely many possible anticipated needs. Instead, and perhaps much more practically, they simply *index what is in the record.* (See also discussion in Fidel, 1994.) In other words, they attempt to provide the most careful and accurate possible description or representation of the contents of the record. This situation differs in many ways from the phenomenological circumstances of the user. We should not be surprised, then, if the user and the indexer use different terminology to describe the record, or, more generally, conceptualize the nature and character of the record differently.

For the indexer, there is no mystery. The record is known, visible before him or her. Factual information can be checked, directly and immediately, to create an absolutely accurate record. The user, on the other hand, is seeking something unknown, about which only guesses can be made. What happens in retrieval if the searcher's guesses have little (or big) inaccuracies in them, and do not match the precise and accurate description provided by the indexer?

Further, the indexer is experienced with the indexing system and vocabulary. Over the years, with any given system, fine distinctions are worked out regarding when one term is to be used and when another for two closely related concepts. Indexers create rules to cover these debatable situations. Eventually, mastery of these rules of application comes to constitute a substantial body of expertise in itself. For example, the subject cataloging manual for the *Library of Congress Subject Headings* (Library of Congress, 1996) runs to two volumes and hundreds of pages (Library of Congress, 1991–). *This manual is not the same as the subject heading listings.* It does not consist so much of general indexing principles as it does of rules for applying individual headings or types of headings. For example, under the subject "Strikes and Lockouts," section H2100 of the manual, four pages of instructions are given for creating headings for strikes in individual industries and for individually-named strikes of various types.

Thesaural indexing systems also frequently have "scope notes" that tell the indexer how to decide which term to use under debatable circumstances.

Often, these rules are not available to searchers, but even when they are, the naive searcher—and that includes Ph.D.s, as long as they are naive about indexing—will usually not realize there are any ambiguities or problems with a term, and will not feel a need to check it. The user has in mind the sense of a term that interests him or her, not the other senses that the indexer is aware of. Only upon retrieving false drops will the user realize there is even any problem.

In short, the user almost always knows less about the indexing issues in a topic area than the indexer does. The user approaches the system with an information need that may be formulated out of the first words that come to mind. (See Markey, 1984b, on the many queries she found that "could be categorized as 'whatever popped into the searcher's mind'" p. 70.) Consequently, the user's input is liable not to be a good match with the indexer's labeling, which is derived from years of experience and analysis. The indexer, on the other hand, cannot undo his/her far greater knowledge of the indexing issues. After indexers have been at work for one day, or attended one training session, they know more, and have thought more, about indexing issues than even the most highly educated typical user has. Already, an expertise gap is forming between the user and the indexer that nearly guarantees some mismatches between user search terms and indexing terms on records.

The same phenomenological gap will hold true for the match between the system user and bodies of data that have been automatically indexed by some algorithm as well. The creator of the algorithm has likewise thought more and experimented more with the retrieval effects of various algorithms than the typical user has, before selecting the particular algorithm made available in a given system. Yet, at the same time, the full statistical consequences of such algorithms can never be anticipated for every circumstance.

Results achieved through such algorithms will seldom dovetail exactly with what humans would do in similar circumstances. So, the result is a peculiar mix of expert human understanding of indexing with non-sentient statistical techniques, to produce a result that is never just like interacting with another human would be. Again, we have a phenomenologically different experience for the researcher/designer on one side, and the user on the other. Further, no retrieval algorithm has been found to be anywhere near perfectly suitable (more on this later), yet the principles by which the algorithm is designed are seldom made fully available to end users—just as the indexing principles seldom are—so the user could try to find ways around inadequacies.

Still another factor is likely to operate in the behavior of catalogers, indexers, and system designers for manual and automated systems. The information professional has an understandable desire to create, in an indexing vocabulary, classification system, or statistical algorithm, a beautiful edifice. He or she wants a system that is consistent in its internal structure, that is logical and rigorous, that can be defended among other professionals, as well as meet all the usual expectations for creations of human endeavor. After years of working with problems of description, the creators of such systems have become aware of every problem area in the system, and have determinedly found some solution for each such problem. Therefore, the better developed the typical system, the more arcane its fine distinctions and rules are likely to be, and the less likely to match the unconsidered, inchoate attempts of the average user to find material of interest.

This is by no means to suggest that IR systems should be inchoate or unconsidered! Instead, the question is a different one that is usually assumed. That question should not be: "How can we produce the most elegant, rigorous, complete system of indexing or classification?," but rather, "How can we produce a system whose front-end feels natural to and compatible with the searcher, and which, by whatever infinitely clever internal means we devise, helps the searcher find his or her way to the desired information?"

Such clever internal means may include having distinct means of access and indexing. The two functions of indexing and access are not one and the same. It is not necessary to require the user to input the "right" indexing term, which the system in turn uses to search directly on record indexing. The design of the access component of a system can be different from the design of the indexing component, provided these two are appropriately linked.

Thus, the user, with only vague, poorly thought through ideas initially of what is wanted, can be helped, with the right access mechanism, to find his or her way into the portions of the database that have been carefully and rigorously organized. It is unreasonable to demand of system users that they develop the expert indexer's expertise. At the same time, it is unreasonable to demand of the indexers that they be sloppy and fail to note critical, and useful, distinctions. By developing an access mechanism—a user-friendly front-end—for the user, and linking it to the indexing, indexers can maintain standards, and users can benefit from the intellectual work that has gone into the system of description, without having to be experts themselves. (For further discussion, see Bates, 1986a, 1990.)

Multiple terms of access

On this next matter there is a huge body of available research. Several people have written extensively about it (Bates, 1986a, 1989b; Furnas, Landauer, Dumais, & Gomez, 1983; Gomez, Lochbaum, & Landauer, 1990), and yet the results from these studies are so (apparently) counterintuitive that little has been done to act on this information in IR system design. It is as if, collectively, we just cannot believe, and, therefore do not act upon, this data. A few examples of these results will be described here; otherwise the reader is encouraged to explore the full range of available data on this matter in the above-cited references.

In study after study, across a wide range of environments, it has been found that for any target topic, people will use a very wide range of different terms, and no one of those terms will occur very frequently. These variants can be morphological (forest, forests), syntactic (forest management, management of forests) and semantic (forest, woods).

One example result can be found in Saracevic and Kantor (1988). In a carefully designed and controlled study on real queries being searched online by experienced searchers, when search formulations by pairs of searchers *for the identical query* were compared, in only 1.5% of the 800 comparisons were the search formulations identical. In 56% of the comparisons, the overlap in terms used was 25% or less; in 94% of the comparisons, the overlap was 60% or less (p. 204).

In another study, by Lilley (1954), in which 340 library students were given books and asked to suggest subject headings for them, they produced an average of 62 different headings for each of the six test books. Most of Lilley's examples were simple, the easiest being *The Complete Dog Book,* for which the correct heading was "Dogs." By my calculation, the most frequent term suggested by Lilley's students averaged 29% of total mentions across the six books.

Dozens of indexer consistency studies have also shown that even trained experts in indexing still produce a surprisingly wide array of terms within the context of indexing rules in a subject description system (Leonard, 1977; Markey, 1984a). See references for many other examples of this pattern in many different environments.

To check out this pattern on the World Wide Web, a couple of small trial samples were run. The first topic, searched with the Infoseek search engine, is one of the best known topics in the social sciences, one that is generally described by an established set of terms: *The effects of television violence on children.* This query was searched on five different expressions that varied only minimally. The search was not varied at all by use of different search capabilities in Infoseek, such as quotation marks, brackets, or hyphens to change the searching algorithm. Only the words themselves were altered—slightly. (Change in word order alone did not alter retrievals.) These were the first five searches run:

> violent TV children
> children television violence
> media violence children
> violent media children
> children TV violence

As is standard, each search produced 10 addresses and associated descriptions as the first response for the query, for a total of 50 responses. Each of these queries could easily have been input by a person interested in the identical topic. If each query yielded the same results, there would be only 10 different entries—the same 10—across all five searches. Yet comparison of these hits found 23 different entries among the 50, and in varying order on the screen. For instance, the response labeled "Teen Violence: The Myths and the Realities," appeared as #1 for the query "violent media children" and #10 for "violent TV children." The search was then extended a little farther afield to a query on "mass media effects children." That query yielded nine new sites among the 10 retrieved, for a total of 32 different sites—instead of the 10 that might have been predicted—across the six searches.

The previous example varied the search words in small, almost trivial ways. The variation could easily have been much greater, while still reflecting the same interests from the searcher. Let us suppose, for example, that someone interested in freedom of speech issues on the Internet enters this query:

+"freedom of speech" +Internet

This time the search was run on the Alta Vista search engine. The plus signs signal the system that the terms so marked must be present in the retrieved record and the quotation marks require the contained words to be found as a phrase, rather than as individual, possibly separated, words in the record. So, once again, we have a query that is about as straightforward as possible; both terms, as written above, must be present.

Let us suppose, however, that three other people, interested in the very same topic, happen to think of it in just a little different way, and, using the identical system search capabilities, so that only the vocabulary differs, they enter, respectively:

+"First Amendment" +Web
+"free speech" +cyberspace
+"intellectual freedom" +Net

All four of these queries were run, in rapid succession, on Alta Vista. The first screen of 10 retrievals in each case was compared to the first 10 for the other three queries. The number of different addresses could vary from 10 (same set across all four queries) to 40 (completely different set of 10 retrievals for each of the four queries). Result: There were 40 different addresses altogether for the four queries. Not a single entry in any of the retrieved sets appeared in any of the other sets.

Next, the search was expanded by combining the eight different terms in all the logical combinations, that is, each first term combined with each second term (free speech and Internet, free speech and Web, First Amendment and cyberspace, etc.). There are 16 such orders, for a total of 160 "slots" for addresses on first 10 retrievals in each case. All 16 of these combinations could easily have been input by a person interested in the very same issue (as well as dozens, if not hundreds, of other combinations and small variations on the component terms).

The result: Out of the 160 slots, 138 unique different entries were produced. Thus, if each of the 16 queries had been entered by a different person, each person would have missed 128 other "top 10" entries on essentially the same topic, not to mention the additional results that could be produced by the dozens of other terminological and search syntax variations possible on this topic. In sum, the data from these small tests of the World Wide Web conform well with all the other data we have about the wide range of vocabulary people use to describe information and to search on information.

If 85 or 90% of users employed the same term for a given topic, and only the remainder used an idiosyncratic variety of other terms, we could, with a moderate amount of comfort, endeavor to satisfy just the 85 or 90%, by finding that most popular term and using it in indexing the topic. But description of information by people just does not work this way. Even the most frequently used term for a topic is employed by a minority of people. There are generally a large number of terms used, many with non-trivial numbers of uses, and yet no one term is used by most searchers or indexers.

For search engines designed as *browsers* this may be a good thing. The slight variations yield different results sets for searchers, and thus spread around the hits better across the possible sites, thereby promoting serendipity. But for people making a directed search, it is illusory to think that entering that single just-right formulation of the query, if one can only find it, will retrieve the best sites, nicely ranked, with the best matches first.

Under these circumstances, any simple assumption about one-to-one matching between query and database terms does not hold. In million-item databases, even spelling errors will usually retrieve something, and reasonable, correctly spelled terms will often retrieve a great many hits. (In one of my search engine queries, I accidentally input the misspelling "chidlren" instead of "children." The first four retrievals all had "chidlren" in the title.) Users may simply not realize that the 300 hits they get on a search—far more than they really want anyway—are actually a small minority of the 10,000 records available on their topic, some of which may be far more useful to the user than any of the 300 actually retrieved.

Another possible reason why we have not readily absorbed this counterintuitive study data: Interaction with a system is often compared to a conversation. Whether or not a person consciously thinks of the interaction that way, the unconscious assumptions can be presumed to derive from our mental model of conversations, because that is, quite simply, the principal kind of interaction model we language-using humans come equipped with. In a conversation, if I say "forest" and you say "forests," or I say "forest management" and you say "management of forests," or I say "forest" and you say "woods," we do not normally even notice that different terms are used between us. We both understand what the other says, each member of the example pairs of terms taps into the same area of understanding in our minds, and we proceed quite happily and satisfactorily with our conversation. It does not occur to us that we routinely use this variety and are still understood. Computer matching algorithms, of course, usually do not generally build in this variety, except for some stemming, because it does not occur to us that we need it.

Experienced online database searchers have long understood the need for variety in vocabulary when they do a thorough search. In the early days of online searching, searchers would carefully identify descriptors from the thesaurus of the database they were searching. The better designed the thesaurus and indexing system, the more useful this practice is. However, searchers soon realized that, in many cases where high recall was wanted, the best retrieval set would come from using as many different terms and term variants as possible, including the official descriptors. They would do this by scanning several thesauri from the subject area of the database and entering all the relevant terms they could find, whether or not they were official descriptors in the target database.

In some cases, where they had frequent need to search a certain topic, or a concept element within a topic, they would develop a "hedge," a sometimes-lengthy list of OR'd terms, which they would store and call up from the database vendor as needed. (See, e.g., Klatt, 1994.)

Sara Knapp, one of the pioneers in the online searching area, has published an unusual thesaurus—not the kind used by indexers to identify the best term to index with, but one that searchers can use to cover the many terms needed for a thorough search in an area (Knapp, 1993). Figure 1 displays the same topic, "Child development," as it appears in a conventional thesaurus, the *Thesaurus of ERIC Descriptors* (Houston, 1995), and in Knapp's searcher thesaurus. It can be seen that Knapp's thesaurus provides far more variants on a core concept than the conventional indexer thesaurus does, including likely different term endings and possible good Boolean combinations.

A popular approach in IR research has been to develop ranking algorithms, so that the user is not swamped with hundreds of undifferentiated hits in response to a query. Ranking will help with the 300 items that are retrieved on the term-that-came-to-mind for the user—but what about the dozens of other terms and term variations that would also retrieve useful material (some of it far better) for the searcher as well? IR system design must take into account these well-attested characteristics of human search term use and matching, or continue to create systems that operate in ignorance of how human linguistic interaction in searching actually functions.

```
CHILD DEVELOPMENT          Jul. 1966        Child development. Child development.
   CIJE: 4101      RIE: 3775    GC: 120      Choose from: child(ren,hood), juvenile, pedi-
   BT    Individual Development              atric, infant(s), bab(y,ies), neonat(e,es,al),
   RT    Child Behavior                      adolescen(t,ce), psychosocial, psychosexual,
         Child Development Centers           emotional, personality, physical, cognitive,
         Child Development Specialists       moral, intellectual, social, language, auton-
         Child Health                        omy, motor, sexual, psychophysiological,
         Child Language                      psychomotor, speech with: development(al),
         Child Rearing                       develop(ed,ing), growth, matur(ed,ing,ation),
         Child Responsibility                immatur(e,ity), transition(s,al), stage(s).
         Children                            Consider also: oral, anal, phallic, genital with
         Delayed Speech                      stage(s). See also Adolescent development;
         Developmental Delays                Age differences; Autism; Bonding (emo-
         Developmental Stages                tional); Child development disorders; Child
         Developmental Tasks                 language; Child nutrition; Childrearing; Cog-
         Failure to Thrive                   nitive development; Delayed development;
         Family Environment                  Developmental disabilities; Developmental
         Parenthood Education                stages; Early childhood development; Ego-
         Piagetian Theory                    centrism; Emotional development; Failure to
                                             thrive (psychosocial); Home environment;
                                             Human development; Individual differences;
                                             Infant development; Life cycle; Motor
                                             development; Object relations; Oedipus
                                             complex; Perceptual development; Physical
                                             development; Psychomotor development;
                                             Socialization.
```

FIG. 1. *Comparison of "child development" in two thesauri.*

NOTE: *Entry on left reprinted from James E. Houston (Ed.). (1995). Thesaurus of ERIC Descriptors, 13th Edition, Oryx Press, p. 43. Entry on right reprinted from Sara D. Knapp (Ed.). (1993). The Contemporary Thesaurus of Social Science Terms and Synonyms: A Guide for Natural Language Computer Searching, Oryx Press, p. 52.*

All subject vocabulary terms are not equal

There is considerable suggestive evidence that the human mind processes certain classes of terms differently from others, i.e., that certain terms are privileged in comparison with others. If so, we can ask how we might take advantage of these characteristics in IR system design.

Folk classification

There is a substantial body of linguistic and anthropological research into what are called "folk classifications," the sets of categories used by various cultures for plants, animals, colors, etc. (See, e.g., Brown, 1984; Ellen & Reason, 1979; Raven, Berlin, & Breedlove, 1971.) As Raven, Berlin, and Breedlove note: "In all languages, recognition is given to naturally occurring groupings of organisms. These groupings appear to be treated as psychologically discontinuous units in nature and are easily recognizable" (p. 1210).

These they refer to as *taxa*. Across many cultures, these groupings have been shown to fall into a few class types, which the authors label, going from general to specific: "Unique beginner, life form, generic, specific, varietal" (p. 1210).

Of these, the "generic" is pivotally important, containing readily recognizable forms such as "monkey" or "bear." The more specific forms, "specific" and "varietal," are generally few in number, and "can be recognized linguistically in that they are commonly labeled in a binomial or trinomial format that includes the name of the generic or specific to which they belong" (p. 1210), such as—in Western cultural terms—"howler monkey" or "Alaskan grizzly bear."

The generics are so readily recognized because there are many physical discontinuities that distinguish one from another (Brown, 1984, p. 11). For instance, the shape and appearance of a cow (generic level) is very different from the shape and appearance of a fox (generic level), while the same for a Guernsey cow (specific or varietal) is not so different from the shape and appearance of a Hereford cow (specific or varietal).

Raven, Berlin, and Breedlove (1971) go on to say:

> Folk taxonomies all over the world are shallow hierarchi-
> cally and comprise a strictly limited number of generic
> taxa ranging from about 250 to 800 forms applied to
> plants and a similar number applied to animals. These
> numbers are consistent, regardless of the richness of the
> environment in which the particular people live. (p. 1213)

So the English-speaking Californian will have a set of names for plants or animals that falls in the same number range as the Yapese speaker on an island in Micronesia or an Eskimo in Canada. (And, no, in contrast to what is commonly stated, even in serious scientific works, Eskimos do *not* have hundreds of words for "snow," trouncing English with just one or two words for the same phenomenon. Read Pinker, 1994, p. 64ff, as he skewers what he calls the "Great Eskimo Vocabulary Hoax.")

A striking discovery in this research on folk classifications has been the observation that formal scientific taxonomies of biological taxa started out, and remained for some time, folk classifications in structure. Several generations of biological taxonomies, including, above all, that of Linnaeus, resemble folk classifications on several structural features. "In broad outlines . . . the system of Linnaeus was a codification of the folk taxonomy of a particular area of Europe" (Raven, Berlin, & Breedlove, 1971, p. 1211).

Both linguistic and anthropological research are more and more frequently demonstrating common underlying patterns across cultures and languages, whatever the particulars of the expression of those patterns in given cultures. I believe, even, that an argument can be made that the Dewey Decimal Classification also betrays some of these same folk classification characteristics.

But whether or not Dewey or other formally constituted classifications retain folk classification roots, we can certainly expect the average information system user to approach that system with a mind that creates—and expects to find—classifications with such characteristics.

What would these classifications look like? Research was not found that links this research in anthropology with IR research, but we might at least expect, and test for, the pattern described above: Shallow hierarchy (few levels), with the generic level of prime significance. In any one area that generic level might contain 250 to 800 terms. If we were to find this pattern in information-seeking behavior—that is, people are found to favor use of systems with categories numbered in this range—then the implications for design of access in automated information systems are clear.

Basic level terms

Other research has been conducted in psychology that also supports the "not all vocabulary terms are equal" idea. Eleanor Rosch and her colleagues (Rosch, Mervis, Gray, Johnson, & Boyes-Braem, 1976; Rosch, 1978) have done extensive research supporting the idea that, in natural language vocabulary grouping and use, there are what she calls "basic-level" terms. As a psychologist, Rosch has endeavored to identify patterns, not to compare across cultures, but rather to discover as fundamental human patterns of cognitive processing. She, too, identified the importance of natural discontinuities. She states:

> A working assumption of the research on basic objects is that (1) in the perceived world, information-rich bundles of perceptual and functional attributes occur that form natural discontinuities, and that (2) basic cuts in categorization are made at these discontinuities. (Rosch, 1978, p. 31)

In a long series of studies, she found that these basic-level terms are the ones that are learned first by children, and are easiest to process and identify by adults (Rosch et al., 1976; Rosch, 1978). Both Rosch (1978, p. 32) and

Berlin (1978, p. 24) note the likely correspondence between the generic level in folk classifications and the "basic-level" in the psychological studies.

She (Rosch et al., 1976) and Newport and Bellugi (1978) even found that the centrality of basic-level terms appears in sign language for the deaf. Research throughout the Rosch studies was done on basic-level terms (e.g., chair) plus superordinate (e.g., furniture) and subordinate (e.g., kitchen chair) terms. Newport and Bellugi (1978) state, regarding the signs in American Sign Language, that "superordinate and subordinate signs are usually derived from signs at the basic-level: They contain basic-level signs as their components. In short, Rosch's basic-level is formally basic in American Sign Language" (p. 52).

When we turn to information science, we do not know if there are basic-level search terms used by information system users. Rosch's work has tantalized the field for many years, but it is not easy to find a way to identify basic-level terms when people are talking about topics of interest in information seeking in contrast to Rosch's very carefully controlled laboratory studies. (See Brown's [1995] efforts to study subject terms from a more psychological perspective.) However, the task should not be insurmountable. Looking at how college students search for material on a topic when assigned to write a paper might reveal patterns in the level of generality of their search terms, for instance. Much more research is needed in this area.

However, it would seem to be a reasonable assumption that we would find that certain terms come more commonly to mind for the general user of the Web browser or database, terms that are neither the broadest nor narrowest (i.e., that are "basic-level"), and if we could find a way to identify and use those terms for access, system users would make a match much more readily in their searches.

Folk access

The discussion above was about "folk classification." We in information science might also talk about "folk access." There is some evidence that there are identifiable patterns in what people expect of information systems, though much more needs to be studied on this matter. In their study of online catalog design, Kaske and Sanders (1980a, 1980b) found that focus groups responded positively to the idea of some sort of classification tree being available to users at the beginning of their search. My dissertation research (Bates, 1977, p. 371) also uncovered a substantial amount of spontaneous classification behavior on the part of the student participants in a study of the *Library of Congress Subject Headings* (Library of Congress,

1996). That is, a substantial minority of the students frequently used broad terms with narrower topical subdivisions, despite the fact that such topical subdivisions were forbidden at that time in indexing with Library of Congress subject headings.

There are many problems with attempting to offer classified access in the design of subject access systems in manual and automated information systems, and I am not suggesting that access systems should necessarily offer that approach, at least in the conventional sense of classified access in library systems. Rather, I suggest that some sort of design that enables people to approach a digital information system with the *feel* of classified access may be helpful for users. There will be more on this matter later in the article.

Finally, there is another body of evidence about the nature of "folk access." It is an anecdotal truism among reference librarians that users frequently do not say what they really want when they come to a reference desk, but rather ask broader questions. The user who really wants to find out Jimmy Hoffa's birth date instead asks where the books on labor unions are.

In an empirical study of reference interviews, Lynch (1978) found that 13% of the several hundred interviews she observed involved shifts from an initial presenting question to a different actual question. Although Lynch did not analyze these shifts in terms of breadth, she did find that the great majority of the 13% were cases in which the user presented either a directional question ("Where are the . . .") or a holdings question ("Do you have [a specific item]"), and it turned out that the person really wanted information on a subject not specific to a particular book.

Thomas Eichman has argued persuasively (1978) that this is a quite reasonable approach for users to use in the actual circumstances of the reference interview, and should be expected rather than bemoaned by reference librarians. Usually, the person with a query is approaching a total stranger, and has no idea how much the librarian might know about the subject of interest, or how helpful she will be able or willing to be. Initial interactions constitute "phatic" communication, wherein the user is opening up a channel of communication, sizing up and getting to know the person on the other side of the desk.

Eichman argues that in asking an initial broad or general question, the user is much more likely to be able to establish some point of contact with the stranger behind the desk. Consider: If the user asks, "Where are the psychology books?" or "Do you have so-and-so's *Introduction to Psychology*?," can he not have a higher expectation of the librarian's being able to answer than if he asks for his true information need, a book that can tell him about the Purkinje Effect?

Let us suppose, further, that the librarian has, indeed, never heard of the Purkinje Effect. If the user asks for this point-blank, the librarian cannot immediately help him, without asking more questions. The user anticipates that there will be a socially awkward moment, as he gets a blank look from the librarian. If, on the other hand, he starts with the question about psychology books, and the conversation proceeds well, he and the librarian will move through a conversation that makes it clear that the user is interested in visual perception, and the Purkinje Effect is a topic within that area. The librarian, having been given this necessary context, can now, in fact, direct him to the right books in the psychology section, even though she still may not know specifically what the Purkinje Effect is.

Starting general, then, would seem to be an effective strategy in the information-seeking conversation between librarian and user. Librarians sometimes fail to recognize the value of this approach from the user, because they (the librarians) are focusing on the technical, professional matter of getting the question answered, just as some physicians bypass the phatic and contextual interactions in a patient interview to get at what they see as the "real business" of diagnosis and treatment. Unfortunately, the patient does not yield up private matters to total strangers so easily, and the professional's "short" route to the technical content of the interview often founders on its failure to recognize how the interview feels to the user/patient.

In broad outline, this movement from general to specific in the course of the reference interaction sounds rather like the pattern of broad term/ narrower term noted above in some of the student subject headings. It is as though they expect to connect with the information system by starting broad and working down to the specific: Psychology—Visual Perception— Purkinje Effect. If, as assumed, people carry conversation patterns over into interaction with information systems, then enabling the human user to survey the territory, to size up the system's offerings before settling down directly to business might equip the searcher with a better understanding of the system's capabilities, and therefore enable that searcher to submit queries better matched to the strengths of the system.

Another part of my dissertation analyzed the match between the student-generated terms and the library subject headings actually applied to the test books. The students without library training more frequently used terms *broader* than the actual heading applied than they used terms narrower than the correct heading (Bates, 1977, p. 370ff).

Other data in my study supported the idea that use of broader terms was a wise (if probably unconscious) strategy on the part of the students. One might expect, a priori, that broader search terms would be easier to match to index terms than narrower ones, because they are usually shorter, simpler, and more generally agreed-upon in phrasing. This indeed proved to be the case. That half of the students who erred most by using broader terms were compared with the half who used the fewest broad terms. The match rates of the former were higher (Bates, 1977, p. 373).

In a study of different design, Brooks (1995) also confirmed my result, finding that "narrower descriptors are harder for subjects to match to bibliographic records than the other two types" (p. 107). The "other two types" were what he called "topical-level" and "broader." The former were terms assigned to a record by an indexer; broader and narrower terms were those that were broader and narrower in relation to the assigned term.

Statistical indexing properties of databases

A fair amount of data exists on the statistical properties of databases (though we could benefit from quite a bit more), but these data have seldom been brought to bear on the discussion of indexing and access in IR system design. Here, three statistical features of databases that have implications for indexing and access to digital records will be discussed: Bradford's Law, vocabulary scalability, and the Resnikoff-Dolby 30:1 rule.

Bradford's Law

The first point about statistical properties of databases is that there are very robust underlying patterns/distributions of vocabulary and index terms to be found in bibliographic and full-text databases. It is likely that many people involved with information organization and retrieval have not known or acted upon this fact.

Most information-related phenomena have been found to fall into a class of statistical distributions known as Zipfian distributions, named after George Zipf, who published data on the relationship of word frequency to word length (Zipf, 1949). In information science, Samuel Bradford developed what came to be known as Bradford's Law in describing the distribution of articles on topics through the journal literature (1948). Subsequently, Bradford's Law was found to appear in a variety of other information-related phenomena (see Chen & Leimkuhler, 1986; Rousseau, 1994).

Other Zipfian formulations besides Zipf's and Bradford's are the distributions of Yule, Lotka, Pareto, and Price (Fedorowicz, 1982). Over the years, there has been extensive debate on the nature of the social processes that produce these distributions, and how best to represent them mathematically (e.g., Brookes, 1977; Chen & Leimkuhler, 1986; Qiu, 1990; Rousseau, 1994; Stewart, 1994). The intention here is not to justify any one Zipfian formulation—for our purposes they look similar—but rather to draw attention to the fact that information-related phenomena fall into this general class of distributions, as do many other distributions associated with human activity.

Zipfian distributions have a characteristic appearance which is quite different from the familiar bell-shaped normal distribution that is the usual focus of our statistics courses. Zipfian distributions are characterized by tong tails and must often be presented on log paper in order to capture all the data produced in a research study. See Figure 2.

Zipfian distributions are presented as rank-frequency and frequency-size models (Nelson & Tague, 1985). For instance, a rank-frequency distribution of number of index terms assigned in a database displays the frequencies of application of the terms against their rank, with the most frequent being the highest rank (i.e., first). A frequency-size model shows the number of terms assigned in a database at each frequency level. In either case, there is generally a small number of terms with a very high frequency, and a large number of terms with a very low frequency. In Nelson and Tague's data, for example, approximately 1% of the terms were in the high frequency portion of the distribution (p. 286). At the other end, the great majority of terms in a typical database might have been applied just once or twice.

These distributions are quite robust and defy efforts of thesaurus designers and indexers to thwart them. For instance, librarians have historically used some subdivisions in the *Library of Congress Subject Headings* to break down large sets of records indexed under the popular high-end terms into smaller sets. For example, "U.S.—History," an enormously popular term, would get another layer of subdivisions to produce headings like "U.S.—History—Revolution, 1775–83," and "U.S.—History—Civil War, 1861–65," and the like. However, the self-similar nature of this type of data indicates that the distribution of the subdivisions will *again* fall out into a Bradford form within the set of all headings beginning with "U.S.—History" (R. Rousseau, personal communication, 1996). Thus some of the combined headings will be very popular and some will have few or one application each, for a mini-Bradford distribution within the larger Bradford distribution.

In fact, Zipfian distributions are so common in information-related phenomena that there would be more surprise in finding that such data did *not* express a Zipfian pattern. To show how far afield this pattern can go, Brookes (1977) reports data from a 3-day-long closed conference with 50 people in attendance (pp. 207ff). One of the attending members kept a

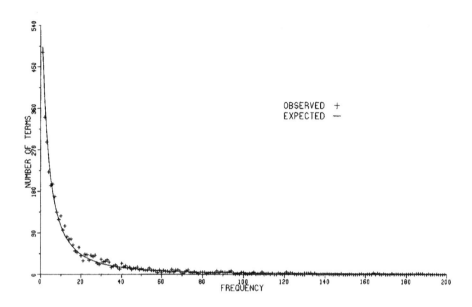

FIG. 2. *A frequency-size Zipfian distribution.*
NOTE: *This is Fig. 2, reprinted from Nelson, M. J. and Tague, J. M. (1985). Split size-rank models for the distribution of index terms.* Journal of the American Society for Information Science, 36(5), 291.

record of who contributed how many times each to the conference discussion. The results fell into a Bradford pattern, similar to what we have all experienced in school, where some students in class speak very frequently and many hardly at all.

To better understand the implications of these distributions for information retrieval, it may be helpful to visualize the Bradford distribution in a different way. When Bradford originally developed his data, he studied the rates at which articles relevant to a certain subject area appeared in journals in those areas. (His two test areas were applied geophysics and lubrication.) He identified all journals that published more than a certain number of articles in the test area per year, as well as in other ranges of descending frequency. He wrote:

> If scientific journals are arranged in order of decreasing
> productivity of articles on a given subject, they may be divided
> into a nucleus of periodicals more particularly devoted to
> the subject and several groups or zones containing the same

number of articles as the nucleus, when the numbers of periodicals in the nucleus and succeeding zones will be as 1:n:n^2.
(Bradford, 1948, p. 116)

In principle, there could be any number of zones, with the number
of articles in each zone being the total number of articles divided by the
number of zones. In his empirical data, however, Bradford identified just
three zones, and three will be used here for simplicity's sake. Bradford found
in his empirical data that the value of "n" was roughly 5. Suppose, then, that
someone doing an in-depth search on a topic finds that four core journals
contain fully one-third of all the relevant articles found. If the value for n
is 5, then $4 \times 5 = 20$ journals will, among them, contain another third of all
the relevant articles found. Finally, the last third will be the most scattered
of all, being spread out over $4 \times 5^2 = 100$ journals. See Figure 3.

Figure 3 shows that one could find a great many relevant articles on
a topic nicely concentrated in a few core journals. But finding the rest of
the relevant articles involves an increasingly more extensive search, as the
average yield of articles per additional journal examined becomes smaller
and smaller the farther out, i.e., the more remotely from the core topic
one goes. The Bradford data thus tell us that desired material is neither
perfectly concentrated in one place, as we might hope, nor is it completely
randomly distributed either, as we might fear.

If we assume that Bradford-type distributions of numbers of relevant
hits per term in a database could also be arrayed as in Figure 3, then there are
some predictable consequences in searching that can be anticipated. When
searching with core, "right-on" terms, many relevant hits are retrieved, a
high precision result. If, however, some high percentage of all the relevant
articles are to be found "farther out," under still related but somewhat more
remotely connected terms, then the percentage of good hits per added term
goes down, the more remotely related the search term is.

The pattern in Figure 3 would thus reflect the classic recall/precision
trade-off. The better the recall, the lower the precision, because, as one
incorporates more and more remotely related (OR'd) terms in the query,
fewer and fewer relevant hits are found. To be confident in finding *all*
relevant items, one would have to go very far afield, scooping up large
numbers of records, with more and more remotely related terms, in order
to find the occasional relevant item. The new system user who may never
have thought about problems of retrieval may assume that a simple query
will retrieve all relevant records: the experienced searcher knows that one
must go very far afield to catch all relevant materials, and must tolerate
increasingly many irrelevant records the farther out one goes.

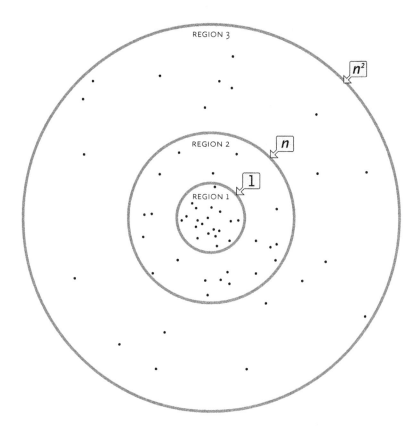

FIG. 3. *Bradford scatter of hits across three zones.*
NOTE: *Hits are sparser in sources in outer zones, therefore more sources must be covered—hence larger territory in each successive zone. Each zone contains the same total number of hits.*

Bradford's work was very important for special librarians to know about. It demonstrated that an organization that specializes in a certain subject area can readily purchase a good percentage of all relevant materials in its area by buying a small set of core journal subscriptions. But the higher the percentage of relevant materials the library seeks to capture through additional purchases, the smaller the payoff per journal added. The same can be said, of course, of the recall/precision trade-off in IR.

So, what are the implications of this discussion for indexing digital resources? First, we can expect that even the most beautifully designed system of indexing—whether human or automatic—will produce Zipf-type distributions. If a system has a 10,000-term thesaurus, and a 100,000-record database, and each record has just one term applied to it, each term would then have 10 hits, if the distribution of term applications across the database were perfectly even. The research on these distributions, however, suggests that the distribution will be highly skewed, with some terms applied thousands of times, and a large number of the 10,000 terms applied just once.

Further, there is some evidence (Nelson, 1988) that frequencies of term applications in a database are significantly correlated with frequency of terms in queries, i.e., terms popular in indexing are also popular in information needs expressed as queries. So, those terms with lots of hits under them will also be used frequently among the queries coming into the database. This question needs much more research, however.

Finally, even in the best-designed database, users will usually retrieve a number of irrelevant records, and the more thorough they are in trying to scoop up every last relevant record by extending their search formulation with additional term variants, the greater the proportion of irrelevant records they will encounter. However, as the "core" terms will probably retrieve a relatively small percentage of the relevant records (certainly under half, in most cases), they must nonetheless tolerate sifting through lots of irrelevant records in order to find the relevant ones. It is the purpose of human indexing and classification to *improve* this situation, to pull more records into that core than would otherwise appear there, but it should be understood that even the best human indexing is not likely to defeat the underlying Zipfian patterns.

Indexers and system designers have to find a way to *work with* these database traits, rather than thinking they can, through good terminology design, produce a database full of terms, each of which falls in some ideal range of 10 to 50 hits. The latter, desirable as it may be, is not likely.

How then can we design systems to satisfy users, given this robust configuration of database term applications? I do not have any miracle solutions for it, but as long as these patterns are not recognized or understood, we will not even know how to begin to improve retrieval for users.

Vocabulary scalability

Scalability in the development of digital resources is one of the issues currently being discussed (Lynch & Garcia-Molina, 1995). Scalability deals with questions of "scaling up" systems from smaller to larger. Can a system that functions well at a certain size also function well when it is 10 or 100 times larger? This is an important question in information system design, because there is ample reason to believe that there are problems with scaling in this field. Small systems often do not work well when database size expands. New and different forms of organization and retrieval have to be introduced to maintain effectiveness.

Evidence of the need to change with growth in size can be detected in the longer history of information organization and access. In the 19th century, Charles Cutter developed alphabetical subject indexing ("subject headings") to make growing book collections more accessible. In the 1950s, when the conceptually broader subject headings began producing too many hits, especially in journal and report collections, "concept" indexing, which forms the basis of most current Boolean-searchable databases, was developed. When manual implementation of concept indexing bogged down on collections of even modest size, computer database searching was developed in the 1970s for faster searching.

Now that databases are exploding into the tens of millions in size, it can be guessed that new responses will again be needed. The purpose in this section is to draw attention to just one statistical feature that bears on scalability in indexing and/or full-text term matching as a means of retrieval from digital resources—the limitations of human vocabulary.

It is harder than it might at first seem to estimate the vocabulary size of the average person. Should the words one can produce be counted, or the much larger set one can recognize? Are proper noun names of products, people's names, etc., counted, or only "regular" lower-case words? How does one count the many morphological variations language creates for many words (e.g., compute, computes, computing, computed)? Here is Pinker (1994) on this question:

> The most sophisticated estimate comes from the psychologists William Nagy and Richard Anderson. They began with a list of 227,553 different words. Of these, 45,453 were simple roots and stems. Of the remaining 182,100 derivatives and compounds, they estimated that all but 42,080 could be understood in context by someone who knew their components. Thus there were a total of 44,453 + 42,080 = 88,533 listeme words. By sampling from this list and testing the sample, Nagy and Anderson estimated that an average American high school graduate knows 45,000 words. (p. 150)

This estimate did not include proper names, numbers, foreign words, and other such terms.

Not all of the 45,000 words would be suitable for searching for information. On the other hand, college graduates might know more words, including some that are technical terms useful for searching and not in the general vocabulary. So, just to make a general estimate, let us take the closest round-number figure, 50,000, as the vocabulary size of an average information seeker on the Internet or in a digital collection.

A recent study found that 63% of the search terms employed by scholar searchers of databases were single-word terms (Siegfried, Bates, & Wilde, 1993, p. 282). (Solomon, 1993, also found that children overwhelmingly used single-word search terms.) So if users mostly employ single-word terms, let us, for the moment deal with just single-word indexing terms. Let us further assume that we have a million-item database—small by today's standards. We did arithmetic like this in the previous section—with 50,000 core terms available for searching by the user, and if the frequency in the database for each term were precisely even across the database, then each index term would have to have been applied to exactly 20 records (1,000,000/50,000). Such multiple uses of each term cannot be avoided when the size of the database is so much larger than the size of the indexing vocabulary.

But that assumes that only one term is applied per record. In fact, it is common for anywhere from 10 to 40 terms to be applied per record in human-indexed bibliographic databases, and, of course, indefinitely many— easily hundreds or more—words are indexed in each record in full-text databases. Let us suppose our little million-item bibliographic database has an average of 20 index terms per record. Then, if the distribution of terms across the database were again exactly level, *each term would have 400 hits.*

This is a very problematic hit rate—it is far more than most people want. But we have only just begun. With natural-language indexing of the abstracts, let us suppose there are 100 indexable words per record, then if the application of words across the million-item database is level, there will be 2,000 hits for every indexable term used in the database. With digital libraries and the Internet, where tens of millions of records are currently involved, 20,000 or 50,000 or 100,000 hits per word can easily become *the minimum* on the assumption of level application of terms across the database.

There is no avoiding these statistics. As a database grows, the number of words a human being knows does not grow correspondingly. Consequently, the average number of hits grows instead.

It can be expected from the Bradford data, however, that the actual number of hits will be highly skewed, so some will have tens of thousands of hits and other terms very few. Further, if the popular terms are also popular in queries, per Nelson's data (1988), then a high proportion of all the queries will be pulling up that small set of terms with the huge numbers of hits.

To be sure, a searcher is not limited in most cases to single-word terms. The use of implicit or explicit Boolean logic in a query makes possible the combination of two or more words and usually drastically reduces the number of retrievals. Indeed, based on my own experience, I would estimate that a study on databases in the 1-million to 5-million item range would find that the best starting point for a search is to use two words or two concepts; that is, such a combination will most often produce sets of tolerable size. One-word searches produce too many high-hit searches and three-word (or -concept) searches produce too many zero or low-hit searches. It remains to be seen whether three-word queries are optimal for searches on mega-databases of tens of millions of records.

Other problems arise at this point, however. There are astronomically many different combinations possible for even just two- and three-word phrases. If every one of our searcher's 50,000 words can be combined with every other one, then there will be just under 2.5 billion possible combinations for the two-word combinations alone. As we learned in an earlier section, varying the search terms by just morphological changes (not even included in that 50,000 figure)—"violence" to "violent," for example, produced substantial changes in the retrieved set, and varying by synonymous or near-synonymous terms often produced results that were entirely different.

So, by using more than one term, we succeed in reducing the retrieved set, but in ways that are quite unpredictable in relation to the question of which set of records will most please the searcher. How can I know a priori whether I should use "violent" or "violence" to find the hits that would most please me, if I could somehow look at all the records and determine which ones I would like? What if I think of "freedom of speech" and "cyberspace" and do not think of the other 15 combinations discussed earlier for this topic? Brilliant ranking algorithms for the retrieved set will have no impact on the many relevant unretrieved records.

The distribution of frequency of use of two-word combinations will probably fall out into a Bradford distribution too, so there will be the usual problem of some combinations with very many hits and many combinations with few or no hits. The "perfect 30-item search" that we all want from databases—actually, say, a range of 10–50 items—will likely occupy a small part of the entire distribution of hits in a database of almost any size, with most of the match rates being substantially larger or smaller.

For browsing purposes, the current indexing along with the ability to go in any of thousands of directions—sometimes with just the change of a character or two in a search statement (and, of course, also by following up hypertextual links)—makes the World Wide Web entertaining and sometimes informative. But active, directed searching for even a moderately focused interest, has yet to be provided for effectively, for data collections of the size available on the Net. The time has clearly arrived to develop a next round of innovations as information stores scale up another explosive level.

The general assumption has been that the needed innovations will be all automatic. Certainly, the solution will require substantial automated production, but what has been discussed so far in this article surely indicates that some role for human intervention is needed too. Algorithms based on current designs, or even enhancements of current designs, cannot deal with the many issues raised here.

Resnikoff-Dolby 30:1 rule

Earlier, in discussing Bradford-type distributions in information-related phenomena, we had to contemplate the possibility that our many individual actions and decisions as information system designers, and information providers and users, however motivated by individual choice and need, nonetheless fall out into remarkably persistent and robust statistical patterns. In examining the Resnikoff-Dolby 30:1 rule, we will discover an even more striking and hard-to-credit statistical pattern, which is nonetheless backed up by considerable data.

Under a grant from the Department of Health, Education, and Welfare, Howard Resnikoff and James Dolby researched the statistical properties of information stores and access mechanisms to those stores (Dolby & Resnikoff, 1971; Resnikoff & Dolby, 1972). Again and again, they found values in the range of 28.5:1 to 30:1 as the ratio of the size of one access level to another. For mathematical reasons, they used $K = 29.55$ as the likely true figure for their constant, but they and I will use 30 for simplicity's sake in most cases. They found from their data:

- A book title is 1/30 the length of a table of contents in characters, on average (Resnikoff & Dolby, 1972, p. 10).

- A table of contents is 1/30 the length of a back of the book index, on average (p. 10).

- A back of the book index is 1/30 the length of the text of a book, on average (p. 10).

- An abstract is 1/30 the length of the technical paper it represents, on average (p. 10).

- Card catalogs had one guide card for every 30 cards on average. Average number of cards per tray was 302, or about 900 (p. 10).

- Based on a sample of over 3,000 four-year college classes, average class size was 29.3 (p. 22).

- In a test computer programming language they studied, the number of assembly language instructions needed to implement higher-level generic instructions averaged 30.3 (p. 96).

All these results suggest that human beings process information in such a way as to move through levels of access that operate in 30:1 ratios. Resnikoff and Dolby did not use this term, but I think a good name for it would be: *Information Transfer Exchange Ratio.* Something about these size relationships is natural and comfortable for human beings to absorb and process information. Consequently, the pattern shows up over and over again.

But Resnikoff and Dolby's research did not stop there. They found that book superstructures, as well, tended to cluster around multiples of 30. Drawing on library statistical data, they found that junior college libraries clustered around 29.55^3 volumes, or 25,803; university libraries clustered around 29.55^4, or 762,483. The next level up, 29.55^5, or 22,531,361, represented what they called a national library (Library of Congress) level. We would now add bibliographic utilities, such as OCLC, and, of course, Web browsers. With the spectacular growth of the Internet, we may soon expect to need to be able to provide access to resources in the 29.55^6 range, or, in the 660-million range.

Of course, not all libraries or books fit the above averages. Libraries are constantly growing, and figures could be expected not to rest strictly on average points. But Resnikoff and Dolby did find that the data clustered fairly tightly around these means (1972, p. 92). The largest item at one level seldom exceeded the smallest item at another (p. 90).

Resnikoff and Dolby (1972) suggested that the line between two access levels should be drawn in the following manner: "Mathematically, the natural way to define a boundary between two values on an exponentially increasing scale is to compute the geometric mean of the two values" (p. 12). Their table listing these range values (p. 12) is adapted as Table 1.

Resnikoff and Dolby (1972) bring mathematical and physical arguments to bear in support of why this pattern appears, which will not be reproduced here. As they note:

> The access model presented in this chapter is not restricted to the book and its subsystems and super systems. There is considerable evidence that it reflects universal properties of information stored in written English form, and, in a slightly generalized version, may be still more broadly applicable to the analysis and modeling of other types of information systems such as those associated

with the modalities of sensory perception. These wide ranging and difficult issues cannot be examined here in a serious way; moreover, we do not yet have sufficient data upon which a definitive report can be based. (p. 93)

To demonstrate results with such wide-ranging significance would indeed require vast amounts of data, more than one funded study could possibly produce. But Resnikoff and Dolby do bring forth a great deal of data from a wide variety of environments—more than enough to demonstrate that this is a fertile and very promising direction for research to go. (See also Dolby & Resnikoff, 1971. Later, Resnikoff, 1989, pursued his ideas in a biophysical context, rather than in library and information science applications.) While there are hundreds, if not more, papers pursuing questions related to Bradford distributions, this fascinating area of research has languished.[1]

Indeed, one may ask why these promising data have not been followed up more in the years since. When I have presented them, there is a common reaction that these relationships sound too formulaic or "gimmicky," that there could not possibly be such remarkable regularities underlying the organization of information resources. There has also been a strong shift in the years since from physical interpretations of information to constructivist views, which see each event or experience as uniquely constructed by the person doing the experiencing. I would argue that there are nonetheless regularities underlying our "unique" experiences, that while the individual construction of a situation generally cannot be predicted, there are often strong statistical patterns underlying human behavior over a class of events. We will find that there is no fundamental contradiction in the physical/statistical and the social/constructivist views; only a failure to accept that they can, and do, operate at the same time.

Equipped with the ideas in the Resnikoff-Dolby research, it is possible to see how certain results in the research literature—done independently of Resnikoff and Dolby's work—in fact, fit nicely within the framework of their model of information. Wiberley, Daugherty, and Danowski did successive

---

1   For those unable to access the ERIC technical report, White, Bates, and Wilson (1992) have a brief summary and discussion on p. 271. White says there that in writing my paper "The Fallacy of the Perfect Thirty-Item Online Search" (Bates, 1984), I did not know of Dolby's work. That is not strictly true. I took a class from Dolby when I was a graduate student at the University of California at Berkeley, where he mentioned the 30:1 ratio and some of the instances where the ratio had been found. The class preceded the publication of the technical report, however, and I did not know until White wrote his chapter that Dolby's figure was based on extensive data and had been published through ERIC. Had I known of the work, I would have addressed it in my own analysis of book indexes, tables of contents, etc. (in Bates, 1986b).

TABLE 1. *Resnikoff and Dolby's "ranges in level structure."**

LEVEL	TYPE	NO. OF VOLUMES		
		MINIMUM	MEAN = K^n	MAXIMUM
1	Encyclopedia	5	30	161
2	Personal	161	873	4,747
3	Junior college	4,747	25,803	140,266
4	University	140,266	762,483	4,144,851
5	National	4,144,851	22,531,361	122,480,276

*Their Table 2, Resnikoff & Dolby (1972, p. 12). Used by permission.

studies on user persistence in displaying online catalog postings, first on a first-generation online catalog (1990), and later on a second-generation online catalog (1995). In other words, they studied how many postings users actually examined when presented with a hit rate of number of postings found when doing a search in an online catalog. They summarize the results of both studies in the abstract of the second (1995):

> Expert opinion and one study of users of a first-genera-
> tion online catalog have suggested that users normally
> display no more than 30 to 35 postings. . . . Analysis of
> transaction logs from the second-generation system
> revealed that partially persistent users typically displayed
> 28 postings, but that overloaded users did not outnumber
> totally persistent users until postings retrieved exceeded
> 200. The findings suggest that given sufficient resources,
> designers should still consider 30 to 35 postings typical
> persistence, but the findings also justify treating 100 or
> 200 postings as a common threshold of overload. (p. 247)

Note the parallels between this data and that in Table 1. Resnikoff and Dolby's level 1 shows a mean of 30 items, with a maximum of 161. In the Wiberley, Daugherty, and Danowski research, people feel comfortable looking at 30 items, and will, if necessary go up to "100 or 200" (ideally, 161?), but beyond that figure go into overload.

Another parallel appears in the research on library catalogs. Time and time again, when asked, catalog users say they want more information, an abstract or contents list, on the catalog record (Cochrane & Markey, 1983).

Resnikoff and Dolby discuss at some length questions of the role the catalog plays, in terms of levels of access, to the collection. The argument will not be made here in detail, but both bodies of data converge on the idea that people need another 30:1 layer of access between the catalog entry and the book itself. This need shows up in the request for an abstract or summary, presumably 30 times as long in text as the average book title or subject heading. The Resnikoff and Dolby research also clearly needs to be related to the research on menu hierarchies in the human computer interaction literature (e.g., Fisher, Yungkurth, & Moss, 1990; Jacko & Salvendy, 1996).

Finally, at many points in their analysis, Resnikoff and Dolby (1972) work with the lognormal distribution: "These examples and others too numerous to report here prompt us to speculate that the occurrence of the lognormal distribution is fundamental to *all* human information processing activities" (p. 97). That distribution is one of the common candidates for modeling Zipfian distributions (see Stewart, 1994). Those with more mathematical expertise than I will surely be able to link these two bodies of data in a larger framework of analysis.

It may yet be found that human information processing characteristics are the underlying driving force behind many other seemingly random or unpredictable statistical characteristics of the information universe. If so, it may be discovered that the two seemingly disjoint approaches taken so far in this article, the "Human Factors" and the "Statistical Indexing Properties of Databases," are, in fact, very closely linked and both derive from common sources.

Domain-specific indexing

Research emanating from two areas of study strongly indicates that attention to subject domain in the design of content indexing and access has potentially high payoff in improved results for users. Research in computational linguistics and automatic translation has increasingly been looking to sub-domains of language as more productive venues for improving effectiveness in application of automatic techniques (Grishman & Kittredge, 1986; Kittredge & Lehrberger, 1982). The value of sublanguage analysis is beginning to be recognized and studied in information science as well (Haas & He, 1993; Liddy, Jorgensen, Sibert, & Yu, 1993; Losee & Haas, 1995).

Research in library and information science on domain vocabularies for indexing and retrieval has likewise demonstrated the importance of domain in the provision of access to resources. Stephen Wiberley has demonstrated that the character of the humanities vocabulary does not match the conventional assumptions that such vocabulary is fuzzy and hard to pin down (Wiberley, 1983, 1988). Nor is the vocabulary similar in character to natural and social scientific vocabulary, according to a study carried out at the Getty Information Institute (Bates, Wilde, & Siegfried, 1993; Bates, 1996b). That study found several classes of vocabulary types used in the humanities literature that were virtually non-existent in the science literature. Tibbo (1994) surveys the distinct issues associated with humanities indexing, Swift, Winn, and Bramer (1979) draw attention to unique characteristics of social science vocabulary, and Pejtersen (1994) applies domain analysis to fiction classification.

Weinberg (1988) also makes a strong case for a whole different class of access to information, viz., *aspect,* or *comment,* as distinct from the usual "aboutness" that index-descriptive terms are intended to provide. This sort of information would be particularly valuable for the humanities and the "softer" social sciences. Yet it is the characteristics of scientific and engineering vocabulary that have driven most of the theory of indexer thesaurus development since World War II.

Likewise, Mavis Molto, who was interested in developing automated techniques for genealogical literature, found that the distribution of term types in that literature is very different from general text at large, and that means of optimizing retrieval in such text may be quite different from those assumed previously (Molto, 1993). These results suggest dramatic differences in the character of vocabulary and information needs across the various intellectual domains. Techniques that work well in one may not work well in another.

There are other reasons, as well, for suspecting that treatment of the various intellectual domains as though all vocabularies are equal is an ineffectual and sub-optimal approach. Research in the sociology of science (Meadows, 1974; Merton, 1973) and scholarly communication (Bakewell, 1988; Bates, 1994, 1996a; Morton & Price, 1986) demonstrate a number of fundamental differences in how scholars and scientists conceptualize their research problems, in how paradigms do and do not function in various domains, in how social processes and relationships among researchers function differently in one domain as compared to another, and on and on. We should rather assume that these many differences *do* make a difference in means to optimize access to recorded materials than that they do not—at least until such time as we have much more research in hand on the effectiveness of various access techniques and vocabulary types.

Recently, Hjørland and Albrechtsen (1995) made an extensive and cogent argument for the value of domain analysis in information science. Their argument will not be adumbrated here, except to quote them briefly:

The domain-analytic paradigm in information science (IS) states that the best way to understand information in IS is to study the knowledge-domains as thought or discourse communities, which are parts of society's division of labor. Knowledge organization, structure, co-operation patterns, language and communication forms, information systems, and relevance criteria are reflections of the objects of the work of these communities and their role in society. The individual person's psychology, knowledge, information needs, and subjective relevance criteria should be seen in this perspective. (1995, p. 400)

Much could be written and hypothesized, well beyond the scope of this article, on how domain factors might affect retrieval. The goal here, however, is rather simply to establish, in general, the importance and value of paying attention to domain as a way to improve retrieval. So, the final argument to be brought forth is a practical, real-world one, a description of a database that uses domain analysis and has met the test of the marketplace.

BIOSIS, the database of biological periodicals, is just one of several that might serve as examples, but illustrates particularly well the points being made in this section. The database contains over 10 million records and adds over half a million records per year (*BIOSIS Search Guide*, 1995, p. A-3), so it represents a very large body of information with, as we shall see, substantial value added in the handling of its indexing, both human and automatic.

The developers of BIOSIS studied the literature of the field and the needs of their users, and created a resource that serves many of the distinctive needs of the biological research community. Articles are coded for whether they describe a new species, for example, a likely important question for many biologists searching the database.

But the analysis of the literature of the field goes much deeper than that. In the end, the database makes available two broad classes of information—*taxonomic* (descriptions of species and broader classes of flora and fauna) and *general subject* information. These are, in turn, broken out in ways likely to be of particular value in the study of biology.

The Biosystematic Index provides searchable codes for taxonomic levels discussed in articles above the genus-species level. At the species level, species can be searched by the user as free text on the subject-related fields of the record. Retrieval is improved, however, by the indexers at BIOSIS, who add species names to the basic bibliographic description of the article in every case that they are mentioned in the text of the article, but not in the title or abstract.

CC07006 ANIMAL COMMUNICATION

Frequencies Major (6760) Minor (540)

Applications This code retrieves studies on nonverbal human communication and on physical and biochemical animal communication pathways and patterns.

Examples Studies on • echolocation • pheromones • displays • animal sounds • infant noises

Strategy Recommendations

- For comparative studies on animal communication, use this code with appropriate keywords and the *General and Comparative Behavior* code CC07002.
- For human speech or verbal communication, use the *Deafness, Speech and Hearing* code CC20008.

Coverage Note This code was introduced in 1971.

FIG. 4. *BIOSIS concept code for animal communication.*
NOTE: Concept code taken from BIOSIS Search Guide *(1995, p. F-11). Reprinted by permission of BIOSIS.*

General subject topics are, likewise, approached at both broad and specific levels. Broad, popular concepts, the sort that recur frequently in the biological literature, have been identified and carefully described and analyzed for both indexers and searchers. Such broad concepts include things like animal distribution, wildlife management, and reproduction. Because these are both common and broad, searching on these terms alone or with a species name could lead to very large and wildly varying retrieval sets, depending on which particular terms for the concept had been used by the article's writer, the indexer, or the searcher. Because of the importance of these concepts (they are clearly at the upper end of the Bradford distribution), it has paid off for BIOSIS to analyze these terms closely and define them precisely for both indexers and searchers. These terms are called "concept codes." For example, Figure 4 displays the entry in the BIOSIS search manual for the concept code for Animal Communication.

On the other hand, less common subject terms, those that are more specific and narrowly applicable, and often at the low end of the Bradford distribution, do not receive this elaborate analysis. They are, instead, not even indexed in any formal way; they are just made free-text searchable. BIOSIS helps the searcher improve results, however, by providing a search manual containing the more popular of these free-text terms. For the less popular terms, or terms newly appearing since the last manual, the searcher knows to use them anyway, because the list of terms in the manual is explicitly stated to include only the more popular terms, and not all legitimate ones, as is usual with thesauri.

BIOSIS has thus cleverly worked simultaneously with the character of the domain and its practitioners' information needs, the character of the terminology important in the domain, and the statistical character of the literature in the domain, to produce a database that enables fast, high-recall, high-precision retrieval.

Discussion and conclusions

Having reviewed these various issues, we come to the next natural question: How can these things we have learned be applied to improve IR system design for the new digital information world?

In the previous section, the BIOSIS database of biological literature was brought forth as an example demonstrating a good understanding of and use of domain factors in the design of indexing for very large databases. Special indexes and retrieval capabilities probed precisely the kinds of information of most interest and use to biologists. Further, as was noted there, BIOSIS also effectively uses the Bradfordian statistical properties of its material, by indexing deeply and carefully the core concepts in biology that recur frequently in the literature, and therefore constitute the high frequency end of the Bradford curve.

The BIOSIS database constitutes one solution that integrates both database statistical factors and subject domain factors in its design. It demonstrates that the seemingly intractable Bradfordian characteristics—the massively skewed distributions that typically characterize meaningful collections of information—need not be defeated in order to effectuate good information retrieval. Rather, these statistical characteristics can be *worked with,* the system design ingeniously set up to invest high indexing effort in the high-demand end of the curve, and low effort, largely automatic, in the low-demand end.

There are no doubt other such inspired mixes of human and system effort possible throughout the information world, once the underlying factors are understood. One area that remains to be studied much more is that of the Resnikoff-Dolby 30:1 rule. If, as the evidence to date suggests, people often like to move down through a hierarchy of some sort as they access information, various kinds of hierarchical arrangements could be developed with layers sized in a 30:1 ratio.

Many systems currently are being developed with the structure of classical hierarchical (family-tree style) classification schemes. In library and information science, however, such classifications are frequently seen to be less effective than classifications based on faceted principles, developed some decades ago by S.R. Ranganathan (1963) but only now coming into their full fruition. Examples of faceted approaches can be seen in the Getty *Art & Architecture Thesaurus* and in the Predicasts business database. Faceting provides a flexibility and power much in excess of the limited character of conventional hierarchical schemes—not unlike the advance represented by relational databases in the database world. (A brief, simplified comparison of the two types of classification scheme is provided in Bates, 1988. See Rowley, 1992, or Vickery, 1968, for more thorough introductions.) Using this and other indexing techniques, in combination with a sensitivity to database and domain factors, can produce great retrieval power. Whether and how these techniques can be used to good effect in multi-million-item collections remains to be seen.

However, of all the issues raised in this article, those in the first section, on human factors, have been least attended to in system design (see also Chen & Dhar, 1990). Little research in information science has examined the various folk classification issues raised in this article—whether people spontaneously use terms that fall into groupings fitting the characteristics of folk classifications, whether there are Roschian "basic-level" terms (see also Brown, 1995), and so on.

Many design changes need to be made in information systems in response to the research on the great variety of terms generated by people for a given topic. Until we fully accept that reality, and build information retrieval systems that intelligently incorporate it, systems will continue to under-perform for users. It is interesting to note, however, that two different information systems, designed for two radically different environments, independently came up with solutions involving the collecting and clustering together of variant terms around core concepts.

The Los Angeles Department of Water and Power, with more than 10,000 employees, needed to solve a thesaurus problem for their multi-million item records management database. The records would be input into the system by clerks who often had only a high school education and no concept of vocabulary control, and retrieved by any and everyone in the organization, up to and including the General Manager. The content range of the vocabulary needed for retrieval was very wide—engineering, real estate, customer relations, construction, names of organizations, officers, etc.

The solution proposed (Bates, 1990), which was subsequently implemented, was to use highly skilled human labor to create and update continuously a cluster thesaurus of closely related term variants, based on a close monitoring of database contents and relevant technical thesauri. (In this way, only one person, the thesaurus developer, needed to have lexicographical expertise, rather than expecting every clerk in the organization to develop it.) When a searcher used any one of the terms, the variants could be called up too. The searcher was then given the option of searching on all or selected terms from the cluster. The person searching on "transmission line right of way" might think no variants are needed until the cluster appears with a dozen or more other ways the concept has been described in the database (some examples: transmission line easements, T/L Right of Way, T/L ROW).

Meanwhile, at the Getty Information Institute, the rarefied world of art historical scholarship was likewise being served by a database developed to cluster term variants—in this case, various forms of artists' names, in the *Union List of Artist Names* (1994). Just as it was impractical at the Water and Power Department to get all the department's memo and report writers to use the same word for the same concept, it is also undesirable to try to search on an artist's name under just one form. Artists have frequently been known by both vernacular and Latin names, by different names in different languages, and by nicknames and formal names. They may be referred to in all these forms in the literature of interest to a researcher, and the researcher may not initially be aware of all the forms that have been used. Consequently, provision of a database containing all those forms not only aids in retrieval effectiveness, but is an important scholarly resource in its own right.

The Getty Information Institute has been experimenting with making this and two other thesaural databases, *Art & Architecture Thesaurus* (Peterson, 1994), and *Thesaurus of Geographic Names,* available on the Internet. As of this writing, two of the three are combined in an online thesaurus named "a.k.a." which can be used during an experimental period by people searching the Getty bibliographic databases via the World Wide Web (http://www.ahip.getty.edu/aka/). Searching on the artist "Titian" yielded the names of five different individuals who have been known by this name, as well as all the variants found on each individual's name. One of these five, Tiziano Vecellio, has been known by at least 46 different names, according to the *Union List of Artist Names*. Examples include the following: Detiano, Titsiaen, Tizzani, Vecelli, and Ziano. This term-variant database provides a nice example of ways in which online access can be improved in real time for Internet or other online searchers.

A number of other experimental systems and approaches are currently being developed to improve vocabulary for users for search and retrieval as well (Chen & Lynch, 1992; Chen & Ng, 1995; Chen, Yim, Fye, & Schatz, 1995; Johnson & Cochrane, 1995; Jones et al., 1995; Kristensen, 1993; Larson,

McDonough, O'Leary, Kuntz, & Moon, 1996; Schatz, Johnson, Cochrane, & Chen, 1996).

Both the Water and Power and the Getty systems rely on a valuable aspect of human cognition that is unfortunately much ignored in the information system design world: People can *recognize* information they need very much more easily than they can *recall* it. The average person will recall (think up) only a fraction of the range of terms that are used to represent a concept or name, but can take in a screen full of variants in an instant, and make a quick decision about desired terms for a given search. Most current information systems require that the searcher generate and input everything wanted. People could manage more powerful searches quickly if an initial submitted term or topic yielded a screen full of term possibilities, related subjects, or classifications for them to see and choose from (see also Bates, 1986a).

These and other experiments in improved access are made possible if *indexing* is separated from *access* in the design of an information system. By separating these two, the user front-end can be designed around the distinctive traits and evolutionary adaptations of human information processing, while the internal indexing describing the document may be different. Changes in our developing understanding of human cognition in information-seeking situations, and changes in vocabulary can relatively quickly be accommodated in a user-oriented front-end, without requiring the re-indexing of giant databases.

In sum, the pieces of knowledge reviewed here have yet to be unified into a single grand model. Much research remains to be done. However, there are tantalizing hints that seemingly dramatically different features presented herein—such as the human and statistical factors—may indeed ultimately be given a unified formulation, once research and theory development have progressed far enough.

From what is already known, however, it can be seen that we need to design for the real characteristics of human behavior as people have information needs and confront information systems to try to meet those needs. We know, further, that robust underlying statistical properties of databases demand that we find ingenious ways to work with these statistical patterns, rather than deny or ignore them. Finally, indexing and information system design needs to proceed within the context of a deep understanding of the character of the intellectual domain, its culture, and its research questions. Any design lacking understanding of these human, database, and domain elements will almost certainly sub-optimize information retrieval from digital resources and the Internet.

REFERENCES

Bakewell, E. (1988). *Object, image, inquiry: The art historian at work.* Santa Monica, CA: Getty Art History Information Program.

Bates, M.J. (1977). System meets user: Problems in matching subject search terms. *Information Processing & Management, 13*(6), 367–375.

Bates, M.J. (1984). The fallacy of the perfect thirty-item online search. *RQ, 24*(1), 43–50.

Bates, M.J. (1986a). Subject access in online catalogs: A design model. *Journal of the American Society for Information Science, 37*(6), 357–376.

Bates, M.J. (1986b). What is a reference book? A theoretical and empirical analysis. *RQ, 26*(1), 37–57.

Bates, M.J. (1988). How to use controlled vocabularies more effectively in online searching. *Online, 12*(6), 45–56.

Bates, M.J. (1989a). The design of browsing and berrypicking techniques for the online search interface. *Online Review, 13*(5), 407–424.

Bates, M.J. (1989b). Rethinking subject cataloging in the online environment. *Library Resources & Technical Services, 33*(4), 400–412.

Bates, M.J. (1990). Design for a subject search interface and online thesaurus for a very large records management database. In *Proceedings of the 53rd ASIS Annual Meeting, 27,* 20–28.

Bates, M.J. (1994). The design of databases and other information resources for humanities scholars: The Getty Online Searching Project report no. 4. *Online & CDROM Review 18*(6), 331–340.

Bates, M.J. (1996a). Document familiarity in relation to relevance, information retrieval theory, and Bradford's Law: The Getty Online Searching Project report no. 5. *Information Processing & Management, 32*(6), 697–707.

Bates, M.J. (1996b). The Getty end-user online searching project in the humanities: Report no. 6: Overview and conclusions. *College & Research Libraries, 57*(6), 514–523.

Bates, M.J., Wilde, D.N., & Siegfried, S. (1993). An analysis of search terminology used by humanities scholars: The Getty Online Searching Project report no. 1. *The Library Quarterly, 63*(1), 1–39.

Belkin, N.J., Oddy, R.N., & Brooks, H.M. (1982). ASK for information retrieval: Part 1: Background and theory. *Journal of Documentation, 38*(2) 61–71.

Belkin, N.J., Kantor, P., Fox, E.A., & Shaw, J.A. (1995). Combining the evidence of multiple query representations for information retrieval. *Information Processing & Management, 31*(3), 431–448.

Berlin, B. (1978). Ethnobiological classification. In E. Rosch & B.B.Lloyd (Eds.), *Cognition and categorization* (pp. 9–26), Hillsdale, NJ: Lawrence Erlbaum.

BIOSIS Search Guide. (1995). Philadelphia, PA: BIOSIS.

Blair, D.C. (1996). STAIRS redux: Thoughts on the STAIRS evaluation, ten years after. *Journal of the American Society for Information Science, 47*(1), 4–22.

Borgman, C.L. (1996). Why are online catalogs still hard to use? *Journal of the American Society for Information Science, 47*(7), 493–503.

Bradford, S.C. (1948). *Documentation.* London: Crosby Lockwood.

Brookes, B.C. (1977). Theory of the Bradford Law. *Journal of Documentation, 33*(3), 180–209.

Brooks, T.A. (1995). People, words, and perceptions: A phenomenological investigation of textuality. *Journal of the American Society for Information Science, 46*(2), 103–115.

Brown, C.H. (1984). *Language and living things: Uniformities in folk classification and naming.* New Brunswick, NJ: Rutgers University Press.

Brown, M.E. (1995). By any other name: Accounting for failure in the naming of subject categories. *Library & Information Science Research, 17*(4), 347–385.

Chen, H., & Dhar, V. (1990). User misconceptions of information retrieval systems. *International Journal of Man-Machine Studies, 32*(6), 673–692.

Chen, H., & Lynch, K.J. (1992). Automatic construction of networks of concepts characterizing document databases. *IEEE Transactions on Systems, Man, and Cybernetics, 22*(5), 885–902.

Chen, H., & Ng, T. (1995). An algorithmic approach to concept exploration in a large knowledge network (automatic thesaurus consultation): Symbolic branch-and-bound search vs. connectionist Hopfield net activation. *Journal of the American Society for Information Science, 46*(5), 348–369.

Chen, H., Yim, T., Fye, D., & Schatz, B. (1995). Automatic thesaurus generation for an electronic community system. *Journal of the American Society for Information Science, 46*(3), 175–193.

Chen, Y.S. & Leimkuhler, F.F. (1986). A relationship between Lotka's Law, Bradford's Law, and Zipf's Law. *Journal of the American Society for Information Science, 37*(5), 307–314.

Cochrane, P.A., & Markey, K. (1983). Catalog use studies—before and after the introduction of online interactive catalogs: Impact on design for subject access. *Library & Information Science Research, 5*(4), 337–363.

Dolby, J.L., & Resnikoff, H.L. (1971). On the multiplicative structure of information storage and access systems. *Interfaces: The Bulletin of the Institute of Management Sciences, 1*, 23–30.

Eichman, T.L. (1978). The complex nature of opening reference questions. *RQ, 17*(3), 212–222.

Ellen, R.F., & Reason, D. (Eds.). (1979). *Classifications in their social context.* New York: Academic Press.

Ellis, D. (1996). The dilemma of measurement in information retrieval research. *Journal of the American Society for Information Science, 47*(1), 23–36.

Fedorowicz, J. (1982). The theoretical foundation of Zipf's Law and its application to the bibliographic database environment. *Journal of the American Society for Information Science, 33*(5), 285–293.

Fidel, R. (1994). User-centered indexing. *Journal of the American Society for Information Science, 45*(8), 572–576.

Fisher, D.L., Yungkurth, E.J., & Moss, S.M. (1990). Optimal menu hierarchy design—Syntax and semantics. *Human Factors, 32*(6), 665–683.

Furnas, G.W., Landauer, T.K., Dumais, S.T., & Gomez, L.M. (1983). Statistical semantics: Analysis of the potential performance of keyword information systems. *Bell System Technical Journal, 62*(6), 1753–1806.

Gomez, L.M., Lochbaum, C.C., & Landauer, T.K. (1990). All the right words: Finding what you want as a function of richness of indexing vocabulary. *Journal of the American Society for Information Science, 41*(8), 547–559.

Green, R., & Bean, C.A. (1995). Topical relevance relationships. II. An exploratory study and preliminary typology. *Journal of the American Society for Information Science, 46*(9), 654–662.

Grishman, R., & Kittredge, R. (Eds.). (1986). *Analyzing language in restricted domains: Sublanguage description and processing.* Hillsdale, NJ: Lawrence Erlbaum.

Haas, S.W., & He, S. (1993). Toward the automatic identification of sublanguage vocabulary. *Information Processing & Management, 29*(6), 721–732.

Harter, S.P. (1992). Psychological relevance and information science. *Journal of the American Society for Information Science, 43*(9), 602–615.

Hert, C.A. (1996). User goals on an online public access catalog. *Journal of the American Society for Information Science, 47*(7), 504–518.

Hjørland, B., & Albrechtsen, H. (1995). Toward a new horizon in information science: Domain-analysis. *Journal of the American Society for Information Science, 46*(6), 400–425.

Houston, J.E. (Ed.). (1995). *Thesaurus of ERIC descriptors* (13th ed.). Phoenix, AZ: Oryx.

Jacko, J.A., & Salvendy, G. (1996). Hierarchical menu design—breadth, depth, and task complexity. *Perceptual and Motor Skills, 82*(3), 1187–1201.

Johnson, E., & Cochrane, P. (1995). A hypertextual interface for a searcher's thesaurus. In *Proceedings of Digital Libraries '95, Austin, Texas* (pp. 77–86). College Station, TX: Hypermedia Research Laboratory.

Jones, S., Gatford, M., Robertson, S., Hancock-Beaulieu, M., Secker, J., & Walker, S. (1995). Interactive thesaurus navigation: Intelligence rules OK? *Journal of the American Society for Information Science, 46*(1), 52–59.

Kaske, N.K., & Sanders, N.P. (1980a). Evaluating the effectiveness of subject access: The view of the library patron. *Proceedings of the 43rd Annual ASIS Meeting, 17*, 323–325.

Kaske, N.K., & Sanders, N.P. (1980b). On-line subject access: The human side of the problem. *RQ, 20*(1), 52–58.

Kittredge, R., & Lehrberger, J. (1982). *Sublanguage: Studies of language in restricted semantic domains.* New York: Walter de Gruyter.

Klatt, M.J. (1994). An aid for total quality searching: Developing a hedge book. *Bulletin of the Medical Library Association, 82*(4), 438–441.

Knapp, S.D. (Ed.). (1993). *The contemporary thesaurus of social science terms and synonyms: A guide for natural language computer searching.* Phoenix, AZ: Oryx.

Kristensen, J. (1993). Expanding end-users' query statements for free text searching with a search-aid thesaurus. *Information Processing & Management, 29*(6), 733–744.

Kuhlthau, C.C. (1993). *Seeking meaning: A process approach to library and information services.* Norwood, NJ: Ablex.

Larson, R.R., McDonough, J., O'Leary, P., Kuntz, L., & Moon, R. (1996). Cheshire II: Designing a next-generation online catalog. *Journal of the American Society for Information Science, 47*(7), 555–567.

Leonard, L.E. (1977). *Inter-indexer consistency studies, 1954–1975: A review of the literature and summary of the study results* (occasional papers no. 131). Champaign-Urbana, IL: University of Illinois Graduate School of Library Science.

Library of Congress. (1991–). *Subject cataloging manual. Subject headings* (4th ed.). Washington, DC: Cataloging Distribution Service, Library of Congress.

Library of Congress. (1996). *Library of Congress subject headings* (19th ed.). Washington, DC: Cataloging Distribution Service, Library of Congress.

Liddy, E.D., Jorgensen, C.L., Sibert, E.E., & Yu, E.S. (1993). A sublanguage approach to natural language processing for an expert system. *Information Processing & Management, 29*(5), 633–645.

Lilley, O.L. (1954). Evaluation of the subject catalog. *American Documentation, 5*(2), 41–60.

Losee, R.M., & Haas, S.W. (1995). Sublanguage terms: Dictionaries, usage, and automatic classification. *Journal of the American Society for Information Science, 46*(7), 519–529.

Luhn, H.P. (1957). A statistical approach to mechanized encoding and searching of literary information. *IBM Journal of Research and Development, 1*(4), 309–317.

Lynch, C., & Garcia-Molina, H. (1995). *Interoperability, scaling, and the digital libraries research agenda: A report on the May 18–19, 1995 IITA Digital Libraries Workshop.* Retrieved from http://www.diglib.stanford.edu/diglib/pub/reports/iita-dlw/main.html.

Lynch, M.J. (1978). Reference interviews in public libraries. *The Library Quarterly, 48*(2), 119–142.

Markey, K. (1984a). Interindexer consistency tests: A literature review and report of a test of consistency in indexing visual materials. *Library & Information Science Research, 6,* 155–177.

Markey, K. (1984b). *Subject searching in library catalogs: Before and after the introduction of online catalogs.* Dublin, OH: OCLC Online Computer Library Center.

Meadows, A.J. (1974). *Communication in science.* London: Butterworths.

Merton. R.K. (1973). *The sociology of science: Theoretical and empirical investigations.* Chicago, IL: University of Chicago Press.

Molto, M. (1993). Improving full text search performance through textual analysis. *Information Processing & Management, 29*(5), 615– 632.

Morton, H.C., & Price, A.J. (1986). The ACLS survey: Views on publications, computers, libraries. *Scholarly Communication, 5,* 1–16.

Nelson, M.J. (1988). Correlation of term usage and term indexing frequencies. *Information Processing & Management, 24*(5), 541–547.

Nelson, M.J., & Tague, J.M. (1985). Split size-rank models for the distribution of index terms. *Journal of the American Society for Information Science, 36*(5), 283–296.

Newport, E.L., & Bellugi, U. (1978). Linguistic expression of category levels in a visual-gestural language: A flower is a flower is a flower. In E. Rosch & B.B.Lloyd (Eds.), *Cognition and categorization* (pp. 49–71). Hillsdale, NJ: Lawrence Erlbaum.

O'Connor, B.C. (1996). *Explorations in indexing and abstracting.* Englewood, CO: Libraries Unlimited.

Pejtersen, A.M. (1994). A framework for indexing and representation of information based on work domain analysis: A fiction classification example. In H. Albrechtsen & S. Oernager (Eds.), *Knowledge organization and quality management* (pp. 161–172). Frankfurt am Main, Germany: Indeks Verlag.

Peterson, T. (1994). *Art & architecture thesaurus* (2nd ed.). New York: Oxford.

Pinker, S. (1994). *The language instinct.* New York: Harper Perennial.

Qiu, L. (1990). An empirical examination of the existing models for Bradford's Law. *Information Processing & Management, 26*(5), 655–672.

Ranganathan, S.R. (1963). *Colon classification: Basic classification* (6th ed.). New York: Asia Publishing House.

Raven, P.H., Berlin, B., & Breedlove, D.E. (1971). The origins of taxonomy. *Science, 174,* 1210–1213.

Resnikoff, H.L., & Dolby, J.L. (1972). *Access: A study of information storage and retrieval with emphasis on library information systems.* Washington, DC: U.S. Department of Education. (ERIC ED 060 921).

Rosch, E. (1978). Principles of categorization. In E. Rosch & B.B. Lloyd (Eds.), *Cognition and categorization* (pp. 27–48). Hillsdale, NJ: Lawrence Erlbaum.

Rosch, E., Mervis, C.B., Gray, W.D., Johnson, D.M., & Boyes-Braem, P. (1976). Basic objects in natural categories. *Cognitive Psychology, 8*(3), 382–439.

Rousseau, R. (1994). Bradford curves. *Information Processing & Management, 30*(2), 267–277.

Rowley, J. (1992). *Organizing knowledge: An introduction to information retrieval.* (2nd ed.). Brookfield, VT: Ashgate.

Saracevic, T., & Kantor, P. (1988). A study of information seeking and retrieving. III. Searchers, searches, and overlap. *Journal of the American Society for Information Science, 39*(3), 197–216.

Schatz, B.R., Johnson, E.H., Cochrane, P.A., & Chen, H. (1996). Interactive term suggestion for users of digital libraries: Using subject thesauri and co-occurrence lists for information retrieval. In *Proceedings of the 1st ACM International Conference on Digital Libraries* (pp. 126–133). New York: Association for Computing Machinery.

Siegfried, S., Bates, M.J., & Wilde, D.N. (1993). A profile of end-user searching behavior by humanities scholars: The Getty Online Searching Project report no. 2. *Journal of the American Society for Information Science, 44*(5), 273–291.

Soergel, D. (1985). *Organizing information: Principles of database and retrieval systems.* Orlando, FL: Academic Press.

Solomon, P. (1993). Children's information retrieval behavior: A case analysis of an OPAC. *Journal of the American Society for Information Science, 44*(5), 245–264.

Stevens, M.E. (1965). *Automatic indexing: A state-of-the-art report* (NBS monograph no. 91). Washington, DC: United States G.P.O.

Stewart, J.A. (1994). The Poisson-lognormal model for bibliometric/scientometric distributions. *Information Processing & Management, 30*(2), 239–251.

Swift, D.F., Winn, V.A., & Bramer, D.A. (1979). A sociological approach to the design of information systems. *Journal of the American Society for Information Science, 30*(4), 215–223.

Tibbo, H.R. (1994). Indexing for the humanities. *Journal of the American Society for Information Science, 45*(8), 607–619.

Union list of artist names. (Version 1.0) [computer file] (1994). New York: G.K. Hall/ Macmillan.

Vickery, B.C. (1968). *Faceted classification: A guide to construction and use of special schemes.* London: Aslib.

Weinberg, B.H. (1988). Why indexing fails the researcher. *The Indexer, 16*(1), 3–6.

White, H.D., Bates, M.J., & Wilson, P. (1992). *For information specialists: Interpretations of reference and bibliographic work.* Norwood, NJ: Ablex.

Wiberley, S.E., Jr. (1983). Subject access in the humanities and the precision of the humanist's vocabulary. *The Library Quarterly, 53*(4), 420–433.

Wiberley, S.E., Jr. (1988). Names in space and time: The indexing vocabulary of the humanities. *The Library Quarterly, 58*(1), 1–28.

Wiberley, S.E., Jr., Daugherty, R.A., & Danowski, J.A, . (1990). User persistence in scanning postings of a computer-driven information system: LCS. *Library & Information Science Research, 12*, 341–353.

Wiberley, S.E., Jr., Daugherty, R.A., & Danowski, J.A. (1995). User persistence in displaying online catalog postings: LUIS. *Library Resources & Technical Services, 39*(3), 247–264.

Wilson, P. (1968). *Two kinds of power: An essay on bibliographical control.* Berkeley, CA: University of California Press.

Zipf, G.K. (1949). *Human behavior and the principle of least effort: An introduction to human ecology.* Cambridge, MA: Addison-Wesley.

8

The cascade of interactions in the digital library interface

ABSTRACT

Each design element or layer in an information system interacts with every other design layer in a synergistic, neutral, or conflicting manner. This cascade of interactions culminates in the interface, where all the prior interactions have either worked to produce effective information retrieval or to produce a hodgepodge of system elements working at cross-purposes. Very large networked and World-Wide-Web-based online databases and online public access catalogs provide numerous illustrative examples of how the cascade works. Good design requires that these interactions be well understood and properly designed for the purposes of the information system in question. Interactions among metadata and indexing systems, information system front-ends, user search capabilities, and interface design are discussed and used as illustrations for the effective design of digital library access.

Keywords: Digital library design; Information retrieval systems; Interface design; Information system design; Online information systems

First published as Bates, M. J. (2002). The cascade of interactions in the digital library interface. *Information Processing & Management, 38*(3), 381–400.

Introduction

The creation of means of access to large bodies of digitized information has rightly been viewed in our society as a major development in the history of human knowledge use. The elimination or reduction of prior constraints of distance, fragility of resources, or limited physical access to resources promises a freedom and flexibility in information access unprecedented in human history. However, we have a way to go yet in creating systems that are both easy to use and truly effective in retrieval. The very growth in computing power and design options for the latest systems also means that there are more opportunities to get it wrong—to design systems that have some wonderful individual design features, but which do not comprise an effectively integrated information system that works well as a whole.

In the 1970s—the early days of mounting databases such as online catalogs and abstracting and indexing services for searching purposes—developers were generally happy to get a database functioning in any reasonable way possible. Information systems often consisted of a body of information, originally selected and indexed for the paper environment, being mounted for electronic access with a search engine and system front-end designed entirely independently from the body of information being retrieved. The resulting systems were often crude, but faster than the paper alternatives, and so represented an important step forward. Most computing in those days was directed toward running large numbers of operations on relatively small bodies of information. Appropriate technology and software were slow to develop where few operations and very large bodies of textual information were concerned.

Major amounts of money and attention are at last flowing into studying questions of information management and retrieval from large bodies of heterogeneous textual and image databases. The landscape of information retrieval is changing in fundamental ways. Much more power, variety of options, and flexibility are now available for each layer of an information system's design.

Deep expertises are developing in each of the design layers. In practice, that means that it is harder and harder for any one person to have sufficient knowledge of all the design layers to see the entire forest for the trees. That, in turn, means that systems are prone to being designed with many different objectives in mind and with little understanding between the several groups of professionals addressing the design.

The purpose of this article is to present a model of some of the typical important layers in the design of information systems, and to show how those layers interact in operation. It is argued that these layers are in the way of a cascade—what is done, well or poorly, at one layer affects the next, which then affects the next layer, and so on. Thus, if designers do not understand the ways in which the layers interact, and they design and develop the layers independently of each other, then these information system layers may end up actually working at cross-purposes with each other. The result will be ineffectual or sub-optimized information systems.

In this article, a model is presented of this cascade of interactions in information systems. Several examples—from networked databases, online catalogs, and a Web-based information system—are presented in detail to illustrate the subtle and complex ways in which the design layers may interact, for good or ill. Finally, it is argued that staff working on all design layers *must* work together, sharing their expertise and design decisions, or face the likelihood of producing a sub-optimal information system.

Though the discussion is largely about integrating designer expertises, a fundamental assumption throughout the article is that this is *user-centered design*. The choices made at each one of the design layers should draw on what is known of prospective user needs and interests, their capabilities in system use, and their attitudes. A good, user-centered information system is not just a pretty interface. Design choices based on knowledge of users should penetrate deep into the system, should shape each one of the design layers and affect how those layers can best be integrated. (See also Bates, 1990a, 1994, 1998; Butler, Bahrami, Esposito, & Hebron, 2000; Dillon, 1994; Hayman & Elliman, 2000; Kilker & Gay, 1998; Payette & Rieger, 1998; Zhang & Fine, 1996; Zhu, 2001.)

Background: information system design models

Researchers and system developers have used a variety of sorts of models to aid in the process of designing and developing information systems. Here, some of the types are described and contrasted with the approach to be taken in the Cascade Model.

In automated information systems, there are three major components that appear in many different forms and permutations: (1) the computer/network system, i.e., the technical infrastructure, (2) the information or "content" that is supported and transmitted by the system, and (3) the user and his/her interaction with the system. Many models of automated systems emphasize the technical infrastructure necessary to make the system work. For example, the seven-layer Open Systems Interconnection Reference Model was designed to clarify relationships and support standards for inter-networking between computer systems. (See description in ISO/IEC 7498-1, 1994; Shor, 1991.)

The emphasis in this discussion is on the non-technical components of the Cascade Model—the information and the user. The layers of the model are identified from the perspective of the person who must attend to user-centered design and to optimizing the effective delivery of information in the development of some sort of information retrieval system. In particular, integrating these two components—the user and the information—*together* in modern, particularly Web-based, information retrieval system design deserves, as I hope to demonstrate, much more attention than has generally been given.

The Cascade Model describes the several design layers that have to be taken into account in the process of developing and implementing an information system in an automated environment. *Starting with the interface, imagine turning that interface on its side and pulling it apart, like an accordion, to reveal the several design layers backing that interface and culminating in the interface.* Those dovetailing layers will appear as in Fig. 1. The body of this article will elaborate the Cascade Model in more detail, but in the meantime, to sharpen its profile, let us compare it to other common types of information system models.

One type of model is the *design process model*. The purpose of these models is to lay out the various steps in sequence that designers should take in creating their system. Examples of these are to be found in Damodaran (1991), Galitz (1997, p. 46ff), Gardner (1991), Shneiderman (1998) and Syan and Menon (1994). For example, Gardner describes six design stages, from project initiation through product phase-out. The Cascade Model depicts the layers of a system that are simultaneously operating in a functioning system. The presence of layers in the Cascade Model is *not* to imply that one should design first one layer, then the next, in sequence. All layers need to be designed for in relation to each other. How the work then proceeds sequentially is another question—for another model.

Another type of model is the *human-computer interaction model*. There is a huge literature on the subject of human-computer interaction. (See, for example: Bødker, 1991; Card, Moran, & Newell, 1983; Carroll, 1991; Dix, Finlay, Abowd, & Beale, 1993; Galitz, 1997; Norman & Draper, 1986; Shneiderman, 1998.) Many researchers and designers have attempted to develop general principles of human-computer interaction design. The interface is indeed the pivotal point where people interact with automated information systems, but it is by no means the only point of interest here. The interface

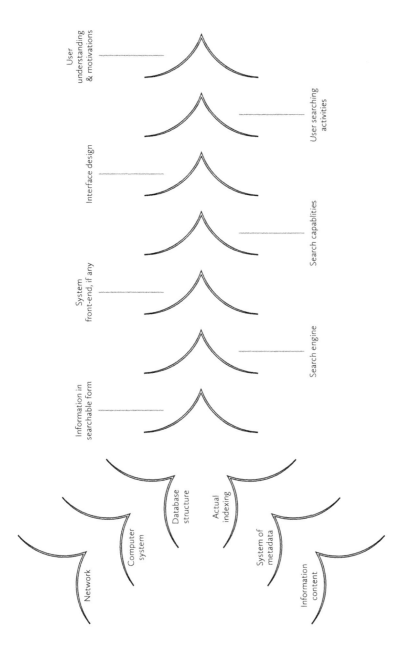

FIG. 1. The cascade of interactions in the digital library interface. The diagram presents example layers, even including use patterns and use environment at the right, that determine the overall functional effectiveness of a digital library information retrieval system. Design decisions at each layer have a cascading impact on subsequent layers; poor design at later layers can block products of earlier layers.

is just one layer of the Cascade Model; user-centered design of information systems must be informed by a knowledge of general information seeking behavior on the part of the human users, and it must also be informed with a knowledge of the many layers behind the interface that go into creating an effective information retrieval system.

The Cascade Model is also not an *information retrieval model*. Decades of research and thousands of articles have been produced around various theories of optimal automatic information retrieval techniques. (See Ellis, 1996; Robertson, 1977; Salton & McGill, 1983). In these cases, the focus is on varying the design characteristics of the search engine and sometimes the search capabilities, and testing which system does best. These testing methods frequently control for the queries put to the system and the relevance assessments on the retrieved records. In other words, in order to compare the information retrieval systems, all the layers of the Cascade Model except the search engine are held constant in order better to test the comparative effectiveness of the searching algorithms. Here, with the Cascade Model, we are considering all the design layers that actually affect the real-world performance of an information retrieval system, and are giving particular attention to the way variations in the layers affect other layers' performance.

Next, the Cascade Model is not a model of *interaction in information retrieval research*. In recent years, the information retrieval research community has become increasingly interested in the importance of human interaction with the system, in addition to search algorithm performance. Attention is being paid to the patterns and characteristics of human-system interaction, and the influence of these patterns on information system performance is being recognized (Beaulieu, 2000; Belkin, Brooks, & Daniels, 1987; Ingwersen, 1992; Saracevic, 1996, 1997; Spink, 1997).

Unquestionably, this perspective enriches both the information retrieval research and the human-computer interaction research. More of the full picture involved in the creation of a successful information searching experience is being incorporated into a single model.

I would argue, however, that still more needs to be incorporated into our thinking about means of creating effective online information search experiences. I will argue for each of the other layers in the Cascade Model as having crucial impacts on the resulting system success. These other layers must also be a part of the design and evaluation.

Finally, where digital resources and Internet-based resources are concerned, the Cascade Model is relevant in any case where the system user is expected to be able to search on any collection in excess of a few dozen items in number. Currently, there are countless commercial and non-profit efforts to create good, high-impact websites, Intranets, CD-ROMs, and other electronic resources. The Cascade Model is not a *website design model*, nor an *Intranet design model*, nor a model for any other specific technology. Rather, the Cascade Model refers to *any information retrieval component of an electronic resource*. So when a website has a dozen features, one of which is the ability to search on some collection or database of information, then the Cascade Model refers to that information retrieval component.

Currently, in the general discussion regarding website design, there is frequently a failure to differentiate the information retrieval component from the rest of the design. We know a lot of things about how people act and how systems need to be designed to be effective specifically in the context of information retrieval. This knowledge is distinct from the questions Web designers address when they consider advertising, chat rooms, screen design, and the other features of sites independent of a search capability. This is not to say that in design thinking for a site, information retrieval should be utterly independent of all other design considerations for the site. What is needed, however, is a recognition that when information retrieval capabilities are to be provided to users, the expertise we have about that area of design of electronic systems needs to "kick in" and not be drowned out by the other considerations that inevitably play a role in site design.

So, in sum, the Cascade Model is *not* a design-process model, a human-computer interaction model, an information retrieval model, an interaction in information retrieval model, nor a website design or other specific technology design model. The Cascade Model *is* a design model for operational online information retrieval systems. The model emphasizes the many design layers that should be considered in relation to each other in the process of designing and implementing an automated information system.

The model describes the layers in the design and is labeled "Cascade," because the layers interact in a cascading manner. Design features of earlier layers inevitably affect the success of later design features. Later features, if poorly designed, can block the effectiveness of the earlier layers. Either way, without integrated good design across all layers, *and constantly considering the layers in relation to each other in design and development*, the resulting information system is likely to be poor, or at least sub-optimal. In the new world of information systems—those associated with digital libraries and databases on the Internet, particularly—we need a unified model, for design purposes, of the underlying network, hardware, information, database structures, search capabilities, interface design and social context.

The cascade layers

Each design element or layer in an information retrieval system interacts with each other design layer in a synergistic, neutral, or conflicting manner. This cascade of interactions culminates in the interface, where all the prior interactions have either worked to produce effective information retrieval or to produce system elements working at cross-purposes. Each layer cannot be laid on top of the lower layers as if there were little or no relationship between those layers.

This point may be relatively obvious in some cases—a search engine cannot be used with a server that is not powerful enough to process records in real time, for example—but is much less obvious in other cases. In particular, there are problems of integrating the underlying information and its metadata with the user search capabilities and other features for the user in the interface. (For an extensive discussion of user search capabilities in the interface, see Bates, 1990a.)

Fig. 1 illustrates a number of the layers in a typical information system. (The model builds on Hildreth's model for online catalog searching, Hildreth, 1982, p. 114, Fig. 12.) These layers could be broken out in a different manner, or even put in different orders relative to each other, depending on the specific system being analyzed, but this figure will do as a general example.

There are actually four areas to the figure. When the figure is oriented to be right-reading, the upper left wing presents the technical infrastructure supporting the system, the lower left wing represents the information, or content, combined with the metadata structuring necessary to make it accessible in an information system. The middle wing, from "Information in searchable form" to "Interface design," represents the information retrieval system itself—supported by the technical infrastructure and containing the structured information. Finally, the two far-right layers, "User searching activities" and "User understanding and motivations," are the fourth area, representing the human portion of the overall system. So we see the technology, the information, and the human being all brought together in the larger system that represents a person actually using an information system.

The various layers in Fig. 1 will now be described. The upper left wing will be relatively slighted in this discussion; the emphasis here is on the information, information system, and user portions of the figure. The upper left wing composes the computer infrastructure—communications network, hardware and software platforms, and database structures. The strengths and constraints of that infrastructure will, to some extent, determine what can be done with the superstructure of information and interface. In particular, there are often crucial decisions made at the stage of selecting software and designing database structure that promote or limit the power of the overall information retrieval system tremendously. Here, it is crucial that the "technical people" and the "information people" understand each other's domains enough to work out the best information system possible within resource constraints.

Starting from the lower left of the diagram, the "Information content" layer is of fundamental importance, though it is often taken for granted. Beautiful systems have been designed and built to access the wrong information for the intended users. We will return later to this matter of matching the information to the user.

"System of metadata" refers to the intellectual and organizational system for description of the digital information. As people have begun to recognize the wide variety of types of information, and contexts of information use, a corresponding variety of metadata schemes are being developed to meet those various needs (see, e.g., Digital Object Identifier, 2001; Encoded Archival Description, 2001; Text Encoding Initiative, 2001; Weibel & Lagoze, 1997). Where subject description is concerned, it has long been recognized in information science that the character of the information to be indexed should be analyzed, and that targeted thesauri and classification schemes should be developed that are adapted to that information. This lesson has not yet been completely absorbed in the digital library world.

In particular, understanding that *systems* of metadata are used in assigning metadata is key to effective metadata use. It is not uncommon in the digital library literature to treat all descriptive terminology—especially terminology for subject content—as if all thesauri or term lists were simple aggregations of independent terms, and not part of an intellectual system whose integrity should be respected for optimal retrieval performance. Explanatory examples will be given in the following section.

The "Actual indexing" of objects and texts is distinguished from the "System of metadata" to draw attention to the importance of the quality and character of the indexing as actually carried out. Great variability is possible in the actual description done of digital objects, compared to what the rules of any one theoretical system allow or encourage. Variability in *depth of indexing* (average number of descriptive elements applied) and in quality of indexing can have an enormous influence on quality and power of results at the point of actual searching. That which is not indexed, either by algorithmic or human means, cannot be retrieved.

"Information in searchable form" refers to the first point where the information and database structure come together as a part of the actual information retrieval system. A library, for example, may use a particular computer platform, have a particular body of catalog or other data to put into the system, and buy or develop an online catalog, which functions as the information system. Almost invariably, bringing these three together—platform, data, and information system—requires local configuring of various types, as well as "massaging" of the data structure in order to make the information actually searchable.

The "Search engine" provides the core retrieval facility in the system. It determines how and whether fields can be searched, and how efficiently they are searched.

"System front-end" refers to any of a variety of types of systems interposed between the interface and the information system proper, whose purpose is to assist the user in searching in any of several ways. Such front-ends may be gateways employing a single search command language for accessing several different database vendor systems, interrogators helping searchers better identify and specify their queries (Vickery & Vickery, 1993) vocabulary support systems that suggest additional and related terms to use in searching (Bates, 1986, 1990b), or others. Efthimiadis (1990, 1996) reviewed some of the literature on such front-ends and gateways. In the digital library environment, the potential of such assistive systems has only begun to be exploited.

"Search capabilities" are the searching mechanisms made available to the user of the system. This term does not refer to whatever underlying methods are used by the search engine, but rather refers to what the user can do from his/her perspective. For instance, internal storage and indexing mechanisms may vary from system to system, but if they provide the same end result capability to the user, then the underlying differences do not matter for this discussion. For the discussion here, those internal mechanisms are considered to be a part of the search engine. Typical search capabilities offered to the user include keyword searching, proximity searching, Boolean combination, searching by field, and many more.

"Interface design" is pivotal to the effective use of an information system by users. As noted earlier, much of the interface literature represents an effort to identify general principles for interface design for all kinds of systems. The application environment of information retrieval systems, however, also has its own distinctive needs and characteristics that need to be understood and addressed in design.

Finally, we come to the two right-hand layers of Fig. 1, those representing the user role in the overall system. Commonly, in information system design models, these two layers are left out. Efforts may be made to identify in advance what people need and what features they would use in an information system. But from that point, it is often assumed that the performance of the system is measured by how well actual use matches what the system was designed for. However, there is much unpredictability in even the best-designed and planned system. The final, final measure of performance will always be how people actually use a system, not how one expected them to.

Consider, for example, two organizations which have each introduced computer-based information systems that are intended for the same purpose and role in the organizations. In the one organization, use of computer systems is viewed as the prerogative of the senior management. In the other organization, the management consider computers to be secretarial devices and disdain using them. In these contrasting cases, system use, including types and content of information queries, will have dramatically different profiles—with possibly major consequences for the perceived and actual effectiveness of the information system in the organization. So we need to consider the "using person" or "using community" as a part of a larger system, which is the actual functioning unit consisting of system, information, and user. For these reasons, the two right-hand layers are included as functional elements of the information retrieval system in Fig. 1.

Examples of cascade interactions

Now let us examine how the cascade of interactions works in practice. To date, the greatest expertise in the mounting and accessing of very large bodies of structured machine-readable information has accumulated in the areas of online public access catalogs and online and CD-ROM commercial databases. Online catalogs of major library systems routinely exceed 10 million records in size; some of the online databases, such as *BIOSIS* (1997) and *Chemical Abstracts* (Chemical Abstracts, 1907–) are also very large. Many of the digital library experiments to date, exciting and pioneering as they are, still do not yet fully challenge our skills in designing methods of retrieval from very large structured databases. We can thus learn from these earlier experiences. (At the same time, it is important not to be limited by earlier practices.)

Below, after discussing a simple, introductory example from the world of database searching, I present three further, more complex examples, one each from online catalogs, online databases, and a Web-based database and query expansion tool.

In the examples, the emphasis is on the interactions of indexing, search-ing, and interface features, as that is the author's area of expertise. These correspond to the lower left branch, as well as the middle and right-hand parts of Fig. 1. In illustrating how decisions and design features at earlier stages influence later stages, and vice versa, the cascading of interactions through the layers of the system is demonstrated.

Example #1
Database producer and database vendor designs conflict

We begin with a very simple example. Biological Abstracts, in the early days of producing its database of biological literature, *BIOSIS*, discovered that its users were having problems in searching terms such as "Vitamin B 6." Searching on the Boolean statement "Vitamin AND B AND 6" would pick up the three elements from all over records and would yield many "false drops" (retrievals of unwanted senses of the search terms). Proximity searching (allowing the searcher to require that search terms be in a designated proximity to each other), which would solve most of the problems, was not initially available in database vendor systems, such as DIALOG®. Biological Abstracts solved their problem by hyphenating "B-6" and a select group of other subject terms in their records. In principle, searchers could then use the hyphenated terms and eliminate the many false drops they were otherwise retrieving.

At that same time, however, DIALOG had the practice of stripping hyphens, among other punctuation, to make searching simpler and more consistent across the many databases, including *BIOSIS*, that DIALOG offered to its customers. So Biological Abstracts went to the human and automatic effort necessary to add the hyphens, and DIALOG turned around and stripped them out again. Both organizations had good reasons for what they did, but, needless to say, the end result was a conflict between two laudable objectives that left searchers at a loss. In terms of Fig. 1, the transition between "Actual indexing" and "Information in searchable form" conflicted, work being done at the former stage (to assist users ultimately employing search capabilities in the interface) being undone at the latter stage.

Now, let us consider three more complex examples.

Example #2
Boolean search system being superimposed
on non-Boolean indexing system in online catalogs

The most common type of searching available in automated information systems of all kinds is some form or another of Boolean searching, that is, the combining of search terms with the Boolean operators AND, OR, and

NOT. The use of Boolean operators is a "natural" in computer systems, because it echoes so much of the deeper structure of computer design. However, Boolean logic for information searching actually predates modern computer searching applications by decades. It was first promoted in a big way in the early 1950s (Taube, 1953), with cumbersome manual paper systems.

For our purposes here, the important point about Boolean searching in those manual and online systems, was that it was associated—*necessarily*—with a system of indexing called "concept" indexing. With concept indexing, each distinct important concept used in the record was to be indexed separately. These one-concept-only terms have come to be called "descriptors." In the indexing process, as many as 30 or 40 such descriptors might be applied to a single short article or report. Then, at the time of the search, Boolean logic would be used to combine selected concepts in any way desired by the searcher. So, for example, using concept indexing, a Boolean search could be designed as follows:

Digital libraries AND Information retrieval AND Distance learning

Concept indexing contrasts with an older system of indexing that involves the use of what are known as "subject headings". In particular, subject headings found in the Library of Congress Subject Headings (Library of Congress, 1999) and Sears Subject Headings (Miller, 1994) are used virtually universally by academic and public libraries in the US. As examples, two different children's books on the US Civil War might be indexed as below. Dashes separate the main heading and each subsequent subdivision.

US—History—Civil War, 1861–1865—Campaigns—Juvenile literature

US—History—Civil War, 1861–1865—Naval operations—Juvenile literature

Online databases have generally been indexed by some form or other of descriptor. Boolean search systems became standard for accessing these databases. It seemed natural, then, to use implicit or explicit Boolean search capabilities as well for accessing library catalogs when they went online in the 1980s.

There was a major problem, however—still only partially solved—in using Boolean searching with library subject headings. The theory of the design of subject headings was that they were *not* to be single-concept terms. For lack of a better word, we might call them "whole-document" indexing terms. (See also Bates, 1988; Rowley, 2000; for more detail on differences in underlying indexing systems.) That is, the subject heading string (main heading plus subdivisions) applied to a book was to describe—all by itself—the entire book.

Consequently, the subject heading, even including the subdivisions, was generally quite broad, often much broader than individual concept index terms. Instead of the 30 or 40 terms per record used with concept indexing languages, just one or two subject headings were typically applied, as each heading was assumed to describe all or most of the book. The types of subdivisions allowed were strictly controlled, as was their order of appearance in the subject heading.

Under these circumstances, it makes no sense to search on subject-heading–indexed records with Boolean logic. If most of the records have only one subject heading, then the searcher will almost always come up with no hits on a search that combines more than one subject heading. Yet Boolean search systems have routinely been superimposed on subject-heading-indexed catalogs.

Not surprisingly, these systems did not work very satisfactorily (Markey, 1984; Matthews et al., 1983) until keyword searching, especially on titles, was allowed. Early on, users had more success searching by subject with such keyword searching than with subject-heading searching, and use of keywords shot up in the profile of online public access catalog use (Larson, 1991). But keyword searching has its own limitations. If a title does not use a word, then the entire document is missed, even if it is exactly on the subject desired. In other words, all the benefits of controlling and standardizing vocabulary in indexing is lost, if the searcher must rely only on automatic searches for keyword matches.

How, then, to solve these problems? There is no one best solution that has been employed, and a number of ideas are still floating around for ways to improve things. One of the responses is that the Library of Congress has taken to applying more, and shorter, subject headings, thus creating a hybrid indexing system more responsive to Boolean searching.

Keyword searching on subject headings can also be very helpful, though it is not a fully satisfactory solution, because the headings are typically quite broad, conceptually. With the keyword-search capability the searcher can cherry-pick words and phrases from within the long strings of subject headings and combine them with Boolean logic. However, neither of these solutions has had the flexibility and power of the concept-indexing/Boolean logic combination.

Since the strength of the subject heading approach lies in its combination of elements to describe the whole document in a single string, some online catalog designers have made it possible for the user to see a segment of the alphabetized main headings plus subdivisions in the interface. In this way, the searcher can see a list of the main headings grouped alphabetically and then differentiate among different heading/subdivision combinations to find the most relevant search phrase. (The example above is such a list, just two headings long.)

This method brings its own limitations, however. For example, it can be seen that in a real catalog of any size, a person searching for juvenile Civil War literature would find that the two "Civil War" subject headings listed above would be separated by many other subject headings on *adult* literature of the Civil War. All the adult literature on the Civil War that uses subdivisions falling alphabetically between "Campaigns" and "Naval operations" would fall between the two juvenile literature headings.

These are just some of the problems encountered when an indexing system designed for a paper card catalog has imposed on it a search system that is not compatible with it. The consequences ripple through the layers of the entire system, all the way to, and including, the interface.

Considering it from the searcher and interface design perspective, should there be keyword searching on subject headings? Boolean searching? Searching on subdivision segments? Alphabetical listing of subject headings on the screen? Batching of subject heading levels so as to group main heading and subdivisions in successive hierarchical displays? Provision of searcher front- ends to assist with vocabulary and/or grouping of records? All these and many other solutions have been proposed and experimented with by designers of online public-access catalogs (Bates, 1977, 1986; Cochrane & Markey, 1983; Drabenstott & Weller, 1996; Hildreth, 1989; Kristensen, 1993; Larson, McDonough, O'Leary, Kuntz, & Moon, 1996; Schatz, Johnson, Cochrane, & Chen, 1996).

All of these have implications at the interface layer. Forms of assistance that could be provided to users, such as those mentioned in the preceding paragraph, may not be considered at all, if system designers do not understand the underlying conflict between the conceptual organization of the indexing language and the retrieval methods provided to the user.

Example #3
Structure of online retrieval system designed for one searching style conflicts with needs of those with different searching style

In the 1990s, the Getty Information Institute (now absorbed into the Getty Research Institute, a part of the Getty Trust, which also supports the Getty Museum in Los Angeles, CA, USA) carried out a program of study, in which the author was involved, on online database use by Visiting Scholars at the Getty Research Institute (Bates, 1994, 1996a,b; Bates, Wilde, & Siegfried, 1993, 1995;

Siegfried, Bates, & Wilde, 1993). For two years of the Visiting Scholar program, scholars willing to participate were taught to do online searching through DIALOG. The entire protocols of their searches were captured by a computer program, and the scholars were interviewed extensively about their experiences. This abundant data formed the basis of the six articles that resulted from the project. In examining the scholars' queries, their actual search strategies as input to the system, their overall search histories, and their reactions and attitudes regarding their experiences, we learned, without initially intending to, the importance of the interactions at every step of the cascade. The full results are available in the article reports, but a number of the interactions are illustrated below:

Information content Databases for the humanities literature had been developed in parallel to the design of databases for the sciences. Emphasis in such databases is on recent secondary literature in each humanities subject field. The scholars consistently wanted more original (primary) materials—the sort likely to be mounted in future years as digital libraries—rather than secondary materials, and they wanted older materials. They felt they uncovered relevant references adequately other ways besides database searching, and wanted to use computer databases for research on things that were not easy for them to find. Database searching as currently constituted had some uses for them, though of a somewhat different nature than assumed in the design of the databases. (See especially discussion in Bates, 1994.)

So, all the way back at the very first design layer—selection of information content—database providers were not meeting the needs of the anticipated users of the information. Not surprisingly, then, no matter how well mounted for the user, secondary databases have proven to be of relatively less interest to humanities scholars than to scientists. It became apparent through this study and through examination of the literature on humanities information seeking that the mix of motivations and objectives of humanities scholars demands a different type of information be selected for mounting and searching than is common for the sciences. Once that problematic selection of information content had been made, the consequences cascaded through the rest of the system design and use.

System of metadata and actual indexing of objects The analysis of the scholars' natural language queries and the terms used in the actual search formulations demonstrated that the character of humanities queries and search terms are quite different from those in the social and natural sciences. (See especially discussion in Bates et al., 1993.) We found that whole classes of subject terms were routinely used in the humanities that were virtually non-existent in the sciences. Names of individuals, historical periods, and geographical locations are very common and important in the humanities, and seldom used in the sciences.

In the Getty study, commonly, a scholar would create a query out of several broad terms, one or more drawn from each of the different typical classes of subject term in the humanities. A query topic from the Getty study is illustrative: "Image of the tree in literature, art, science, of medieval and renaissance Europe" (Bates et al., 1993, p. 18). A typical science topic, by contrast, might use solely conventional common terms, few or none of which fall in the common humanities term categories. An example from a National Science Foundation funded study: "Occurrences, causes, treatment, and prevention of retrolental fibroplasia" (Saracevic & Kantor, 1988, p. 195).

The different character of humanities subject terminology has dramatic consequences for indexing of such material. A different design from either concept indexing or subject headings, known as faceted classification, lends itself very well to the terminology of humanities literature. In fact, the Getty Information Institute, finding the faceted approach effective, had already committed itself to that approach in the design of its *Art & Architecture Thesaurus* (Petersen, 1994).

In faceted classifications, recurrent types of terms, or facets, are developed independently of other classes of terms with which they might be combined in conventional hierarchical classification. For example, in the arts, historical period might be one facet, geographical location another facet, style another, materials used still another, and so on. In this manner whole classes of terms are grouped together in facets, so it is easy for a searcher to find and use a relevant term of the desired type.

However, most of the database producers, again drawing on the concept-indexing/Boolean-logic-searching model, had developed descriptor-type indexing, rather than faceted. The scholars had a hard time using Boolean combination—its logico-mathematical character did not sit well with their very different mental strengths. Further, they had difficulty finding and combining the types of terms they needed to properly express their queries. (See Bates, 1996b; Bates et al., 1993.)

In fact, the conventions of descriptor indexing actually militated against successful searching for the scholars in some characteristic elements of their searching. The example above, "the image of the tree...," uses some very broad terms—Medieval and Renaissance, Europe, literature, science. Descriptor indexing generally requires the use of specific concepts, because otherwise far too many hits are returned in a typical search. So, frequently, terms of such breadth either do not exist in descriptor thesauri or are used very sparingly in indexing practice. For the humanities scholar, however, it is the combination of perhaps a half-dozen of such very broad terms that produces, in the end, a highly specific topic that should retrieve manageably few hits. So the development of indexing vocabularies along the science descriptor model had actually inhibited good indexing of humanities materials. The scholars' discomfort with Boolean logic further hamstrung them, to the point where the searches were often only incidentally rewarding.

System front-end, search capabilities, and interface design Interactions among the above-mentioned layers and those in this section can be seen in several ways. With respect to the design of the search interface, two things from the above considerations become very evident. First, a way must be found to enable humanities searchers *not* to have to use and understand Boolean logic. Second, the underlying information should be facet indexed, and the searcher helped to use those facets explicitly in the search interface design.

These two needs could be met simultaneously by designing the search interface for humanities scholars so that it both presented the comfortable, familiar conceptual facets to the searcher, *and* enabled the searcher to use these facets without appearing to do Boolean searching. This could be achieved by presenting the searcher with labeled prompt boxes for each facet. Vocabulary assistance associated with each prompt box could enable the searcher to select good terms from within each facet to express the element(s) of the query relevant to that facet. The searcher chooses which facet prompt boxes to fill in—all would not be necessary. In this fashion, the entire query could be expressed effectively, and collectively, through the various prompt boxes actually used.

Once terms are selected and entered in the prompt boxes, searchers then simply click on "Search," and the system does the Boolean combining for them. What the system could actually do in these circumstances, is conduct Boolean searching according to an algorithm, based on experience and testing, that optimally and sequentially uses the various logical combinations until a satisfactory set size is retrieved for the searcher. Low-priority facets could be left out entirely, if the retrievals were few from the use of initial core facets. Subsequent requests by the user to increase or reduce the retrieved set could lead to further Boolean searching behind the scenes for the humanities searcher.

Example #4
Design of Web-based retrieval system
conflicts with design of indexing system

A final example is drawn from an experimental Web-based vocabulary support and query expansion tool created by the Getty Information Institute. (The Information Institute has now been absorbed into the Getty

Research Institute.) The tool was known as "a.k.a." (for "also known as") and was available for a time at the Getty website.

The purpose of the system was to provide the searcher access to the rich vocabulary resources of two Getty databases, the *Art & Architecture Thesaurus* (Petersen, 1994), and the union list of artist names (ULAN) (Bower & Baca, 1994). The intent was that the user could identify alternative or additional search terms in the vocabulary databases, either subject terms or artist names or both, and then use those terms to search several Getty databases, such as the *Bibliography of the History of Art* (1999–), also accessible from within a.k.a.

The system was designed in such a way as to give the searcher, at the interface, the option of using vocabulary assistance or not. Further, the searcher who chose vocabulary assistance could turn the task over to the system for automatic query expansion or explore the vocabularies on his or her own and select desired terms.

This was a powerful idea and was well implemented in many ways. At the behest of the Information Institute, I led a group to evaluate the system extensively. We studied actual use by 36 users with a variety of backgrounds, using a carefully designed activity protocol that combined unstructured and directed searching on a.k.a. We studied both local and remote users. Yet with all this power, a.k.a. did not work very well in the study cases. We ultimately discovered that the problems were due, to a substantial degree, to conflicts between design layers. Here, I will describe two high-impact design layer conflicts that we discovered.

First, as noted earlier, the *Art & Architecture Thesaurus* is a faceted system; in fact, it probably represents the best-developed faceted indexing system in the world. So the general system of indexing used was well suited to the information content and to the needs, particularly, of arts researchers.

Yet with all this power, a.k.a. did not work well in our study. Frequently, users did better without using the vocabulary enhancement than with. Why? We found that the most serious problem concerned the interaction between the system of indexing and the structure of the interface.

The power of faceted classification lies, jointly, in (1) its grouping of terms of a similar type into facets, and in (2) its ability to combine terms from different facets (usually with Boolean AND) to create a total query. As noted earlier, humanities queries characteristically draw terms from several facets. So, for the "image of a tree" example mentioned earlier, a searcher might want to draw a term or terms for Europe from a geographical facet, terms for "Medieval" and/or "Renaissance" from a historical period facet, and so on through the various facets touched on in the query statement.

The online a.k.a. system, however, as originally designed, only permitted the searcher to explore and select terms from one facet at a time.

Once terms from a facet had been selected, it was not possible to move to another facet and select additional terms to AND with the terms selected from the first facet. The searcher could only move on to a completely new search. Clearly, in the image of the tree example, and in many other humanities queries, it is not enough to search on just one facet of a subject. Of what use would it be to search to bring up every record in the database on the Renaissance, without also limiting that search by image of the tree, "Europe," and so on?

This was a crucial flaw in the original design of a.k.a. The main purpose of the system was to enable people to expand queries with the rich and carefully researched vocabulary resources of the Getty. But the query expansion capabilities were designed without adequately incorporating a core feature of the intellectual structure of faceted vocabularies—facet combination, a feature that was crucial to effective operation for many real queries. We learned that there had been inadequate communication between technical staff and vocabulary staff at critical design phases of the project.

The a.k.a. system was a daring experimental design (a design, incidentally, similar to what I have been recommending [Bates, 1986]—and implementing [Bates, 1990b]—for a number of years), and, as such, was bound to have start-up problems that needed to be ironed out. But this particular new-system glitch might not have happened with a design process that required frequent and detailed communication between the representatives of the various design layers.

The second example problem with a.k.a. reflected what was probably another communication mix-up. In this case the problem arose with the ULAN (Bower & Baca, 1994). Artists may be known by literally dozens of names—names in different languages, nicknames, and the like. We found, for example, that the painter Titian had more than 40 name variants in his entry. The material available on name variants in the ULAN represents extensive research by the developers of the vocabulary at the Getty, and can be of great value to scholars who may not realize at the beginning of a scholarly project on an artist how many names they may need to use in their research.

It therefore seemed to make sense to offer ULAN to searchers as a part of the a.k.a. system. However, the evaluation found that ULAN-enriched queries did not seem to help people find more references in the Getty bibliographic databases, such as the *Bibliography of the History of Art* (1999–) (BHA). We soon discovered why. The indexers who prepared the entries for the BHA database, for example, themselves used ULAN to identify the standard preferred name for the painters referenced in the database.

So, even if Titian was described by the variant name "Ticiano" or "Ziano" in the record indexed, the catalogers would also always add the standard name "Titian". They thus eliminated the need for the end-user to identify the alternative names for searching purposes. That was an excellent use of ULAN, but it defeated the point, for the most part, of including ULAN in a.k.a. Here, in this second example from the a.k.a. evaluation, we see a conflict, or misunderstanding, between the people at the "actual indexing" layer and those designing the "system front-end" and "search capabilities" layers.

After the evaluation project, a number of changes were made in a.k.a. to solve these layer conflicts, and before it was taken down from the Web, a.k.a. performed closer to its potential.

Implications for digital libraries

The elaboration of these various examples and their proposed solutions in the previous section has not been done principally to suggest solutions to those specific problems. Others may have different solutions. Rather, the purpose was to illustrate how the mix of circumstances in a particular information system design situation can lead to implications and interactions that cascade throughout the layers of the structure of an information system.

In the first example, two entities that manipulated the database contents—the database producer (Biological Abstracts) and the database vendor (DIALOG)—worked at cross-purposes to each other. In that case, the database producer and vendor had different motivations: the producer to create a unique resource, shaped to the distinctive needs of its audience, and the vendor to create as uniform a set of databases as possible, to make it easier for searchers moving from one database to another.

It is not hard to imagine these same sorts of conflicts arising again and again in the digital library world. The producing institution shapes and develops its own distinctive mix of types of metadata, which some search engine or interoperability mechanism overrides or ignores.

This is not (or, at least, not always) an insoluble problem, however. Ultimately, proximity searching capabilities added to DIALOG made it possible for searchers to require that the components of these multi-element biological concepts be found together or not be retrieved.

In the second example, the use of Boolean search mechanisms with subject headings, the important lesson to learn is that the conflict between user search capability and underlying indexing principles can go very deep.

Because subject headings were designed for a different environment, they did not mesh well with the Boolean searching requirements of typical online catalogs. This is one case where the solutions have been halting, expensive, and not wholly satisfactory.

Yet much of the discussion in the digital library world regarding metadata seems to presume that the intellectual structure guiding the design and application of the metadata is of little import. In the Dublin Core, "subject" is just one generic category among 15 (Weibel & Lagoze, 1997). If there are four different types of subject description applied to each document—a situation not at all unlikely—each designed on different principles, they will all be lumped together in the repeating fields of that category. For good retrieval, however, they may each need a different kind of retrieval mechanism and presentation in the interface.

In the third example in the previous section, given what was learned about the character and structure of the information in the humanities, and about the nature of query formation by humanities scholars (elements in the far left and far right of Fig. 1), conclusions were drawn about the nature of the indexing that should be done in the humanities (faceted), and, consequently, about the nature of presentation of search capabilities (prompt boxes with hidden Boolean searching) in the interface. Choices made at every layer of the system design culminated in the final look of the information system interface.

For the end user attempting to use subject access in the system interface, it is desirable, first, to provide search capabilities to the searcher that are appropriate for the type of intellectual structure contained in each type of subject metadata, and second, to represent those capabilities in the interface so that their function is as self-evident and as easily usable as possible.

The challenges of designing a system so that all the layers work together effectively is amply illustrated by the fourth example, the a.k.a. system. The system deserves to be revived and refined, to take full advantage of the rich and deeply researched information available in the Getty vocabularies and databases. But for it to work in the end, that revival must be done in a way that truly integrates the complex expertises of the personnel working at each layer of the system. The kind of information, the systems of description used for that information, the search mechanism(s) used on that information, and the manifestation of search capabilities in the user interface all have to dovetail for effective retrieval to result.

The four examples provided above—as well as many others encountered in a long career of consulting on the design of real-world information systems—illustrate two key points of this article. First, excellent design at individual layers of a system can nonetheless work completely at cross-purposes and thwart the purpose of the overall system. Second, deep expertises are developing at every design layer in Fig. 1. Work necessarily must be compartmentalized to some degree to achieve the objectives of a project. People working at each layer cannot become experts at every other layer. Therefore, genuine, ongoing communication must take place between designers working on the several layers throughout the development and implementation process. That communication must go deeper than a memo passed around or an occasional meeting. Cooperative interaction needs to take place frequently, and be built into the administrative and social structure of the organization.

That information exchange, by the way, should take place on an equal footing. Human nature being what it is, it is not uncommon for competitiveness and domination struggles to interfere with genuine openness between the representatives of the various layers.

Conclusions

Changing even seemingly small things at one information system design layer can have huge implications for the other layers. Since the layers themselves interact in a cascade from system and information content chosen (left-hand side of Fig. 1) all the way through interface design and characteristics of use (right-hand side of Fig. 1), the design of such systems must also manifest mutual knowledge between those layers.

In the development of digital libraries, the layers are proliferating and the potential for conflict between layers multiplying (Kramer, Nikolai, & Habeck, 1997; Lynch & Garcia-Molina, 1995). It is not uncommon nowadays for information systems to be designed collectively by several different individuals or groups, some of which either never talk to each other or talk past each other. Now that so much computing power and sophistication is entering the information world, especially in the development of digital libraries, deep expertises are developing in each of the layers displayed in Fig. 1. One person cannot know all that is needed to put such a system together effectively.

Unfortunately, people working at each layer may do an excellent job in their own area of expertise but may fail to recognize or influence the design issues interacting between their layer and the other layers. As a consequence, individual layers may function very well, but work at cross-purposes with the functions of other layers.

Digital libraries cannot be fully effective as information sources for users until the entire design process is done in a manner that involves genuine conceptual and practical coordination among the people working on the system layers. The information content, its database structure, and retrievable elements, should not be selected without full consultation with experts in the subject domain and in the information seeking behavior and context of use of the proposed digital library information.

The interface design should meet not only general criteria of good interface design, but should also draw on expertise in *information system interface design*. That expertise will include understanding of various options in the provision of search capabilities for the user, including front-ends, as well as understanding of the underlying indexing and metadata structure, and how that structure can best be represented and used in the interface.

In sum, all layers of the system for accessing and displaying digital library information should be simultaneously designed with knowledge of what is going forward in the other layers. It takes only one wrongly placed layer to thwart all the clever work done at every other layer. For effective information retrieval to occur, all layers of a system must be designed to work together, and the people doing the designing must genuinely communicate.

REFERENCES

Bates, M.J. (1977). System meets user: Problems in matching subject search terms. *Information Processing & Management, 13*(6), 367–375.

Bates, M.J. (1986). Subject access in online catalogs: A design model. *Journal of the American Society for Information Science, 37*(6), 357–376.

Bates, M.J. (1988). How to use controlled vocabularies more effectively in online searching. *Online, 12*(6), 45–56.

Bates, M.J. (1990a). Where should the person stop and the information search interface start? *Information Processing & Management, 26*(5), 575–591.

Bates, M.J. (1990b). Design for a subject search interface and online thesaurus for a very large records management database. In *Proceedings of the 53rd ASIS Annual Meeting, 27*, 20–28.

Bates, M.J. (1994). The design of databases and other information resources for humanities scholars: The Getty Online Searching Project report no. 4. *Online & CDROM Review 18*(6), 331–340.

Bates, M.J. (1996a). Document familiarity in relation to relevance, information retrieval theory, and Bradford's Law: The Getty Online Searching Project report no. 5. *Information Processing & Management, 32*(6), 697–707.

Bates, M.J. (1996b). The Getty end-user online searching project in the humanities: Report no. 6: Overview and conclusions. *College & Research Libraries, 57*(6), 514–523.

Bates, M.J. (1998). Indexing and access for digital libraries and the Internet: Human, database, and domain factors. *Journal of the American Society for Information Science, 49*(13), 1185–1205.

Bates, M.J., Wilde, D.N., & Siegfried, S. (1993). An analysis of search terminology used by humanities scholars: The Getty Online Searching Project report no. 1. *The Library Quarterly, 63*(1), 1–39.

Bates, M.J., Wilde, D.N., & Siegfried, S. (1995). Research practices of humanities scholars in an online environment: The Getty Online Searching Project report no. 3. *Library & Information Science Research, 17*(1), 5–40.

Beaulieu, M. (2000). Interaction in information searching and retrieval. *Journal of Documentation, 56*(4), 431–439.

Belkin, N., Brooks, H., & Daniels, P. (1987). Knowledge elicitation using discourse analysis. *International Journal of Man-Machine Studies, 27*(2), 127–144.

Bibliography of the History of Art (1999–). Los Angeles, CA: J. Paul Getty Trust, Vandoeu-vre-les-Nancy; France: Centre National de la recherche scientifique. (See description at: http://library.dialog.com/bluesheets/html/b10190.html).

BIOSIS Search Guide (1997). Philadelphia, PA: Biological Abstracts, Inc.

Bødker, S. (1991). *Through the interface: A human activity approach to user interface design.* London: Lawrence Erlbaum Associates.

Bower, J.M., & Baca, M. (1994). *Union list of artist names. Computer file Version 1.0.* New York: G.K. Hall/Macmillan. (See also http://www.getty.edu/research/tools/vocabulary).

Butler, K.A., Bahrami, A., Esposito, C., & Hebron, R. (2000). Conceptual models for coordinating the design of user work with the design of information systems. *Data and Knowledge Engineering, 33*(2), 191–198.

Card, S.K., Moran, T.P., & Newell, A. (1983). *The psychology of human-computer interaction.* London: Lawrence Erlbaum Associates.

Carroll, J.M. (Ed.). (1991). *Designing interaction: Psychology at the human-computer interface.* New York: Cambridge University Press.

Chemical Abstracts (1907–). Easton, PA: American Chemical Society.

Cochrane, P.A., & Markey, K. (1983). Catalog use studies—before and after the introduction of online interactive catalogs: Impact on design for subject access. *Library & Information Science Research, 5*(4), 337–363.

Damodaran, L. (1991). Towards a human factors strategy for information technology systems. In B. Shackel, & S.J. Richardson (Eds.), *Human factors for informatics usability* (pp. 291–324). New York: Cambridge University Press.

Digital Object Identifier. (n.d.). (Home page). http://www.doi.org. (Retrieved April 27, 2001).

Dillon, A. (1994). *Designing usable electronic text: Ergonomic aspects of human information usage.* London: Taylor & Francis.

Dix, A., Finlay, J., Abowd, G., & Beale, R. (1993). *Human-computer interaction.* New York: Prentice-Hall.

Drabenstott, K.M., & Weller, M.S. (1996). Failure analysis of subject searches in a test of a new design for subject access to online catalogs. *Journal of the American Society for Information Science, 47*(7), 519–537.

Efthimiadis, E.N. (1990). Online searching aids—A review of front ends, gateways and other interfaces. *Journal of Documentation, 46*(3), 218–262.

Efthimiadis, E.N. (1996). Query expansion. *Annual review of information science and technology, 31,* 121–187. Medford, NJ: Information Today.

Ellis, D. (1996). *Progress and problems in information retrieval* (2nd ed.). London: Library Association.

Encoded Archival Description. (n.d.). (Home page). http://www.loc.gov/ead. (Accessed: April 27, 2001).

Galitz, W.O. (1997). *The essential guide to user interface design.* New York: Wiley.

Gardner, A. (1991). An approach to formalised procedures for user-centred system design. In B. Shackel, & S.J. Richardson (Eds.), *Human factors for informatics usability* (pp. 133–150). New York: Cambridge University Press.

Hayman, A., & Elliman, T. (2000). Human elements in information system design for knowledge workers. *International Journal of Information Management, 20*(4), 297–309.

Hildreth, C.R. (1982). *Online public access catalogs: The user interface.* Dublin, OH: OCLC.

Hildreth, C.R. (1989). *Intelligent interfaces and retrieval methods for subject searching in bibliographic retrieval systems.* Washington, DC: Library of Congress Cataloging Distribution Service.

Ingwersen, P. (1992). *Information retrieval interaction.* London: Taylor Graham.

International Organization for Standardization. (1994). *Information technology—Open systems interconnection—Basic reference model: The basic model.* (ISO/IEC 7498-1). Retrieved from http://www.iso.ch/cate/d20269.html.

Kilker, J., & Gay, G. (1998). The social construction of a digital library: A case study examining implications for evaluation. *Information Technology and Libraries, 17*(2), 60–70.

Kramer, R., Nikolai, R., & Habeck, C. (1997). Thesaurus federations: Loosely integrated thesauri for document retrieval in networks based on Internet technologies. *International Journal on Digital Libraries, 1*(2), 122–131.

Kristensen, J. (1993). Expanding end-users' query statements for free text searching with a search-aid thesaurus. *Information Processing & Management, 29*(6), 733–744.

Larson, R.R. (1991). The decline of subject searching—long-term trends and patterns of index use in an online catalog. *Journal of the American Society for Information Science, 42*(3), 197–215.

Larson, R.R., McDonough, J., O'Leary, P., Kuntz, L., & Moon, R. (1996). Cheshire II: Designing a next-generation online catalog. *Journal of the American Society for Information Science, 47*(7), 555–567.

Library of Congress. (1999). *Library of Congress subject headings* (22nd ed., 5 Vols.). Washington, DC: Cataloging Distribution Service, Library of Congress.

Lynch, C., & Garcia-Molina, H. (1995). *Interoperability, scaling, and the digital libraries research agenda: A report on the May 18–19, 1995 IITA Digital Libraries Workshop.* Retrieved from http://www.diglib.stanford.edu/diglib/pub/reports/iita-dlw/main.html.

Markey, K. (1984). *Subject searching in library catalogs: Before and after the introduction of online catalogs.* Dublin, OH: OCLC Online Computer Library Center.

Matthews, J.R., Lawrence, G.S., & Ferguson, D.K. (Eds.). (1983). *Using online catalogs: A nationwide survey: A report of a study sponsored by the Council on Library Resources.* New York: Neal-Schuman.

Miller, J. (Ed.). (1994). *Sears list of subject headings* (15th ed.). New York: Wilson.

Norman, D.A., & Draper, S.W. (1986). *User centered system design: New perspectives on human-computer interaction.* London: Lawrence Erlbaum Associates.

Payette, S.D., & Rieger, O.Y. (1998). Supporting scholarly inquiry, Incorporating users in the design of the digital library. *Journal of Academic Librarianship, 24*(2), 121–129.

Peterson, T. (1994). *Art & architecture thesaurus* (2nd ed.). New York: Oxford.

Robertson, S.E. (1977). Theories and models in information retrieval. *Journal of Documentation, 33*(2), 126–148.

Rowley, J., & Farrow, J. (2000). *Organizing knowledge: An introduction to managing access to information* (3rd ed.). Aldershot, Hampshire: Gower.

Salton, G., & McGill, M.J. (1983). *Introduction to modern information retrieval.* New York: McGraw-Hill.

Saracevic, T. (1996). Modeling interaction in information retrieval (IR), A review and proposal. In *Proceedings of the 59th annual meeting of the American Society for Information Science, 33,* 3–9.

Saracevic, T. (1997). The stratified model of information retrieval interaction: Extension and application. *Proceedings of the 60th annual meeting of the American Society for Information Science, 34,* 313–327. Medford, NJ: Information Today.

Saracevic, T., & Kantor, P. (1988). A study of information seeking and retrieving. II. Users, questions, and effectiveness. *Journal of the American Society for Information Science, 39*(3), 177–196.

Schatz, B.R., Johnson, E.H., Cochrane, P.A., & Chen, H. (1996). Interactive term suggestion for users of digital libraries: Using subject thesauri and co-occurrence lists for information retrieval. In *Proceedings of the 1st ACM International Conference on Digital Libraries* (pp. 126–133). New York: Association for Computing Machinery.

Shneiderman, B. (1998). *Designing the user interface: Strategies for effective human-computer interaction* (3rd ed.). Reading, MA: Addison-Wesley Longman.

Shor, R. (1991). A uniform graphics front-end. *Computers in Libraries, 11*(11), 48–51.

Siegfried, S., Bates, M.J., & Wilde, D.N. (1993). A profile of end-user searching behavior by humanities scholars: The Getty Online Searching Project report no. 2. *Journal of the American Society for Information Science, 44*(5), 273–291.

Spink, A. (1997). Information science: A third feedback framework. *Journal of the American Society for Information Science, 48*(8), 728–740.

Syan, C.S., & Menon, U. (1994). *Concurrent engineering: Concepts, implementation and practice.* London: Chapman & Hall.

Taube, M. (1953). *Studies in coordinate indexing.* Washington, DC: Documentation, Inc.

Text Encoding Initiative. (n.d.) (Home page). http://www.tei-c.org. (Retrieved April 27, 2001).

Vickery, B., & Vickery, A. (1993). Online search interface design. *Journal of Documentation, 49*(2), 103–187.

Weibel, S.L., & Lagoze, C. (1997). An element set to support resource discovery. *International Journal on Digital Libraries, 1*(2), 176–186.

Zhang, J., & Fine, S. (1996). The effect of human behavior on the design of an information retrieval system interface. *International Information and Library Review, 28*(3), 249–260.

Zhu, Z. (2001). Towards an integrating programme for information systems design: An oriental case. *International Journal of Information Management, 21*(1), 69–90.

Content list of Volumes I, II, and III

INFORMATION AND THE INFORMATION PROFESSIONS: SELECTED WORKS OF MARCIA J. BATES, VOL. I

All entries are by Bates unless otherwise noted.

INFORMATION SEARCHING THEORY AND PRACTICE: SELECTED WORKS OF MARCIA J. BATES, VOL. II

ISBN 978-0-9817584-2-8

All entries are by Bates unless otherwise noted.

INFORMATION USERS AND INFORMATION SYSTEM DESIGN: SELECTED WORKS OF MARCIA J. BATES, VOL. III

ISBN 978-0-9817584-3-5

All entries are by Bates unless otherwise noted.

Index

vocabulary indexing, *continued*
    all subject vocabulary terms are not equal,
    313–19
    See also humanities search terms, vocabu-
    lary, and indexing
vocabulary control, 247, 249, 258–60, 337. *See also* thesauri
vocabulary scalability, 324–28
Vrba, E. S., 9

walls, students posting academic information on their, 162–63, 164t
Walsh, B. C., 203
Walter, Virginia A., 6, 34, 114
Wang, Peiling, 34
Waples, Douglas, 22
Web-based retrieval system. *See* under Internet
Web-searching instruction. *See* SNAPdragon Project

website design model, 351
Weinberg, B. H., 333
Weintraub, K. J., 44
welfare networks, system to link, 193–94
White, H. D., 330n1
Wiberley, Stephen E., Jr., 52, 96, 270, 272, 330–31
Wilde, Deborah N., 43n2, 48, 88, 263n2, 284n2
Wildemuth, Barbara, 27
Williams, Michael, 248
Wilson, Patrick, 33, 330n1
Wilson, Tom, 24
Winn, V. A., 333
Woo, J., 44

Zipf, George, 319
Zipfian distributions, 319–21, 323–24
    frequency-size, 320, 321f

CPSIA information can be obtained
at www.ICGtesting.com
Printed in the USA
BVOW09s2129310717
490777BV00005B/53/P